Macroeconomics

JOHN LINDAUER
Claremont Men's College and
Claremont Graduate School

Macroeconomics
SECOND EDITION

JOHN WILEY & SONS, INC.
New York   London   Sydney   Toronto

275310

\ CC

6000 594806

To Jacqueline Lindauer,

whose efforts and understanding
made this book possible

Preface

Burgeoning ideas and research during the last few years have expanded the material that might be covered in macroeconomic theory and policy courses and reviewed by graduate students preparing for their theory exams. The purpose of this second edition is to present a straightforward and thorough explanation of macroanalysis in a concise, verbal, and graphic manner that will maximize each reader's exposure to its essence.

The development of the revised edition of *Macroeconomics* was encouraged by the very pleasant acceptance of the first edition and the many communications and suggestions that came from throughout the world as a result of its translation into other languages. This edition is substantially expanded as a result of those communications and the additional literature that has come forth since the completion of the first edition.

The first half of this edition describes the tenets of macroeconomics and presents a basic macroeconomic model. Then the model is used to analyze such macroeconomic considerations as inflation, unemployment, growth, fluctuations, and income distribution. Third, there is an examination of both the requirements of stabilization and the monetary, fiscal, and other policies that might be implemented for stabilization purposes. Finally, macroeconomics is put into historical perspective as the macroeconomic postulates of the classical economist are presented and evaluated.

The end of each chapter includes a list of references related to the subject matter presented in the text. The reader should examine at least some of these selections if only to discover that there are aspects of macroeconomics more complex than those described in the text.

Many people have influenced the new edition. I would like particularly to acknowledge the ideas and suggestions of Professors Charles Cole, Sarjit Singh, Thomas Holmstrom, Phillip Coelho, John Hotson, and Gerald Sazama. Mention also should be made of the hundreds of students who have enrolled in my macroeconomic theory courses at Claremont Men's College and the Claremont Graduate School. Their comments and questions were invaluable.

Claremont, California   JOHN LINDAUER
February 1971

Contents

3 Consumption Purchasing 40

7 Fiscal Activities 152

CONTENTS   xv

Macroeconomics

1

Anyone graduating from college or entering the work force from other training has a great stake in the condition of the economy in which he will live in the years ahead. For the condition of the economy governs whether there will be two television sets in every home or "no help wanted" signs and long lines of welfare applicants. When prosperity prevails, jobs are plentiful, and many competing businesses bid up the price for human talents. When times are hard, on the other hand, the specter of unemployment and the threat of want hover over millions of men, women, and children.

Basically, macroeconomics is concerned with the general state of a nation's economy and the degree to which the economy uses and expands its capacity for producing goods and services. As a result, macroeconomics deals with some of the most controversial and challenging issues of our time—inflation, taxes, unemployment, balanced and unbalanced budgets, and the role of government. Furthermore, it is a subject in which passions and prejudices

3

often have resulted in legislators and bureaucrats applying simple but unrealistic policies to complex economic problems. They have sought prosperity with homemade remedies rather than with sophisticated policies based on common sense and logic, let alone any kind of economic analysis, and the consequences have been inevitable. Complex and highly developed countries such as the United States and those of western Europe have been plagued and even overwhelmed at times by inflation, unemployment, low rates of production growth, and balance of payments deficits. These are strong terms, to be sure, but mild in comparison to the conditions associated with them: men have gone hungry and unsheltered; children have been dressed in rags and unable to obtain educations; elderly persons have seen the savings of a lifetime wiped out. But often these conditions could have been prevented by the implementation of appropriate economic policies!

Since it is the amount of goods and services produced in a country that makes it rich or poor, the leaders of every nation have a vested interest in seeing that production is never so low that labor and capital stand idle. Those leaders need to comprehend the causes of problems related to the level of production, for the economy's citizens, disenchanted by the problems, may be inspired to seek other leaders or some other form of economic organization. Solution of the problems while maintaining high levels of production requires the application of policies based on an understanding of the complex factors that affect the general level of economic activity in an economy. Such knowledge, together with the study of related problems that can plague an economy and the policies intended to solve them, is the domain of macroeconomics.

MACROECONOMIC GOALS AND PERFORMANCE

An economy must efficiently produce the maximum amount of goods and services most desired by its participants if it is to attain the basic goal of satisfying as many needs as possible. But the production of the maximum amount of goods and services does not necessarily occur automatically and there are other important goals that may have a significant impact in determining how well an economy attains its basic goal. Some of these goals are macroeconomic in nature in the sense that they are generally related to the economic conditions of the whole economy.

High Levels of Employment and Production

Labor and capital are the factors whose employment generates the goods and services needed to satisfy present needs and provide the basis for the continuation and expansion of production. Ideally all of the labor and capital in an economy that are willing and able to engage in productive activities will be employed unless they are normally moving between jobs or adjusting to changes in the structure of the economy. Such a *full employment* of an economy's factors, when coupled with their efficient use, means that the level of output of goods and services in the economy will be maximized.

If willing and able factors are not employed, there may be general dissatisfaction with the lower than possible levels of production as well as particular dissatisfaction on the part of the individuals who futilely desire to earn incomes with their unemployed factors and must exist on whatever combination of previously accumulated wealth, other incomes, or charity is available to them. Dissatisfactions also exist whenever there is underemployment so that factors work at jobs below their production capacities. For example, the lack of production opportunities may cause an engineer to accept a less productive job as a draftsman and a skilled worker to accept a position as a laborer. This is inefficient.

Employment and production in the United States, for example, have often failed to reach their potentially high levels. Willing, able labor and capital have all too often been either unemployed or underemployed. Underemployment is difficult to measure but throughout the 1950's, 1960's, and early 1970's labor unemployment fluctuated widely from highs in excess of 6.8 percent in 1958 to lows of 2.9 percent in 1953. For the 1950's and 1960's labor unemployment averaged 4.7 percent. Plant utilization during the same period ranged between 72.3 percent and 94.2 percent of capacity with an average utilization of 85.7 percent.

As a result of the unemployment and underemployment that existed in the United States from 1950 to 1970, there was often a substantial gap between actual production in the economy and the level of production that could have occurred if the economy's factors were fully employed. For instance, early in 1970, the Chairman of the President's Council of Economic Advisers observed that $40 billions of production would be lost annually because the labor unemployment rate rose to 5 percent from the 4 percent the chairman estimated to be normally moving between jobs or adjusting to changes in the structure of the economy. And the rate of labor unemployment continued climbing throughout 1970.

Stable Prices

An "inflation" is an increase in the general level of an economy's prices. Such an increase tends to change the distribution of an economy's level of production as it reduces the purchasing power of individuals and other economic units with fixed money incomes or with assets such as cash and bonds that have fixed money values. Inflation also distorts the nature of production to the extent that it causes an increase in the purchase and production of assets whose prices are expected to ride out the inflation by increasing as fast or faster than the general increase. At the same time, inflation tends to reduce the purchase of financial assets such as bonds whose prices are not expected to keep pace with the general increase; thus it tends to reduce the purchasing of the manufacturing and other facilities financed with bonds. Inflation may also reduce savings since income recipients will tend not to delay their purchasing if they expect prices to be even higher in the future. Furthermore inflation changes the nature of purchasing and production to the extent that the products of one economy become more expensive than those of another; when prices in one economy rise more than in other economies, there is a tendency for individuals and other economic units to redirect their purchasing toward those economies not experiencing as much inflation. Popular folklore to the contrary, prices in the United States have not risen rapidly. The wholesale price index went from 86.8 in 1950 to 113.0 in 1969 for a growth rate of approximately 1.5 percent per year. The index of prices for all of the goods and services produced and sold in the economy rose at an average of 2.4 percent during the same period of time.

Economic Growth

Economic growth is traditionally measured in terms of an increase in the amount of goods and services produced in an economy. The annual rate of growth in production in the United States during the 1950's and 1960's averaged about 1.5 percent in the 1950's and 4.35 percent in the 1960's.

During the period 1952–1969, if total production in the United States had not been crippled by periodic conditions of unemployment and underemployment and instead had steadily grown at say, 5 percent, the total value of the economy's production would have been in the order of $11.1 trillion dollars (1958 prices). In fact, the United States' economy only produced goods and services valued at $9.5 trillion. The difference, $1600 billion of goods and services, is thus an estimate of the price that the United States paid for inadequate economic policies that led to low rates of growth and greater than necessary unemployment and underemployment during the 18-year period.

Minimum Standards of Living

Wealth, education, inclination, ability, and opportunity all determine the level of income received by an individual in an economy. Disabled individuals, those without wealth or the skills or abilities, and the owners of productive factors that are capable of working but incapable of obtaining employment all earn no incomes. Individuals with minimal wealth and skills and the partially disabled and underemployed earn low incomes. But low or nonexistent incomes and wealth mean that few goods and services can be purchased to satisfy needs. Sometimes charitable individuals and groups or the governments of an economy respond by transferring purchasing power to such individuals in order that they might attain whatever level of want satisfaction that the donors desire for them. If such transfers are not or can not be made in sufficient amounts, poverty-afflicted individuals have little to lose by encouraging a change in the economy's structure or government.

Should the people on the bottom of an economy's income scale receive a larger share? That is a value judgment. Perhaps a better question would be how much will those at the bottom receive if the economy operates at high levels of production. It may well be that policies leading to sustained prosperity and a growing level of income are better weapons in the war on poverty than policies that change the percentage of income going to the lower income groups. And though it is true that the aged, the disabled, and the unfit still will be unable to earn incomes, the existing amounts of transfer could be concentrated on these individuals and thus increase their incomes toward more acceptable levels.

THE RATIONALE FOR MACROECONOMICS

No economy has ever claimed attainment of a stage of economic development wherein it could meet the ultimate economic goal of producing and distributing enough goods and services to fully satisfy all its citizens' diverse and conflicting desires. Instead, the ultimate goal remains unattained, and the degree to which economies use and expand their productive capacities and the manner in which the production is distributed remain crucially important to all the people of the world. Perhaps the economic wants of man are insatiable and conflicting and thus, unlike the mythical grail quest, never to be satisfied. Nevertheless, each economy tends to have as its basic goal the satisfaction of as many economic needs as possible, and there tends to be a concern for the general economic conditions that exist in each economy, regardless of its structure.

With the goal of improving conditions and more universally achieving the ultimate goal, there is a continual tendency for changes to be advocated in the economies' structures and policies as well as in the governments that make and administer the policies. It goes without saying that most of the advocates of a particular economic policy or form of economic organization are sincere. The dilemma is that hopes and good intentions are not sufficient to ensure that benefits will follow from a particular policy or change. A classic example of this would be the policies of the market-oriented governments of Great Britain and the United States in the late 1920's and early 1930's. These governments wanted to maintain or regain prosperous free-enterprise-oriented economies and thought their policies were appropriate to do so. Though intended to conserve a free-enterprise type of economy, their policies caused their economies' general level of performance to decline so markedly that the socialists were able to come to power in Great Britain and the liberal democrats with their "New Deal" and its increased government intervention in markets to come to power in the United States. Rather than accomplishing their intention of conserving economies based on markets and prices, the "conservative" policies thus, in fact, only conserved socialism and increased governmental interference. As we shall see, many popular and so-called conservative economic policies may well have an adverse effect on market economies and thus be anything but conservative in nature. Economic policies that conserve market economies are those that enhance their economic performances. We shall discuss such policies in detail.

Market-Oriented vs. Planned Economies

The major difference between price-oriented market economies and economies in which production and distribution occur along the lines specified by a government plan is in terms of their unique institutions and different forms of economic organization. Many policies, institutions, and economic forms used by particular economies were initially introduced to eliminate or reduce certain macroeconomic problems that had existed prior to their introduction. This is particularly true, for example, in the case of the socialist economies wherein planning was implemented in an effort to eliminate various macroeconomic problems considered (often inaccurately) to be uniquely associated with price-oriented market economies.

At this point in the evolution of economic conditions and knowledge, both the planning and pricing forms of organizing an economy seem to be capable of providing some degree of growing production and an equitable distribution of that production. The basic question is whether pricing or planning can do the best job when rational policies are being pursued by those who understand how each type of economy operates. In the past, particularly in the market economies such as those of North America or

Western Europe, such understanding did not prevail and the policies may not have encouraged maximum performance. But performance in these economies improved in the 1960's due to the dissemination of economic knowledge, and further improvements are quite possible. As a result of improvement in the performance of the market economies as well as dissatisfaction with some results of planning, several socialist economies began to move back toward pricing and away from planning. On the other hand, unfortunately for the advocates of pricing, the United States' performance in the early 1970's was substantially below the level it had spent the better part of the previous decade demonstrating that it could attain, and the momentum of change from planning to pricing in the socialist economies was reduced.

Macroeconomics emphasizes the theories and policies applicable to market economies rather than planned ones. Nevertheless, in a subsequent chapter a brief description appears of the manner in which Marx derived his forecast that market economies would tend to evolve toward continually more undesirable conditions. Marx's views are included because they provided the philosophical and theoretical basis by which certain economies rationalized leaving the actual and projected problems associated with market-oriented economies for the problems associated with planning-oriented economies. Unfortunately for the followers of Marx, his theories and projections have not been borne out. We shall see in *Macroeconomics* why the conditions Marx projected do not need to be expected in the future. It is important to note, however, that the conditions Marx foresaw certainly could occur in the market economies if inadequate economic policies are implemented by governments not understanding the complex macroeconomic considerations related to market economies.

Market Economies

A market economy with appropriate policies tends to efficiently produce and distribute as much as possible of whatever goods and services are wanted most of all. Production and distribution in market economies occur in response to the affirmative purchasing decisions of buyers. In essence, individuals in such an economy are motivated to obtain the highest possible incomes consistent with their noneconomic motivations and to allocate those incomes to acquire whatever is available that they value the most. Producers seeking incomes respond by bringing together labor and capital to produce goods and services for the buyers. The producers tend to use labor and capital as efficiently as possible in order to keep their expenses down and their incomes up. This tendency toward efficiency is important because the smaller the amount of labor and capital needed to produce a particular product, the more labor and capital will be left over and thus available to produce other goods and services.

The owners of the factors of production also want the highest possible incomes consistent with their noneconomic motivations. They therefore tend to offer their factors to whichever producers will pay them the highest prices for their factors' services. Furthermore, they tend to increase the productivity of their factors whenever possible, for if their factors can produce even more valuable products, their owners can expect to receive large incomes from the producers that employ them. The factor owners tend to get income increases when their factors contribute more to production; if they are not paid what their factors are worth and do not get increases when their factors are worth more, they have the alternative of taking their factors to producers who will pay for them on the basis of what the factors contribute. Competition among the producers to get factors from the limited supply available tends to lead them to pay the factor owners an amount equal to what their factors add to the value of the producers' production.

Inefficient production of less desirable goods and services tends not to occur in a market economy. Producers who seek to produce less desired goods and services will tend not to be able to sell their products for money enough to compete with producers of more valuable products for the labor and capital necessary for production. Furthermore, producers can not use unnecessarily large amounts of labor and capital to produce a product. If they do, other more efficient producers using less labor and capital will have lower costs of production and be able to price low enough to drive them out of business.

The other great genius of a market economy, in addition to its tendency to efficiently produce what is wanted most of all, is its tendency to automatically adopt the most efficient methods of production and to keep what it produces in line with the changing desires of its purchasers. Such economies may not yet have reached the ultimate economic goal of producing enough to satisfy all the economic needs of the participants, but they do tend to continually adjust to provide as much satisfaction of needs as is possible with a given stock of factors and level of technology. For example, if individuals in an economy come more and more to prefer a certain type of product, the price of the product will tend to be bid up as purchasers compete to acquire the available production. The profits of the producers will tend to rise and to cause the existing producers to expand their production while at the same time attracting producers away from the production of the now relatively unfavored items. Labor and capital will then be worth more to the producers of the favored items, and they will be able to bid these factors away from their former employments producing less desired items.

Market Economy Problems

There is no reason to expect that a market economy functioning in response to price changes will automatically adjust to provide either the maximum amount of production, rapid rate of production, or a relatively rapid rate of production growth. For example, purchasing may decline and thus cause production and employment to be reduced since producers will not keep employing labor and capital to produce products that they can not sell. Or prices may rise and eliminate the motivation to produce by reducing the purchasing power of those whose production efforts have enabled them to acquire wealth. Or foreign economies may reduce their purchasing or engage in pricing activities that cause residents of a market economy to purchase abroad instead of in their own economy. Or taxes on earned incomes may be increased, tending to reduce the incentives to provide labor and capital for the production process and tending to reduce purchasing in the economy by decreasing the amount of incomes individuals or businesses have available after taxes. Or the economy's money supply may be expanded too slowly so that the growth of purchasing and production is restricted by the absence of a medium of exchange and by the resulting increase in the level of interest rates and the lack of credit.

The list of problems that can arise in a market economy and keep it from efficiently producing the maximum possible amounts of the goods and services most desired by the purchasers is virtually endless. These problems are as interrelated as the economy's markets; as a result, the solution to one problem may aggravate another. Nevertheless, although general prosperity is not by any means inevitable, it is not necessary to junk the market system. As we shall see, prosperity is attainable in a market economy if rational economic policies are implemented.

The previous discussion of the nature of market economies has assumed competition among the various producers to sell their products and to hire factors of production, and occurrence of adjustments if preferences and conditions change and proper policies eliminate arising problems. But most market economies do not have perfect forms of competition. And ignorance, time, and distance can all combine to keep buyers from buying the best products and from producers with the lowest prices. Also, individuals may be motivated not to seek to improve their productivity or not to move from one occupation or place of employment to another by the psychic (non-economic) incomes they receive from traditional employments or the desire for serenity or their appreciation for leisure and beauty. Self-interest in an economic sense is not the only motivation of man, and competition among buyers and sellers may not be perfect. Still, so long as they are powerful forces within the market economy, the economy's performance will tend toward the optimum described above as long as appropriate economic policies are pursued.

Planned Economies as an Alternative to Market Economies

Over half a century ago the economic structures and institutions of certain price-oriented economies began to be reorganized away from market and prices and into a system wherein their production and distribution were based on planning. In such economies the planners determine what should be produced, how it should be produced, and who should get it; they specify the allocation of the economies' factors of production to ensure the types and amounts of production that the planners desire.

There are certain advantages in such a system. First, since prices do not have the same importance as in market economies, they can be eliminated or arbitrarily fixed so that such economies need never experience inflation. Second, the economies are organized so that production does not depend on purchasing. Thus labor and capital can be engaged in the production processes even if there are no buyers. Consequently, there need never be a condition of general unemployment as might exist in a market economy if purchasing were reduced or not increased as fast as the economy's productive capacity. Advocates of planned economies often emphasize that an advantage of such economies is that they are not subject to purchasing fluctuations and price changes and they do have a capacity for providing incomes for individuals such as the aged or injured who do not have any productive powers. Nevertheless, stable prices, full employment, and charity for the unproductive are not unique to planned economies. They can occur in market economies as well.

The potential dilemmas of a planned economic system are as numerous, albeit in some ways different, as those that can exist in an economy with a market orientation. For example, the planners may arrange to have the economy's labor and capital produce things other than those that people in the economy would prefer to have produced by the economy's labor and capital. In other words, the major problem of planners is to get preferences revealed and the economy's producers to respond efficiently to them. An additional problem in a planned economy is that its producers tend not to be motivated to minimize their use of labor and capital so that there will tend to be as much labor and capital as possible left over for the production of other items. Instead of profits based on market-determined prices and costs, planned economies traditionally use profits based on arbitrarily established prices and costs or other measures such as quotas to measure the efficiency of their productive units. Thus, in a planned economy not only does there tend to be a lack of productive efficiency because of absence of a way to measure it, but there is also no measure of the value of the contribution made by a particular factor. It is therefore quite possible for a planned economy to have all of its labor and capital employed and its nonmarket-established prices stable at the same time its production is low because the economy is inefficiently producing not particularly desired items and growing slowly because its efforts to expand are arbitrarily concentrated in areas that appeal to planners but involve low productive-yield increments. Also inherent in such an economy is the lack of freedom associated with actual or *de facto* government ownership of the factors of production. The government ownership characteristic of planned economies must exist to prevent private owners of labor and capital from ignoring the government plans for production and distribution.

MACROANALYSIS

The desire to improve the performance of economies and to understand how and why they operate has led economists to probe every possible economic nook and cranny. Microeconomists have long examined the behavior and motivation of individual participants in an economy. But it was not until Lord Keynes in the 1930's that Macroeconomics, sometimes called *Keynesian economics* or the *new economics*, arrived. Keynes criticized the primarily microeconomic ideas developed prior to that time as inadequate either to explain the depression of the 1930's or to suggest policies that might restore prosperity without surrendering the advantages and freedoms of market economies. He suggested that market economies as a whole might have unique aspects and problems that should be considered in addition to those of the economies' individual participants, and he presented his macroeconomic view of the basic nature of those aspects and problems.

The macroeconomists who followed Keynes have expanded and modified almost all of the original Keynesian analysis. But like Keynes they are concerned with the economic aspects of the economy as a whole, and they owe an intellectual debt to him for drawing attention to the need to study the economy as a whole and for bringing together and refining the initial concepts and analyses of earlier economists in order to do so.

The present concern of macroeconomists has many facets. They want to know what causes the general level of prices to rise and what policies can stop the increase. They are curious about why an economy's production grows and why the capacities of some economies grow faster than others. Macroeconomists are concerned when production recedes and millions of men lose their jobs. They want to know the effect of various government activities, and they are concerned about the economic relationships between economies. Macroeconomists, in essence, are concerned with the economic state and well-being of the many millions of people who participate in an economy rather than the condition of a particular individual or economic unit.

The Use of Models

The specific concerns of macroeconomists are virtually infinite since a complex market economy such as that of the United States contains many millions of interrelated markets and prices and untold numbers of unique institutional restrictions and personal preferences. This means that many things can change and possibly adversely affect an economy. Specific causes of undesirable circumstances and possible policies that can be implemented to prevent or offset their occurrence require knowledge of the economy in question. Unfortunately, despite the importance of the ability to forecast the effect of a condition that might arise or be caused, the experiences of the past may not be completely applicable to the present or future state of an economy. On the other hand, a multitude of experiments can not be carried out in an economy in advance to determine which potential solution will be most successful in the event of the need for policy.

The only alternative to actual experiences or experiments with an economy is experimentation with a model representing the basic conditions that exist in the economy. Such a model allows economic analysts to test their hypotheses without subjecting an actual economy to possible mistakes. This means that even though a model may oversimplify to some extent from the economy it represents by reducing the number of relationships and variables in order to get the model to a workable size, it must accurately depict the basic relationships of the economy and the nature and size of the basic economic variables. Information about relationships and data for models comes directly from the experiences of the economy or similar economies or from the economic theories that have been presented about such economies. The more applicable the data and the theories, the better the models and the better the conclusions that they may yield. Thus, the better the understanding and policies that can be derived from them.

Since models typically use only what their builders consider to be the key relationships and variables, different models may be constructed to represent the same economic conditions and relationships. And if a model does not adequately represent the actual economic situation, the use of the model may lead to erroneous conclusions as to the effect of a particular policy or condition. This means that projections for tomorrow's economy that merely extend or enlarge present conditions must be approached cautiously if they do not anticipate or allow for changes in the basic relationships or the nature of the variables. Furthermore, it should be remembered that there are more than just purely economic factors that influence an economy; if forecasting is made on the basis of purely economic factors alone, there can be serious miscalculations for technological, social, and political traits can drastically alter economic possibilities.

Despite the problems of using models, they can represent the basic conditions existing in an economy and can be used to determine the effect of a change in an actual economy with the basic characteristics used in the model. It is the sophisticated macroeconomic policies for market economies and the theories and models on which they are based that are discussed in *Macroeconomics*. As you consider the models and theories that follow, remember that the basis for their existence is the economic conditions that they represent; the development of models and their manipulation is the means and not the end of economic analysis. Models and theories are only useful to the extent that they are necessary to analyze an economy or aspects of it.

The purpose of economics and thus of economists is to help society reach its goals. And models are used because in a positive sense they help explain what *has* and what *will* occur and because in a normative sense they help decide policies on the basis of what *should* occur. The positive aspect of models and economists is that they provide understanding; the normative aspect is that they help society reach its goals.

● REFERENCES

de Leeuw, F., "The Concept of Capacity," *Journal of the American Statistical Association*, (Dec. 1962).

Fishman and Fishman, *Employment, Unemployment, and Economic Growth* (Crowell, 1969).

Friedman, M., *Capitalism and Freedom* (University of Chicago Press, 1962).

———, *Essays in Positive Economics* (University of Chicago Press, 1953).

Mundell, R., *Man and Economics* (McGraw-Hill, 1968).

Romano, R., and M. Leiman, Eds., *Views on Capitalism* (Glencoe Press, 1970).

Ulmer, M. J., *The Welfare State* (Houghton-Mifflin, 1969).

The National Income Accounts

2

The various national income accounts of an economy depict the sizes and compositions of some of the basic economic activities occurring in the economy and its principal sectors. Together the accounts indicate the general level of performance provided by a nation's economy. Examined over time the accounts indicate the direction in which the economy and its basic sectors are heading and the speed with which they are moving. Familiarity with the national income accounts is essential to the successful study of macroeconomics because the concepts and data associated with each account provide important foundations for macroeconomic analysis.

GROSS NATIONAL PRODUCT

The purchasing of newly produced commodities is important to an economy because of its influence on the level of production. Business firms will continue to produce goods and services, commodities, only if they can sell what they produce at prices that cover their costs of production. In other words, it is the purchasing of new factories, new homes, haircuts, medical care, education, new cars, and other commodities which causes them to come into being.

The total amount of purchasing occurring in an economy during a given time period, since it represents, in essence, the money expended on the finished new goods and services produced in the economy, equals the money value of all the commodities produced in the economy during that period. The total amount of production in a nation is its *gross national product* or *GNP*. The money value of a nation's GNP equals the amount of money expenditures or their equivalent that occur to purchase the commodities produced in the nation's economy.

To construct accurate GNP estimates, care must be taken not to include purchases of items that are not newly finished goods and services. The inclusion of such items would result in overstating the money value of the new commodities available to meet an economy's needs. For instance, the purchase of a new car for $4,000 is included among the purchases of finished goods and services that are part of an economy's GNP. It is included because, as a result of its occurring, a new commodity which a buyer values at $4,000 is brought into being to satisfy his needs. But intermediate purchases related to the production and sale of the car are not counted. Such excluded purchases could cover, for example: (1) a steel company's purchase of coal and iron ore for $500 for use in making steel; (2) an auto parts company's purchase of steel for $1,400 to make auto parts; (3) an automobile company's purchase of the parts for $2,200 for use in making the car; (4) a dealer's purchase of the car for $3,500. Despite all these transactions, the money value of all the goods and services actually provided to the economy is only $4,000, which is the value of the car. All the other transactions cover only intermediate activities necessary for the production of the commodity. Obviously inclusion of the expenditures involved in intermediate activities would swell the estimated money value of the commodities being produced far beyond their actual value.

Estimates of gross national product provide economists with one of their most useful tools for analyzing the performance of an economy. Two examples of the types of possible performance analysis should be sufficient to emphasize the usefulness of GNP as such a tool. First, gross national product estimates can be used to measure the performance of an economy over time by comparing commodity production during one period with that of other periods. Thus, if an economist finds that the money value of the commodities produced in the United States (GNP) this year is 20 percent higher than last year and that the general level of commodity prices is also 20 percent higher, he quickly deduces that there has been no change in the real level of commodity production in the economy. What has happened rather is that the additional money expenditures have merely purchased the same amount of commodities but at higher prices than the previous year. On the other hand, if the economist finds that total purchasing has risen 20 percent while prices have risen only 5 percent, he knows that commodity production in the economy has risen approximately 15 percent.

Gross national product figures also can be used to analyze the changes in total purchasing required to obtain maximum levels of production. For example, consider an economy in which commodities valued at $1,200 billion have been sold during a given year. If a survey indicates that only three-fourths of the economy's labor and capital was employed to produce those commodities, one may estimate that additional commodities with money values of $400 billion might have been obtained if all the available labor and capital had been employed. This estimate provides the basis for determining one of the requirements for attainment of maximum levels of commodity production: either purchasing would have to be $400 billion higher to induce business firms to produce the potential additional units of production at the existing level of prices, or the general level of commodity prices would have to fall 25 percent so that all the commodities could be purchased with the original level of money expenditures.

The Purchasing Included in Each GNP Component

Because production is important to a nation, governments of market economies typically make efforts to appraise the amount of purchasing of finished goods and services that causes production to occur. In the United States, the Department of Commerce computes and publishes estimates of the sizes of the different components of total purchasing in periodicals such as the *Survey of Current Business*. The categories which the Department of Commerce includes in each major purchasing component are described below. The various factors that determine the size of each component are discussed in subsequent chapters.

Consumption purchasing. Purchasing included in consumption spending involves those expenditures made by households and private, nonprofit institutions, such as private colleges and unions, on the following major types of goods and services: *durable goods*—those items that may be expected to yield benefits to their user for an extended period of time, such as stoves and automobiles; *nondurable goods*—those goods whose values are used up rather quickly, such as shoes and shampoo; *services*—those commodities whose values are obtained as soon as they are purchased, such as haircuts, bus rides, and the use of houses by renters.

Specifically excluded from consumption purchasing are expenditures by households and private, nonprofit institutions for structures such as houses and hospitals. These items are arbitrarily placed in the category of investment purchasing. Nevertheless, their presence does influence the level of consumption purchasing because the valuable services they provide over their lifetimes are considered to be purchased by their users in each time period that such services are received. Determination of the value of this consumption purchasing is no problem when tenants actually are buying housing services with their rent payments; an estimate of the amount of rent tenants pay in order to purchase the services generated by structures is included in the service portion of consumption purchasing. A problem does occur, however, when owners occupy their own structures; they pay no rent even though their structures generate the same kind of services in each time period. However, an estimate of the rental value of the services produced by owner-occupied dwellings during a given period is made by determining the amount of rent owners would have to pay to purchase the services of their structures if they did not own them. This estimate of "imputed rents" is then added to the total value of the economy's production and is considered to be a purchase of a newly produced commodity by the homeowner who is simultaneously the seller of the housing services provided by the dwelling.

Similar methods are used to determine the value of food and fuel produced and consumed on farms and wages and salaries paid in kind. The "kind" aspect of wages and salaries refers to payments in terms of commodities such as housing or food which the recipient is allowed to consume in return for the services he renders. Since these commodities represent something of value that is being consumed in the economy, the commodities in effect are being purchased by the farmer or worker who consumes them. Thus the appropriate subsections of consumer purchasing are increased by an estimate of the cost of producing the commodities that have been paid in kind and an estimate of the payment that the farmer would have received if he had sold commodities instead of consuming them.

Investment purchasing. Investment purchasing comprises those expenditures by households, nonprofit institutions, and profit-seeking businesses for the acquisition of the following types of capital commodities: *structures*—houses and factories; *producers' durable equipment*—machinery; and *changes in business inventories.* Inventory changes are included because the normal operation of a business may require maintaining adequate inventories of the various inputs and final products so that production is not halted or a sale prevented because of the temporary lack of a particular component or product. Since business firms must purchase and hold these inventories in order to operate, the items in them are considered to be finished products and the building up of an inventory is considered to involve investment purchasing.

Specifically not included as investment purchasing are money outlays that, even though commonly called "investments," are for items other than newly produced commodities. A partial list of these items would contain such things as land and all financial instruments such as stocks and bonds. Money outlays to acquire these things are excluded because the expenditures that bring them into existence or cause a change in their ownership do not directly cause productive activity to occur in the economy.

It may be easier to see why expenditures to obtain these items are not viewed as investment if their purchase is considered an investment by the buyer whose act of investment is offset by the *dis*investment of the seller without there being any change in the number of new, productive commodities being purchased in the economy. In the case of new issues of stocks and bonds, even though they may be issued to raise money for investment purchasing purposes, the money outlays merely acquire pieces of paper containing some promise of future performance such as repayment of the money plus interest. Investment purchasing of productive commodities is a separate activity that occurs only when and if the money obtained from the sale of the pieces of paper is used to buy capital assets such as factories, machinery, and inventories. Such purchasing is counted when it occurs.

Government purchasing. Included in government purchasing are the expenditures made by all the governments in an economy to purchase goods and services. This purchasing typically is broken down into those purchases made by the federal government and those made by the state and local governments such as cities, counties, and school districts. The federal purchasing is broken down further into national defense and other purchasing. The "other" purchasing includes nondefense items such as highways, hospitals, the space program, and grants for research and development.

Included in the foregoing components are all government expenditures to obtain the goods and services produced by government workers; all government purchasing of goods and services, no matter how durable; and the gross investment expenditures of government enterprises. The value, however, of any goods and services that are produced and sold by government enterprises is subtracted from the level of government purchasing. This is done so that the level of total purchasing will not be overstated by the counting of both consumer and business purchasing of these items and government purchasing of the services and materials that provided them. The production and sale of water and power by a municipal government is an example of such a government enterprise. The water and power is purchased by its users and their expenditures are part of the GNP. The government expenditures related to the production of the water and power are considered to be of an intermediate nature and are excluded from the GNP in order to avoid overstating the value of the water and power actually produced.

Governments at all political levels also disburse money for other purposes than the purchase of commodities. For example, they may provide charity for the needy or purchase land on which to build schools. Since only the government purchasing of goods and services directly adds to the total purchasing that induces commodity production, all other forms of government spending such as transfer payments (charity), interest on the national debt, subsidies, and loans are not counted as part of government purchasing.

Foreign purchasing. Included in this GNP sector are all expenditures by foreign consumers, governments, and investors for the goods and services which the economy produces for foreign purchasers. Specifically excluded from foreign purchasing are the same items that are excluded from consumption, investment, and government purchasing: land, financial instruments, etc.

GNP Estimates and Modifications

Table 2-1 contains a sample GNP computation for the United States. Notice that a relatively small net figure of $8.8 billion is added for foreign purchasing even though commodities produced in the economy are sold abroad for $73.4 billion. The net figure is used to offset an overestimation of GNP that originates in the other major types of purchasing. Their overestimation occurs because the U.S. Department of Commerce includes purchasing of foreign-produced commodities in its estimates of the total amount of purchasing done by each of the other major types of buyers even though such purchasing of foreign commodities does not directly induce production in the United States' economy or affect the value of the commodities produced in the economy. For instance, in the Table 2-1 example, import purchasing of $64.6 billion has been included in the consumption, government, and investment purchasing figures even though no production has taken place in the economy because of them. Since this amount of purchasing has already been included by overstating the size of the other components, the Department of Commerce need add only the "net export" amount of $8.8 billion to obtain the full effect on total purchasing of having

TABLE 2-1
Gross National Product by Expenditures (Billions of Dollars)

Personal consumption expenditures		943.0
Durable goods	147.4	
Nondurable goods	425.0	
Services	370.6	
Gross private domestic investment		210.4
Structures	115.2	
Producers' durable equipment	82.0	
Net change in business inventories	13.2	
Net exports of goods and services		8.8
Exports	73.4	
Imports	−64.6	
Government purchasing of goods and services		339.2
Federal	183.4	
National Defense	144.4	
Other	40.6	
Government sales	−1.6	
State and Local	155.8	
GROSS NATIONAL PRODUCT		1501.4

foreign purchases of $73.4 billion. The advantage of the "net export" approach is that it allows the government to compute both the economy's GNP and the total value of the commodities which the economy's consumption, investment, and government purchasers have obtained from both domestic and foreign producers.

A somewhat similar situation exists with previously purchased commodities in the form of inventories. It exists because commodities tend to be sold out of the older stocks in existing inventories with the inventories simultaneously being replenished with whatever new items are needed to keep them at the desired levels. But replacement purchasing of commodities continually being sold out of inventories is not inventory investment purchasing. Inventory investment is the purchasing that changes the actual size of an economy's inventories. Thus it is necessary to include only net inventory additions or subtractions as part of an economy's investment purchasing. For example, consider an economy that opens a year with its producers holding inventories that they had previously purchased for $50 billion and that during the year the original inventories are sold out. Fifty-five billion dollars is spent to purchase new commodities and to replenish the depleted inventories. Total purchasing in the year is $55 billion with $5 billion of inventory investment and $50 billion of purchases by the buyers of the original inventory. More will be said about net exports and changes in the levels of business inventories in this and later chapters.

GNP Via Value Added

Another method of estimating GNP involves totaling the value added to a commodity at each stage of production. For example, consider what happens in the production of the $4,000 automobile.

1. One company starts with nothing but ore or mineral deposits in the earth and turns it into coal and iron ore valued at $500.
2. A steel company buys the coal and iron ore for $500 and transforms it into steel valued at $1,400, thus adding another $900 to the value of what was initially taken out of the ground.
3. An auto parts company purchases the steel for $1,400 and makes auto parts which it sells for $2,200. It adds another $800 to the value of the materials that were being made into a car.
4. An automobile company buys the parts for $2,200 and uses them to make the car which it sells to a dealer for $3,500. The automobile company adds $1,300 in value to the materials as it refines them into a finished product.
5. Finally, a dealer buys the car for $3,500 and sells it to a consumer for $4,000. He adds the $500 to the value of the car as he moves it from the automobile company into the hands of the consumer.

The total value added by the various different stages of production in the foregoing example is $4,000. Thus it is possible to estimate an economy's GNP by adding the differences between the value of the material inputs and outputs at each stage of production. This approach is useful not only because it provides a means of checking the GNP estimates obtained by summing the various types of commodity purchasing; also it can be used to identify the degree to which each sector of the economy contributes to the value of the commodities produced and to establish the importance of the intermediate sales that are not included in the national income accounts.

GNP Component Modifications

The purchasing data for each of the major types of buyers include their purchases of used assets such as structures and producers' durable equipment from the other major buying sectors of the economy even though production is not directly induced by such purchasing. For example, if a government sells a used factory to a business firm for $1 million, investment purchasing is increased by that amount. Then, to prevent the value of the commodities actually produced in the economy from being overstated, the figure for government purchasing is reduced by that amount. This procedure has the advantage of identifying the amount of commodities that each sector in the economy actually finishes with and, of course, total GNP remains unchanged. The point to remember is that the estimates resulting from this procedure obscure the importance of each major type of buyer in terms of purchasing newly produced commodities and thus in terms of actually causing production to occur.

A somewhat similar modification is the inventory valuation adjustment used to bring an economy's inventory withdrawals in line with current prices. This is done to get a better measure of the economy's inventory investment purchasing and the profitability of the economy's producers. Consider a firm that sells off or uses part of its inventory of commodities originally costing $8 each but then must replace the 1000 items it has withdrawn with 1,000 replacement commodities for which it must now pay $10. This firm's accounts will indicate that the cost of the items it has used or sold is $8,000 and that its inventory investment purchasing has increased by $2,000 to a total of $10,000. But the firm has not acquired any additional items. In order to reflect the actual stability of the inventories in the economy in which the firm produces, the economy's government reduces the total inventory investment purchasing reported for the economy by the $2,000 and increases by $2,000 its estimate of the costs of producing the goods and services that have been produced and sold to purchasers. The inventory valuation adjustment tends to reduce an economy's reported investment purchasing when the prices of inventory items are rising and to increase the estimate of such purchasing when inventory prices are falling.

Goods and Services Excluded from the GNP

The goal of an economy's gross national product account is to provide an estimate of the value of the production occurring in the economy. But some items are arbitrarily excluded from the United States' GNP estimates on one basis or another. And the estimates of other items are modified in order to improve the accuracy of the GNP account and its components. But whatever goods and services are produced in an economy to satisfy needs should, conceptually at least, be included even if they satisfy the needs of only a few of the economy's participants. Some of the most significant of the United States' exclusions and modifications are discussed below. In a later chapter we shall discuss the possibility of bringing some of the excluded goods and services into the GNP estimates.

Housework and self-service. The valuable services that men purchase from their housekeepers and automobile mechanics are part of their economy's gross national product. But what if the men marry their housekeepers and repair their own cars? The same valuable services occur in the economy, but now these activities are outside the economy's market structure and are excluded from the economy's gross national product. The domestic services of housewives and almost all forms of nonfarm self-serving production are excluded from the official estimates of the value of production occurring in the United States. The source of the exclusion is the difficulty of assigning values to goods and services produced by individuals for themselves since there is no market transaction to examine. Virtually the only exception is in the case of food and fuel produced on farms for consumption by the producing farms. Estimates of the size and market values of these items are used to expand the United States' GNP by assuming that the farmer is both producer and purchaser and is purchasing food and fuel from himself.

Illegal activities. Gambling table losses in Las Vegas are expenditures to purchase recreation goods and services and are included as part of the United States' GNP. The same goods and services in Massachusetts or Illinois are illegal and not included in gross national product. Similar conditions exist for alcoholic beverages that are legal in some areas and not in others. Thus an increase in the production of the legal manufacturers of alcohol raises an economy's GNP while the same increase on the part of bootleggers has no effect at all. The same type of situation exists whenever an illegal act occurs. But many of the illegal activities satisfy the needs of those who voluntarily partake of them. Thus the efforts of a majority to impose its version of morality onto others by declaring illegal those activities that they do not approve does not mean that those activities are not valuable products of the economy's factors of production and should not be part of the economy's gross national product.

Interest payments. Business interest payments are considered to be purchases that acquire valuable financing services. But consumer and government interest payments are not considered to involve the purchase of such services. Consumer interest expenditures were withdrawn from GNP in 1965 on the premise that they are not purchases that cause the production of valuable goods and services to occur. Thus consumer interest is no longer considered to be the price that is paid for the consumer financing services that help provide for the satisfaction of consumers by allowing commodities to be acquired prior to the completion of the required savings. Interestingly enough, consumer interest expenses are still carried as part of the prices that compose the Consumer Price Index. The index thus rises when the interest rates paid to finance automobiles increase because it means that the monthly payment to purchase the services of the autos will increase.

A similar uncounted purchase of valuable financing services exists in the case of interest payments resulting from government debt. The interest payments are, in effect, the price that governments pay for the financing services of banks and financiers; the interest payments induce them to provide and create funds to finance the governments. But such interest expenditures are not counted as purchases even though expenditures to buy paper and presses and the services of printers are added to the GNP estimates. Thus an economy's GNP increases if a government buys paper and prints money to create the funds that it needs but does not expand if a government makes an interest payment to a bank in order to induce the bank to create the funds that the government needs.

Transfers. A "transfer" occurs when purchasing power is given or transferred without obtaining something of value in return. In the United States, for instance, transfers are given by persons, businesses, and governments to such recipients as the poor, the infirm, the unemployed, the aged, and the agrarian enfarmed. Such expenditures are not counted as part of the economy's GNP even though, as in the case of disabled veterans, they may well be considered by their recipients as a form of delayed payment for services rendered.

In any case why should the expenditure of a dollar to acquire a hot fudge sundae be considered as a purchase of a valuable commodity whose provision by an economy tends to expand its GNP while the alternative of giving the dollar to someone in need is not part of GNP? If it can be assumed that rational men allocate their incomes to maximize utility or satisfaction, then it must be assumed that the transfer expenditures provide more satisfaction to the donors than the donors could obtain by allocating the funds to purchase other goods and services. Perhaps the act of making a transfer provides a form of satisfaction because it makes the donor feel successful and powerful. Perhaps the donor receives satisfaction from the security of knowing that he may be helping to establish or perpetuate a tradition that he can depend on if he ever becomes impoverished. But if the donors receive such satisfaction from their transfer expenditures, then the recipients of the transfers are producing a service comparable in value to that provided by other producers in the economy and perhaps the value of transfers should be included as part of an economy's GNP.

Leisure and the quality of life. Blue skies and racial peace and leisure may yield more satisfaction to some people than do shiny new cars and bottles of beer. But no effort has yet been made to add the value of leisure and the quality of life produced by an economy to the economy's gross national product. Yet it is difficult to say that two economies are doing equally well in producing goods and services if both have identical gross national products but one is continually providing relatively cleaner skies and rivers. The same reasoning applies to such situations as where leisure is valued and more leisure is provided by one economy, where greater confidence and satisfaction is produced by the social policies of an economy's governments, and where more satisfaction is produced by an economy's ancient traditions and heritage. For example, as the GNP estimates are presently constructed, an economy with a two percent annual rate of increase in its GNP would appear to be more successful than an economy with the same GNP that could have raised its GNP 10 percent during the same period of time but did not do so because the economy's participants desire more leisure. The economy's participants, in other words, value the additional leisure in excess of the value of the alternative of a 10 percent increase in goods and services other than leisure. There is no measure of the quality of life or the value of leisure in the gross national product estimates as they are presently constructed.

Subsidies. Benefits from the production of certain products may accrue to individuals other than the purchasers. For example, the benefits of a rapid transit system are received by both the purchaser who rides on the system and the public generally who benefit from the resulting less crowded streets and less polluted air. But the latter beneficiaries do not directly participate in the purchasing. Thus a highly valued product may be produced in inadequate quantities if at all. Governments, in an attempt to encourage more production than would otherwise occur in response to the purchases of the direct users, may transfer additional funds to the producers in order to subsidize their productive activities and encourage them to produce additional commodities. The producers earn both the subsidies and the money spent by the direct users and thus both are part of national income. But only the purchases of the direct users are used to estimate the value of an economy's gross national product even though the governmental subsidies occur in order that the economy might obtain commodities that are particularly valued. Conceptually, however, there is no difference between a government subsidy that causes production to occur and a government purchase that causes production to occur.

NATIONAL INCOME

Producers receive payments from purchasers when the producers sell goods and services to them. The receipts that are obtained from the sale of newly produced goods and services, barring some exceptions, constitute the "earned income" of the owners of the factors of production used to produce these commodities. All the receipts tend to become earned income since they either are paid out to the owners of the labor and property employed by the firms for their use in the productive process or are left to the owners of the producing firms as payment for the labor and property which they themselves contributed. The total of this income earned by the production of commodities in a nation's economy within a given period of time is the nation's *national income* (NI).

An economy's national income tends to be equal in size to the economy's gross national product.[1] The equality exists because each dollar spent by purchasers tends to be received as income by the producers of the purchased commodity. Since the payments made by purchasers tend to be equal to the incomes received by the owners of the labor and property to compensate them for the use of their labor and property in the production process, it is possible to determine the value and amount of commodity production occurring in an economy in two ways: via the product approach that examines commodity purchasing or value added; or via the income approach that examines the income earned producing the commodities.

Estimates of gross national product and national income are computed periodically in most modern countries such as the United States. This two-fold approach provides a means of doublechecking the accuracy of the estimates and thus helps to assure a more adequate depiction of the size and money value of the commodity-producing activity occurring in the economy.

---

[1] The estimates are not exactly equal for reasons that will presently be discussed in some detail.

The Components of National Income

In computing national income the U.S. Department of Commerce lists the types of income received for producing goods and services in the following categories. (An estimate of national income is presented in Table 2-2.)

TABLE 2-2
National Income by Type of Income (Billions of Dollars)

Compensation of employees		850.6
Wages and salaries	774.2	
Supplements to wages and salaries	76.4	
Proprietors' income		141.2
Business and professional	105.2	
Farm	36.0	
Rental income of persons		34.6
Corporate profits		151.6
Net interest		77.0
NATIONAL INCOME		1245.0

Compensation of employees. This largest component of national income includes the total amount of *wages and salaries* and *supplements to wages and salaries* that persons receive as remuneration for their work. Wages and salaries cover the money receipts commonly received as wages and salaries as well as commissions, tips, and bonuses. Payments in kind are included on the basis of their money value in the market or their cost of production. Supplements to wages and salaries refer to various items of value which persons receive as a result of their productive efforts but which traditionally are not included as wages and salaries. Among such receipts are employer contributions for social security, private pensions and welfare funds, compensation for injuries, and the pay of military reservists.

Proprietors' income. This component of national income includes the monetary value of the cash and kind payments received by sole proprietorships, partnerships, and producers' cooperatives for their productive efforts.

Rental income of persons. Rental income includes the monetary receipts of persons who actually rent real property to tenants as well as an estimate of the rent payments which the owner-occupants of nonfarm dwellings would have received for the services of their dwellings had they rented them to tenants. (Estimates of the rental incomes that would have been received for the service of owner-occupied farms and business structures are included in the other components of national income.) Additionally, this item includes all royalty earnings from patents, copyrights, and mineral and water rights.

Specifically excluded from rental incomes are the rents received by persons in the real estate business; their rent receipts are considered to be part of their business income and therefore are included under proprietors' income.

Corporation profits. Money received by corporations for the commodities they provide either is passed on to persons and proprietors in payment for the services that their factors of production have performed for the corporation or retained by the corporation as profit. The money that is passed on is counted as income when it is received by persons and proprietors. The profits that remain are the only portion of corporation receipts that are not counted elsewhere. These profits are earned before corporate income taxes are paid and are counted as part of national income before such taxes are deducted. Capital gains and losses are specifically excluded from such profits since they do not represent income earned from the production of commodities.

Net interest. The interest payments received from private business are included as a part of national income. Interest payments received from governments and consumers, however, are not included as part of national income on the already discussed premise that such payments are unrelated to the purchase and production of commodities and therefore are not income earned in producing commodities.

Why National Income Differs from Gross National Product

Despite measuring fundamentally the same thing, gross national product and national income estimates may not necessarily yield identical totals since one estimates how much is spent and the other how much is received. Differences occur whenever business firms do not receive all the purchasing expenditures, or do not pass on all their receipts to pay for the labor and property they have used, or receive income from sources other than purchasing. The causes of the differences are reviewed in the next several paragraphs, and an example reconciling the discrepancy in GNP and NI estimates is presented in Table 2-3.

TABLE 2-3
Gross National Product and National Income Estimates (Billions of Dollars)

Gross National Product: Purchasing			National Income: Receipts		
Personal consumption			Compensation of employees		850.6
expenditures		943.0	Wages and salaries 774.2		
Durable goods	147.4		Supplements to		
Nondurable goods	425.0		wages and		
Services	370.6		salaries	76.4	
Gross private domestic			Proprietors' income		141.2
investment		210.4	Business and pro-		
Structures	115.2		fessional	105.2	
Producers' durable			Farm	36.0	
equipment	82.0		Rental income of persons		34.6
Change in business			Corporate profits		151.6
inventories	13.2		Net interest		67.0
Net export of goods and			NATIONAL INCOME		1245.0
services		8.8			
Exports	73.4		*Purchasing Not Received as Income*		
Imports	−64.6		Capital consumption		
Government purchasing of			allowances		123.6
goods and services		339.2	Indirect business taxes and		
Federal	183.4		nontax liabilities		133.8
National defense	144.4		Business transfer payments		6.8
Other	40.6		Statistical discrepancy (errors		
Government sales	−1.6		in reconciling GNP		
State and local	155.8		and NI)		−5.8
			Subsidies *less* current surplus		
			of government		
			enterprises		−2.0
			Net Purchasing Not Received		256.4
			NATIONAL INCOME and Net		
GROSS NATIONAL PRODUCT		1501.4	Purchasing Not Received		1501.4

Capital consumption allowances. One segment of purchasing that is not received as income results from capital either being deliberately used up in the production process or becoming obsolete or accidentally destroyed during the time period under consideration. Thus a producer who receives money from the sale of what he produces may need to use some of it to replace worn-out, obsolete, or destroyed equipment. In this case, only the balance of the money he receives is available to pay to the owners of labor and property for their contributions to the production process. The value of the capital used up during each period of time is, therefore, subtracted from total purchasing expenditures in the computation of the size of income earned by an economy's factors of production.

For example, if a producer supplies commodities having a money value of $10 but in doing so uses up $2 worth of capital, he really has received only $8 that can be distributed to the owners of the labor and property used in production. The money value of commodities produced over and above the amounts needed to replace the capital used up during the production is the *net national product* (NNP). It is a most appropriate measure since it shows the net value of the commodities that can be consumed in an economy during a given period of time without reducing the economy's stock of capital. It should be noted, however, that the value of the capital used up during the period of production is based on its original costs[1] and that the cost of replacing the capital may have changed. There is nothing equivalent to the inventory valuation adjustment. Thus net national product and profits may be overstated during periods of rising prices.

Indirect taxes. Another element of purchasing not received as income is indirect taxes: the sales, excise, and property taxes paid by a purchaser when he buys a taxable commodity. Thus, though a buyer spends a given amount of money to purchase a commodity, some of the money goes to a government and is not available for payment to the owners of labor and property. For example, the $20 spent to purchase a commodity is part of total purchasing, but if $3 of it is taken by a government, only $17 is left to be distributed to the owners of labor and property as part of their income.

The figures for "indirect taxes" also include an estimate of certain *nontax liabilities* such as licenses, fines, and fees. These items have the same effect as the business taxes; they are costs that the purchaser must cover if he wants the commodity to be produced but which are not available to be distributed as part of national income to the owners of the factors of production.

Subsidies. Subsidies are government payments that tend to increase the amount of income earned in producing commodities without requiring an increase in the amount of purchasing. These tend to make the level of national income higher than that of gross national product. For

---

[1] Except for capital used up on farms which is valued at its replacement costs in order to give bigger tax deductions to farmers.

example, the $30 that a consumer spends to purchase a commodity is part of total purchasing, GNP; but if the government gives a subsidy of an additional $5 to the producers because it particularly wants that commodity produced, the producers have received $35 for the owners of labor and property, and national income thus is $5 higher than gross national product. The Department of Commerce presents the figures for subsidies minus an estimate of the *current surplus of government enterprises*. The latter refers to the money obtained from private purchases of government-produced goods which is not paid out to the owners of the labor and property that produced the goods. For example, $40 used to purchase a government-produced commodity is part of GNP. But if the government pays only $30 to the owners of the labor and capital that produce the commodity, NI will tend to be $10 lower than GNP. Specifically, NI is lower by the amount of the $10 surplus which the government enterprise has accumulated.

Business transfer payments. These payments are transfers of purchasing power from businesses to individuals. Such transfers usually are in the form of gifts to nonprofit institutions and consumer bad debts that occur when goods and services are delivered but payment is not received. National income is lower than gross national product by the amount of any such voluntary or involuntary charity payments since the money received from the purchasers is not passed on to the factors of production as part of their earnings. For example, $60 used to purchase a commodity is part of GNP, but if $15 is donated to a needy student, only $45 is left for the owners of labor and property. Involuntary charity payments occur whenever the firm provides commodities but does not receive payment. This, for example, occurs when the commodities are stolen or are sold to a purchaser who goes bankrupt before making payment.

Statistical discrepancy. Any difference between the independent estimates of GNP and the sum of NI, on the one hand, and the various difference-causing components, on the other, is a "statistical discrepancy." It is included in order to reconcile the estimates completely and to provide some idea of the degree of error involved in making the estimates. The sources of the difference are the inaccuracies in the estimating procedures as well as the underreporting of incomes that tends to occur in response to the existence of income taxes.

INCOME AVAILABLE FOR PURCHASING

Despite the fact that it is the income earned from producing commodities during a given period, national income may not exactly equal the amount of income actually received by persons and available to them for use in purchasing newly produced consumer commodities.

Why Income That Persons Receive May Differ from Income Earned

Certain activities preclude a portion of the income that people's labor and capital have earned from being distributed to them. On the other hand, other activities, such as government charity payments, add to the income that persons actually receive. The total income that people receive, their actual receipts from all sources, is *personal income* (PI). It includes the portion of the national income earned in producing commodities that actually is distributed to people as the owners of labor and property plus all the other payments they receive for reasons other than the production of commodities. The "nondistributed" earnings and "unearned additions" that cause earned incomes (NI) to differ from received incomes (PI) are examined in the following paragraphs.

Excess of wage accruals over disbursements. Personal income is less than national income by the amount that income earned but not yet paid exceeds income paid in advance. For example, consider a man who every Saturday is paid the money he has earned during the week. It is possible that the time period for which national income and personal income are being computed may end in the middle of the week so that the man has earned income (national income) during the time period which actually will not be received by him until after that time period ends.

Corporate income taxes. Incorporated producers receive income for the products that they sell. But they must pay income taxes if their operations are profitable. Every dollar earned as income that goes to a government as a result of corporation taxes obviously cannot be passed on to individuals in the economy to become part of their personal incomes.

Corporate after-tax profits. Corporate profits are part of national income but are not counted as part of personal income since they may be retained by the corporation rather than distributed to its owners who would receive them as part of their personal income. Corporations, as legal individuals, may desire to retain earnings (save) for some of the same reasons that individuals do. For instance, they may do so in order to be prepared for unknown events, to carry out large ventures, to prepay their debts, to pay their taxes, or to be prepared to grasp any profitable opportunity that might arise. The portion of profits that is distributed is discussed in the section on dividends as a separate item that tends to expand personal income without affecting national income.

Contributions for social insurance. Social security payments paid by the employee are deducted from the income he earns. Thus the amount he actually receives, personal income, is smaller by the amount of such contributions than the amount of income he has actually earned—national income.

Government transfer payments to persons. Government charity payments to persons increase personal income without changing the amount of national income earned in producing commodities. There is no change in the amount earned since no commodity purchasing and thus no additional production take place.

Net government interest. Governments pay interest on their debts and also receive interest from their debtors. Since they are usually net interest payers, these payments expand the amount of personal income. On the other hand, these payments are not made to buy commodities, so they have no effect on the amount of national income earned in producing commodities.

Dividends. Corporations earn profits and then distribute them to the owners of the corporation in the form of "dividends." These dividends increase personal income when they are received. Since profits, however, may be earned and thus contribute to national income in one time period and be distributed as dividends and so increase personal income in the next time period, the two components are separated for purposes of analysis.

Business transfer payments. Business firms can earn income in one time period and give it away as charitable contributions in another. When it is earned by the business, it is part of national income; when it is received by a transfer recipient in the local economy, it expands personal income.

Why Income Available May Differ from Income Received

The amount of income actually available for an individual to use in purchasing commodities for consumption is called *disposable income* (DI or Y_d). It tends to differ from personal income because of personal income taxes. These taxes arbitrarily remove a portion of the personal income received by individuals and thus leave a smaller amount for disposal by the income recipients. Included with the estimates of personal income taxes are estimates of nontax receipts from persons. These receipts include voluntary payments to the government as well as fines and penalties. Such nontax payments have the same effect as personal income taxes in that they leave less income available for purchasing.

TABLE 2-4
The Relationship of National Income, Personal Income, and Disposable Income (Billions of Dollars)

National Income		1245.0
minus:	Corporate income taxes	72.2
	Corporate after-tax profits	79.4
	Social insurance contributions	83.8
	Excess wage accruals over disbursements	2.0
plus:	Government transfer payments to persons	108.6
	Net government interest	29.2
	Dividends	56.0
	Business transfer payments	6.8
Equals Personal Income		1208.2
minus:	Personal income taxes and nontax receipts	151.8
Equals Disposal Income		1056.4

PERSONAL SAVINGS: DISPOSABLE INCOME NOT USED FOR CONSUMPTION PURCHASING

All of the disposable income that individuals have available may be used for consumption purchasing. The portion they actually use to obtain new, domestically produced consumer goods and services is their consumption purchasing, whereas the remainder is considered to be their *personal savings* no matter what use they make of it. This all-or-nothing relationship between the consumption and savings uses of disposable income often is presented algebraically through the formula: $Y_d - C = S$, where Y_d represents disposable income, C, consumption purchasing, and S, personal savings.

Among the many possible forms of savings to which disposable income can be allocated are such activities as buying common stock, buying used or foreign commodities, buying land, making bank deposits, buying insurance policies, and buying bonds. Even though such activities may be for the purpose of financing consumption or other types of purchasing, all of the foregoing activities and acquisitions are part of savings since they involve no firsthand consumption purchasing of new, domestically produced commodities; any purchasing that such savings activity ultimately allows is counted only when it actually occurs, which, of course, may be immediately. This approach prevents the overcounting that would occur if funds were counted as they were lent and then again as they were used to purchase commodities. Furthermore, it prevents errors associated with delays in making purchases.

For example, during one time period an individual may save part of his disposable income and lend it to someone who plans to use the money to purchase commodities, but the borrower may not actually purchase commodities with it until the next time period, or perhaps never. The purchase of commodities such as used cars is included in savings because it has no direct effect on the number of commodities produced in the economy; all that occurs in the used car purchase is that ownership passes from one individual to another with no change either in the number of cars in the economy or in the income earned by producing cars.

The relationship of consumption purchasing and savings to the other components of the national income accounts is presented in Table 2-5. Notice that in this example economy almost 90 percent of the economy's disposable income is devoted to consumption but that consumption pur-

TABLE 2-5
The National Income Account Relationships (Billions of Dollars)

Gross National Product		1501.4
minus:	Capital consumption allowances	123.6
Net National Product		1377.8
minus:	Indirect business taxes	132.8
National Income		1245.0
minus:	Corporate income taxes	70.2
	Corporate after tax profits	81.4
	Social insurance contributions	83.8
	Excess wage accruals over disbursements	2.0
plus:	Government transfer payments to individuals	108.2
	Business transfer payments	6.8
	Net government interest	29.2
	Dividends	56.0
Personal Income		1208.2
minus:	Personal income taxes and nontax receipts	151.8
Disposable Income		1056.4
	Consumption	943.0
	Personal Savings	113.4

chasing only provides about two-thirds of the purchasing of the economy's gross national product.

A number of factors influence the proportion or amount of disposable income an individual will devote to personal savings. These factors will be explored in the following chapter.

● REFERENCES

Duggan, J. W., "International Comparisons of Income Levels: An Additive Measure," *Economic Journal*, **LXXIX**, pp. 109–116 (March 1969).

Frank, W. G., "A Comparison and Evaluation of Three Interim Income Concepts," *Social Science Quarterly*, **XLIX**, pp. 864–875 (March 1969).

Michaely, M., "Foreign Exchange Rates in National Accounting," *Economica*, N.S., **XXXIV**, pp. 289–297 (Aug. 1967).

National Bureau of Economic Research, *A Critique of the United States Income and Product Accounts*, Studies in Income and Wealth, Vol. 22 (Princeton Univ. Press, 1958).

————, *Measuring the Nation's Wealth*, Studies in Income and Wealth, Vol. 29 (distributed by Columbia Univ. Press, New York). (Originally published by Government Printing Office, Washington, D.C., 1964.)

Ohlsson, I., "National Accounts As An Instrument For Co-ordinating Economic Statistics," *Review of Income and Wealth*, Series 12, pp. 269–280 (Dec. 1966).

Reid, D. J., "Combining Three Estimates of Gross Domestic Product," *Economica*, N.S., **XXXV**, pp. 431–444 (Nov. 1968).

Simpson, J., "Government Transfers, Interest and Subsidies in The National Income Accounts," *Journal of Economic Issues*, **I**, pp. 211–218 (Sept. 1967).

Slinga, P., "The Treatment of Interest and Net Rents in the National Accounts Framework," *Review of Income and Wealth*, pp. 26–35 (March 1967).

Tice, H. S., "Report of a Conference on the Proposals for Revision of the United Nations System of National Accounts," *Review of Income and Wealth*, pp. 36–102 (March 1967).

United Nations Statistical Office, *A System of National Accounts and Supporting Tables*, Studies in Methods, Series F (United Nations, 1964).

VanArkadie, B., and E. Frank, *Economic Accounting and Development Planning* (Oxford University Press, 1966).

Yanovsky, M., *Social Accounting Systems* (Aldine, 1965).

Consumption
Purchasing

3

Individuals in a society like that of the United States may use all or part of their disposable incomes to purchase new, domestically produced consumer goods and services. How much each individual spends on the goods and services he prizes depends on his "propensity to consume," his desire to use income for purposes of consumption. In the United States, the strength of this desire traditionally has made purchasing for consumption the largest of the components composing the total amount of purchasing in the economy. This category of purchasing and some of the factors affecting its size constitute the subject matter of this chapter.

SUBJECTIVE FACTORS

What part of their disposable income people spend on domestically produced television sets and glasses of beer and what part they use to buy stocks and bonds or used and foreign commodities or to put in savings accounts are believed to be influenced by various subjective and objective considerations. Among the subjective factors are those suggested by John Maynard Keynes.[1] He noted that certain psychological drives may lead individuals to save some of their disposable incomes rather than make consumption purchases. Keynes enumerated some of these subjective motivations, and they include "precaution," "foresight," "calculation," and "independence." Saving as a precaution occurs because individuals may want to build up a reserve to protect themselves against unexpected calamities such as unemployment, injury, or illness. Saving motivated by foresight occurs so that the individuals will be able to meet future consumption needs that continue after some portion of disposable income ends. Persons who wish to be able to afford even higher levels of consumption purchasing at some future time may be motivated by calculation to lend part of their income in order to earn interest. Finally, an individual may be led to accumulate savings by his desire to have a sense of independence and an ability to make decisions such as taking a trip or changing jobs.

Keynes also noted psychological drives of "enterprise," "pride," and "avarice" as motivations for persons to allocate a portion of their disposable incomes to nonconsumption uses. Savings might occur, for example, while an individual is acquiring the financial capacity to enter into some speculative or business enterprise. On the other hand, pride may cause him to save some of his income so that he will be able to leave an inheritance; or he may simply be a miser and save part of his income just for the sake of saving.

Social Pressures

Obviously other psychological forces in addition to those enumerated by Keynes tend both to offset and promote high proportions of savings out of disposable incomes. For one thing, individuals may allocate high proportions of their income to consumption because of their feeling of the desirability and necessity of maintaining their position in society. In other words, they may find it psychologically necessary to consume in order to "keep up with the Joneses."

An individual's psychological motivation for savings rather than consumption also may be influenced by his community's traditional method of evaluating success and worthiness. Consider the United States' economy: on one hand, consumption purchasing tends to be expanded as individuals seek the recognition apparently given in some sectors of the economy's

[1] J. M. Keynes, *The General Theory of Employment, Interest and Money* (Harcourt, Brace, 1936), pp. 107–108.

society to the purchaser of big cars and fancy clothes. On the other hand, other sectors of the society apparently consider saving or thrift to be desirable. For example, the populace is exhorted periodically by some speaker or publication to emulate the early immigrants who supposedly prospered in The New World as a result of leaving a portion of their incomes unconsumed. It is difficult to believe that there will be no effect on the level of consumption purchasing in the United States when some of the populace consider such nonconsumption behavior to be socially "good" and worthy of emulation while the conspicuous consumption of large amounts of commodities brings raised eyebrows or even open condemnation.

Expectations

Other subjective or psychological factors that can influence consumption purchasing during a time period are the expectations existing during that time period concerning future incomes and commodity prices. For instance, if an individual expects his income to be lower in the future, he may refrain from making a purchase today: first, because any indebtedness associated with the purchase will have to be paid back later out of his lower income; second, because he may desire to save today in order to be able to continue consumption purchasing in the future when his income declines. Conversely, an individual such as a recent college graduate who is just beginning permanent employment may expect higher levels of income in the future; thus he may go into debt today in order to attain a high level of consumption because he feels that he not only can continue that level of consumption in the future but also can pay off debts incurred as a result of today's consumption out of his higher future income.

No doubt similar reactions occur in regard to expected changes in commodity prices. When prices are expected to fall, consumption purchasing may decline as a larger portion of the income is saved for use in that future time when lower prices will permit more purchases. And the reverse may occur when prices are expected to rise; the portion of income devoted to consumption purchasing may rise because any income saved will be worth less in the future when it will not buy as many commodities as now. Interestingly enough, the increased purchasing that results from expectations of price increases can cause commodity prices to be bid up to higher levels, thus justifying the original expectations. On the other hand, expected price changes may have an opposite effect from those just discussed. For instance, if consumers expect price increases in the future, they may reduce their present level of consumption purchasing so that they will have the financial ability to make purchases in the future when prices are higher.

OBJECTIVE FACTORS

Various other items also might influence the degree to which the disposable income of an economy will be used for consumption purchasing. These nonpsychological influences often are categorized as "objective factors" since they are more specific and quantifiable than the psychological or subjective factors. The following are among the objective factors that have been identified specifically as having some effect on the propensity to consume.

Distribution of Income

The proportion of disposable income that a typical individual will use for consumption purchasing depends, in part, on the size of his income. Families with relatively high disposable incomes apparently save a larger portion of their incomes than families with very small incomes. It is thus reasonable to suppose that the greater the proportion of the economy's disposable income going to the relatively high income recipients, the larger the amount of the economy's disposable income that will be saved. Consider a hypothetical situation of three families whose behavior is average for families in their circumstances. One family receives $1,000 per year and, typical of families in these circumstances, spends all of it; the second receives $6,000 and spends 90 percent of it; the third receives $11,000 and, similar to other families having this level of income, spends 60 percent of it. Total disposable income is $18,000 and total consumption purchasing $13,000. Now consider the alternative that $5,000 less is received by the third family as disposable income and is received instead by the first family. All three families now have disposable incomes of $6,000, and if all three use 90 percent of their income for consumption, total consumption purchasing will be $16,200 ($3,200 higher as a result of a different distribution of disposable income), while total disposable income remains unchanged at $18,000.

Various studies have divided consumers on the basis of their disposable incomes and have attempted to find the typical percentage of disposable income used for consumption purchasing. The results of one such study are presented in Table 3-1. Notice that the percentage of disposable income used for such purchasing exceeds 100 in the families with very low levels of income. These families do not save any of their disposable income; on the contrary, they not only consume all their disposable income but also *dis*save by making purchases with funds obtained by such means as drawing down cash reserves, obtaining credit, or liquidating assets obtained in other time periods.

TABLE 3-1
Degree of Urban Family Consumption Purchasing by Income Class

LEVEL OF FAMILY DISPOSABLE INCOME	PERCENT USED FOR CONSUMPTION
Under $1,000	181.7
$1,000–1,999	106.2
$2,000–2,999	101.7
$3,000–3,999	97.6
$4,000–4,999	95.5
$5,000–5,999	93.5
$6,000–7,499	90.0
$7,500–9,999	83.7
$10,000 and over	69.3

Source: Irwin Friend and Stanley Schor, "Who Saves," *Review of Economics and Statistics*, Supplement, **XLI**, p. 232 (1959).

Liquid Assets

The liquid assets of consumers are composed of their money, such as their checking account deposits, and any other assets that can be converted readily into money, such as bonds and savings account deposits. Such assets provide consumers with a reservoir of potential purchasing ability. It is logical that consumers with large amounts of these assets do not feel under as much pressure to restrict consumption purchasing out of disposable income in order to build up what they deem to be a necessary stock of such assets. The validity of this reasoning has been borne out by several studies showing that consumers with a certain level of income who also have high levels of liquid assets use a larger portion of disposable income for consumption purchasing than consumers with similar incomes but without such assets.

It is also true that if consumers reevaluate downward their need for a reservoir of purchasing power owing to such factors as increased unemployment insurance or retirement benefits, this unneeded portion of their liquid assets becomes available for purchasing in addition to that portion of their income previously allocated to consumption. Several major reevaluations and subsequent expansions of consumer purchasing have occurred in the United States' economy; for instance, during the Second World War patriotism and the lack of commodities to purchase caused individuals to save relatively large portions of their disposable incomes in the form of money and bonds. Then, after the war ended, their reevaluation of the patriotic need to save led them to liquidate some of their accumulated savings and use both the proceeds and their postwar incomes to purchase the consumer goods which they had foregone during the war years. Needless to say, the size of consumption expenditures in the economy was atypically high relative to the size of disposable income in the immediate postwar years.

Consumer Credit

The availability of consumer credit allows an individual to make purchases exceeding those he could make if only his income were available. To get some idea of the importance of credit to purchasing, try to imagine the effect of eliminating credit on automobile sales. Such purchasing then could be financed only out of cash holdings, or by selling other assets, or by saving from disposable incomes until sufficient funds were accumulated to make the purchase. Since many consumers obviously do not have that much cash or liquid assets which they are able or willing to surrender, car sales likely would decline substantially.

Credit purchases often involve relatively high interest charges, but it is now generally accepted that consumers pay little or no attention to this cost. Instead, their chief concern seems to be with the size of the down payment and the amount and duration of the monthly payments. The present lack of emphasis on the importance of the rates of interest as a determinant of the level of consumption purchasing contrasts directly with the beliefs held by certain earlier economists. They had maintained that the possibility of earning interest by lending savings to those who wanted to make immediate purchases was the main reason why individuals saved. It was these economists' position that the amount of disposable income that would be used for consumption purchasing would be determined by the rates of interest that individuals could obtain by temporarily parting with their savings; the higher the rates, the more each individual would be induced to save. Today the level of interest rates in an economy is accepted as one more of the many influences on savings, but certainly not the major determinant of its size.

The Stock of Durable Consumer Goods

An individual's stock of durable consumer goods has a dual effect on the possible level of his consumption purchasing. First, possession of these goods undoubtedly reduces his desire to use a portion of his disposable income to make additional purchases since he already has them. A family with a relatively new refrigerator is less likely to buy another than is a family that has no refrigerator or a relatively worn or obsolete model. On the other hand, the possession of such durables also tends to expand the consumption purchasing that an individual will do in that it encourages other purchasing that would not be made if his stock of durable assets did not exist. These purchases primarily involve commodities of a nondurable nature that complement his stock of durable goods; for instance, the possession of automobiles and television sets tends to induce purchases of gasoline and electricity.

THE CONSUMPTION FUNCTION

The total amount of consumption purchasing that will occur in an economy at each level of disposable income is determined, of course, by the individuals in the economy and their reaction to the various subjective and objective influences existing in the economy. Needless to say, different amounts of consumption purchasing occur in an economy at different levels of disposable income.

The relationship between the various possible levels of disposable income in an economy and the levels of consumption purchasing that accompany them is known as the *consumption function.* Algebraically the basic relationship between an economy's consumption purchasing and the level of its disposable income often is shown as $C = f(Y_d)$, which simply states in mathematical shorthand that the amount of consumption purchasing (C) in an economy is a function (f) of the economy's level of disposable income (Y_d). But since the level of consumption purchasing also depends on the objective and subjective factors described, it is more accurate to present an economy's consumption purchasing as depending on (being a function of) all these items. Thus, $C = f(Y_d$, liquid assets, credit terms, stock of durable goods, expectations, psychological forces, etc.).

The proportion of each addition to the level of an economy's disposable income that will be devoted to additional consumption purchasing is the economy's "marginal propensity to consume" or MPC. For example, if an economy's marginal propensity to consume is 75 percent and its disposable income rises $20 billion from $500 billion to $520 billion, then an increase in consumption purchasing of $15 billion (.75×$20 billion) can be expected. The concept of an MPC differs from the concept of an "average propensity to consume" or APC which refers to the proportion of an economy's total disposable income that is devoted to consumption uses. For example, if the individuals in the economy with a disposable income of $500 billion use $450 billion for consumption purposes, the economy's average propensity to consume is 90 percent ($450/$500) even though its MPC is only 75 percent.

An Example Consumption Function

It is possible to depict algebraically one of the common ways in which the amount of consumption purchasing is related to the level of an economy's disposable income:

$$C = bY_d$$

The equation states that the level of consumption purchasing in an economy (C) will be some proportion (b) of the economy's level of disposable income (Y_d). The size of b (which is both the APC, since it represents the proportion of each level of income that will be devoted to consumption purchasing and the MPC, since the economy's consumption purchasing will increase by that proportion of any increase in the level of disposable income) is set by the subjective and objective influences that affect the recipients of the additional disposable income. As an example of how this equation depicts the relationship of consumption purchasing to disposable income as well as how it can be used to determine the level of consumption purchasing that will occur in an economy with a given level of disposable income, consider the following: if b is 75 percent and the level of disposable income in an economy is $200 billion, a consumption purchasing estimate of $150 billion (75 percent of the disposable income of $200 billion) results for the economy when the data are substituted into the consumption function formula and the equation is solved; if b is 75 percent and the level of disposable income is $300 billion, a consumption purchasing estimate of $225 billion will result.

It is also possible to present an economy's consumption function as a line on a graph. Figure 3-1 presents the linear form of the foregoing consumption function: it shows consumption purchasing at zero when income is zero and then rising at the rate of 75 percent of the level of disposable income. Thus, for example, the line representing the economy's consumption function indicates that the level of consumption purchasing will be $150 billion if the economy's disposable income is $200 billion; $75 billion if it is $100 billion; and $225 billion if it is $300 billion. Other points on the line depict the levels of consumption purchasing that will occur at other levels of disposable income.

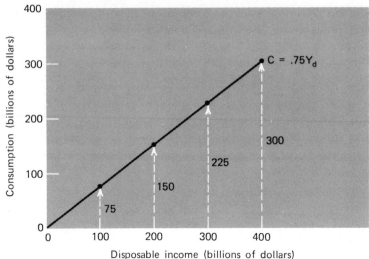

FIGURE 3-1
A consumption function.

The Most Common Consumption Function

Students considering consumption functions for the first time often are confronted with one whose fundamental nature is only slightly more complex than that discussed in the previous section. This type of consumption function is usually presented in terms of two aspects: first, even if there is no disposable income in an economy a minimum amount of consumption purchasing will go on just to sustain life or maintain traditional levels of consumption. Then, as the level of disposable income in the economy gets larger and larger, consumption purchasing increases. How much it grows for each income increase depends on the subjective and objective influences. The proportion of each increase in income used for consumption is, of course, the economy's marginal propensity to consume (MPC).

Algebraically, the relationship of this form of consumption purchasing to the level of disposable income is:

$$C = a + bY_d$$

The equation simply states that the consumption purchasing that will occur in an economy (C) is equal to some minimum level of purchasing (a) that will occur even if there is no disposable income in the economy, plus some proportion (b) of each addition to the economy's level of disposable income (Y_d). The b represents the percentage of each additional amount of the economy's disposable income that will be spent for consumption purposes; it is the MPC. As an example of how this equation depicts the relationship, consider an economy in which a = $30 billion, and b = 75 percent. This economy's consumption function is C = $30 billion + $.75Y_d$. Then, for instance, if the economy's level of disposable income is $200 billion, its consumption purchasing will be $180 billion: $30 billion plus $150 billion (75 percent of the total Y_d of $200 billion). If the level of income in the economy is $300 billion then its consumption purchasing will be $255 billion: $30 billion plus $225 billion (75 percent of the total Y_d of $300 billion).

It is also possible to use a graph to depict this common consumption function. Figure 3-2 does so with the numerical example just presented. It shows consumption purchasing beginning at a level of $30 billion when the economy's disposable income is zero and rising at the rate of 75 percent of each increment in the level of disposable income.

Needless to say, this economy's MPC will always be less than its APC. For example, when the level of its disposable income is $100 billion, consumption purchasing will be $105 billion for an APC of 105 percent, even though the MPC is 75 percent; when the level of disposable income is $200 billion, consumption purchasing will be $180 billion for an APC of 90 percent, while the MPC is still 75 percent; when the level of disposable income is $300 billion, consumption purchasing will be $255 billion for an APC of 85 percent, while the MPC remains 75 percent.

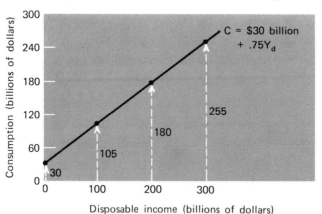

FIGURE 3-2
A common consumption function.

A Declining MPC Consumption Function

The straight-line consumption function presented in Figures 3-1 and 3-2 depicts situations in which a constant proportion of each increment of an economy's disposable income will be used for consumption purposes. It is possible, however, that the MPC of an economy will decline as the level of its disposable income increases. For example, consider an economy in which consumption purchasing will be $90 billion when the level of disposable income is $100 billion, then will rise $65 billion if the level of disposable income in the economy increases from $100 billion to $200 billion; another $40 billion if it increases from $200 billion to $300 billion; and only $25 billion if it increases from $300 billion to $400 billion. Graphically, such a declining MPC consumption function is presented in Figure 3-3. Notice that at the higher levels of disposable income, consumption purchasing in the economy rises little with each subsequent increase in disposable income; the MPC's at the higher levels of income are relatively low and declining.

THE RELATIONSHIP OF SAVINGS AND CONSUMPTION

An alternate approach to depicting the level of consumption purchasing in an economy involves the portion of the economy's disposable income that the individual recipients do not spend for consumption purposes. As we have already seen, all such unconsumed disposable income is referred to as "sav-

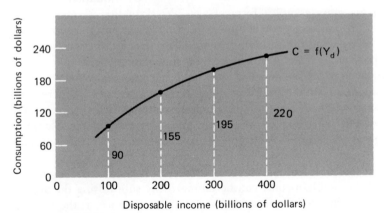

FIGURE 3-3
A declining MPC consumption function.

ings" no matter what use may be made of it. A *savings function*, which depicts the level of personal savings that will occur at each level of disposable income, is directly related to the consumption function; as the disposable income of an economy grows, the amount of income that is not used for consumption purposes—the personal savings of the recipients of the disposable income—also can be expected to grow. Why and how fast savings grows depends on the same set of factors and influences affecting the level of consumption purchasing. The proportion of each increment in the level of disposable income that will be saved is the "marginal propensity to save" or MPS. Since all of each increment of disposable income is either devoted to consumption purchasing or saved, the proportion that is saved, the MPS, and the proportion that is consumed, the MPC, total 100 percent.

The relationship of an economy's savings to its income and consumption purchasing can be expressed as an equation. For example, where consumption purchasing is related to disposable income and the consumption function has the form $C = a + bY_d$, it follows that:

1. $S = Y_d - C$

2. $S = Y_d - (a + bY_d)$

3. $S = -a + Y_d - bY_d$

4. $S = -a + (1 - b)Y_d$

The first equation defines savings (S) as the part of disposable income (Y_d) that is not used for consumption purchasing (C). Equation 2 merely puts C into its more complex form of $a + bY_d$. Equation 3 removes the parentheses and rearranges the components. Finally, Equation 4 shows that savings (S) is equal to the dissavings required to provide the level of consumption purchasing that occurs when income is zero $(-a)$ plus some proportion $(1 - b)$ of the level of disposable income (Y_d). Since b (the marginal propensity to consume) represents the percentage of each increment of income that will be used for consumption purchasing, the percentage that will not be used (the marginal propensity to save) is $1 - b$. For example, if the marginal propensity to consume (b) is 75 percent, then the marginal propensity to save is 25 percent.

Needless to say, the amount of savings that will occur in an economy at each level of disposable income can be estimated by substituting the appropriate data into the savings function formula. For instance, if the level of disposable income is $200 billion in the economy whose consumption function was depicted in Figure 3-2, $20 billion of savings will occur as can be seen from:

$$S = -a + (1 - b)Y_d$$

$$S = -\$30 \text{ billion} + (1.00 - .75)\$200 \text{ billion}$$

$$S = -\$30 \text{ billion} + .25(\$200 \text{ billion})$$

$$S = -\$30 \text{ billion} + \$50 \text{ billion}$$

$$S = \$20 \text{ billion}$$

The savings function and its relationship to the consumption function also can be depicted graphically. The negative amount of savings (dissavings) that occurs in an economy when its disposable income is zero is represented by $-a$. Then as the level of income in the economy rises, its savings rises. In the foregoing economy, personal savings rises at the rate of 25 percent of each increase in disposable income. Figure 3-4 shows this savings function and relates it to the consumption function. Notice that at each level of disposable income the sum of consumption purchasing plus savings adds up to that level of income. For example, when the economy's disposable income is $200 billion, its consumption purchasing will be $180

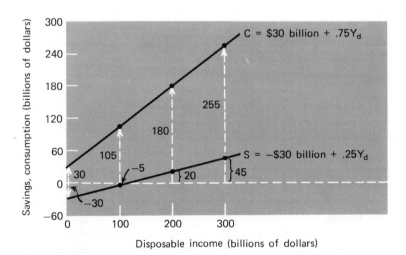

FIGURE 3-4
Savings and consumption.

billion and its savings $20 billion; at $300 billion, its consumption will be $255 billion and its savings $45 billion.

Consumption as a Function of Total Purchasing or National Income

The discussion so far has related the levels of an economy's consumption purchasing and savings to the level of the economy's disposable income. It is possible, of course, to relate them graphically and algebraically to any of the other measures of economic activity such as total purchasing or national income since the level of disposable income also is related to the size of these items.

To understand how consumption and savings can be related to these other measures, consider the relationship of consumption purchasing to the total amount of purchasing (Y) in an economy. Basically, all purchasing expenditures are received as disposable income and used for consumer purchasing except "net business savings" (BS), "net government savings," and "personal savings." Net business savings refers to the net effect of business activities that cause the amount of total purchasing or gross national product to differ from disposable income. We have already discussed retained earnings, accrued wages, and depreciation. They are all part of business savings which tend to make an economy's disposable income smaller than its GNP: they represent the total purchasing that is not passed on by the business sector as disposable income to individuals in the economy. On the other hand, business charity payments have exactly the opposite effect as they tend to make disposable income larger than the gross national product. Net government savings is the difference between an economy's GNP and its disposable income which is caused by the activities of the economy's governments. Tax collections that tend to reduce the amount of disposable income in an economy below the level of its GNP are the major type of government savings, but their effect on the level of disposable income in the economy is offset by government transfers since these tend to raise the level of disposable income. Finally, personal savings is that portion of the disposable income of an economy which individuals do not use for consumption purchasing. Since these forms of savings collectively represent the amount of total purchasing that cannot or will not be used for consumption purchasing, they are in effect the "total savings," voluntary and involuntary, that will occur in the economy at every level of Y.

Since all the purchasing expenditures in an economy are either received by individuals and used for consumption purchasing or are saved voluntarily or involuntarily, the fundamental relationship between consumption purchasing and savings remains intact. Thus it is possible to present a consumption function depicting the level of consumption spending and a savings function depicting the total savings occurring at every level of Y. So far as consumption purchasing is concerned, if the consumption function is of the a + bY variety where a is $30 billion and b is 60 percent, the consumption function becomes C = $30 billion + .60Y. Then if Y is $100 billion, C will be $90 billion; if Y is $200 billion, C will be $150 billion; if Y is $300 billion, C will be $210 billion; and if Y is zero, C will be $30 billion. This is presented graphically in Figure 3-5.

Similarly, it is possible to present a savings function based on total purchasing or gross national product. On the basis of the numerical data used in Figure 3-5, b is 60 percent and a is $30 billion so that the equation for the savings function, S = −a + (1 − b)Y, becomes S = −$30 billion + (1.00 − .60)Y. Thus, when Y is $100 billion, S will be $10 billion; when Y is zero, S will be −$30 billion; when Y is $200 billion, S will be $50 billion; and when Y is $300 billion, S will be $90 billion. Figure 3-6 contains a graphic representation of such a savings function along with the Figure 3-5 consumption function.

Delays in Adjusting Consumption to New Levels of Income

The various consumption functions imply a simultaneous change in the level of an economy's consumption purchasing whenever a change occurs in

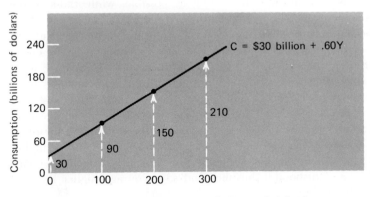

Total purchasing (billions of dollars)

FIGURE 3-5
Consumption and total purchasing.

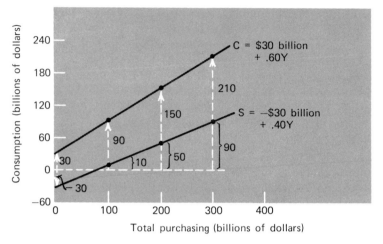

FIGURE 3-6
A savings function.

the level of the economy's disposable income or total purchasing. But there may be temporary delays in the short run before such changes actually result in a change in the level of an economy's consumption purchasing. Two reasons may explain such delays. First and primarily, individuals whose disposable incomes have dropped may attempt to maintain their traditional levels of consumption as long as possible, while those whose disposable incomes have risen may continue to consume at the old levels until they become aware of their new level of disposable income and can adjust their mode of living to it. Second, and only applicable where the level of consumption purchasing is being related to national income or gross national product, the nonpersonal savings activities of an economy's businesses or governments might expand so that the new, higher levels of purchasing or earned incomes do not immediately result in higher levels of disposable incomes that would cause increases in the level of consumption purchasing. For example, higher levels of purchasing may result in higher corporate profits but not in the immediate increase in dividend payments that would expand disposable incomes and so encourage higher levels of consumption purchasing.

Figure 3-7 presents the temporary relationship between the level of consumption purchasing and the level of disposable income (a short-run consumption function) that will exist if there are delays in adjusting an economy's consumption purchasing to changes in its level of disposable income. This figure uses the Figure 3-1 relationship between consumption and income in the long run. Our analysis begins where the economy's disposable income is $200 billion and consumption purchasing $150 billion. The line $C = \$90$ billion $+ .30Y_d$ represents the temporary consumption function; it indicates that the economy's consumption purchasing will temporarily increase very little when its disposable income rises above $200 billion and temporarily decrease little when the level of disposable income in the economy falls below $200 billion. It shows, for example, that consumption purchasing in the economy will temporarily increase by only $30 billion (from $150 billion to $180 billion) when the level of disposable income in the economy moves from $200 billion to $300 billion even though such purchasing eventually will reach $225 billion. It also shows that consumption purchasing will rise only by $60 billion (from $150 billion to $210 billion) when the level of disposable income in the economy rises from $200 billion to $400 billion even though the economy's consumption purchasing eventually will reach $300 billion.

An important question to answer is which consumption function should be used in an analysis that requires knowledge of the nature of the consumption function? Economists often eliminate the problem by assuming that there are no time lags. If, in fact, there are lags, both forms of the consumption function should be considered, with the temporary or short-run one

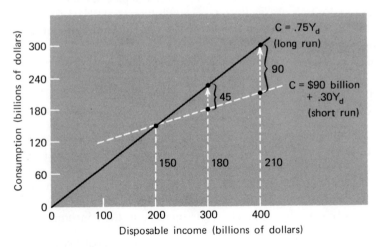

FIGURE 3-7
Short-run and long-run consumption functions.

being used to depict the immediate reaction of an economy's consumption purchasing to a change in its level of income and the regular or long-run consumption function to depict the final result.

Changes in Consumption and Savings Functions

Since the level of consumption purchasing at every level of income in an economy is influenced by a host of subjective and objective factors, it is possible that some occurrence would change the proportions of each level of income devoted to consumption. Such a change could occur, for example, if suddenly there was the expectation that higher commodity prices were inevitable; after all, wouldn't individuals in the economy be tempted to reduce the proportion of their incomes devoted to savings in order to buy commodities before their prices go up? Or, for an example of a different sort of reasoning, is it not possible that the adoption of a large and comprehensive program of retirement benefits might remove some of the need for individuals to continue to accumulate savings for use when retired? In any event, the level of consumption purchasing desired in an economy at every level of income might rise or fall. This would require a change in the line representing the economy's consumption function. The line will move from the position that represented the original relationship of consumption purchasing and income to one depicting the new relationship.

The effect of an increase in the level of consumption purchasing at every level of disposable income is shown in Figure 3-8. It depicts a change in the economy's propensity to consume from $C = \$20$ billion $+ .60Y_d$ to $C = \$30$ billion $+ .75Y_d$. Notice that there is both a new consumption function and a new savings function since the higher level of consumption spending at every level of disposable income also means a smaller amount of savings.

THE SHAPE OF THE CONSUMPTION AND SAVINGS FUNCTIONS

In 1936 J. M. Keynes made the first attempt to describe an economy's consumption function.[1] He noted what he called a "fundamental psychological law": that the level of consumption purchasing in an economy depends on the level of income in the economy because ". . . men are disposed, as a rule and on the average, to increase their consumption as their income increases but not by as much as the increase in their income."[2] Or

---

[1] J. M. Keynes, *The General Theory of Employment, Interest and Money* (Harcourt, Brace, 1936), pp. 89–98.
[2] *Ibid.*, p. 96.

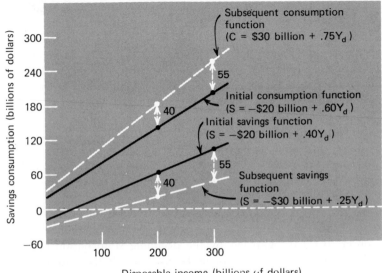

FIGURE 3-8
Changes in the consumption and savings function.

to repeat a typical paraphrasing of Keynes' statement, if the level of income in an economy increases, its consumption purchasing will increase but not by as much. Keynes did not specify what the relationship of consumption purchasing and income would be although he seems to suggest that the average propensity to consume and perhaps even the marginal propensity to consume would decline as income rose. His reasoning apparently was relatively simple: that at higher levels of income more money is available both to save and to spend and, since there is no reason to expect that just one or the other will occur once the requirements of survival are met, probably both will occur.

The Significance of a Declining Marginal Propensity to Consume

The possibility of a declining marginal propensity to consume in an economy is extremely important for such a decline means that it will be increasingly more difficult for the economy to increase its purchasing to keep pace with increases in its productive capacity. (Why a market-oriented economy's production capacity tends to grow is discussed in a later chapter.) Such growing capacity means that purchasing in the economy must increase to keep pace if the economy's factors of production are to be employed producing the maximum capacity level of production. Consider an economy that initially has $225 billion of consumption, a gross national product of $300 billion, and a marginal propensity to consume that declines an average of 5 percent per $100 billion of income from an initial 80 percent of the first $100 billion of income so that consumption is $75 billion out of the second $100 billion, $70 billion out of the next $100 billion . . . . The important characteristic of such an economy is that sources of purchasing other than consumption must contribute progressively larger and larger amounts of purchasing if the economy's level of production is to climb higher and higher.

But can we expect an economy's investment or government or foreign purchasing to continually grow as a proportion of the economy's level of income in order to fill the gap left by the declining contribution of consumption? Investment purchasing might be able to fill the gap since it provides the plant and equipment for the additions to productive capacity. But there is no reason to expect that the additional plant and equipment required to maintain each increment of productive capacity will increase with each successive increment. Foreigners could become ever more important purchasers. But the foreign governments might be opposed to their economies' producers losing purchasing and match the incentives offered by the economy that desires to increase its sales abroad. The only dependable alternative is the economy's governments. Governments can purchase in ever greater amounts even if this requires the purchase of useless products.

Following the publication of Keynes's *General Theory* certain economists used the suggestion of a declining marginal propensity to consume to explain the need to continue and expand the "New Deal" government spending programs that arose in the United States in response to the depression of the 1930's. They felt that increases in purchasing of investors and foreigners were unlikely to be large enough to fill the gap left by the declining contribution of consumption. Whether or not such an expanded role for government is desirable or even necessary will be discussed in detail in this and subsequent chapters.

Budget Studies

Budget studies provided the only data immediately available with which to analyze the nature of the consumption function that Keynes described.

The studies contained information on the proportion of income used for consumption purposes by individuals with different levels of income. (Table 3-1 presented the results of one such study.) The use of these studies to describe the nature of consumption functions was based on the assumption that the differences between the consumption purchasing of different classes of income recipients could be used to analyze the impact of different levels of income on the total level of consumption in an economy. The assumption was thought to be valid since the effect of higher and higher levels of income would mean that more and more individuals would reach higher levels of income and would emulate the consumption patterns of present members of that income group.

The results of such analysis seemed to confirm Keynes on every point. First, people with higher incomes consumed more, presumably proving the idea that consumption purchasing increases as income increases. Second, individuals in successively higher income groups consumed successively smaller proportions of their total income. This observation was accepted as evidence that the average propensity to consume for the economy as a whole would be lower at the higher levels of total income when more people joined the higher income groups. Furthermore, differences between the levels of consumption purchasing became smaller and smaller for each successive income group; this was accepted as indicating that the MPC for the economy as a whole would decline as its income rose since the individuals who received the higher income would emulate the consuming habits of the income group they joined and thus increase their consumption purchasing less and less with each increment in income.

The First Statistics

The first data that actually could be used to relate the level of consumption purchasing to the level of income covered the depression and recovery years of 1929–1941 in the United States. Analysis of the data seemed to confirm Keynes' thoughts regarding the existence of a close relationship between the level of an economy's income and the level of its consumption purchasing. The relationship had the form of an a + bY type consumption function such as was presented in Figure 3-2; basically, the APC declined at the higher levels of income whereas the MPC did not.

The validity of the declining APC inherent in the a + bY type of consumption function yielded by the 1929–1941 statistics was then disputed by new statistics that covered a longer period of time. These later data suggested that a relatively constant proportion of the level of income had been devoted to consumption purchasing. The devotion of a constant proportion of higher and higher levels of income to consumption uses means that there was a constant APC as well as a constant MPC equal to the APC since this is required for the APC to be constant. These results directly conflicted with those implying functions with a declining APC.

The original data suggesting a constant APC and MPC were presented first by Simon Kuznets[1] and then by Raymond Goldsmith[2] and others. Kuznets' findings are presented in Table 3-2. They relate the level of consumption purchasing to gross national product for overlapping decades from

TABLE 3-2
Consumption and Gross National Product, 1869–1938, by Overlapping Decades (Millions of Dollars, 1929 Prices)

YEAR	GROSS NATIONAL PRODUCT*	CONSUMPTION*	PROPORTION CONSUMED
1869–1878	$10,334	$8,056	77.96%
1874–1883	14,842	11,649	78.49
1879–1888	19,462	15,260	78.41
1884–1893	23,143	17,660	76.30
1889–1898	26,747	20,248	75.70
1894–1903	32,929	25,356	77.00
1899–1908	41,197	32,265	78.32
1904–1913	49,847	39,114	78.47
1909–1918	56,526	43,970	77.79
1914–1923	64,543	50,719	78.58
1919–1928	77,791	62,031	79.74
1924–1933	82,820	68,900	83.19
1929–1938	81,745	71,002	86.86

*Source: Simon Kuznets, *National Product Since 1869* (New York: National Bureau of Economic Research, 1946), p. 119.

1869 to 1938. Figure 3-9 presents the relationship between consumption purchasing and GNP which results from plotting the Kuznets data; it indicates that a relatively stable proportion of every level of total purchasing has been used for consumption purposes. Furthermore, the data also depict

[1]Simon Kuznets, *National Product Since 1869* (National Bureau of Economic Research, 1946), p. 119.
[2]Raymond Goldsmith, *A Study of Savings in the United States*, Vol. I (Princeton Univ. Press, 1955), p. 78.

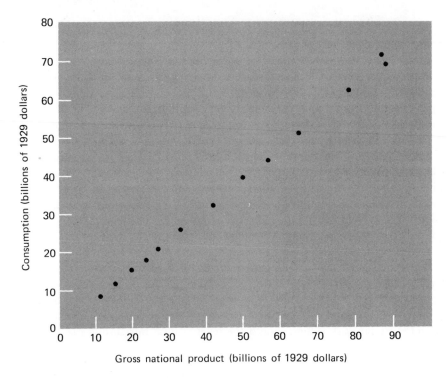

FIGURE 3-9
Consumption purchasing and gross national product, 1869–1938.

the relative importance of consumption purchasing: it apparently provided a major portion of all the purchasing in the United States during the time period examined.

EXPLANATIONS OF THE OBSERVED RELATIONSHIP BETWEEN CONSUMPTION AND INCOME

Various lines of reasoning regarding the nature of the relationship between an economy's consumption purchasing and its level of income have been put forward and examined in light of the seeming contradiction between the implications of the budget studies and the observed relationship of consumption purchasing and income over time. Diverse conclusions have been drawn. Some of the major explanations of the observed relationship are plausible in the sense that they are logical as well as compatible with the conflicting statistics.

Shifting Consumption Functions

Some economists accept the idea that the consumption function for the United States' economy has an a + bY nature and perhaps even has a declining MPC as well. They base their conclusions on the budget-study results which indicate that individuals with higher levels of income devote a smaller proportion of their incomes to consumption purchasing. Their major problem is to reconcile these declining APC conclusions with the apparently constant APC consumption function found with the data provided by Kuznets and others. They accomplish this reconciliation by rejecting the idea that the Kuznets' data depict a consumption function. The higher and higher levels of consumption purchasing which Kuznets and the others found at higher and higher levels of income, they maintain, were not the result of a move along a constant APC consumption function. Rather they were the result of a declining APC consumption function that shifted upward over the years.

Their fundamental reasoning is depicted in Figure 3-10 which contains hypothetical a + bY type consumption functions for the years 1972, 1974, and 1976. To understand their logic, consider the 1974 function and a $400-billion level of total purchasing; consumption purchasing is at the level depicted by point A. Then, should the level of total purchasing rise to $600

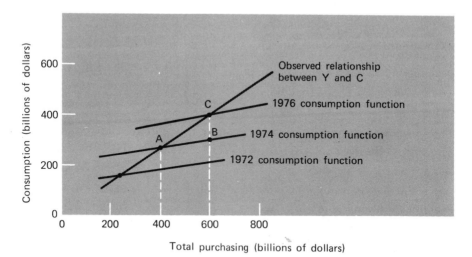

FIGURE 3-10
Shifting consumption functions.

billion in 1974, these economists would expect the level of consumption purchasing to rise as high as the level depicted by point B on the 1974 consumption function. What will happen, they say, and what they assert happened in the period that Kuznets and Goldsmith studied, is that by the time total purchasing in the economy actually reaches the higher level of $600 billion, it will be several years later, such as 1976. By this time, they argue, the economy's consumption function will have shifted up for various reasons so that its consumption purchasing at the higher level of total purchasing will be at that level depicted by point C.

Justification of this explanation requires the existence of causes of the supposed shifts in the consumption function. Several possible causes can be suggested for the periods covered by the Kuznets and Goldsmith studies:

1. *Credit expansion:* An increase in the availability of consumer credit allowed individuals to make even higher consumption purchases in excess of disposable income.
2. *More assets:* Individuals had accumulated both liquid and durable assets and thus did not have to save as much to meet savings goals.
3. *Age composition:* The proportion of the relatively high-saving working-age adults in the population declined as medical advances increased life expectancy and decreased infant mortality.
4. *New goods:* New goods such as airplanes, television sets, automobiles, radios, and dishwashers were developed which induced high levels of purchasing.
5. *Structural:* The proportion of individuals in high-saving occupations such as farming declined.
6. *Social insurance:* The growth of government programs such as Social Security may have removed some of the incentive to save in preparation for nonproductive retirement years.
7. *Migration:* Families moved from the high-saving rural sector of the economy to the relatively low-saving urban sector.
8. *Income distribution:* There was a more equal income distribution. The proportion of income going to the high-saving relatively rich declined.
9. *Luxuries became necessities:* The levels of purchasing required to support a minimum standard of living rose as radios, automobiles, and other goods moved from a luxury class to a necessity class.

Consumption as a Function of Relative Income

The a + bY type of consumption function, which some economists assert has shifted upward over time, is based on the premise that the proportion of income that an individual will devote to consumption uses depends on the absolute size of his income. James Duesenberry disputes both the acceptance of the absolute level of income as the determinant of the level of consumption purchasing and the possibility that the Kuznets' data resulted from upward shifts in the consumption function.[1] He feels that Kuznets' data depict a long-run consumption function with a constant APC. The reason a constant APC occurs at every level of income over time, he argues, is that consumption in the long run is a function of "relative income" which is always constant. It is always constant because there are always the "relatively" rich and the "relatively" poor no matter what happens to the absolute level of income. In these circumstances, individuals in the various income classes always tend to spend the same proportion of any absolute level of income as they continue to attempt to improve or retain their "relative" position in society. The reason the relatively poor and other classes tend to use the same proportion of their incomes for consumption purchasing is that they always feel the same degree of social inferiority no matter what their absolute level of income: the goods they are able to obtain with their absolute incomes are always accepted by society as being relatively inferior in quality and quantity when compared with those consumed by the relatively rich.

This constantly present social inferiority caused by having relatively low incomes along with the desire to overcome them leads the individuals in all but the top income classes to use a greater proportion of their incomes for consumption purchasing than the relatively rich who are not under such pressures. Thus, for example, if the absolute sizes of the incomes of all the individuals in the United States suddenly became ten times larger, the APC for the economy as a whole at this higher absolute level of income still would be the same. It would remain the same because each individual's relative income position would remain the same; there still would be the relatively rich who would not be under as much social pressure to consume and the relatively poor who, having the same relatively inferior position despite the increase, would be under the same degree of social pressure as before and thus would use the same relatively high proportion of their income in an attempt to eliminate their positions of relative inferiority. On this "relative income" basis Duesenberry explains why the APC is constant at every level of income.

---

[1] James S. Duesenberry, "Income-Consumption Relations and Their Implications," *Income, Employment and Public Policy* (Norton, 1948). Reprinted in *Macroeconomic Readings*. J. Lindauer, editor (The Free Press, 1968). Also see his *Income, Saving and the Theory of Consumer Behavior* (Harvard Univ. Press, 1952).

Duesenberry also notes that there can be temporary deviations from the constant proportion of absolute income which he foresees being devoted to consumption uses and that these deviations involve short-run or temporary consumption functions. These short-run functions are based on the long-run function in the following manner: first, a decline in the absolute level of income in an economy will not result in a move down the long-run function to a new and lower level of consumption purchasing. Instead, as income falls, habit causes individuals to resist lowering their consumption expenditures in order to resist a decline in their social status. The level of consumption purchasing thus depends on the highest level of income previously attained in the economy and the consumption associated with it since this is the level which the individuals will attempt to maintain. Of course, consumption purchasing may fall somewhat as the absolute level of income declines in an economy because some individuals' incomes and dissavings will not be enough to allow the previously high levels of consumption purchasing to continue. On the other hand, when the absolute level of income rises, each recipient at first may increase his consumption purchasing only a little on the assumption that any increase will move him ahead of his peers. But when he discovers that they too have increased their consumption purchasing, he will continue to readjust his purchases upward in a futile attempt to get ahead until he is again using the same proportion of his income for consumption purposes which individuals in his income class traditionally use to alleviate the social pressures from those relatively richer and maintain their status above those relatively poorer.

A diagram representing the essence of Duesenberry's long-run and short-run consumption functions appears in Figure 3-11. The figure represents an economy initially in long-run equilibrium at the combination of total purchasing and consumption depicted by point A. To understand the relationship that Duesenberry sees between short-run and long-run consumption functions, consider the effects of a decline in the level of total purchasing from the initial $400 billion to $200 billion. Instead of the level of consumption purchasing being halved, the decline in total purchasing results in a move down short-run function II as the recipients of lower incomes resist cutting their consumption expenditures below the amounts that they enjoyed at the $400 billion level of income.

Specifically, consumption purchasing in the economy will initially be reduced only to $240 billion. The new combination of total and consumption purchasing is represented by point B. On the other hand, an increase in the economy's level of purchasing from $400 billion to $600 billion initially will involve only a slight increase in the level of consumption purchasing as the

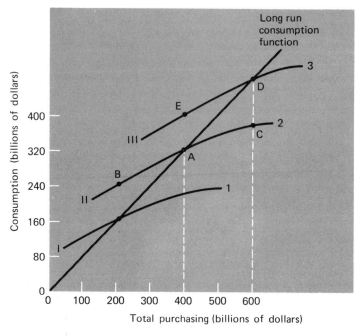

FIGURE 3-11
The nature and relationship of Dusenberry's consumption
functions. Based on James S. Dusenberry, *Income, Saving and
the Theory of Consumer Behavior* (*Cambridge, Mass.*:
Harvard Univ. Press, 1952), p. 114.

economy moves out short-run consumption function 2 to the combination of
income and consumption purchasing depicted by point C. The move occurs
along shortrun function 2 because individuals receiving the increased income
initially expand their purchases only slightly. That is all they think is needed
if they are to move ahead of their peers. Of course, when they see that their
peers also have expanded their purchases so that they have not moved ahead,
they will continue to increase the amount of their purchases until consumption purchasing in the economy finally reaches the level depicted by
point D. This level represents the total amount of consumption purchasing
that will occur when the economy's income is $600 billion and each income
group in the society consumes its traditional proportion of income to alleviate
its feelings of social inferiority.

Consider also the implications of the level of consumption purchasing represented by point D in Figure 3-11. It is another point on the economy's long-run consumption function. But what if the level of income should fall back toward $400 billion again? Will the level of consumption purchasing in the economy decline to the original point A level? No, the economy will move down short-run consumption function III to the level of consumption purchasing represented by point E as individuals in the economy resist cutting their purchases below those they enjoyed when the previous high level of $600 billion existed. Duesenberry refers to the tendency for the new and higher levels of consumption purchasing associated with a previously exceeded level of income as the "ratchet effect"; it explains the tendency for an economy's consumption purchasing not to fall back to earlier levels when its income does.

Consumption as a Function of Permanent and Normal Income

In the view of some economists, the reason the budget studies show a higher proportion of income being used for consumption purposes by the income groups with lower absolute incomes is that some of the people in these groups are those whose absolute incomes have slipped temporarily below their "normal" or "permanent" levels. These individuals continue to consume at their customary levels because, it is held, an individual's consumption purchasing depends primarily on his permanent or normal level of income. On the other hand, included with the individuals in the groups having relatively high levels of absolute incomes are those whose permanent or normal incomes are lower but who have had temporary or "windfall" income increases. These people pull down the proportion of income devoted to consumption purchasing in the group in which they are placed because their consumption purchasing is geared primarily to their lower permanent levels of income.

In any event, it is sometimes held, any increases in consumption purchasing resulting when the actual incomes of some individuals temporarily exceed their permanent levels tend to be offset by the decreases in consumption that occur when the incomes of other individuals temporarily decline below their permanent levels. Thus the relationship between actual consumption and income in an economy tends to be the same as the relationship between the economy's permanent or normal consumption and income. Furthermore, as an explanation of Kuznets' findings, this relationship tends to remain stable over time because individuals in each normal or permanent income class must save the same proportion of their incomes so that after retirement they can continue consuming in the style to which they have become accustomed. Thus, if in a future period the level of income in any economy is at a higher level, the same proportion of the higher level will be saved by its individual recipients so that they too can maintain their customary standard of living after retirement.

Extending the assumptions. Many of the normal or permanent income explanations of the nature of an economy's consumption function assume both that savings occurs during income earning periods in order that dissavings will allow the established pattern of consumption to continue during periods of nonincome such as retirement and that all savings in the economy are dissaved at some time. But the use of an analysis based on savings that occurs in order to maintain a standard of living or a position in society upon retirement does not require that an average individual's savings be completely dissaved by the end of his lifetime. The only requirement for the retention of the normal or permanent income explanations of proportionality when the savings excesses exist is the extension of the behavioral assumptions that are the basis for the explanations: individuals with double the average income will want to average twice the excess of the average individuals in case they live an unexpectedly long life and they will want to bequeath twice as much to their heirs.

Consumption as a Function of the Rate of Growth of Income and Population

The various normal income and permanent income explanations of proportionality emphasize that proportionality exists because income recipients at all income levels tend to save the same percentage of their incomes. Proportionality, under such circumstances, however, also requires that consumption based on dissavings provide a constant proportion of an economy's total consumption purchasing. But a more and more rapidly growing and thus progressively younger population means a growing number of individuals of income-earning and saving ages in relation to the number of dissaving individuals of retirement ages and thus a rising propensity to save in the economy. An increasing rate of growth of individual incomes has the same effect since there can be more savings generated when incomes rise relative to the dissavings that occur out of the earlier savings from lower incomes. The faster the level of individual incomes grows in an economy, the less that the savings occurring will be offset by dissavings and the lower the economy's propensity to consume. The propensity to consume tends to decline as both incomes and populations grow because, even if the income earners of all the income classes save the same proportion of their incomes, there will tend to be relatively less of a contribution to the economy's propensity to consume made by the economy's dissavers since they will become relatively less important in both numbers and accumulated abilities to dissave.

It is important to note, however, that the effects' described above tend to occur only when the rates of growth in incomes and populations are rising. If an economy's rates of population and income growth are steady and the economy's income earners save a constant percentage of their incomes, the portion of total income devoted to consumption in the economy out of both current income and dissaving will remain constant even if growth occurs. It remains constant because a continual growth of population and income means that a constant relationship will exist between the spending abilities of the economy's income earners and those of its dissavers. But if either of the growth rates increase, the economy's propensity to consume will tend to fall. Consider an economy where an amount of consumption occurs that is equal to 70 percent of the economy's income with 60 percent coming from income earners and 10 percent from dissavers. If either the number of income earners or the level of income each earner receives were to double, consumption in the economy would be increased by the additional purchases of the income earners but, in the absence of any change in the level of dissavings, total consumption would decline to 65 percent of the now doubled level of income. Only if an economy's population and income continually grow at a constant rate so that in the long run dissavings is also doubled will a constant relationship be maintained between the sizes of the savings and dissavings sectors so that proportionality can exist between the economy's consumption and income.

The Relationship Between Consumers and Other Purchasers

The various explanations of the observed proportionality between an economy's consumption purchasing and its level of income have proceeded on the premise that the consumption of individuals in an economy tends to be a constant proportion of their incomes. But this explanation requires that an economy's disposable income and gross national product have a constant relationship so that a constant relationship of consumption with disposable income also means a constant relationship of consumption with gross national product. The latter relationship, however, is not inevitable even if consumption is a constant proportion of disposable income. For example, consider an economy with business and government savings of $400 billion coming out of its gross national product of $1,400 billion and an additional $300 billion of personal savings occurring out of the remaining $1,000 billion of disposable income; this economy's initial propensity to consume is 70 percent of disposable income and 50 percent of GNP. Now consider a later time period when the level of gross national product in the economy rises to $1,800 billion with government and business savings rising to $600 billion and personal savings rising to $360 billion out of the $1,200 billion of disposable income. Consumption in the economy is still 70 percent of the economy's disposable income but, because of the disproportionately large growth of business and government savings, consumption as a percentage of GNP declines from 50 percent to less than 47 percent. Obviously the relative, normal, and permanent income explanations of the relationship between consumption and disposable income are inadequate to explain the tendency for a constant relationship to exist between consumption and gross national product unless they can be expanded to explain a constant relationship between personal savings on one hand and the savings of government and businesses on the other.

But the required constant relationship between personal savings and the other forms of savings is quite possible. Business investment occurs in response to actual or expected sales. Therefore, there would be a constant relationship between business savings to finance such investment and the size of the other purchasing components unless there is either a change in the relationship between the investment purchasing needed to acquire the economy's optimum stock of capital and the level of output in the economy or changes in the degree to which investments are financed out of business savings.

Government savings, on the other hand, will tend to be a constant percentage of gross national product so long as the private sector of the economy desires to maintain its importance as a purchaser relative to that of the economy's governments and the governments continue to finance the same proportion of their expenditures with savings as opposed to borrowed or newly created funds. However, if the private sector is prepared to allow the economy's production to shift toward a greater government orientation, consumption as a percentage of GNP would fall even if a constant percentage of the remaining disposable income of persons is devoted to consumption.

In the United States in the 1970's there seem to be impulses toward both a relatively more important savings role for governments and an increase in the importance of business savings as a source of funds for investment. The continuation of the observed proportionality requires that these and other forces tending to reduce the consumption portion of GNP be offset by such forces as decreased rates of population and income growth. There is no inherent reason to expect such an offset to occur, but it seems to be happening. This is important because it means that it will not be increasingly more difficult to obtain progressively higher levels of total purchasing.

● REFERENCES

Ando, A., and F. Modigliani, "The Life-Cycle Hypothesis of Savings," *American Economic Review*, **LIII**, pp. 55–84 (1963).

Bodenhorn, D., "A Note on the Impact of Change in the Marginal Propensity to Consume," *Southern Economic Journal*, **XXX**, pp. 353–357 (1964).

Bonner, J., and D. Lee, "Consumption and Investment," *Journal of Political Economy*, **LXXI**, pp. 64–75 (1963).

Branson, W. H., and A. K. Klevorick, "Money Illusion and the Aggregate Consumption Function," *American Economic Review*, **LIX**, No. 5, pp. 832–849 (Dec. 1969).

Farrell, M., "The New Theories of the Consumption Function," *Economic Journal*, **LXIX**, pp. 678–695 (Dec. 1959).

Feldstein, M., and S. Tsiang, "The Interest Rate, Taxation, and the Personal Savings Incentive," *Quarterly Journal of Economics*, **LXXXII**, pp. 833–835 (Aug. 1968).

Friedman, M., *A Theory of the Consumption Function* (Princeton Univ. Press, 1957).

Goldman, S. M., "Consumption Behavior and Time Preference," *Journal of Economic Theory*, **I**, pp. 1409–1410 (June 1969).

Hamburger, M., "Interest Rates and the Demand for Consumer Durable Goods," *American Economic Review*, **LVII**, pp. 1131–1153 (Dec. 1967).

Houthakker, H. S., and L. D. Taylor, *Consumer Demand in the United States, 1929–1970* (Harvard Univ. Press, 1966).

Hymans, S., "The Cyclical Behavior of Consumer's Income and Spending: 1921–1961," *Southern Economic Journal*, **XXXII**, pp. 23–34 (1965).

Johnson, D., and J. S. Y. Chiu, "The Savings-Income Relation in Underdeveloped and Developed Countries," *Economic Journal*, **LXXVIII**, pp. 321–333 (June 1968).

Juster, T., and R. Lipsey, "A Note on Consumer Asset Formation in the United States," *Economic Journal*, **LXXVII**, pp. 834–847 (Dec. 1967).

Leland, H., "Savings and Uncertainty: The Precautionary Demand For Saving," *Quarterly Journal of Economics*, **LXXXII**, pp. 465–473 (Aug. 1968).

Liviation, N., "Multiple Future Consumption as an Aggregate," *American Economic Review*, **LVI**, pp. 828–840 (1966).

Lubell, H., "Effects of Redistribution of Income on Consumers' Expenditures," *American Economic Review*, **XXXVII**, pp. 157–170 (1947).

Marty, A. L., "Inside Money, Outside Money, and the Wealth Effect: A Review Essay," *Journal of Money, Credit and Banking* **I**, (Feb. 1969).

Mincer, J., "Labor Supply, Family Income and Consumption," *American Economic Review: Papers and Proceedings*, **L**, pp. 574–583 (1960).

Morgan, J. M., "Consumer Investment Expenditures," *American Economic Review*, **XLVIII**, pp. 874–902 (1958).

Perry, G. L., "Consumer Demand in the United States (A Review Article)," *American Economic Review*, **LVII**, pp. 832–840 (Sept. 1967).

Renshaw, E., "The Future Income Hypothesis," *Southern Economic Journal*, **XXXIV**, pp. 40–52 (July 1967).

Spiro, A., "Wealth and the Consumption Function," *Journal of Political Economy*, **LXX**, pp. 339–354 (1962).

Swamy, S., "A Dynamic, Personal Savings Function and its Long-Run Implications," *Review of Economics and Statistics*, **L**, pp. 111–122 (Feb. 1968).

Thurow, L. C., "The Optimum Lifetime Distribution of Consumption Expenditures," *American Economic Review*, **LIX**, pp. 324–330 (June 1969).

Tobin, J., "Relative Income, Absolute Income, and Savings," *Money, Trade, and Economic Growth* (Macmillan, 1951), pp. 135–156.

Wright, C., "Some Evidence on the Interest Elasticity of Consumption," *American Economic Review*, **LVII**, pp. 850–855 (Sept. 1967).

Yaari, M. E., "On the Consumer's Lifetime Allocation Process," *International Economic Review*, **V**, pp. 304–314 (Sept. 1964).

Investment and Capital

4

Capital assets are commodities that can be used in the production process to produce goods and services. They include plants, equipment, and inventory. At any given time a country like the United States possesses a *stock* of capital assets. These assets result from earlier investment purchases by individuals, governments, and business firms. Essentially two things happen to affect this stock during any period of time: part of it vanishes through depreciation, obsolescence, and destruction, while new investment purchasing furnishes a continual *flow* of new capital assets to replace those that are consumed and to expand the size of the stock.[1]

---

[1] An economy's stock of human capital is the sum of all the inherent and acquired production abilities of the economy's residents. Investment in human capital includes expenditures on health, housing, medical care, education, on-the-job training, and migration to more productive employments. Such purchases, however, are specifically excluded from investment purchasing according to the definition used by the national income accounts. But the marginal efficiency of investment purchases that tend to expand an economy's stock of human capital can be measured and analyzed just as the efficiency of any other investment expenditures. The analysis of capital and investment in this chapter is thus also applicable to human capital and investment.

THE DECISION TO INVEST

The purchase of a new capital asset occurs primarily because an investor expects returns over its life which will cover all the costs of purchasing and operating the asset while also yielding a net return at least equal to the interest he would have to pay if he borrowed the money to purchase it. The return anticipated must be that high or the potential investor would not want to borrow the money to purchase the asset. For instance, who would be willing to purchase an asset expected to yield a net return of $500 over its life if he had to pay $600 in interest to obtain the money needed to make the purchase? Additionally, the expected return must be greater than the interest payment even if the investor has sufficient funds of his own; otherwise he would choose to lend his money to someone else to obtain the higher interest payment in preference to the lower return from a capital purchase.

Investment purchasing does *not* occur merely because there have been savings. An individual may save, for example, by putting his money in a commercial bank, but there is no guarantee that the bank will lend it in the same time period to someone who wants to make an investment purchase. The bank, for instance, may lend the money to someone who wants to buy a car or pay an old debt, or it may not lend it at all, keeping it in the vault for safety's sake in case a large number of people wish to withdraw their deposits at once. On the other hand, not all investment purchasing occurs because the acquired assets are expected to yield high enough returns. Instead, investment purchasing may occur by mistake. This possibility exists because of the treatment accorded inventories, which are considered to be acquired through investment purchasing because they are needed for the operation of business firms just as plant and equipment are needed. For example, consider a firm that produces 100 commodities because it expects to sell 80 to consumers and desires, in effect, to purchase the remaining 20 for its own use in order to increase the size of its inventory. If the firm foresees incorrectly and the consumers buy only 70, the firm's holdings of these commodities, its inventory, will be expanded by 30 instead of the desired 20. In other words, the firm's actual investment purchasing of commodities for its inventory will exceed the amount that the firm intended.[1]

---

[1] It should be recalled from the discussions in Chapters 2 and 3 that the expenditures made to obtain used commodities are not considered as purchasing but, because they do not directly induce production, as a form of savings. For this reason, the sales that draw down the previously purchased items in an economy's inventories are not actually a part of the economy's total purchasing. To accurately reflect the reassignment of these commodities to their ultimate users, however, governments often arbitrarily reduce their estimates of investment purchasing by

Three Approaches for Determining Whether to Invest

There are three conceptual approaches that an investor may use to determine whether to deliberately purchase a specific new capital asset. The first method involves computing the rate of return exclusive of interest costs which the asset is expected to earn and then comparing it to the interest rate that must be paid to finance the purchase; the second involves computing the asset's "present value" and comparing it to the price that must be paid to obtain it; the third involves the comparison of total costs and total revenues. Discussion of all three approaches follow.

The marginal efficiency of investment (MEI). The "marginal efficiency of investment" or MEI is the rate of return that a potential new capital asset is expected to earn after all its costs, except the interest expenses, are covered. For instance, consider a new capital asset that could be purchased in the present time period with an investment of $1,000 and whose use is expected to yield $5,100 in additional revenues and $4,000 in additional noncapital costs during the one year of its life. The MEI of such an asset is 10 percent. After covering the noncapital costs, the purchaser of such an asset expects to have not only enough revenue left to replace the original $1,000 but also a net addition or return of $100; he expects to receive an annual rate of return of 10 percent on the $1,000 investment.

More specifically, the MEI can be defined as the rate of return that equates the expected flow of revenues in excess of expected noncapital costs (efficiency) from one additional (marginal) newly constructed asset to the cost of purchasing (investment) the asset. This cost is the "supply price" or "replacement cost." The expected noncapital costs are all those additional costs such as labor, normal profits, and materials which the investor anticipates if he acquires and operates the asset. Specifically excluded from these additional costs are the capital costs of interest and depreciation. The total amount of revenues in excess of the noncapital costs is what the potential investor expects to have available to pay the capital costs. As he decides whether to make an investment purchase in the face of a given supply price and interest rate, the investor must estimate both revenues and non-

their estimate of the net amount of such "disinvestment" and then include the purchases of such disinvestment items as part of the ultimate recipients' purchasing. Although such an inventory valuation adjustment tends to maintain an accurate estimate of total purchasing, it also tends to misstate the importance of investment purchasing in causing production to occur during a particular period of time.

capital costs. This requires his appraising how many additional commodities the asset will produce, how long it will produce, what the commodities can be sold for, and what effect the sale of any additional commodities will have on the prices of, and thus the revenues from, commodities he already is producing. By the same token, the investor also must estimate the change in noncapital costs that will result from its operation. This requires his assessing such things as how many workers will be needed to operate the asset, how much they will be paid, and the size of any cost changes that may occur in his existing operations as a result of operating the new asset.

A potential new capital asset's MEI can be calculated if its supply price is known and it is possible to estimate the returns over noncapital cost in each of the time periods of its life. The following algebraic formula, in which "r" represents the MEI, can be used to solve for the value of the MEI:

$$\text{Supply price} = \frac{\begin{array}{c}\text{Return over}\\\text{noncapital}\\\text{costs,}\\\text{Period 1}\end{array}}{1 + r} + \frac{\begin{array}{c}\text{Return over}\\\text{noncapital}\\\text{costs,}\\\text{Period 2}\end{array}}{(1 + r)^2} + \cdots + \frac{\begin{array}{c}\text{Return over}\\\text{noncapital costs}\\\text{in last period (n th)}\\\text{of asset's life}\end{array}}{(1 + r)^n}$$

Consider a new capital asset costing $1,000 which is used up at a uniform rate during its life span of two years; at the end of the first year it is expected to yield a net return of $550 and the second year a net return of $605. In this case we have:

$$\$1,000 = \frac{\$550}{(1 + r)} + \frac{\$605}{(1 + r)^2}$$

Thus: $r = 10$ percent.

This equation simply states that at the end of the first year the capital asset is expected to return $500 of the original $1,000 investment plus an additional $50; the $50 means that the asset is expected to yield a 10 percent return on the $500 that will be committed for one year. The second year it is expected to return the second $500 of the investment plus an additional $105 for the $500 that will be committed for two years. The second $500 also earns 10 percent per year: $50 for the first year when $500 is tied up, and 10 percent or $55 the second year when the investor has $550 tied up (the original $500 plus $50 interest from the first year). Thus, exclusive of interest costs, the investment purchase of this asset is expected to yield a 10 percent return on each dollar per year committed to the investment.

Whether this asset actually will be purchased depends on the rate of interest involved in acquiring the dollars needed to make the investment.

The investment will be made if the MEI is equal to or higher than the rate of interest; it will not be made if it is lower. For instance, if the MEI is 10 percent and the interest rate needed to finance the purchase is only 6 percent, then the purchase will be made to obtain the asset because a profit equal to 4 percent of the dollars committed in each time period is expected after all costs have been covered. How much investment purchasing occurs in an economy, then, depends on both the MEI's of various potential new capital assets and the rates of interest at which money can be borrowed for the purpose of purchasing the assets. Algebraically this relationship is $I = f(\text{MEI}, i)$. The formula simply states that the level of investment purchasing in an economy during a given time period (I) is a function (f) of the marginal efficiency of investment (MEI) and the level of the economy's interest rates (i). Notice that in this instance investment decisions are made by comparing the expected rate of return to the rate of interest. The same decision can be made by comparing present dollars to future dollars.

Present value. The "present value" of a potential new capital asset equals the additional revenues it is expected to generate in the future minus an estimate of all the additional costs it will incur except depreciation. The interest needed to finance the purchase is specifically included as a cost. In other words, an asset expected to yield $130,000 in additional revenues and to incur $80,000 of additional noncapital costs and $2,830.19 in interest costs has a present value of $47,169.81 ($130,000 − $80,000 − $2,830.19).

The investment purchase needed to obtain a potential new capital asset will be made any time that the present value of the asset exceeds its supply price—the price the investor has to pay to obtain the asset. For example, assume that an investor is considering the purchase of a new capital asset which he expects, after covering all costs except interest and depreciation, to yield $50,000 in the one year of its life. Also assume that it will cost 6 percent interest to finance the purchase of the asset. The present value of the asset is the dollar amount of the revenue remaining after paying the non-capital costs ($50,000) minus the interest cost. Put another way, the present value of the asset is the maximum amount on which the investor can pay 6 percent interest if he expects the asset to generate $50,000 which can be used to cover its capital costs. Algebraically applying the formula for determining the present value (V) to these data, we see that

1. $$V \cdot (1.06) = \$50,000$$

2. $$V = \frac{\$50,000}{1.06} = \$47,169.81$$

The required interest payment is then equal to

3. $\qquad$ $6\% \times \$47,169.81 = \$2,830.19$

The computation shows the present value of the potential capital asset to be $47,169.81 at 6 percent. This means that if the investor buys the asset for $47,169.81 and pays the $2,830.19 in interest to borrow that amount to make the purchase, he breaks even because the asset will yield (he expects) $50,000 which is neither more nor less than the total of the asset's price plus the interest he has to pay to finance the purchase of the asset. But what if the supply price of the asset were lower, such as $40,000? The investor would borrow the money at 6 percent and make the purchase because the asset has a higher present value at 6 percent than the $40,000 it costs to obtain. In fact, he would be paying out a total of $42,400 ($40,000 plus 6 percent interest on the $40,000) and receiving $50,000 for a profit of $7,600.

Consider the same situation except that the investor does not expect to get the $50,000 until the end of a two-year period. The approach is the same except that now he will have to pay the 6 percent interest compounded for two years. This means he will pay 6 percent on the amount borrowed during the first year and then for the second year again pay 6 percent on the borrowed amount plus another 6 percent on the first year's interest. Thus:

1. $V \cdot (1.06) \cdot (1.06) = \$50,000$

2. $V = \dfrac{\$50,000}{(1.06)^2}$

3. $V = \$44,499.82$

Then, since the required interest payment to finance $44,499.82 at 6 percent for two years is $5,500.18 ($50,000 − $44,499.82), the investor will purchase the asset if its supply price is less than $44,499.82.

Now expand the example to an asset that will yield $25,000 in each of the two years of its life and for which our investor again will have to pay 6 percent interest. The present value of this asset then is the sum of the one-year and two-year present values. Or:

$$V = \frac{\$25,000}{(1.06)} + \frac{\$25,000}{(1.06)^2} = \$45,834.82$$

The basic procedure for determining present value, which was followed in the foregoing examples, can be depicted with an algebraic equation that shows the expected returns (R), such as the $25,000, and interest rate (i), such as the 6 percent, for each time period until that one (n) when the asset no longer is expected to produce returns. Specifically it has the form

$$V = \frac{R_1}{(1 + i)} + \frac{R_2}{(1 + i)^2} + \cdots + \frac{R_n}{(1 + i)^n}$$

Total cost vs. total revenues. The total cost of using an asset is the sum of the additional noncapital operating costs including normal profits that its use causes, the interest expenses of financing its acquisitions, and the actual cost of purchasing the new asset less any salvage value. Consider a producer already operating five machines producing a total of 80,000 units of production that sell for $12 each. This producer's investment purchase of a sixth machine will only occur if the expected additional costs associated with the sixth machine are equal to or less than the additional revenue the machine is expected to generate.

Assume that the producer expects the sixth machine to last two years and add $127,915.98 to his total cost: $74,000 of direct operating costs resulting from operating the machine; $1,000 of normal profits to induce the producer to bear the additional burdens of an expanded operation; $4,000 because the producer's efforts to secure the additional labor and material to operate the sixth machine will bid up the prices he must pay to acquire labor and materials for the first five machines by 5¢ per unit of production; $45,000 for the use of the sixth machine because it can be purchased for $50,000 and is expected to have a salvage value of $5,000 after two years; $3,915.98 of interest to finance the purchase of the machine over its two-year life.

The sixth machine would be purchased if it is expected to produce 14,000 units of production that can be sold for $11 for a profit of ($154,000.00 − 127,915.98) $26,084.02. But the sixth machine might not be profitable enough to purchase if there are other cost and revenue effects. For example, it may only increase the producer's total output by 13,500 units if its installation and operation in close proximity to the other five machines causes their combined production to fall by a total of 500 units. And the $148,500 increase in the producer's revenues that the 13,500 increment yields at $11 may not all be a net addition to the producer's revenues if the sale of the additional output drives down the price that the producer receives for the output of his first five machines from $12 to $11 and thus reduces the producer's revenue by another $80,000.

The Effect of Purchasing Subsequent New Capital Assets

More than one new unit of a particular type of capital asset may be considered for purchase at one time. For example, the manager of a firm may consider adding from one to ten new machines. The question confronting him is, what will be the MEI or present value of each subsequent new machine? It may be reasonable to expect that at any point in time the MEI or present value of each additional unit of a potential new capital asset will be lower than those of the new units that precede it. Thus, for example, the MEI of the second new machine may be 6 percent while that of its predecessor, the first new machine, may be 8 percent. Some of the several possible reasons for such a decline are discussed below.

Declining revenues. The additional revenue generated by the employment of each subsequent new capital asset may be expected to be lower than the increase in revenues provided by the preceding new assets. This tends to occur if each subsequent capital asset is expected to result in the production of fewer additional commodities or if the additional production resulting from the operation of each subsequent asset is expected to cause a reduction in commodity prices. Such expectations are not inevitable. The flow of revenues to each subsequent new asset would tend not to decline if the demand for the product were perfectly elastic. In this case all additional production from subsequent new assets would be purchased at the same prices as the production of preceding new assets. Maintenance of the price level also would occur if the increase in the supply of commodities caused by each subsequent new asset were offset by an increase in the demand for the commodities which the asset produces. Such a demand increase could result either from the higher levels of commodity purchasing possibly resulting from an increase in factor income generated by the additional asset's production or from some unrelated circumstances such as a change in those governmental activities that affect the level of purchasing.

Increased noncapital costs. An increase may occur in the amount of additional noncapital costs attributable to each subsequent new unit of capital. Such increases can occur if the prices of cost items are bid up as a result of the demand for additional materials and factors of production created by the operation of each new asset. For example, each new asset may require labor to operate it; if so, the demand for labor will increase as each subsequent new asset is put into operation. This increase in demand could cause the additional wage payments (a noncapital cost) to rise to levels higher than the comparable additional costs caused by preceding new assets since the owner of this asset will have to pay more not only for the labor required for its operation but also for the labor he uses to operate all his existing assets. It is also possible, of course, that each additional capital asset will be substituted in place of other items used in the production process rather than require more of them; if this occurs, noncapital costs may even fall. In this case, subsequent new capital assets would be purchased as long as the reductions in noncapital costs exceed the expected increase in capital costs.

The production costs of a subsequent new asset also tend to be higher if the asset causes the firms using it to reach a size where there are diseconomies of scale. In other words, with the addition of a subsequent new asset a firm may become too large for maximum efficiency and thus require more non-capital items to achieve the same additions to production provided by previous new assets. Such declining productivity will not occur, of course, if there are no diseconomies of scale associated with the use of the asset, or if the number of firms employing it increases so that subsequent new units of the asset can be used in the most efficient-sized firms.

Increasing supply prices. The purchase of each subsequent potential new capital asset may be expected to cause the supply price of each new asset to be higher. This could occur for two reasons. First, the increased demand for capital assets may cause their prices to be bid up. Additionally, there may be rising costs associated with the higher levels of production needed to produce each subsequent new capital asset. This tends to mean that the producers of the capital assets will be willing to supply each subsequent asset only if they can get a higher price for it. For example, to produce a tenth new machine, the machine producer may have to begin working his labor force overtime or on Sundays and holidays. In other words, although physically capable of building that machine, the producer may not be willing to produce it unless he can get a higher price so that he can cover the additional costs resulting from its production.

The MEI Schedule for an Economy

In any one time period in an economy, investment purchasing opportunities may exist for various potential new capital assets with low MEI's as well as for other potential new assets with higher MEI's. Each subsequent potential new capital asset of a specific type may tend, of course, to have a lower MEI for the reasons discussed. Additionally, the MEI's of each subsequent potential new asset might decline as a result of the investment purchases of other types of new capital assets. For instance, the MEI of a potential new asset of one type might be lower if its supply price were affected by the suppliers' production of other types of assets or if its operating costs were expected to be higher as it competed with other types of new assets for raw materials and labor.

Table 4-1 presents an example MEI schedule depicting the relationship that might exist in an economy at any one point in time between investment purchasing and the MEI of potential new capital assets. It shows the amounts of investment purchasing in an economy which would be needed in a given time period to acquire the capital assets having each MEI level.

Figure 4-1 graphically presents the schedule of MEI values from Table 4-1 and connects them with a line. The resulting "MEI curve" shows, for example, that all the capital assets acquired through $40 billion of investment purchasing are expected to have MEI's of at least 8 percent, whereas all those acquired through $70 billion of such purchasing are expected to have MEI's of at least 5 percent.

TABLE 4-1
An Example MEI Schedule

MEI, PERCENT	BILLIONS OF DOLLARS
11	10
10	20
9	30
8	40
7	50
6	60
5	70
4	80

The MEI Curve as an Investment Demand Curve

Because investment purchasing occurs whenever the MEI of a potential new capital asset exceeds the rate of interest at which the investment purchase can be financed, an economy's MEI curve is also its investment demand curve when the economy's rate of interest is measured on the vertical axis along with the MEI's of the capital assets that would be acquired with each increment of investment purchasing. Needless to say, the use of such a single rate of interest oversimplifies matters considerably since many different rates of interest can exist simultaneously in an economy.[1] In order to handle

---

[1] For example, one investor might have to pay 10 percent to obtain the funds he needs to purchase a unique new type of capital asset, while another investor has to pay only 5 percent for the funds to acquire an asset of a type that has already been operated successfully. Why different interest rates exist simultaneously in an economy is discussed briefly in Chapter 7.

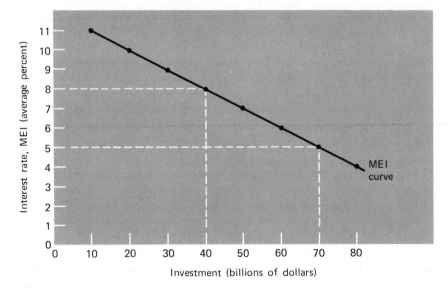

FIGURE 4-1
An MEI curve.

the existence of different interest rates, it is necessary to think in terms of the investment purchasing that will occur in an economy at each general level of interest rates. We shall continue, however, to identify economies' investment demand curves as MEI curves because the amount of new capital assets acquired by an economy's investors during a particular period of time depends on the various possible assets' MEI's and the interest rates at which they can be financed. Thus, for example, we might find that $50 billion of investment purchasing will occur in an economy if the interest rates in the economy average 7 percent. Investment purchasing will not cease before reaching $50 billion because the expected returns would exceed the interest costs of acquiring the funds needed to make the purchases. It will not exceed that amount because the returns expected from any additional asset would be less than the rates of interest needed to finance their purchase.

The Shape of the MEI Curve

The MEI curve of Figure 4-1 slopes down and to the right to indicate that more investment purchasing will occur at lower rates of interest. Such a shape exists when supply prices and noncapital costs rise or product prices and production fall at higher and higher levels of investment purchasing. Various reasons why productive efficiency, product prices, and noncapital costs may not be affected by increases in the level of investment purchasing have already been discussed. If revenues and costs do remain unchanged by higher levels of investment purchasing, the elasticity of an economy's MEI curve will only be related to whatever changes occur in the supply prices of capital as investment purchasing increases. The rate of return expected for each additional unit of capital will then decline only as the prices necessary to obtain each additional unit of capital increase. But an economy's MEI curve is not a mirror image of the economy's capital supply curve since the MEI of an increment of investment purchasing changes more than proportionally when the supply price of capital is changed. For example, the MEI of an increment of investment purchasing is more than halved when the supply price is doubled. It is more than halved to whatever extent the higher supply prices mean additional capital costs to be covered out of the revenues remaining after the payment of noncapital costs. An economy's MEI for additional increments of investment purchasing would be halved should supply prices double under only two conditions: if revenues from each additional capital asset rise enough; or if the cost of operating the assets falls enough to keep the same net amount of revenue left over to be a return on investment after covering the now higher capital costs caused by the higher supply prices.

Figure 4-2 presents examples of the MEI and supply price relationship when revenues and operating costs are unaffected by additional investment purchasing. MEI_1, for example, indicates that the rate of return on additional investment purchasing would decline from 10 percent to below 5 percent if investment purchasing in the economy increases and causes the supply price of the average unit of capital to rise from \$20,000 when there is \$100 billion of investment purchasing to \$21,000 when there is \$200 billion of investment purchasing. An even more inelastic MEI curve will exist if revenue reductions and operating cost increases are associated with levels of investment purchasing in excess of \$100 billion. If, on the other hand, reductions in operating costs and increases in revenues are associated with the higher levels of investment purchasing, the economy's MEI curve would be more elastic than MEI_1 and could conceivably be more elastic than the supply curve of the economy's capital producers. This could occur, for example, if additional increments of investment purchasing allow the economy's producers either to reach levels of production and capital use which enable them to obtain quantity discounts for inputs into the production process or

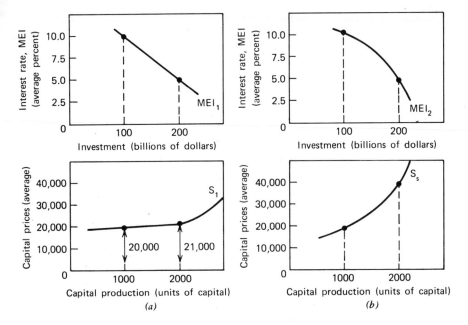

FIGURE 4-2
(*a*) The MEI and supply price relationship (nonmirror image). (*b*) The MEI and supply price relationship (mirror image).

to reach a higher volume of production sufficient to enable the producers to compete for large-scale orders at higher prices.

If the sales and operating cost benefits from an additional increment of investment are great enough, the additional returns could offset the higher capital costs associated with the higher supply prices that might have to be paid to get the additional capital items produced and thus cause the same amount of net returns to be earned by a capital asset as are expected for the assets acquired at lower levels of investment purchasing. MEI_2 in Figure 4-2*b* depicts the special case of an economy's MEI curve as the mirror image of its capital supply curve that would occur under such circumstances. The special case exists whenever the expected rate of return changes in proportion to the supply price of capital because each increment of investment purchasing is expected to be associated with enough of an increase in revenues and decrease in operating costs to cover the higher capital costs caused by higher supply prices. Only under such circumstances would the doubling of a supply price halve the MEI so that the economy's MEI curve would be a mirror image of its capital supply curve.

Shifts in the MEI Curve

Once all the potential new capital assets with MEI's in excess of the rates of interest required to finance their purchase have been obtained, no further investment purchasing will occur in an economy unless either the economy's interest rates fall or something happens to raise the MEI's of other potential new capital assets. Graphically, the effect of investment purchasing is to shift an economy's MEI curve to the left to show that less investment purchasing will occur in the economy at every level of interest rates now that some of the potential new assets actually have been acquired.

Figure 4-3 depicts this situation. It contains an example MEI curve representing the demand for investment purchases at each level of interest rates before such purchases occur. Then, to depict the effect of investment purchases on the MEI curve, assume that the average interest rate has been 7 percent and that the $50 billion in investment purchasing appropriate at that level actually has occurred; now all the remaining potential investment opportunities involve new assets with MEI's lower than the existing

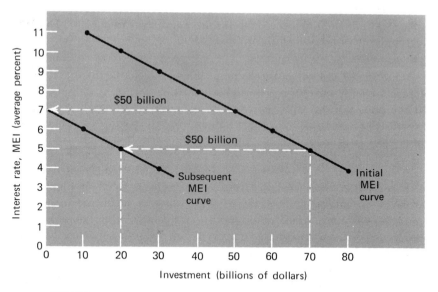

FIGURE 4-3
MEI curves before and after investment purchasing.

7 percent rate. The MEI curve thus shifts to the left by $50 billion since the amount of additional investment purchasing that would have occurred initially at the lower interest rates has been cut by the $50 billion that has taken place. For example, if the initial interest rates in the economy had averaged 5 percent, $70 billion in investment purchasing would have occurred. Now that $50 billion of the $70 billion has been made, only $20 billion more will occur if the level of interest rates in the economy falls to an average of 5 percent. Notice also that the new MEI curve begins at the 7 percent level. That is because there are no more potential investment purchases with MEI's in excess of the interest rates that average 7 percent. All of the original $50 billion at that level of interest rates has been made.

Once investment purchasing occurs at some level of interest rates, increases in the MEI's of other potential new capital assets are necessary if additional investment purchasing is to occur at that level of interest rates. Such MEI increases are desirable because they ensure that investment expenditures, an important component of total purchasing, can continue without a reduction in an economy's rates of interest. Various factors can cause MEI increases, and thus have the effect of shifting the MEI curves to the right.

Factors related to the level of purchasing. The use of existing capital assets to produce commodities may cause some of them to become so dilapidated that they can no longer produce profitably. The completion of their productive life has an important side effect: it tends to induce investment purchasing by opening vacancies for potentially profitable new assets to replace those no longer useful. How much investment purchasing occurs in an economy for replacement purposes during a given period of time depends on the level of interest rates and the current level of production in the economy. The current level of production is a factor since more machines tend to wear out, and thus more vacancies are created, at higher levels of production. The rates of interest are also a factor because the vacancies can have different MEI's; merely because they were once filled at some prior interest rate does not mean they will be filled at the rate existing in the time period in which they expire.

Since the current level of production determines how many vacancies occur in a given period of time, and since the level of production depends on the level of total purchasing, the number of vacancies created and the level of *replacement investment* purchasing (I_r) to fill them depends on the existing level of total purchasing. Needless to say, more vacancies and thus more replacement investment purchasing occur when total purchasing is higher.

The effect of higher levels of total purchasing is depicted by shifting the MEI curve to the right to indicate that more potentially profitable investments will exist at every level of interest rates. How far the curve shifts to depict the vacancies associated with a given level of total purchasing depends on the number of vacancies created and the MEI's of the potential new assets that could replace them. More important, however, is the fact that replacement investment means a different MEI curve for each level of total purchasing because the amount of existing assets that finally expire and cause vacancies, and thus the amount of investment expenditures that will occur at every level of interest rates to fill them, will be different for every level of total purchasing. Figure 4-4 presents MEI curves for an example economy during a given period of time. The curves indicate that more and more investment purchasing would occur in the economy at higher and higher levels of total purchasing. They show, for example, that if the average rate of interest at which investments can be financed is 4 percent, $20 billion of investment purchasing will occur if the level of total purchasing in the economy is $400 billion, $40 billion if the economy's total purchasing is $600 billion, and $60 billion if its total purchasing is $800 billion.

Factors unrelated to the level of total purchasing. Potential new capital assets may become profitable enough to prompt their acquisition through investment purchasing as a result of factors that are "autonomous" of or unrelated to the replacement needs associated with a given level of

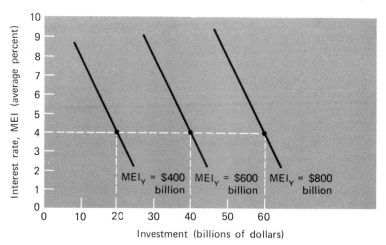

FIGURE 4-4
MEI curves at different levels of total purchasing.

total purchasing. Investment purchasing of this type generally is identified as *autonomous investment* (I_a). The autonomous causes of higher MEI's and present values include:

1. *New purchasers:* Additional customers might be located for existing types of products. This could occur for diverse reasons ranging from population increases and improved transportation facilities to political agreements and expanded sales opportunities caused by increases in the size of total purchasing. For instance, the advent of the railroad and the western markets which it opened for the eastern steel producers tended to increase the MEI's of potential new steel mills. Similarly, the discovery of oil in various Middle East sheikdoms undoubtedly increased the MEI's of potential new assets of the oil machinery firms having access to these markets.

   Specifically included among autonomous investment purchases are those expenditures on the new capital assets required to produce the additional commodities necessitated by a move to higher levels of total purchasing. How much of such investment will occur depends on the sizes of the old and new levels of total purchasing and the amount of idle capital that can be activated to increase commodity production when total purchasing rises. Such autonomous investment purchases often have been designated *induced investment* (I_i) because they are induced by the economy's moving to higher levels of total purchasing. Even though all investment purchasing is induced by something, we shall reserve induced investment for the autonomous investment purchasing associated with changes in a given level of total purchasing. This procedure has the merit of not mixing the different causes of autonomous investment.

2. *New products:* The nature of newly developed products in terms of expected revenues and noncapital costs may be such that the MEI's of the capital assets needed to produce them are high enough to induce their purchase. For instance, the invention of television and the demand for it as a product must have increased the MEI's of certain capital assets used in the electronics industry. After all, the electronics firms acquired these assets and used them to produce television sets; they certainly would not have done so had they not expected profits from them.

3. *New technologies:* The MEI's of potential new capital assets will rise if more efficient (lower cost) methods of operating them are devised. The same effect occurs if a new type of capital asset is devised which allows a new and more efficient method of production. For instance, it is

reasonable to believe that the MEI's of some potential new assets used in water distillation will increase with every new technique lowering the cost of producing a gallon of water. Additionally, new technologies also can affect MEI's by lowering the supply prices of the capital assets. For instance, a new technique for making machine tools more efficiently might be adopted by the industry and passed on to buyers when competition among the tool producers causes the price of the tools to be driven down to the point where the competitors are merely covering their costs.

4. *Lower noncapital costs:* The noncapital costs of production may decline because of a fall in the cost of obtaining some ingredient of production. For example, the government might remove the excise taxes that previously had been levied on some input required in the operation of a particular capital asset. Or perhaps the price of some fuel might decline owing to the discovery of new sources of supply.

5. *Lower capital costs.* The possible effects of improved technologies on the supply prices of capital assets already have been mentioned. It should also be noted, however, that the supply prices of capital assets also may be reduced by the completion of investment programs to expand the stock of capital assets in an economy to new optimum levels. In other words, the prices of the capital assets may be bid down when the expansion is completed and new capital assets are being demanded only for replacement purposes.

Interest is the other major capital cost and it can affect the level of autonomous investment purchasing in two ways even though it has no direct effect on the nature of an economy's investment demand. First, it is the level of an economy's interest rates that determines the amount of autonomous investment purchasing that will occur in the economy under a given set of potential supply prices and expected returns over noncapital costs. Second, the level of interest rates in an economy can rise or fall and thus cause changes in the amount of investment purchasing that results from the existing demand for newly produced capital assets. For instance, the level of interest rates could decline and cause an increase in investment purchasing if more new capital assets are expected to yield rates of return in excess of the interest rates that would have to be paid to finance their purchase. Because such investment purchasing is related to a change in the level of an economy's interest rates instead of the level of purchasing, it is typically part of autonomous investment even though it may involve the replacement of capital assets whose productive lives ended in earlier time periods.

Supply Prices and the Nature of the Capital Goods Industry

As we have seen, the shape of an economy's MEI curve is directly related to the supply prices of capital in the economy. Such supply prices depend upon both the cost structure and competitive nature of the economy's capital goods industry and the ability of existing labor and capital in the economy to move from one productive sector to another. But an economy's supply curve does not necessarily have the upward sloping shape depicted in Figure 4-2. For example, there could be idle capacity in an economy's capital goods industry ready to go to work and produce additional capital assets at the existing level of prices. On the other hand, the economy's supply curve for capital assets could also be perfectly elastic up to a level of capital production that fully employs all of the economy's labor and capital. This would be the unlikely case when there are no diseconomies of scale and there is an immediate transfer of factors into the capital goods industry whenever capital prices tend to rise relative to other prices. At full employment the capital supply curve would become perfectly inelastic to indicate that no additional capital assets could be produced no matter how high their prices rise. Alternately, the economy's capital goods industry could have constant, increasing, or decreasing costs over different ranges of capital goods production. If the capital goods sector's prices were either competitively determined or administered at levels sufficient to cover the costs of production, the economy's MEI curve could conceivably slope upward for the investment purchasing associated with those levels of production where economies of scale resulted in lower costs and thus lower supply prices of capital.

MEI_1 in Figure 4-5 is an example of an economy's MEI curve when the prices of capital assets acquired by each increment of investment purchasing are affected by the level of capital goods sales and there are sufficient economies of scale to reduce costs and increase revenues so that the mirror image relationship exists. MEI_2 is a modified version of MEI_1 to depict the effects of even more extensive economies of scale that further reduce non-capital operating costs and increase revenues. Thus, MEI_2 rises when supply prices are constant and its elasticity throughout is never directly related to the elasticity of the curve representing the economy's supply of capital.

Relative and Absolute Prices

If an economy's capital supply prices increase as the result of higher levels of investment purchasing, the MEI of each increment of investment purchasing will tend to be reduced if there are not sufficient offsetting changes in the

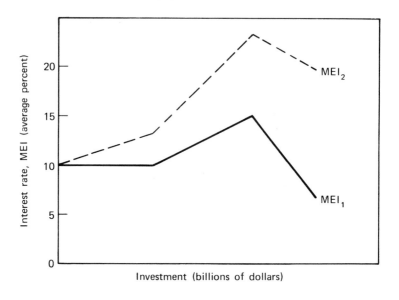

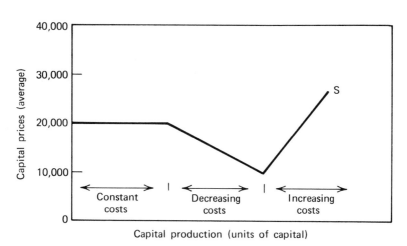

FIGURE 4-5
MEI curves and supply prices.

revenues and operating costs of the assets acquired by the purchases. But the marginal efficiency of investment purchases of such capital will not be decreased by increases in supply prices if the other prices in the economy that affect the assets' profitability also rise in the same degree. For example, if the supply prices of the capital assets acquired by each subsequent unit of investment purchasing are doubled, as are the prices at which their products can be sold and the prices of the noncapital items purchased for their operation, then the MEI of each subsequent dollar spent to purchase subsequent capital assets will remain unchanged even though the level of money expenditures required for the investment purchase of the capital assets will double. Under these circumstances, such an increase in the general level of prices in an economy will cause twice as much investment purchasing to be profitable at every rate of interest. Thus a general increase in prices will cause the economy's MEI curve to shift to the right in proportion to the change in prices. It is only when the supply prices of potential new capital assets increase relative to the other prices in the economy as a result of additional investment purchasing that the rate of return on the additional investment is reduced so that the economy's MEI curve slopes downward.

THE STOCK OF CAPITAL

The purpose of investment purchasing is to acquire and maintain a profit-maximizing stock of capital. Thus the optimum stock of capital for an economy is that amount at which the profits of the economy's producers will be maximized with the existence of a given set of conditions involving technology, prices, capital costs, and noncapital costs. Needless to say, an economy's stock of capital will tend to be expanded so long as the rates of return which additional units of capital are expected to yield exceed the rates of interest that must be paid to finance their purchase.

So far investment purchasing has been discussed in terms of MEI's or the rates of return on potential new capital assets if they are purchased in one particular time period. But a potential investment purchase that is not feasible in one time period because its MEI is too low may have an MEI in a subsequent time period that is high enough for investment purchasing to occur. Specifically, the MEI of a potential new asset may be too low in one time period because of high supply prices caused by investment purchasing for both replacement and expansion purposes, whereas in a later time period the MEI may be high enough because supply prices are no longer being affected by investment purchasing for the purpose of expanding the economy's stock of capital.

The expected rate of return on increments to an economy's stock of capital when its supply prices, noncapital costs, and revenues are normal in that they are not being affected by efforts to change the stock is the "marginal efficiency of capital" or MEC. Furthermore, because it is profitable to acquire capital assets so long as they are expected to yield rates of return in excess of the interest rates that must be paid to finance their purchase, it is possible to use "MEC curves" to graphically depict the profit-maximizing or optimum stock of capital for an economy at each level of interest rates. Figure 4-6 presents an MEC curve for an example economy. It shows, for example, that the optimum stock of capital for this economy is $400 billion when the interest rate level averages 8 percent; $450 billion when the average interest rate is 6 percent; and $500 billion when the level of interest rates in the economy averages 4 percent.

Figure 4-6 indicates that the optimum stock of capital is larger at lower levels of interest rates. But why? It could be because of the lower commodity prices and higher supply prices of capital and higher operating costs that might occur if the economy operates more capital assets and produces more commodities. But, as has already been discussed, additional units of capital do not necessarily mean either higher supply prices and higher noncapital costs or lower commodity prices. Instead, although any higher costs and lower prices that occur will tend to make an economy's MEC curve more

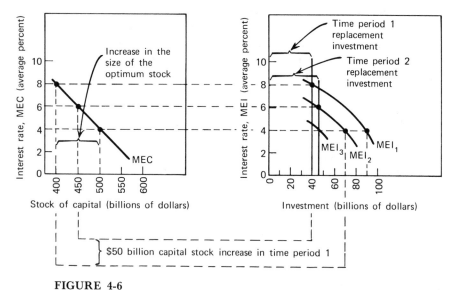

FIGURE 4-6
Investment and capital accumulation when the level of interest rates declines.

inelastic than it would otherwise be, the basic answer is related to the role of capital in the production process and the fact that it may be profitable for an economy's commodity producers to use larger amounts of capital at lower rates of interest. Specifically, a reduction in an economy's rates of interest means a reduction in the cost of using capital in the economy's production processes. Thus, when interest rates decline, an economy's industries tend to become more capital intensive as some capital users find it profitable to increase their stock of capital and substitute the relatively inexpensive capital for the other factors of production. Whether a producer will be able to do so, of course, depends on the technology available and the degree to which it will allow capital to be substituted for labor and land. Needless to say, no such substitution will ocur if there is only one possible combination of capital and the other factors of production.

For an example of how lower interest rates result in a larger optimum stock of capital, consider the two production processes whose cost aspects are described in Table 4-2. They both provide the same level of production, but one uses more capital and less labor than the other. Examination of the data in the table indicates that at the highest of the three interest rates, the relatively labor-intensive process will be preferred because of its lower costs. It also shows that both the production processes will have the same costs at the middle rate of interest and that the production process using relatively large amounts of capital will have the lowest costs at the lowest rate of interest.

TABLE 4-2
Interest Rates, Production Processes, and the Optimum Stock of Capital

INTEREST RATE	PRO-DUCTION PROCESS	STOCK OF CAPITAL	ANNUAL DEPRE-CIATION	ANNUAL INTEREST COST	ANNUAL NON-CAPITAL COST	TOTAL COST
8%	Process C	$5,000	$500	$400	$200	$1,100
	Process L	$1,000	$100	$80	$840	$1,020
6%	Process C	$5,000	$500	$300	$200	$1,000
	Process L	$1,000	$100	$60	$840	$1,000
4%	Process C	$5,000	$500	$200	$200	$900
	Process L	$1,000	$100	$40	$840	$980

Changes in the Level of Interest Rates

A reduction in the Figure 4-6 economy's level of interest rates from an average of 8 percent to an average of 4 percent means an increase of $100 billion in the optimum size of the economy's stock of capital. According to our previous discussions of investment demand, investment purchasing of $140 billion would seemingly occur in the next time period if the useful life of 10 percent of the economy's capital stock is ended in each time period so that an additional $40 billion of investment purchasing is needed for replacement purposes. But what if the economy's capital goods industry has a maximum production capacity in each time period of $100 billion? At best, this industry's producers will be able to replace only the $40 billion of capital assets whose useful lives expire in each time period and provide a net addition of $60 billion to the economy's stock of capital.

This leads us back to the previously discussed MEI or investment demand curves to see how much "net" investment purchasing will occur in each time period to expand the economy's stock of capital. The curves in the right-hand graph of Figure 4-6 depict the investment demand that will exist in the example economy at each level of interest rates in each time period. Consider curve MEI_1. It represents the amount of investment purchasing that would occur at each level of interest rates in the first time period when investment purchasing can occur to expand the economy's stock of capital toward the new optimum level. It is affected, of course, by the various factors that influence the rate of return expected of a potential new capital asset. Consequently, the more that the supply prices of potential new capital assets rise when there is capital asset production in excess of the amount needed in the economy for replacement purposes, the more inelastic the investment demand curve for a particular time period.

Curve MEI_1 indicates that total investment purchasing will be $90 billion in the first time period after the economy's level of interest rates is reduced to an average of 4 percent. Thus the economy's stock of capital will expand from $400 billion to $450 billion. The stock of capital expands by only $50 billion despite the economy's capacity for higher levels of capital production because supply prices and other conditions will change so much by the time the economy's capital output reaches $90 billion that the rates of return on any additional new capital assets that might be acquired in this time period would be exceeded by the interest rates that would have to be paid to finance their purchase.

The net addition of $50 billion of capital, as depicted in the lefthand

---

graph of Figure 4-6 reduces the marginal rates of return on the economy's existing stock of capital (the economy's MEC) to those sufficient to cover interest expenses averaging 6 percent.[1] Thus the investment demand for the next time period (MEI_2) is reduced to indicate that zero net investment will now occur at the level of interest rates averaging 6 percent and that only $70 billion of investment purchasing will occur in the second time period if the level of interest rates in the economy averages 4 percent. Since $45 billion will be needed for replacement purposes when the economy's stock of capital is $450 billion, the $70 billion of investment purchasing means that only an additional $25 billion of capital will be added to the economy's stock of capital assets in the second time period. In each subsequent time period, the process will be repeated until the economy's stock of capital reaches the $500 billion optimum at a level of interest rates averaging 4 percent. Investment purchasing will then be $50 billion for replacement purposes. This occurs in time period n in the example economy of Figure 4-6.

An increase in an economy's level of interest rates would have the opposite effect on its optimum stock of capital and demand for investment. A portion of the economy's stock of capital assets would tend to be excessive due to the resulting tendency for the now relatively less expensive factors such as labor to be substituted for capital in the production process. The economy's users of capital would then tend to allow their stocks to depreciate without replacement until the new and lower profit maximizing level of stocks is attained. Only then would investment purchasing for replacement resume. Such a reduction in the stock of capital, however, does not mean that all investment necessarily ceases in the economy. New opportunities expected to yield a high enough rate to cover the now higher interest rates may open up in specific areas and replacement opportunities may continue to exist in sectors of the economy where the interest rate increases do not reduce the optimum stock of capital enough to completely eliminate investment purchasing.

[1] The differences between the MEI and MEC concepts are purely definitional, but some form of distinction must be made. For example, only $50 billion of investment purchasing will occur in the Figure 4-6 economy during the first time period because the expected rates of return on any additional investment purchases in that time period (MEI) would be below the rates of interest that would prevail when the average rate of interest in the economy is 4 percent. On the other hand, additional net investment purchasing can be expected in the next time period because the $50 billion will reduce the marginal rates of return on the economy's existing capital stock (MEC) to a level sufficient to cover interest rates averaging 6 percent at the supply prices that would exist if investment purchasing were occurring to maintain the $450 billion stock of capital.

Long-Run and Short-Run Investment Demand

The Figure 4-6 economy experienced a $100 billion increase in its optimum stock of capital when the economy's level of interest rates declined from 8 percent to 4 percent. Initially, investment purchasing increased from the $40 billion required for replacement purposes at 8 percent to $90 billion. In subsequent time periods the level of investment purchasing declined as the economy got closer and closer to its new optimum stock of $500 billion. When the new optimum stock is obtained, the economy's investment purchasing will decline to the $50 billion required for replacement purposes.

The move from $40 billion of investment purchasing to $50 billion of purchasing is the long-run change that occurs as a result of the lower level of interest rates when the economy's supply prices are no longer being affected by efforts to expand the stock of capital. A curve representing the Figure 4-6 economy's long-run investment demand at each interest rate would depict $40 billion of investment purchasing at 8 percent and $50 billion at 4 percent. Such a curve represents the level of investment purchasing that would occur in the economy at different rates of interest when no effort is being made to change the size of the economy's stock of capital.

Figure 4-7 depicts the Figure 4-6 economy with the addition of a long-run MEI curve. The elasticity of the long-run curve depends upon the replacement requirements of the economy's optimum stock of capital for each level of interest rates. The elasticity of the MEC curve depends on the degree to which a reduction in interest rates causes capital to be substituted for other factors of production and the degree to which an increase in the

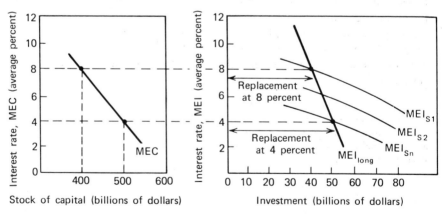

FIGURE 4-7
Long-run and short-run MEI curves.

size of the stock causes lower revenues or higher operating and capital costs. The more rigid the techniques of production are in terms of not allowing factor substitution and the less important interest is as a cost of production, the less the optimum stock of capital will change as the level of interest rates changes and the more inelastic the economy's MEC and long-run investment demand.

An economy's short-run MEI curve is positioned in each time period by the rate of return (MEC) expected from an increment to the economy's stock of capital and the replacement requirements of that stock. The elasticity of the curve from that position is determined, as we have already seen, by the same things that affect the elasticity of the MEC curve, changes in the supply prices of capital, for example. Figures 4-6 and 4-7 depict an economy where less investment purchasing occurs in each subsequent period during the expansion. The economy's short-run MEI curves continually shift down to the lower rates of return associated with the larger stocks of capital that exist in each subsequent time period until the optimum stock is obtained.

The downward or upward shift in investment demand is not the only way in which investment is influenced during a period of changing optimum stock. If all short-run efforts to expand an economy's capital stock cause supply prices to be higher than they would be in the long run, an economy's short-run MEI curves would be more inelastic during the period of expansion than they would be in the long run when the expansion is complete. Whether the elasticity of an economy's short-run MEI curve changes as the economy moves toward the long-run level of investment purchasing appropriate for a new optimum stock depends on the price structure of the economy's capital goods industry and the way in which revenues and non-capital operating costs are affected by either the new stocks of capital or the efforts of the economy's producers to obtain them. If capital goes into the capital goods sector as the stock expands, then more capital assets may be produced at the same prices at each interest rate level in subsequent periods so that the short-run MEI curve becomes more elastic during expansion. On the other hand, supply prices may rise at lower levels of investment purchasing in subsequent time periods if capital is bid out of the capital goods sector due to the shortages temporarily caused by the new optimum stock not being reached. An economy's short-run MEI curve becomes less elastic during expansion if the economy's supply prices tend to rise at lower levels of production in subsequent time periods during an expansion.

An economy's short-run MEI curve becomes perfectly inelastic at the levels of investment at which the economy's capital goods industry will be operating at maximum output since no additional output can be induced with higher prices for capital goods. On the other hand, if there are no diseconomies of scale and there is either idle capacity in the economy's capital goods sector or an immediate transfer of factors to efficient capital goods production whenever there is a tendency for capital prices to rise relative to other prices, then the economy's short-run MEI will be perfectly elastic in the absence of cost and revenue changes. The elasticity of the short-run curve depends on the degree to which additional production can occur during the period of expansion without causing supply prices and operating costs to rise or revenues per unit of capital to fall.

An Increase in the Marginal Efficiency of Capital

An increase in the rate of return expected on each stock of capital that might exist in an economy is depicted by an upward shift in the MEC curve which represents the economy's optimum stock of capital at each level of interest rates. Such a change would occur, for instance, if an economy's noncapital costs decline or if the operating lives of its capital assets are prolonged. Figure 4-8 presents an example of such an increase. It begins with an interest rate level averaging 4 percent and the economy's possessing an optimum stock of capital valued at \$500 billion. Then the curves depicting the optimum stock of capital and short-run demand for investment purchasing shift upward from MEC_1 and MEI_1 to MEC_2 and MEI_2. They do so to depict that the marginal rates of return for the economy's existing \$500 billion stock of capital are now sufficient to cover an 8 percent level of interest rates and that substantial increments to that stock can be anticipated because they are expected to yield rates of return in excess of the current 4 percent rate of interest.

As a result of the initial changes depicted in Figure 4-8, the optimum-sized stock of capital for an interest rate level averaging 4 percent rises to \$600 billion. MEI_2 depicts the demand for investment that exists in the first time period after the initial change in the optimum amount of capital stock for each rate of interest. It indicates that \$50 billion of new capital assets will be purchased for replacement purposes in the first time period if the interest rate level averages 8 percent and that there also will be enough additional investment purchasing to cause a \$40 billion increase in the economy's stock of capital if the interest rate remains at an average of 4 percent. This investment purchasing will increase the economy's stock of capital to \$540 billion and, according to the Figure 4-8 depiction of the conditions in the economy, will reduce the marginal efficiency of the

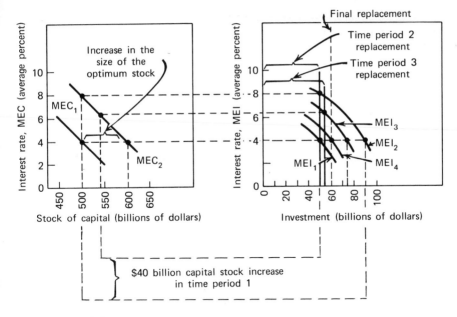

FIGURE 4-8
Investment and capital accumulation when there is an increase in the marginal efficiency of capital.

economy's stock of capital to a level sufficient to cover interest rates averaging slightly above 6 percent. MEI_2 represents the willingness to make investment purchases that will exist at each level of interest rates in the subsequent time period. Finally, in the long run, the new optimum capital stock of $600 billion will be reached and investment purchasing again will be only for replacement purposes (MEI_4).

AN INVESTMENT FUNCTION

There is a similarity between investment purchasing and consumption purchasing: not only do both contribute to the total amount of purchasing, but also how much they contribute is determined in part by the level of total purchasing. More investment purchasing tends to occur at higher levels of total purchasing because the higher levels of production associated with the higher levels of purchasing will result in more capital assets being worn out or otherwise consumed. Consequently, just as a consumption function relates the level of consumption purchasing to the level of total purchasing, an *investment function* relates the sum of autonomous and replacement investment purchasing to the level of total purchasing. Thus, since there will be a different amount of investment purchasing in an economy at every level of interest rates, there will be a different investment function for an economy at every level of interest rates.

Figure 4-9 depicts an economy's investment function when its interest rates average 6 percent. The curve indicates, for example, that when the level of total purchasing in the economy is $300 billion, autonomous investment purchasing will be $30 billion and replacement investment purchasing will be $45 billion; when its Y is $500 billion, autonomous investment will still be $30 billion but replacement investment will be $75 billion. The economy's marginal propensity to invest is .15 at 6 percent; its investment purchasing will be $30 billion higher if its total purchasing rises $200 billion.

The effect of a lower level of interest rates is to increase the amount of investment purchasing occurring at every level of income. For instance, at an interest rate level averaging 4 percent, the foregoing economy's autonomous investment purchasing might become $40 billion while its replacement investment becomes 20 percent of the level of income in the economy. The dotted line in Figure 4-9 represents an investment function of this kind. The curve is higher at every level of income than the 6 percent curve because the effect of a lower level of interest rates is a higher level of both autonomous and replacement investment at every level of total purchasing.

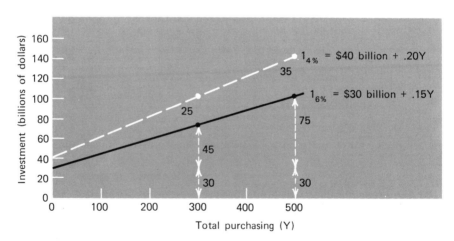

FIGURE 4-9
Investment functions and the level of interest rates.

THE INSTABILITY OF INVESTMENT PURCHASING

In an economy such as the United States' the amount of investment spending tends to fluctuate proportionally more than the amount of total spending. This instability may be the result of several factors. First, changes in the level of interest rates may occur to cause the amount of investment purchasing at every level of total purchasing to change, even if the MEI's of potential new assets remain the same. Then there is the possibility that capital assets whose usefulness is being exhausted may not wear out at a constant rate.

Another important potential cause of instability is the possibility of changes in expectations. The basis for the instability is that no investor knows for certain what revenues he will obtain from new assets acquired by a particular investment or what additional costs will be caused by operating it. Instead, he can only estimate them as best he can. His estimates may be based on experience, knowledge, and even contractual agreement, but even so there is still an element of uncertainty.

Furthermore, since man cannot predict the future with any certainty, it may be that the expectations of investors are guided by the present and near-past circumstance of each factor that influences the level of profits. And then, to the extent that such circumstances change, the expected rate of return on potential new assets changes. For example, low revenues and high costs in an economy's steel industry due to present business conditions or government policies might cause the expected rate of return for a new steel mill to be very low even though the mill would not be operational until years in the future when the business conditions and government policies may be quite different.

Changes in the size of investment purchasing also can be induced by changes in the level of total purchasing. Such changes in investment usually are discussed in terms of their "accelerator effect." The term *accelerator* is used in conjunction with the induced investment portion of autonomous investment because an increase or decrease in investment purchasing may move or accelerate an economy to even greater changes in investment and total purchasing.

For instance, consider an economy with a stock of $100 billion in capital assets, 10 percent of which wear out in each time period. Begin in a period in which there is $30 billion of investment purchasing of which $10 billion is replacement investment and $20 billion is autonomous investment which increases the economy's stock of capital. In the next period, replacement investment purchasing will reach $12 billion: $2 billion to replace 10 percent of the additional $20 billion of capital acquired through autonomous investment in the previous period and $10 billion to replace the other assets that have worn out in the present period. But if no additional autonomous factors such as an increase in the level of total purchasing occur, there will be no autonomous investment in this period, and the total amount of investment purchasing in the economy will fall from $30 billion to $12 billion.

Moreover, total purchasing in the economy not only will fall $18 billion below the level of total purchasing of the first period, it also will decline further as consumption spending falls because of the decline in income earned in selling commodities to investors. Indeed, it is possible that total purchasing will decline so much that in the next period there will be no need for induced investment to replace the 10 percent of the economy's stock of capital assets whose profitable life has expired; the assets that remain will be sufficient to produce all that will be purchased. Investment spending thus falls to zero, and both total and consumption purchasing again will decline. Finally, the economy will reach the point where either more autonomous investment occurs due to some reason unrelated to changes in the level of total purchasing (such as the development of a new product) or replacement investment occurs as enough capital wears out to necessitate replacement assets.

This higher level of investment purchasing then will cause an increase in the level of consumption purchasing as it drives the level of total purchasing upward. Subsequently, investment and total purchasing will increase as autonomous investment occurs to provide any additional new capital assets made profitable by the higher levels of total purchasing. The upward move in total purchasing will continue until the size of autonomous investment stops expanding from one time period to the next so that the level of total purchasing stops growing. Once this occurs, only replacement assets are needed, and the level of investment purchasing again begins to decline. Much more will be said about the accelerator and the relationship between investment purchasing and the level of income in subsequent chapters.

● REFERENCES

Almon, S., "Lags Between Investment Decisions and Their Causes," *Review of Economics and Statistics*, **L**, pp. 193–206 (May 1968).

Angell, J. W. "Uncertainty, Likelihoods and Investment Decisions," *Quarterly Journal of Economics*, **LXXIV**, pp. 1–28 (Feb. 1960).

Bowman, M., "Principles in the Valuation of Human Capital," *Review of Income and Wealth*, pp. 217–246 (Sept. 1968).

Campagna, A., "Capital Appropriations and the Investment Decision," *Review of Economics and Statistics*, **L**, pp. 207–214 (May 1968).

Dorfman, R., "An Economic Interpretation of Optimal Control Theory," *American Economic Review*, **LIX**, pp. 817–831 (Dec. 1969).

Eisner, R., "Investment: Fact and Fancy," *American Economic Review*, **LIII**, pp. 237–246 (1963).

Gehrels, F., and S. Wiggins, "Interest Rates and Fixed Investment," *American Economic Review*, **XLVII**, pp. 79–92 (1957).

Harcourt, G., "Some Cambridge Controversies in the Theory of Capital," *Journal of Economic Literature*, **VII**, pp. 369–405 (June 1969).

Hirshleifer, J., *Investment, Interest and Capital* (Prentice-Hall, 1970).

Jorgenson, D., and J. Stephenson, "Issues in the Development of the Neoclassical Theory of Investment Behavior," *Review of Economics and Statistics*, **LI**, pp. 346–352 (Aug. 1969).

————, "Investment Behavior in U.S. Manufacturing, 1947–60," *Econometrica*, **XXXV**, pp. 169–220 (April 1967).

Kendrick, J., "Some Theoretical Aspects of Capital Measurement," *American Economic Review Papers and Proceedings*, **LI**, pp. 102–111 (1961).

Keynes, J. M., *The General Theory of Employment, Interest and Money* (Harcourt, Brace, 1936), Chapters 11, and 12.

Knox, A. D., "The Accelerator Principle and the Theory of Investment: A Survey," *Economica*, **XIX**, pp. 269–297 (1952).

Lerner, A. "On Some Recent Developments in Capital Theory," *American Economic Review Papers and Proceedings*, **LV**, pp. 284–295 (1965).

————, "On the Marginal Product of Capital and the Marginal Efficiency of Investment," *Journal of Political Economy*, **LXI**, pp. 1–14 (Feb. 1953).

Meyer, J., and E. Kuh, *The Investment Decision* (Harvard Univ. Press, 1957).

Phelps, E., "The New View of Investment: A Neoclassical Analysis," *Quarterly Journal of Economics*, **LXXVI**, pp. 548–567 (Nov. 1962).

Schultz, T., "Investment in Human Capital," *American Economic Review*, **LI** (March 1961).

Solow, R., *Capital Theory and the Rate of Return* (Rand-McNally, 1964).

Tarshis, L., "The Elasticity of the Marginal Efficiency Function," *American Economic Review*, **LI**, pp. 958–985 (Dec. 1961).

White, W. H., "Interest Inelasticity of Investment Demand—The Case from Business Attitude Surveys Re-examined," *American Economic Review*, **XLVI**, pp. 565–589 (1956).

White, W. H., "Lags Between Actual and Reported Fixed Investment," *International Monetary Fund, Staff Papers*, **XVI**, pp. 240–266 (July 1969).

Foreign Purchasing

5

Individuals, businesses, and governments may purchase commodities produced in other economies. Such foreign purchases have an effect on the producing economies' incomes and behavior similar to the effect of any other form of purchasing. The only difference is that now the economies' producers are responding to the existence of offers of payment from foreign purchasers and the owners of the economies' factors of production are earning income producing for foreigners.

THE DETERMINANTS OF FOREIGN PURCHASING

Commodities are purchased in foreign economies because the purchasers are unable to obtain comparably priced items in their own economy. First, the foreign economy may have a unique ability to supply the particular commodities desired. For example, French wines are a product only of France, and Jaguar automobiles are produced only in England; anyone from another economy who wants these items must purchase them abroad and import them. Second, lower production costs may enable the other economy to sell at lower prices certain commodities that can be produced in the domestic economy. These costs may be lower because of a relatively advantageous endowment of the factors needed to produce the commodities in question. For example, high-quality coal and iron-ore deposits may be readily available so that there are relatively low raw-material costs involved in the production of steel. Furthermore, costs and prices may be lower because of the efficient way the factors are used to produce the commodities. Producers in the United States, for example, are able to export certain products constructed with relatively expensive labor because they use the labor so efficiently: through their utilization of the latest technology, they get more output for each unit of labor used in the productive process than do the foreign producers with whom they compete.

Exchange rates. Producers in an economy inevitably tend to conduct their economic affairs with the local variety of money. Thus a foreign purchaser may have to use the money of the local economy when he purchases its commodities. To do this, a German, for example, might exchange marks for dollars in order to obtain the dollars he needs if he is to make purchases in the United States. Alternately, of course, the exporter may accept foreign money in payment for what he produces. He will do so only if he can exchange such receipts for the type of money required to finance the operation of his productive facilities. For example, an American exporter might accept marks from a German purchaser because he can exchange them at his bank for the dollars he needs to pay his labor and capital.

The rate at which different types of currencies are exchanged is the exchange rate. For instance, the exchange rate is 4 to 1 if it takes 4 German marks to acquire 1 United States dollar. The rate of exchange is important because it determines whether prices of comparable commodities are lower in the local economy or in a foreign economy.

Consider a commodity priced at 3.5 marks in Germany and 1 dollar in the United States. If the exchange rate is 4 to 1, the Germans will not buy the commodity in the United States because they would have to trade 4 marks for the dollar needed to purchase it, whereas they can buy it in their own country for 3.5 marks. Conversely, purchasers in the United States also would buy the commodity in Germany since they can get 3.5 marks for less than the dollar required to purchase it in their own economy. On the other hand, the situation will be exactly reversed if the exchange rate is 3 to 1. The purchasers in the United States will buy from their own producers because the $1 price at home is less than the amount of dollars they would have to give to get enough marks to buy the commodity in Germany. Similarly, the German buyers will buy in the United States because they can get the required 1 dollar for 3 marks as opposed to the 3.5 marks they would have to pay for the commodity in Germany.

Balance of payments. A "balance of payments" account records both the amount of money coming into an economy from abroad and the amount of money going abroad from the economy. Of course, money comes and goes between economies for more reasons than just the buying and selling of newly produced commodities. For instance, it can come in to buy old commodities or noncommodities such as stock shares in local corporations, or it can come in as loans or as gifts. Needless to say, the recipients of such foreign money may exchange it for the local money of those who want foreign money to send abroad for the same purposes. Further complicating the situation is the possibility that at any one exchange rate there may be more (or less) foreign money coming into the economy for such purposes than the economy desires to use abroad.

When more funds are coming in than going out during a given period, an economy is said to have a balance of payments surplus; when less is coming in than is paid out, the economy has a balance of payments deficit. When an economy has a deficit, it must find some way of getting additional foreign money if it is to purchase as much abroad as it desires. Such an economy can do this by selling any gold it possesses to holders of the desired foreign money, by using foreign money accumulated during earlier periods of balance of payments surpluses, or by engaging in any other activity that results in foreigners sending in more of their money and residents sending out less. For instance, an economy desiring additional amounts of foreign money can raise the interest rates which its banks pay on deposits in order to encourage deposits from abroad. Alternately, an economy might accomplish the same result by changing the rate at which its money exchanges for the money of other economies. For example, suppose that the exchange rate between the monies of the United States and Germany is 4 German marks to 1 United States dollar and the United States is running a balance of payments deficit and Germany a surplus because the United States purchasers are exchanging their dollars for marks and buying German products while the United States' producers are not selling commodities to German purchasers. If the rate of exchange between marks and dollars is then changed to 3 to 1, the United States balance of payments deficit and the German surplus might tend to be eliminated as fewer German commodities would be purchased by United States purchasers because they would now have to give up more dollars to get enough marks. At the same time German purchasers would find it more attractive to purchase commodities produced in the United States because they would now need fewer marks to get enough dollars.

It is important to note that such a "devaluation" of the dollar in terms of the number of marks that can be acquired in exchange for it may aggravate rather than eliminate a balance of payments deficit as it changes the number of commodities purchased and produced in the different economies. What happens when exchange rates are changed depends upon the elasticities of purchasers' demands. For example, if the Germans were previously spending 4 billion marks to purchase products of the United States when the exchange rate was 4 to 1 and then responded to the 3 to 1 rate by increasing the number of commodities they purchased in the United States by 10 percent, the number of marks spent in the United States by the German purchasers would be reduced to 3.3 billion and the United States' balance of payments deficit would tend to be increased. More importantly, whether the balance of payments deficit is eliminated or not, the United States economy would end up with fewer commodities since its producers would be sending more commodities to Germany while its purchasers would not be able to buy as many from the German producers.

THE NET EXPORTS APPROACH

The effect of foreign purchasing on the level of an economy's total purchasing can be approached in two ways: first, in terms of the economy's "net exports" (the difference between the economy's expenditures to import commodities produced abroad and the amount that foreigners spend on commodities exported by the economy) ; second, in terms of the total amount of foreign purchasing made to obtain the commodities exported by the domestic economy.

The main advantage of the net exports approach is that it is consistent with the statistics used in countries like the United States. As should be remembered from discussion of the GNP statistics in Table 2-1, the data reported for United States' consumption, investment, and government purchasing include expenditures to import commodities produced in other economies. This inclusion means that it is only necessary to add the amount of foreign purchasing in excess of United States purchasing abroad to obtain an estimate of the total amount of purchasing of U.S.-produced commodities.

On the other hand, the same estimate of total purchasing can be obtained if all export sales to foreign purchasers are included as part of foreign purchasing and the purchases abroad by local buyers are excluded from consumption purchasing. The main advantage of this approach is that it realistically limits each purchasing component to purchases that induce production in the economy and cause income to be earned in the production process. The use of this approach means that all consumer, investment, and government expenditures abroad are considered to be part of savings just like all other nonpurchasing uses of income. Such an approach is realistic since expenditures abroad, even though included in the statistics, do not directly cause production to occur or contribute to the income earned from producing commodities. For example, increased consumer purchases of Volkswagens and Fiats do not directly cause more Fords and Chevrolets to be produced in the United States or cause incomes earned in the United States to rise. In fact, if the buyers reduce their purchases of American-made cars in order to purchase cars produced abroad, fewer cars will be produced in the United States and the levels of income earned in the United States will tend to fall.

AUTONOMOUS AND INDUCED FOREIGN PURCHASING

It is possible that some foreign purchasing would go on in an economy no matter what happens to the level of total purchasing in the economy. After all, the desires and abilities of foreigners are not determined *in toto* by the amounts of money that they receive from the exporting economy. And the foreigners may be able to get credit from various sources or pay the economy's producers with foreign money or be able to spend money that is obtained from the exporting economy when it is sent abroad for any purpose without regard to the level of income in the exporting economy. On the other hand, it is also possible that the level of foreign purchasing in an economy is at least partially related to the level of total purchasing in the economy. The latter relationship may exist because the amount of money that an economy sends abroad can then be used by the foreign recipients of the money to buy commodities produced in the economy. Thus an economy's exports may rise as its level of income rises due to the higher levels of purchasing that occur abroad when an economy's income rises and the subsequent return of the additional money sent abroad that further increases purchasing in the economy whose income initially increased.

To represent the two possibilities, foreign purchasing (F) can be subdivided into two components: autonomous foreign purchasing (F_a), whose size is unaffected by the level of total purchasing in the exporting economy, and induced foreign purchasing (F_i), whose size changes as the economy's level of purchasing changes. Thus, $F = F_a + F_i$.

AN EXPORT FUNCTION

Just as its consumption and investment functions relate the amount of each of these types of purchasing to the level of total purchasing, an *export function* relates the level of foreign purchasing to the level of total purchasing in the exporting economy. Furthermore, just as the MPC and MPI are the changes in consumption and investment that will occur when the level of purchasing changes, the "marginal propensity to export" (MPX) relates changes in the level of foreign purchasing to changes in the level of total purchasing. For example, consider an economy in which \$10 billion in foreign purchasing will occur no matter what the level of total purchasing, while additional foreign purchases are induced at the rate of 5 percent of the total purchasing that occurs in the economy. If the economy's Y is \$200 billion, its F is \$20 billion; if its Y is \$300 billion, its F is \$25 billion.

The relationship of foreign purchasing and total purchasing also can be presented graphically. Since the amount of autonomous foreign purchasing does not change at different levels of total purchasing, a perfectly horizontal line will result when the points that represent the level of autonomous foreign purchasing occurring at each level of total purchasing are joined. Based on the data from the foregoing example, such a line appears in Figure 5-1; it shows that autonomous foreign purchasing will be \$10 billion no matter whether total purchasing is as low as \$100 billion or as high as \$400 billion. On the other hand, if additional foreign purchasing is induced at

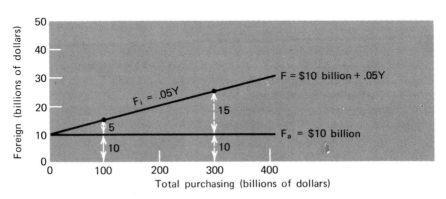

FIGURE 5-1
Foreign purchasing.

higher levels of total purchasing, a line representing total foreign purchasing will slope upward to show that more of such purchasing will occur at higher levels of Y. Such a line also is depicted in Figure 5-1. It is based on induced foreign purchasing occurring at the rate of 5 percent of Y, and autonomous foreign purchasing of $10 billion.

THE INSTABILITY OF FOREIGN PURCHASING

Foreign purchasing is the smallest purchasing component of the United States' economy. Typically it provides only 5 or 6 percent of the total purchasing that occurs in the economy. But, despite its relatively small size in some economies, foreign purchasing does have an important influence on the level of income that occurs in market economies. Foreign purchasing is important because substantial fluctuations in foreign purchasing can originate abroad and affect production in the economy and the income earned by its factors. Purchasing by the economy's participants may also fluctuate at the same time in response to changes that occur in the foreign economies.

There are many sources of instability originating abroad. They include:

1. *Interest Rate Changes.* If a foreign economy increases its interest rates it may attract from another economy deposits of money that would otherwise be used to purchase commodities produced in the other economy or deposited in the other economy's domestic financial institutions and available for them to loan to purchasers. On the other hand, if the foreign economy lowers its interest rates, its deposits may flow into the economy and increase the amount of money available for purchasing.
2. *Exchange Rate Changes.* A foreign economy, as we have already seen, may affect purchasing in a local economy if it changes the exchange rate between its money and that of the local economy. For example, the exchange rate is 4 to 1 if Germany stands ready to buy and sell gold at 140 marks per ounce and the United States buys and sells at 35 dollars per ounce. If Germany reduces the price at which it will buy and sell gold to 70 marks per ounce it will have devalued the dollar from being worth 4 marks to being worth 2 marks. The effect of such a downward devaluation of the dollar and upward revaluation of the mark on the total foreign expenditures in each economy will depend on the price elasticities of demand for the commodities produced in each economy.
3. *The Imposition of Tariffs and Quotas.* A tariff is a tax levied on commodities and other items that are imported into an economy. If an economy raises the tax on the products imported into it from another economy or

just arbitrarily imposes a quota to limit that amount, then the foreign purchasing to obtain the imported commodities will tend to be reduced.

4. *Changes in Prices.* If one economy's level of commodity prices changes more rapidly than the price level of another economy, the total amount of purchasing in both economies will tend to be affected. For example, consider what would happen if the United States and France were each initially purchasing the same amount of commodities from each other and then, over time, commodity prices rose 10 percent in the United States and 2 percent in France. French purchasers would tend to stop buying in the United States and switch their purchasing to the now relatively less expensive commodities of France. Additionally, United States purchasers who used to buy goods and services in the United States would also tend to switch to French products. Whether the money amount of foreign purchasing would go up or down in either economy when the number of commodities they sell abroad is changed depends, of course, on the price elasticity of the foreigners' purchasing desires. Purchasing would tend to rise in the United States, for instance, if the French demand for commodities produced in the United States is inelastic so that a 10 percent increase in United States' prices results in a 1 percent reduction in the number of commodities sold to the French. French purchasing in the United States would fall, on the other hand, if the French demand was elastic so that the 10 percent increase in prices caused a 50 percent reduction in the amount of commodities being purchased by the French.

INTERNATIONAL TRADE AND THE LEVEL OF INCOME

The existence of foreign purchasers and local buyers purchasing in foreign economies provides a tempting solution for economies with problems caused by inadequate amounts of total purchasing. For example, if an economy's production is depressed due to a lack of purchasing, the economy could change its exchange rates, tariffs, quotas, or interest rates in an effort to solve its problem by getting more purchasing both from abroad and from its own residents who otherwise would have purchased abroad. But the foreign economies may not accept a reduction in the purchasing of commodities produced by their producers in order to solve the problems of the first economy. They may retaliate in kind and further reduce the volume of trade and the benefits of specialization.

Even if there are no problems related to its total purchasing, an economy with fixed exchange rates may act in such a manner to avoid a balance of payments deficit or to gain a surplus so that it can accumulate reserves of gold or other assets in return for the commodities that it produces and sends abroad. Balance of payments deficits can not go forever because an economy will eventually run out of reserves with which to cover them. Yet economies may hesitate to admit that their money and products are not valued by foreigners to the extent suggested by the fixed exchange rate. As a result, they may hesitate to move to the uncertainty of fluctuating exchange rates where the value of their money in exchange for other types of money would be determined in money markets by the willingness of those who hold it to give it up.

Sometimes an economy's policies to protect a fixed exchange rate and eliminate a balance of payments deficit are compatible with its desires for foreign products and levels of purchasing that will lead to maximum levels of production at home. Sometimes they are not. The way an economy's balance of payments considerations constrain its policies to attain domestic prosperity will be discussed in later chapters dealing with stabilization and macroeconomic policies.

● REFERENCES

Bowman, C., "Employment Related to Exports," *Monthly Labor Review*, **XCII,** pp. 16–20 (June 1969).

Chown, J. and R. Valentine, *The International Bond Market in the 1960's: Its Development and Operation* (Praeger, 1968).

Davis, T., "Exchange Rate Adjustments Under the Par Value System, 1946–68," *Federal Reserve Bank of Kansas City Review* (Sept.–Oct., 1969).

Floyd, J., "International Capital Movements and Monetary Equilibrium," *American Economic Review*, pp. 472–492 (Sept. 1969).

Hamada, K., "Optimal Capital Accumulation by an Economy Facing an International Capital Market," *Journal of Political Economy*, **LXXVII,** pp. 684–697 (July–Aug. 1969).

Hansen, N., "America's Challenge and Europe's Response," *Journal of Economic Issues*, **II,** pp. 157–165 (June 1968).

Johnson, H., "The Case For Flexible Exchange Rates, 1969," *Federal Reserve Bank of St. Louis Review*, **LI** (June 1969).

Krueger, A., "Balance of Payment Theory," *Journal of Economic Literature*, **VII,** pp. 1–26 (March, 1969).

Mishan, E., "A Note on the Costs of Tariffs, Monopolies and Thefts," *Western Economic Journal*, **VII,** pp. 230–233 (Sept. 1969).

Mundell, R. A., "A Theory of Optimum Currency Areas," *American Economic Review*, **LI**, pp. 657–665 (Sept. 1961).

———, "Flexible Exchange Rate and Employment Policy," *Canadian Journal of Economics and Political Science*, **XXVII**, p. 516 (Nov. 1961).

———, "Real Gold, Dollars and Paper Gold," *American Economic Review*, **LIX**, pp. 324–331 (May 1969).

Ophir, T., "The Interaction of Tariffs and Quotas," *American Economic Review*, **LIX**, pp. 1002–1005 (Dec. 1969).

Scitovsky, T., *Money and the Balance of Payments* (Rand-McNally, 1969).

Timberlake, R., "The Fixation With Fixed Exchange Rates," *Southern Economic Journal*, **XXXVI**, pp. 134–146 (Oct. 1969).

Walker, F., "The Restrictive Effects of the U.S. Tariff," *American Economic Review*, **LIX**, pp. 963–966 (Dec. 1969).

The Equilibrium
Level of Income

6

The all-important total amount of purchasing that occurs in an economy typically is referred to as the economy's "level of income." The use of the term "income" in place of "total purchasing" is traditional in economics. Such an interchange of names is valid because the expenditures made to purchase commodities in an economy tend to be received as income by the owners of the factors of production used to produce the commodities.[1] Needless to say, the level of total purchasing or income in an economy is

[1] The possibility that indirect business taxes and capital consumption may keep an economy's national income from being identical with its gross national product has already been discussed. Furthermore, an economy's businessmen may not have perfect foresight and thus always produce an amount of commodities exactly equal to sales. It is likely that they will make errors in forecasting sales just as consumers will err in estimating incomes that they will earn. But it should be recalled that commodities that are not sold become undesired additions to inventory and are considered to be purchased by their owners as part of inventory investment. Thus the basic equality between income earned and purchasing is retained even though there may well be adjustments in purchasing and production in subsequent time periods to offset the effects of the unintended inventory investment.

equal to the sum of the various purchasing components. Algebraically, $Y = C + I + G + F$ or, with the $a + bY$ description of consumption purchasing, $Y = a + bY + I + G + F$.

Complicating any attempt to calculate the size of an economy's level of income simply by summing its purchasing components is the fact that these components not only *affect* the level of income but also *depend* on it. For example, the level of income in an economy is determined by the level of consumption purchasing that occurs, and the level of consumption purchasing in the economy is determined by the economy's level of income. Fortunately, there are several ways to calculate the level of income in an economy without initially knowing the sizes of all its purchasing components. These approaches will be examined, initially on the simplified basis that only the level of consumption purchasing changes as an economy's level of income changes, and then on the basis that the level of income also affects the other purchasing components. To simplify the discussion further, we shall assume temporarily that there are no government activities in order to postpone consideration of the influence of government purchasing, taxes, or transfers. These will be discussed in the next chapter.

The Basic Equation

One way to determine the level of income is to substitute the values of known purchasing components into the basic equation for the level of income so that they can be added together. For example, consider an economy during a given period in which investment purchasing is fixed at $80 billion, foreign purchasing is $10 billion, and consumption purchasing is $10 billion plus 60 percent of each increment of income. Determining that the level of total purchasing or income in this economy will be $250 billion during the period of time under consideration requires the following steps:[1]

1. $Y = a + bY + I + F$ (basic equation).
2. $Y = \$10 + .60Y + \$80 + \$10$ (putting in data).
3. $Y = .60Y + \$100$ (combining numerical values).
4. $Y - .60Y = \$100$ (combining values of Y).
5. $.40Y = \$100$ (relating Y to numerical values).
6. $Y = \$250$ (and $C = \$160$ since it is $10 plus 60 percent of Y).

[1] The term "billion" has been removed from this and certain subsequent income determination examples for the sake of clarity. In some cases the term will be designated with a "B"; thus, $400B.

The equilibrium level of income in this economy is $250 billion; it is the only level of income that can be maintained in subsequent periods. And it will be maintained as long as there are no changes in the nature of the purchasing components because in each subsequent time period there will be $160 billion of consumption purchasing ($10B plus 60 percent of $250B) plus $90 billion of foreign and investment purchasing. All other levels of income are disequilibrium levels. They cannot occur except temporarily while the economy is moving toward the equilibrium level of income. For example, consider the impossibility of the example economy's maintaining a higher level of purchasing or income such as $300 billion. With an income of $300 billion, the economy's consumption purchasing would be $190 billion ($10B plus 60 percent of the level of income) for a total amount of purchasing of only $280 billion when there is $90 billion of investment and foreign purchasing ($190B + $80B + $10B). Thus the economy would be unable to maintain a $300 billion level of purchasing.

Neither could $280 billion be maintained because at that level of income, its consumption purchasing would fall to $178 billion ($10B plus .60 of $280B) for a total of $268 billion when investment and foreign purchasing are included. Needless to say, the level of income in the economy would continue to decline until it reached $250 billion. On the other hand, a level of income lower than $250 billion also could not be maintained in this economy. For example, if the level of income in the economy were $160 billion, consumption purchasing of $106 billion ($10B plus .60 of $160B) would occur to drive the level of income to $196 billion including the $90 billion of investment and foreign purchasing. But the level of income would not stop rising there. After all, when the level of income is $196 billion, consumption purchasing would be $127.6 billion ($10B plus .60 of $196B) for a total of $217.6 billion including the investment and foreign purchasing. And the level of income would keep rising to the equilibrium of $250 billion.

Every time an income level of $250 billion occurs in the example economy, it will result in $160 billion of consumption purchasing ($10B plus .60 of $250B). That level of consumption purchasing means that the economy will have a $250-billion level of purchasing or income in every subsequent period so long as there is $90 billion of foreign and investment purchasing in the economy. In a sense, the equilibrium level of purchasing recurs in each period because the $90 billion of income that is saved rather than re-spent for consumption purposes is balanced by the additional $90 billion in purchasing from the nonconsumption components such as investment and foreign purchasing. In other words, *equilibrium occurs at the specific income level that causes or generates a total amount of savings that is exactly offset by the amount of the nonconsumption purchasing occurring in the economy.*

That the equilibrium level of income is indeed the only one generating a total amount of savings just equal to the size of the nonconsumption purchasing is demonstrated by the following steps:

1. $Y = C + I + F$.
2. Thus, $Y - C = I + F$.
3. And since $Y - C = S$,
4. Then, $S = I + F$ (because both are equal to $Y - C$).

Quite often the equilibrium requirement that savings be exactly offset by the amount of nonconsumption purchasing is analyzed in terms of a simple economy in which investment is the only purchasing component other than consumption. Then the condition existing when the economy's level of income is in equilibrium is $S = I$. Alternately, the portion of an economy's income that is saved or not respent for consumption purposes is said to have leaked away from the economy's total spending while nonconsumption purchasing is said to be injected into its spending. The equilibrium condition is then, needless to say, "leakages" equal "injections." The only difference between these equilibrium conditions are those of terminology.

Equilibrium Income Determination through Savings

Since the equilibrium level of income can occur only when the amount of nonconsumption purchasing ($I + F$ in an economy in which there is no government purchasing) equals the amount of income not used for consumption purchasing (savings), the equilibrium level of income also can be determined if the amount of nonconsumption purchasing is known. Examples of how this can be accomplished both algebraically and graphically follow.

Algebraically finding the equilibrium level of income. Since an identity exists between savings and the nonconsumption purchasing components, it is possible to substitute the amount of nonconsumption purchasing into an economy's savings function and solve for the equilibrium level of Y, the only one that yields the necessary amount of savings. Consider the example economy described earlier in which $I = \$80$ billion, $F = \$10$ billion, $a = \$10$ billion, and $b = .60$. This economy's savings function is $S = -\$10B + .40Y$. Since it is known that the level of savings at the equilibrium level of income will be equal to the total amount of nonconsumption purchasing, the appropriate equation is $90B = -$10B + .40Y$. Solving this equation yields $Y = 250 billion; this is the only level of Y for this economy which will provide the required $90 billion in savings.

Graphically determining the equilibrium level. It is also possible to determine an economy's equilibrium level of income with the aid of a graphic form of the savings function. Figure 6-1 presents a savings function depicting the amount of savings that would occur in the example economy at each level of income. Another line in the figure, the $I + F$ line, represents the total amount of nonconsumption purchasing that will occur in the economy at each level of income. It is perfectly horizontal in this figure to indicate that the economy's nonconsumption purchasing does not change as its level of income changes. The equilibrium level of income ($250 billion) is identified by the intersection of the savings function representing the amount of savings that will occur in the economy at each level of income and the $I + F$ line representing the amount of investment and other nonconsumption purchasing that will occur in the economy at each level of income. The level of income associated with the point on the savings function where the two lines intersect is the only one that will generate an amount of savings equal to the level of nonconsumption purchasing.

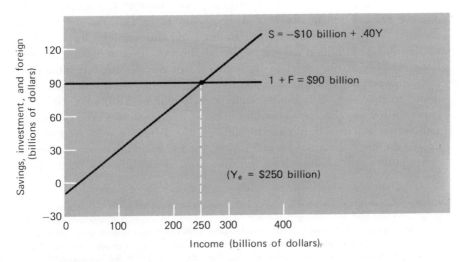

FIGURE 6-1
The equilibrium level of income.

The Forces That Move an Economy to Its Equilibrium Level of Income

Actual (or *ex post*) consumption and investment purchasing is the purchasing that actually occurs in an economy. Intended (or *ex ante*) consumption and investment purchasing is that amount of purchasing which an economy's consumers and investors desire to have occur. Needless to say, any time there is a difference, the consumers and investors will adjust their actual purchasing to bring it in line with the purchasing levels they desire. It is just such adjustments that cause the level of purchasing in an economy to change until the equilibrium level of income is reached and nonconsumption purchasing is exactly offset by savings. In terms of consumption, the move toward the equilibrium level of income occurs because the amounts of actual and intended consumption purchasing differ at all disequilibrium levels of income and the differences cause adjustments in actual consumption purchasing that not only move the economy closer to the equilibrium level of income, but also provide the basis for subsequent adjustments in that direction. There are no differences, and thus no further adjustments, once the equilibrium level of income is reached.

To see how differences between actual and intended consumption purchasing move the level of income toward equilibrium[1] consider the example economy already described in which I = $80 billion, F = $10 billion, a = $10 billion, and b = .60. Obviously, even without consumption purchasing related to the level of income, the I, F, and "a" portions of consumption will yield a total purchasing (and thus income) level of $100 billion. But $100 billion cannot be the equilibrium level of income because the recipients of that level of income will not merely use $10 billion for consumption purposes and save the remaining $90 billion. Instead, they will desire to save only $30 billion and use $70 billion ($10B plus .60Y) for consumption purchasing. Thus the actual savings (*ex post* savings) of $90 billion that will exist if all but $10 billion of the $100 billion is saved will far exceed the desired savings (*ex ante* savings) of $30 billion, whereas the actual consumption purchasing (*ex post* consumption) of $10 billion is far less than

---

[1] These differences and the income moves they cause are related to similar differences between actual and intended investment that have the same effect. Investment differences are related to consumption differences because the unsold commodities that exist when actual consumption purchasing falls below the levels expected by producers results in unintended (*ex post*) investment in the form of unintended inventory buildups. On the other hand, unexpectedly large consumption purchases cause inventories to be drawn down so that actual investment purchasing for the inventory purposes falls below the intended (*ex ante*) levels.

the $70 billion that is desired (*ex ante* consumption). The additional purchasing that will occur when the income recipients increase consumption purchasing by $60 billion and decrease savings by $60 billion will raise the level of total purchasing to $160 billion. Thus the earlier level of $100 billion cannot be an "equilibrium" level because the reaction to the difference between actual and intended consumption and actual and intended savings drives the level of income upward. But even though additional consumption purchasing occurs, the new level of income will still be a disequilibrium level: at $160 billion, the actual level of consumption purchasing will be only $70 billion, and the actual level of savings, $90 billion. But when the level of income is $160 billion, the income recipients will desire to use more than $70 billion of their $160 billion income for consumption purchasing and save less than $90 billion; they will want to use $106 billion ($106B is $10B plus 60 percent of $160B) for consumption purposes and save only $54 billion. $160 billion is thus a disequilibrium level of income because the $106 billion of consumption purchasing which it causes will increase the economy's total purchasing to $196 billion. But even this higher level of income is a disequilibrium level because if the level of income is $196 billion, the recipients will want to use $127.6 billion for consumer purchasing rather than $106 billion; thus total purchasing in the economy will rise to $217.6 billion. It is for these reasons and in this fashion that the level of income continues to rise until it reaches the equilibrium level of income of $250 billion, the level at which the desired level of consumption purchasing (*ex ante* consumption) will be the same as the actual amount of consumption purchasing (*ex post* consumption) and the desired amount of savings equal to the actual amount of savings. Then there will be no more changes in the level of income.

Further, consider why the equilibrium level of income cannot exceed $250 billion. For example, if the level of income is $300 billion, only $190 billion ($10B plus .60 of $300B) will be desired for consumption purposes. But $190 billion of consumption purchasing along with the usual $90 billion of nonconsumption purchasing means that the level of income in the economy will fall to $280 billion. When the level of income is $280 billion, however, the desired level of consumption purchasing will be only $178 billion ($10B plus .60 of $280B). With $90 billion of nonconsumption purchasing, total purchasing in the economy thus will fall to $268 billion as consumers adjust their purchasing to the income level of $280 billion. Of course, consumption purchasing will then decline again because the old actual level of consumption purchasing is again higher than the amount desired for the resulting lower level of income. Consumption purchasing will continue to decline in this economy until the economy reaches an income level of $250 billion.

The Effect of Income-Related Nonconsumption Purchases

It is possible to estimate the equilibrium level of income when replacement investment purchasing and induced foreign purchasing are included. It simply requires the expansion of the basic formula of $Y = a + bY + I + F$ to include both autonomous and income-related nonconsumption purchasing. Notice also the similarity between the components; each has an autonomous subcomponent whose size is independent of the level of income (a, I_a, F_a) and an income-related sub-component whose size is some percentage $(b,$ for consumption; $v,$ for investment; $x,$ for foreign) of the level of income. $Y = a + bY + I_a + vY + F_a + xY.$

Using the previous data with the addition of replacement investment purchasing equal to 10 percent of the level of income and induced foreign purchasing equal to 5 percent of the level of income, we see that the equilibrium level of income in the example economy becomes $400 billion instead of $250 billion:

1. $Y = a + bY + I_a + I_r + F_a + F_i.$
2. $Y = a + bY + I_a + vY + F_a + xY.$
3. $Y = \$10 + .60Y + \$80 + .10Y + \$10 + .05Y.$
4. $Y = .75Y + \$100.$
5. $Y - .75Y = \$100.$
6. $.25Y = \$100.$
7. $Y = \$400.$

The savings function. The same results can be obtained by setting the savings function $(S = -\$10B + .40Y)$ equal to the sum of the income-related and autonomous nonconsumption purchasing components (I, F) and solving algebraically for the level of income that yields an amount of savings just equal to the sum of the nonconsumption purchases. Thus, using the same data:

1. $-a + (1 - b)Y = I_a + vY + F_a + xY.$
2. $-\$10 + .40Y = \$80 + .10Y + \$10 + .05Y.$
3. $.25Y = \$100.$
4. $Y = \$400.$

The savings function also can be used graphically to depict the equilibrium income level when income-related investment and foreign purchasing occur. Figure 6-2 presents this for the example economy already described. Notice that the savings function has exactly the same form as that depicted in Figure 6-1. The only difference is that the I + F line slopes upward since replacement investment and induced foreign purchasing mean more non-consumption purchasing occurring at the higher levels of income.

Equilibrium in a More Complex Economy

The situation in the previous discussion is one in which 60 percent of all purchasing is used for consumption. In other words, the estimation procedure lumped together all business and personal savings, and related the level of consumption purchasing directly to the level of total purchasing. It is possible, however, to expand the fundamental equation to relate an economy's propensity to consume directly to the level of its disposable income. Such an approach has the additional merit of allowing the independent inclusion of net business savings (and, as we shall see later, net government savings). For example, consider an economy in which $10

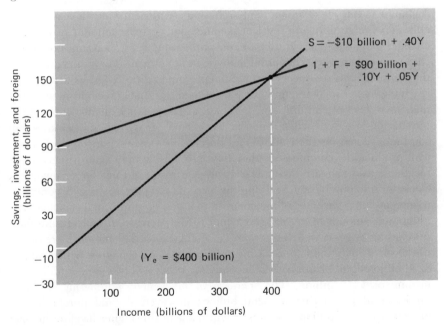

FIGURE 6-2
The equilibrium level of income with replacement investment purchasing and induced foreign purchasing.

billion plus 60 percent of all disposable income is used for consumption purchasing, investment purchasing is $80 billion, foreign purchasing is $10 billion, there is no government activity, and net business savings (BS) is 10 percent of the level of total purchasing so that only 90 percent of total purchasing is received as disposable income. Algebraically, the economy's disposable income is Y − BS. Thus the level of income in the economy is $217.39 billion:

1. $Y = a + b(Y − BS) + I + F$.
2. $Y = \$10 + .60(Y − .10Y) + \$80 + \$10$.
3. $Y = \$10 + .60Y − .06Y + \$80 + \$10$.
4. $Y = \$100 + .54Y$.
5. $.46Y = \$100$.
6. $Y = \$217.39$.

THE MULTIPLIER

A change in the size of any of the purchasing components may have a greater effect on the equilibrium level of income than just the amount of its own change. For instance, if investment purchasing rises, consumption purchasing also may rise: the initial increase in investment purchasing goes into the hands of the producers of investment commodities who, as a result of receiving higher incomes, may use part of their additional receipts to increase their own level of consumption purchasing. (How much their consumption purchasing rises depends on the recipients' marginal propensities to consume.) Then, as their additional purchasing raises the incomes of those who produce the commodities they buy, purchasing may again rise as these recipients also increase their purchasing as a result of their larger incomes. Consumption purchasing, and thus the level of total purchasing, will continue to increase until the level of income rises to a new equilibrium level where an additional amount of savings just equal to the increase in nonconsumption purchasing is generated. For example, if there is a $10 billion increase in the level of investment purchasing in the foregoing economy which had a $250 billion equilibrium level of income, the result will be a new equilibrium income of $275 billion. The increase in investment purchasing initially pushes total purchasing to $260 billion; however, if total purchasing is increased by $10 billion, consumers will react to this higher level of income by increasing their consumption purchasing by $6 billion so that the economy's total level of purchasing will reach $266 billion. If total purchasing increases by $6 billion, however, consumption purchasing will rise another \$3.6 billion to \$269.6 billion, etc., until \$275 billion, the new equilibrium level of income, is reached. In this case, the initial increase of \$10 billion causes the level of purchasing in the economy to rise by \$25 billion and the level of savings to rise by \$10 billion (MPS × \$25 billion).

The Multiplier Formula

It is possible to compute the degree to which an economy's level of purchasing will change as a result of a change in the level of one of its purchasing components. Called the "income multiplier" or the "purchasing multiplier," and often designated by the letter k, it is computed through the following formula when consumption purchasing is the only type of purchasing in an economy whose size depends on the level of income in the economy:

$$k = \frac{1}{1 - MPC} = \frac{1}{1 - b}$$

which, for our example, is:

$$k = \frac{1}{1 - .60} = 2\tfrac{1}{2}$$

The multiplier indicates that a change in the size of one of the example economy's purchasing components is going to change the economy's equilibrium level of purchasing by an amount $2\tfrac{1}{2}$ times larger than the original change in the purchasing component. Thus an increase of \$10 billion in investment purchasing will raise the economy's total purchasing by \$25 billion; and an increase of \$20 billion will raise it by \$50 billion; and a decrease of \$40 billion will reduce it by \$100 billion.

The multiplier formula is derived from the equilibrium income-estimating formula in the following fashion when ΔY represents the change in the size of an economy's total purchasing resulting from a change in the size of its investment purchasing (ΔI):

1. $Y = a + bY + I + F.$

2. Or, $Y - bY = a + I + F.$

3. Or, $Y(1 - b) = a + I + F.$

4. Or, $Y = \dfrac{1}{1 - b}(a + I + F).$

And since an economy's purchasing will rise by some amount (ΔY) if more investment purchasing (ΔI) occurs:

5. $Y + \Delta Y = \dfrac{1}{1 - b} (a + I + F + \Delta I)$.

Then, subtracting the original Y from both sides of the equation (by subtracting Y itself from the left side and the various components of Y from the right) leaves only the change in total purchasing and the cause of the change:

$$\Delta Y = \dfrac{1}{1 - b} (\Delta I)$$

Total pur-   this   of a change
chasing will multiple in investment
change by   (or any other type)
                            purchasing

Thus: $\dfrac{1}{1 - b}$ is the value of the multiplier.

A change in the size of one of the purchasing components and its effect on the economy's level of purchasing also can be shown graphically. Figure 6-3 represents the Figure 6-1 economy before and after an additional $40

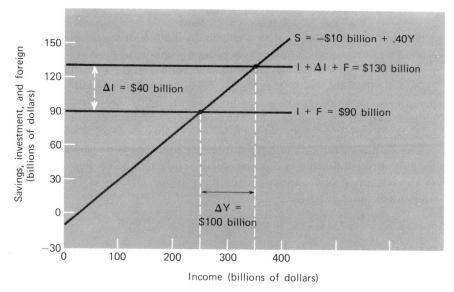

FIGURE 6-3
Changes in the level of income.

billion of investment purchasing. The new equilibrium level of total purchasing ($350 billion) is represented by the intersection of the savings curve and the new $I + F$ curve. ΔI represents the $40 billion increase in investment.

A More Complex Multiplier

Since it is possible that more investment and foreign purchasing will occur in an economy at higher levels of income, an initial change in the size of one of an economy's purchasing components could cause the economy's total purchasing or income to increase by an amount larger than the original increase plus subsequent increases in the level of consumption purchasing. For instance, if the amount of autonomous foreign purchasing (or any other type of purchasing not related to the level of income) should increase, the initial increase in total purchasing could cause the following changes: more consumption purchasing as the recipients of the additional purchasing react to their higher levels of income; additional investment purchasing to replace capital consumed as a result of increased production; and more foreign purchasing as the higher levels of income lead to more funds being sent abroad where foreigners can obtain them. This additional purchasing then will induce even more consumption, investment, and foreign purchasing. Total purchasing will continue to rise in the economy until an income level is reached which generates enough total savings to offset the nonconsumption purchasing (I_a, I_r, F_a, F_i) occurring at that level of income.

The Multiplier Formula with Income-Related Nonconsumption Purchasing

When there is replacement investment and induced foreign purchasing in an economy, the size of the multiplier effect on the economy's equilibrium level of income accompanying an initial change in the size of one of the purchasing components can be computed with the following formula:

$$\text{Mult. (k)} = \frac{1}{1 - \text{MPC} - \text{MPI} - \text{MPX}}$$

Or the same formula with the notation representing the MPC, MPI, and MPX percentages:

$$\text{Mult. (k)} = \frac{1}{1 - b - v - x}$$

Thus, for the example economy in which the MPC is 60 percent, the MPI is 10 percent, and the MPX is 5 percent:

$$k = \frac{1}{1 - .60 - .10 - .05} = 4$$

This multiplier tells us that an initial change in the size of one purchasing component will change the equilibrium level of income in the economy by an amount four times greater. Thus an initial increase of $10 billion in the autonomous portion of the economy's foreign, investment or even consumption purchasing will raise its total purchasing by $40 billion; an increase of $20 billion will raise its total purchasing by $80 billion; and a decrease of $15 billion will reduce the economy's purchasing by $60 billion.

This purchasing multiplier formula is derived from the basic equilibrium income-estimating formula in the following way:

1. $Y = a + bY + I_a + vY + F_a + xY$.

2. Or, $Y - bY - vY - xY = a + I_a + F_a$.

3. Or, $Y(1 - b - v - x) = a + I_a + F_a$.

4. Or, $Y = \dfrac{1}{1 - b - v - x} (a + I_a + F_a)$.

Since total purchasing will change by some amount (ΔY) if the amount of a component such as autonomous foreign purchasing (ΔF_a) changes,

5. $Y + \Delta Y = \dfrac{1}{1 - b - v - x} (a + I_a + F_a + \Delta F_a)$.

Then, removing the original level of Y from both sides of the equation,

6. $$\Delta Y = \frac{1}{1 - b - v - x} (\Delta F_a)$$

| Total pur- chasing will change by | this multiple | of an initial change in foreign (or any other type) purchasing |

Thus, $\dfrac{1}{1 - b - v - x}$ is the value of an economy's multiplier when there is replacement investment and induced foreign purchasing in the economy.

The Multiplier Time Period

The multiplier formula indicates the degree to which an economy's equilibrium level of income will change when there is a permanent change in the size of one of the economy's purchasing components. But the formula does not indicate what length of time will elapse between the initial change and the attainment of the new equilibrium level of income. Instead, the formula assumes an instantaneous adjustment in the level of income in response to an initial purchasing change. Examination of the past responses of various economies to initial purchasing changes, however, suggests that weeks and months and even years may pass before an income adjustment is completed. The length of time depends upon the speed with which an economy's purchasing units react to the income changes they experience and forecast.

Consider an increase of $100 billion of investment purchasing in an economy that has an initial $500 billion level of income and a 60 percent marginal propensity to consume with no other purchasing components affected by changes in the level of income. The multiplier formula indicates that the new equilibrium level of income in the economy will be $750 billion. In the first time period purchasing rises to $600 billion with the addition of the $100 billion of additional investment purchasing. Then, in the next time period (2nd), the consumers react to the higher earnings caused by the $100 billion increase in investment by increasing their consumption purchasing by $60 billion so that the level of total purchasing rises to $660 billion. In the next time period (3rd), consumers react to the even higher levels of income caused by the addition of $60 billion of consumption and increase their consumption purchasing by another $36 billion to bring the total to $696 billion. The expansion continues until enough time periods have passed to get the economy's purchasing up to $750 billion.

The total elapsed time in the example economy depends upon the number and length of each of the time periods as the economy moves from $500 to $750 billion. The length of each period, in turn, depends upon the speed of the reaction of the economy's consumers to the observed increases in the economy's level of income. But changes in consumption, however fast they occur, may not just occur in response to *ex post* changes in the level of income. Instead, consumers may forecast their incomes to the $750 billion level when they observe the initial change and immediately adjust their consumption purchasing to that level. Obviously, the better the forecasts and the more willing consumers are to adjust to what they expect as opposed to what they experience, the faster the multiplier effect will be completed and the faster the economy will attain the new equilibrium level of income.

Permanent and One-Time Changes

The full multiplier effect of an initial change in purchasing only occurs when the change is permanent. Thus, in the previous example, an additional

$100 billion of investment purchasing had to occur in each subsequent time period in order to raise the equilibrium level of income to $750 billion. If the $100 billion of additional investment had not occurred in each period, the level of income in the economy would have initially increased to $600 billion but would have subsequently declined back to $500 billion as investment purchasing and its subsequent consumption purchasing declined in the time periods following the initial increase.

Figures 6-4 and 6-5 depict the time period by time period reaction of consumers to the level of income that occurred in the previous time period. Figure 6-4 depicts the effect of continuously adding the $100 billion of investment purchasing while Figure 6-5 depicts the effect of a one-time increase of the same magnitude.

COMMODITY MARKET EQUILIBRIUM CURVES

The equilibrium level of income in an economy is determined by types of purchasing whose sizes may be affected, in part, by the level of interest rates.

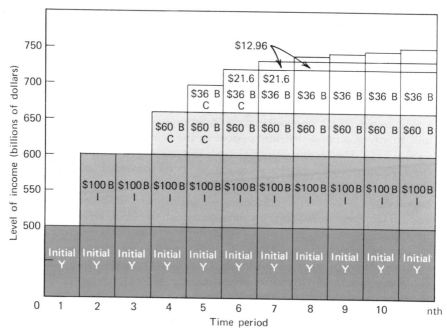

FIGURE 6-4

A permanent increase in investment purchasing.

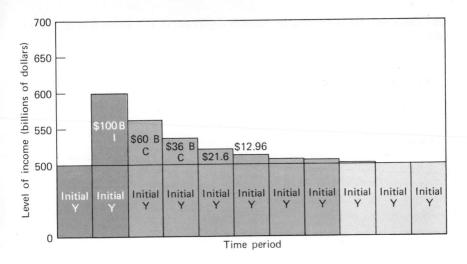

FIGURE 6-5
A one-time increase in investment purchasing.

Thus a different equilibrium level of income may exist in an economy for each level of interest rates.

The various combinations of interest rate levels and equilibrium incomes that can occur in an economy can be depicted graphically by a curve. Such a curve often is identified with the abbreviation IS because it depicts each combination of income and interest rates that fulfills the income equilibrium condition of the amount of investment (I) and other nonconsumption purchasing equaling the total amount of savings (S). Alternatively, the curve may be referred to as the "commodity market equilibrium curve" because it depicts the various equilibrium levels of commodity purchasing which are possible in the economy at various levels of interest rates. Whatever its name or designation, the curve is important because it represents the level of commodity purchasing which an economy can attain with each level of interest rates.

The shape and position of an economy's IS curve can be constructed in several ways. One approach uses the equilibrium income-determining formula $Y = a + bY + I + F$. Each level of income estimated with this formula and the level of interest rates associated with it provide one point on an IS curve. For example, when the various levels of interest rates and resulting equilibrium levels of income in an economy are those depicted in the Table 6-1 IS schedule, the economy's IS curve will be as it is in Figure 6-6.

TABLE 6-1
A Hypothetical IS Schedule

INTEREST RATE (PERCENT)	LEVEL OF INCOME (BILLIONS OF DOLLARS)
20	100.0
15	112.5
10	125.0
5	137.5

The second approach derives IS curves with the aid of three other curves representing conditions in an economy. Together these curves represent the commodity market portion of the graphical model being developed. They include MEI curves, which show how much investment purchasing will occur at each level of interest rates; injection curves, which aggregate the various types of purchasing that must be offset by savings before an equilibrium

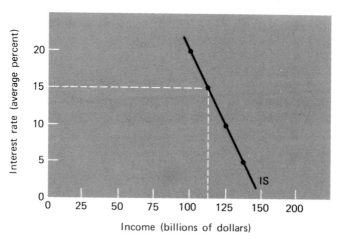

FIGURE 6-6
An example IS curve.

level of income can be reached; and savings functions, which, as they indicate the level of savings that will occur at each level of income, provide the basis for identifying the level of income at which each level of nonconsumption purchasing will be offset by an equal amount of savings.

All the diagrams of the commodity market have been discussed previously except injection curves. An example of these curves is presented in Figure 6-7. Notice that the level of all nonconsumption purchasing is measured on the vertical axis, whereas only investment purchasing is measured on the horizontal axis. The injection curve itself is a 45-degree line from that point on the vertical axis representing the sum of all of the nonconsumption purchasing components except investment. The 45-degree line ensures that the level of investment spending can be added to the sum of the other nonconsumption purchasing components on the vertical axis by drawing a straight line from the level of investment on the horizontal axis, up to the injection curve, and then horizontally to the vertical axis. For example, if the economy's interest rate level is such that $30 billion of investment purchasing will occur in addition to $10 billion of foreign purchasing, the injection curve will indicate a total of $40 billion of nonconsumption purchasing. Thus, the equilibrium level of income at the particular level of interest rates considered is that which will generate $40 billion of savings.

Other levels of income can be generated similarly for other levels of interest

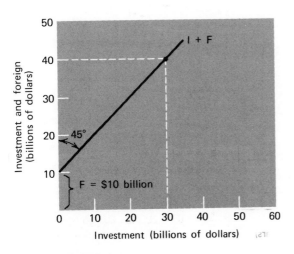

FIGURE 6-7
An injection curve.

rates by the same process. The result is an IS curve for the economy whose commodity market conditions are depicted in Figure 6-8.

The Effect of Replacement Investment Purchasing

Replacement investment purchasing means there will be a different MEI curve for each level of income and thus that different levels of investment purchasing can occur at each level of interest rates. Despite such differences, it is still possible to construct an IS curve showing the equilibrium level of

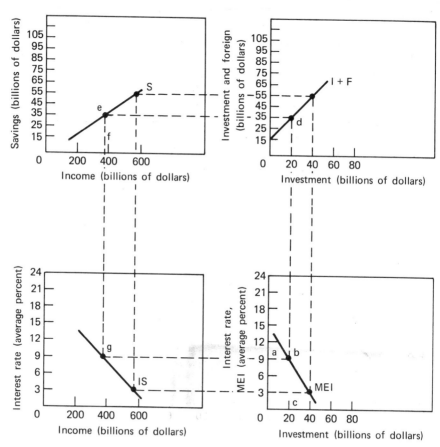

FIGURE 6-8
The commodity market.

income that will occur in an economy at each level of interest rates. Figure 6-9 presents such a curve. It is constructed in the following manner from the relationships depicted in the figure. First, the economy's savings function is used to determine the level of savings that will occur in the economy at a particular level of income such as $400 billion. The economy's level of savings has to be exactly offset by nonconsumption purchasing $(I + F)$ if the level of income is to be an equilibrium one. Thus, the injection curve is examined to see how much investment purchasing is needed to make the sum of the economy's investment and foreign purchasing equal to the level of savings. Then the MEI curve for this level of income is used to determine

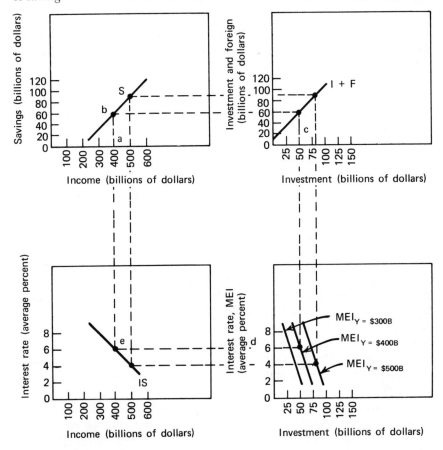

FIGURE 6-9
The commodity market when there is replacement investment purchasing.

the level of interest rates that will result in the level of investment purchasing required for that level of income. The combination of the original level of income and the required level of interest rates are represented by one point on the economy's IS curve. Points representing other combinations are derived by repeating the process for other levels of income.

The Effect of Induced Foreign Purchasing

Induced foreign purchasing means that different amounts of foreign purchasing will tend to occur at each level of income and thus a different injection curve will exist for every level of income. Despite such differences, it is possible to construct an IS curve graphically. For example, consider the economy depicted by Figure 6-10. An IS curve for this economy can be constructed in the following manner. First, arbitrarily select a level of income. Then move up to the savings function to determine the level of savings that will occur at that level of income. Third, move to the injection curve for that level of income to determine how much investment purchasing is needed to provide an amount of nonconsumption purchasing just equal to the amount of savings that will occur at that level of income. Fourth, use the MEI curve for that level of income to determine the level of interest rates that will yield the desired level of investment purchasing. This interest rate level and the initial level of income constitute one point on the IS curve. Other points can be derived by repeating the process for other levels of income.

Interest Rate Considerations

The IS curve analysis has proceeded as if only investment purchasing is affected by the rates of interest. But it is also possible that an economy's interest rates will affect the economy's propensities to consume and save. If they do, there may be a different savings function for every level of interest rates. Furthermore, the amount of foreign purchasing that will occur at each level of income also may be affected by interest rates in the economy selling the commodities. Should this be the case, foreign purchasing will have to be represented by a different injection curve for each level of income and level of interest rates.

The graphic representations of the commodity market still can be used to derive IS curves even though different savings and injection curves exist for each level of interest rates. Basically, the procedure involves arbitrarily selecting a level of income and then examining the curves that exist for a specific level of interest rates to see if the amount of savings will be equal to

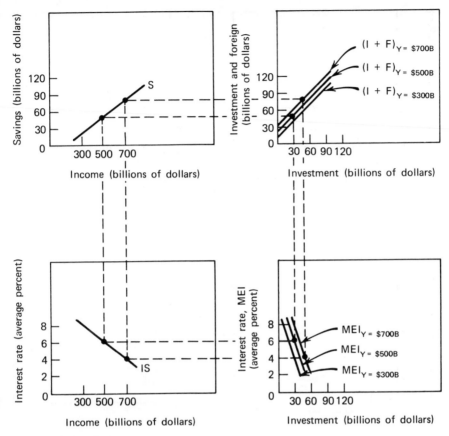

FIGURE 6-10
The commodity market when there is replacement investment purchasing and induced foreign purchasing.

the amount of nonconsumption purchasing. If they are equal, that combination of income and interest represents one point on the IS curve; if not equal, the procedure has to be repeated for another level of interest rates until the equilibrium level of interest rates for this level of income is found. Other points on the IS curve then can be determined by repeating the procedure for other levels of income.

Figure 6-11 presents an example of how such effects of different interest rates can be taken into consideration in an economy's IS curve. It depicts the conditions in which different savings functions exist for each level of

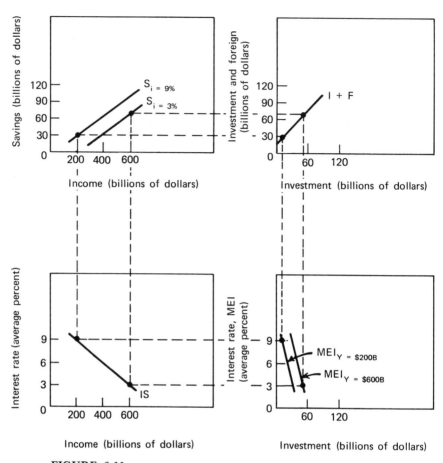

FIGURE 6-11
The commodity market when there is replacement investment and when the level of interest rates affects savings.

interest rates. For the sake of exposition, only savings and investment purchasing are depicted as being affected by the level of interest rates and the level of income.

Shifts in the IS Curve

An IS curve shows the equilibrium levels of income that will occur in an economy at different levels of interest rates. Thus the effects of the different levels of investment or foreign or consumption purchasing which might be caused by different rates of interest or levels of income are already depicted on the curve. On the other hand, changes in other factors that might influence the equilibrium level of income in an economy are not depicted on the economy's IS curve. For instance, the amount of foreign purchasing may change for reasons unrelated to the level of income or the rates of interest (the injection curves shift), or greater or lesser portions of income may be saved at each level of interest rates (the savings functions shift), or more or less investment purchasing may occur for each level of income at every level of interest rates (the MEI curves shift).

Consider the effect of an increase in foreign purchasing. Such a change will tend to cause a multiple increase in the equilibrium level of income for every level of interest rates. The initial change in foreign purchasing and the multiple increase in the equilibrium level of income for each interest rate level are depicted in Figure 6-12 for an economy in which there is neither an interest rate effect nor induced foreign or replacement investment purchasing. The injection curve has shifted up by the amount of the increase in foreign purchasing, ΔF, and the new IS curve lies to the right of the old since there will be a higher equilibrium level of income at every level of interest rates. Similar results will occur with any other change that tends to increase the level of purchasing at each interest rate level. Exactly opposite effects occur when something tends to drive the level of purchasing lower.

Long-Run and Short-Run Curves

The analysis up to this point has proceeded as if an economy only has one set of interest and income combinations to depict with an IS curve. But long-run and short-run relationships have been identified for both consumption and investment. Figure 6-13 depicts the short-run and long-run savings functions, MEI curves, and IS curves for an economy that is initially in long-run equilibrium at an interest rate of 9 percent and an equilibrium level of income of $400 billion. Notice that the tendency for larger short-run levels of investment purchasing at interest rates below 9 percent is partially offset by the short-run delays of consumers in adjusting to the higher levels of income. The existence of such an offset reduces the need in the short run to use different IS curves to identify an economy's possible equilibrium combinations of interest rate levels and levels of income. Notice also that the economy's short-run IS curve indicates that a level of income higher than the long-run level would exist in the short run for interest rates below

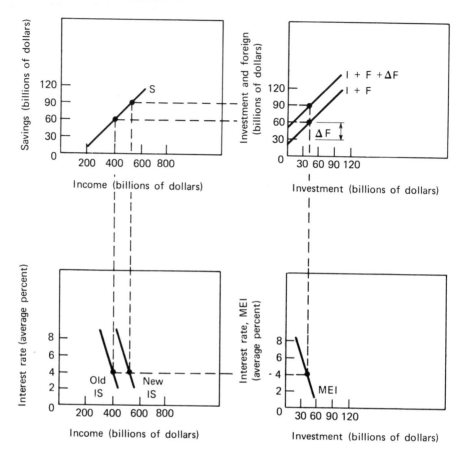

FIGURE 6-12
Shifts in the IS curve.

9 percent. If interest rates decline to 3 percent, for example, the long-run equilibrium level of income would be $600 billion and the short-run level $800 billion. But as time passes and the economy moves through the multiplier time periods toward higher levels of income, the economy's consumers and investors will get closer to their long-run patterns of behavior, and the short-run IS curve will rotate back into the long-run curve as its components take on more and more of the long-run characteristics. Thus, even though the economy's interest rate declines to 3 percent, the level of income in the economy may never exceed $600 billion.

It should be noted that the factors that influence purchasing in an economy are continually changing: they are dynamic rather than unchanging or static. For instance, new markets and products are located, new processes are developed, and capital is consumed through use or accident. These circumstances make it difficult to believe that all purchasing will remain constant long enough for a specific equilibrium level of income to be actually attained. They also make it difficult to believe that the level of income observed at any one point in time is actually an equilibrium level. Instead, the most we can expect in a dynamic situation is that the level of income in an economy is always moving toward an equilibrium level. Studies of the

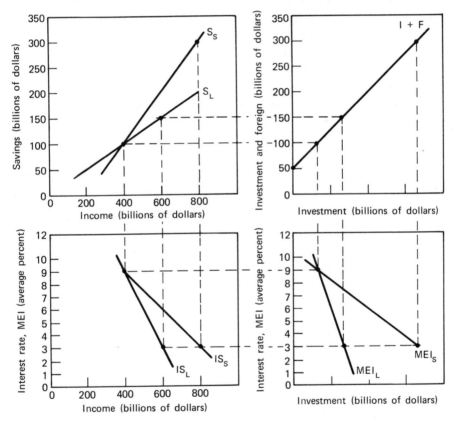

FIGURE 6-13
Long-run and short-run IS curves.

level of purchasing and attempts to understand the equilibrium level of income and what influences it are important, however, even though no exact final estimates can be stated; they provide a general idea of the state of the economy, its direction, and how much farther a particular change will tend to carry it than it otherwise would go.

● REFERENCES

Ackley, G., "The Multiplier Time Period: Money, Inventories, and Flexibility," *American Economic Review*, **XLI,** pp. 350–368 (1951).

Goodwin, R., "The Multiplier," in *The New Economics*, ed. by S. Harris (Knopf, 1947), pp. 482–499.

Hansen, A., *A Guide to Keynes* (McGraw-Hill, 1953), pp. 108–114.

Keynes, J., *The General Theory of Employment, Interest and Money* (Harcourt, Brace, 1936), Chapter 10.

Kurihara, K., *Introduction to Keynesian Dynamics* (Allen and Unwin, 1956), Chapters 5, 6, and 9.

Samuelson, P., "The Simple Mathematics of Income Determination," in *Income, Employment and Public Policy* (Norton, 1948), pp. 133–155.

Fiscal Activities

7

Among the largest contributors to total purchasing in most economies are the governments. At every political level they spend vast sums of money on new goods and services such as missiles and transportation and roads and schools. Governments also disburse money for purposes other than the purchase of commodities—for example, to provide charity (transfers) for the needy. In addition to their purchases of new goods and their provision of transfers, governments collect taxes and borrow money to finance their affairs. All four of these major types of fiscal activities affect the level of total purchasing. In this chapter these activities are considered in terms of why they occur and their impact on the equilibrium level of income.

GOVERNMENT PURCHASING

It is a characteristic of certain types of commodities such as streets and highways, sewer lines, and police protection that their benefits can be received by more than one individual. There is thus no necessity for each individual to act alone in purchasing these commodities. Instead, the potential beneficiaries of these goods and services have a vested interest in banding together (forming a government) to purchase these items since each individual will receive benefits from them but will have to bear only a portion of their purchase price.

Commodities whose benefits can be shared are referred to as "collective" or "public" commodities as distinguished from "private" commodities such as soft drinks, shirts, and shoe shines whose benefits accrue only to one user so that there is no incentive for joint purchasing action. Public commodities generally are held to be one of the major reasons why government purchasing occurs, but there are additional reasons such as the need to have fiscal activities other than purchasing; to have antitrust activities to promote competition between producers where competition is possible but otherwise would not occur; to regulate business practices to promote competitive-like behavior by producers where competition is impossible; and to influence and participate in otherwise private transactions that involve social costs and social benefits. Even though these types of activities may not directly involve purchasing, they require that the governments of an economy buy certain commodities such as offices, supplies, and the services of administrative staffs.

The appropriate amount of government purchasing (and transfers) is obviously neither more nor less than whatever will acquire the commodities which individuals in the economy, acting together as governments, choose to have devoted to those uses. Needless to say, the willingness of individuals to authorize governmental expenditures may change as the circumstances confronting them change. For example, in the United States the amount of commodities being purchased by the various governments has grown over the years, both absolutely and as a proportion of total commodity purchasing. A few observers have mystically decried this as an indication of "national weakness," and even as "creeping socialism" despite the fact that the commodities purchased have not been produced by government-operated facilities in accordance with a government plan.[1]

Fortunately, there are more lucid explanations of the growth in government outlays. Basically, various occurrences have caused individuals in the

[1] The very essence of socialism is production in government-operated facilities in response to a government plan rather than in response to purchasers who are buying whatever they prefer. In the United States, the economy remains fundamentally free enterprise in nature. The government-purchased commodities are supplied primarily by private producers responding to the existence of purchasers rather than to governmental directions or plans.

economy to want their governments to purchase more public goods and provide more transfers. But what are these occurrences? One has been the threat of war: national defense spending now constitutes a substantial portion of all government spending; it did not prior to the Second World War. Also, the nation has accepted the responsibility of assisting injured servicemen and individuals who suddenly find themselves unemployed or disabled. Furthermore, various inventions have contributed to the need for government activity: the advent of the automobile created a need for more streets and highways; and the advent of planes, radio, and television introduced the need for government regulations to ensure that planes do not fly toward the same place at the same altitude or that radio and television stations do not broadcast on the same channel. In addition, rising aspirations for health and education have led individuals to act together through their governments to obtain more schools and hospitals. Finally, growing urbanization has caused a need for large-scale sewage and water systems and modern police and fire facilities.

It is interesting to note, however, that despite the observed growth in the absolute size of government purchasing in the United States and the tendency to blame the federal government for increases in government spending, the proportion of total production purchased by governments during the last 10 or 15 years has remained surprisingly constant in the United States. Furthermore, the share of total production taken by the federal government has tended to decline. It is the rapidly growing purchasing activities of state and local governments that have kept the government proportion constant.

It may be that the desires for government-purchased commodities such as education and highways are income elastic in the sense that the desire for them rises faster than the rate at which an economy's income grows. If the desires are income elastic but government remains proportional, it means that as an economy's income grows the economy will tend to build up an ever-increasing backlog of unattained public goods relative to private goods. Such a "social imbalance" of production would exist due to noneconomic constraints that restrict government purchasing relative to nongovernment purchasing. One such constraint could be public fears of losing individual liberty and freedom to big government. The economy's individual participants, in other words, may be motivated by noneconomic commodities such as freedom to prevent the power of governmental administrative bodies from growing in importance relative to individuals. And this may occur even though the individuals desire additional government goods more than they desire additional private goods.

The Effect of Government Purchasing

Government purchasing of commodities has the same multiplier effect on the level of total purchasing as any other type of purchasing; it increases the total directly by the amount of the government purchasing and indirectly as consumers and investors are induced to make additional purchases with the incomes they earn producing the goods and services purchased by the government. For example, consider the economy without fiscal activities where I is fixed at $80 billion, F = $10 billion, a = $10 billion, there is no business savings so that all purchasing is received as disposable income, and the marginal propensity to save is 40 percent. We have seen previously that the equilibrium level of income will be $250 billion under these conditions. Then, if government purchasing (G) of $20 billion is added to the economy, the resulting equilibrium level of income will become $300 billion:

1. $Y = a + bY + I + G + F$.
2. $Y = \$10 + .60Y + \$80 + \$20 + \$10$.
3. $Y = .60Y + \$120$.
4. $.40Y = \$120$.
5. $Y = \$300$.

The same effect of government purchasing can be shown graphically. Figure 7-1 presents an economy's commodity market before and after government purchasing. Notice that the addition of government purchasing is represented by a new injection curve and causes the economy's IS curve to shift to the right; the new IS curve represents the higher equilibrium levels of income that will exist at each level of interest rates when the government purchasing is added to the investment and other purchasing that will occur at these interest rates.

GOVERNMENT TRANSFERS

"Transfers" are unearned receipts such as charity and gifts which individuals may receive in addition to any income earned by their factors of production. For example, students receive transfers when they get money from home or scholarships from a school or government. The fundamental basis for transfers is the inability of some individuals to obtain "enough" commodities because of a lack of assets or earnings due to circumstances related to age, sickness, occupation, or location. Of course, transfers also are given for less humanitarian reasons such as improving the lot of certain types of voters or rewarding financial institutions and other lenders for loaning money to governments.

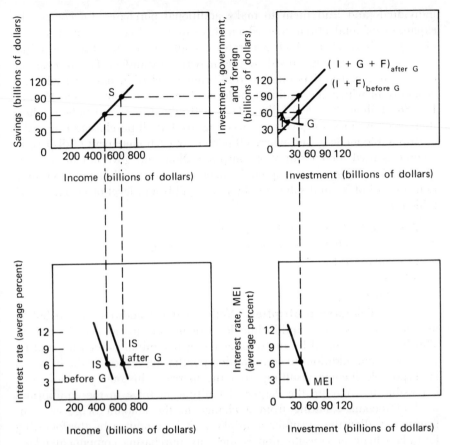

FIGURE 7-1
Government and the commodity market.

The Effect of Government Transfers

Government (and business and foreign) transfers tend to increase consumption purchasing in an economy because they increase the total amount of the disposable income (Y_d) available for consumption purchasing.[1] Furthermore, any initial increase in purchasing which the additional disposable income causes will tend to raise the disposable incomes of other

---

[1] Transfers also can be made by individuals in an economy. Such "personal transfers," however, leave the total amount of disposable income in the economy unchanged even though they do change its distribution and thus may affect the propensity to consume of the economy's consumers as a group.

individuals and lead them to make additional purchases. Of course, the expansion of total purchasing which this causes will continue until a level of income is reached which generates enough savings to offset the initial increase in purchasing caused by the increase in transfers. For an example of the effect of transfers on the equilibrium level of income, consider the economy in which the equilibrium level of income is $300 billion because $I = \$80$ billion, $F = \$10$ billion, $G = \$20$ billion, $a = \$10$ billion, where there is no business or government savings so that all purchasing is received as disposable income, and where 60 percent of each increment of disposable income is used for consumption purposes. Now add government transfers (Tr) of $50 billion to the disposable income already available for consumption use (all of Y) and solve for the new equilibrium level of income ($375 billion):

1. $Y = a + b(Y + Tr) + I + G + F.$
2. $Y = \$10 + .60(Y + \$50) + \$80 + \$20 + \$10.$
3. $Y = .60Y + \$150.$
4. $.40Y = \$150.$
5. $Y = \$375.$

Transfer multiplier. Notice that the addition of $50 billion in transfers causes the equilibrium level of income to rise by $75 billion. This increase is caused by the transfer recipients' initial purchasing and by the subsequent additions to consumption purchasing caused by the increases in disposable income resulting from the increases in total purchasing. It is possible to compute the degree of multiple increase in the equilibrium level of income resulting from a change in the amount of government transfers. Called the "transfer multiplier," it is computed by the following formula whenever consumption is the only purchasing component whose size increases with level of income:

$$\text{Transfer multiplier} = \frac{\text{MPC}}{1 - \text{MPC}} = \frac{b}{1 - b}$$

Thus, where the MPC is 60 percent,

$$\text{Transfer multiplier} = \frac{.60}{1 - .60} = 1\tfrac{1}{2}$$

This multiplier indicates that a change in the amount of government transfers will change the size of the equilibrium level of income in the example economy by $1\tfrac{1}{2}$ times the initial change. Thus an increase in transfers of $10 billion will raise total purchasing by $15 billion; an increase of $40 billion will raise it by $60 billion; and a decrease of $20 billion will cut it by $30 billion. Thus $b/1 - b$ is the value of the transfer multiplier.

Relation to other multipliers. Notice that the value of the transfer multiplier ($1\frac{1}{2}$) derived when the MPC is .60 is exactly one less than the purchasing multiplier ($2\frac{1}{2}$) that would exist under the same economic circumstances. This difference occurs because a change in the size of government or some other type of purchasing would directly change the level of total purchasing by the full amount of the initial change. A change in the size of transfers, on the other hand, has no such initial effect on the level of purchasing. There are no other differences between the effects of transfers and purchasing since once they occur, both transfers and government purchasing will have the same effect on the level of disposable income and thus on the subsequent changes in consumption and other forms of purchasing. On the other hand, an economy's transfer multiplier will not be exactly one less than its purchasing multiplier if comparable changes in transfers and purchasing do not have the same subsequent effect on the level of the economy's disposable income. Such would be the case in an economy in which there is net business savings. Then the economy's disposable income would initially change by the full amount of any change in transfers, but it would not change by the full amount of any initial change in the level of government purchasing.

More complex considerations. The foregoing discussion of transfers and the transfer multiplier typically is presented in intermediate level approaches to macroeconomic theory. Misleading oversimplification, however, may be inherent in the use of such an approach. After all, transfers often are based on the existence of need, and thus it is reasonable to expect that they tend to be placed in the hands of recipients who, on comparison with the individuals who earn their disposable incomes in the productive process, will use relatively large proportions of them for consumption purposes. If transfer recipients have higher or lower marginal propensities to consume in comparison to other recipients of disposable income, it is inappropriate to lump the earned and transfer components of disposable income together and assume that the same proportion of each is used for consumption purposes. Instead, they should be separated so that a different value of b can be assigned to each.

Thus, using a conventional form of the consumption function, the amount of consumption purchasing in an economy would be depicted as $C = a + bY + bTr$ instead of $C = a + b(Y + Tr)$. The advantage of this approach is that it is conceptually possible for a different value of b to be assigned to each portion of the economy's disposable income. (Since the values of b may differ, the MPC of disposable income received from transfers shall be identified hereinafter as b'. Thus, $C = a + bY + b'Tr$.) For an example of how the more appropriate separation of Y and Tr can be handled in order to allow for transfer recipients' higher propensities to consume, consider the economy with conditions that resulted in an equilibrium income of $300 billion when there were no transfers. Now add $50 billion of transfers and also include the condition that 80 percent of the disposable income provided by transfers will be used for consumption purposes while only 60 percent of the balance of the economy's disposable income is used for consumption purposes. The resulting equilibrium level of income becomes $400 billion:

1. $Y = a + bY + b'Tr + I + G + F$.
2. $Y = \$10 + .60Y + .80(\$50) + \$80 + \$20 + \$10$.
3. $Y = .60Y + \$160$.
4. $.40Y = \$160$.
5. $Y = \$400$.

The new equilibrium level of income is $100 billion more than the pre-transfer level. Thus the increase of $50 billion in transfers increases the level of income by a multiple of 2 instead of the original $1\frac{1}{2}$. The same basic transfer multiplier formula can be used to suggest these results when the transfer recipients' MPC is used in the numerator. For example,

$$\frac{b'}{1 - b} = \frac{.80}{1 - .60} = 2$$

Graphical effect of transfers. Transfers have the same basic effect as government, foreign, or investment purchasing; at some point they all cause increases in an economy's level of purchasing, and these are followed by further increases in purchasing brought about by the initial increase in level of income. Since the initial increase in an economy's purchasing caused by transfers is only that portion of the transfers initially spent, their effect on the level of purchasing in an economy can be presented graphically by adding the initial increase in consumption purchasing which they cause to the amounts of the other types of purchasing. (Remember that the recipients of transfers may not use the entire amount of the transfers for purchasing; all that should be added, therefore, is the portion that is used, b'Tr.) Figure 7-2 presents such a situation. It depicts the economy just described before and after the $50 billion of transfers. Basically, the figure shows that a higher equilibrium level of income, $400 billion instead of

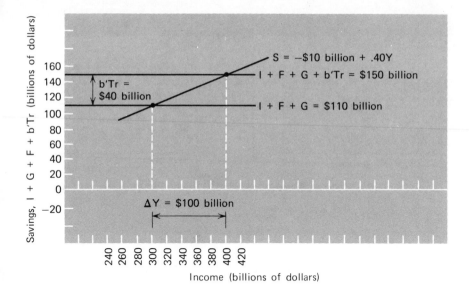

FIGURE 7-2
Transfers and the equilibrium level of income.

$300 billion is required to generate the savings needed to offset the additional injection of purchasing so that equilibrium can be reached.

Transfers and the commodity market. Transfers tend to increase the equilibrium level of income occurring at each level of interest rates. Their effect on the conditions existing in an economy's commodity market is depicted in Figure 7-3. Notice that the IS curve shifts to the right as a result of adding the purchasing of the economy's transfer recipients (b'Tr) to the I, G, and F purchasing that is already occurring at each level of interest rates and income.

TAXES

In order to make their purchases and transfers, governments need funds. They usually obtain a major portion of these from "taxes": the various required payments that governments levy on the economy's private sector. Taxes have additional uses besides financing government purchases and transfers, however. A government may, for example, impose such high tax rates on certain types of imports that no commodities are purchased abroad.

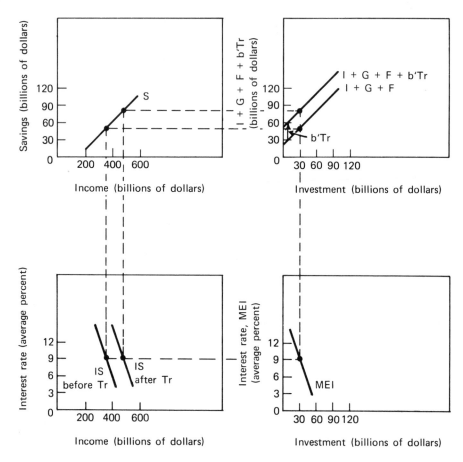

FIGURE 7-3
Transfers and the commodity market.

Since no imports occur, no taxes are collected; instead, the effect is purely regulatory in that it cuts off importation of commodities. Similar tax regulation may occur to discourage the consumption of domestically produced commodities that are deemed "undesirable" for some reason or another. (Is it not possible that for this reason the United States taxes alcohol and tobacco products at rates generally higher than those levied on other commodities?)

Taxes and the Level of Purchasing

One way by which the various types of taxes may affect the level of purchasing in an economy is by reducing the disposable income that individuals have available for consumption uses.[1] How taxes reduce disposable income was shown in Chapter 2 where disposable income was related to gross national product, national income, and personal income. However, let us review: first, all expenditures to purchase commodities that are part of gross national product may not be received as part of national income because of such indirect business taxes as sales and excise taxes. For example, a $10 excise tax on a commodity whose purchase price is $30 leaves only $20 to be earned by the producer as part of national income. Furthermore, not all of this $20 may become personal income because of such business taxes as corporate income taxes and inventory taxes. If business taxes are $5, for instance, there will be only $15 available for distribution to individuals as part of personal income. Finally, not all of the $15 may become disposable income because of the imposition on individuals of personal taxes such as personal income taxes and personal property taxes. Thus, if the governments' taxes take $5 of the $15 in personal income, only $10 of disposable income will be available for consumption or personal savings uses.

Taxes and the equilibrium level of income. Taxes tend to cause a decline in an economy's total purchasing when they reduce disposable income. How much of a decrease in total purchasing results from the imposition of a tax depends on the size of the tax, the degree to which it reduces the level of disposable income, and the marginal propensity to consume of the individuals whose disposable incomes are cut by the tax. It is possible, of course, that an increase in taxes would have no effect because it would be completely paid out of that portion of an economy's

[1] Of course, taxes also can influence an economy's equilibrium level of income in other ways. Consider three such possibilities. First, taxes may cause a decline in investment purchasing if they cut the flow of revenue which the potential new assets are expected to yield. Second, taxes on exports may discourage foreign purchasers because they have to pay both the tax and the price of the producer. Third, taxes on imports may discourage domestic purchase of the foreign-produced commodities and cause an increase in the purchase of similar commodities produced in the domestic economy because these are not affected by the higher import taxes. Additionally, taxes may directly affect an economy's ability to produce. Since taxation absorbs a proportion of disposable income, it tends to reduce the ability of each taxpayer to meet his needs and, therefore, may lessen incentives and the desire to produce. Thus the long-run effect of taxes could be to cause a gap between an economy's potential and actual productive capacity.

income that would otherwise be devoted to some other form of savings. In any event, the initial decrease in purchasing caused by a tax will be equal to the amount that otherwise would have been used for purchasing consumption commodities. For example, consider the economic conditions that initially resulted in an equilibrium level of income of $400 billion: I = $80 billion, F = $10 billion, G = $20 billion, a = $10 billion, b = .60, BS = $0, Tr = $50 billion, and b′ = .80. Since the addition of taxes (Tx) means that disposable income will decline by the amount of the taxes, the level of disposable income available for consumption will be reduced from Y to Y − Tx. If taxes of $50 billion are levied in the economy just described, the resulting equilibrium level of income will be $325 billion:

1. $Y = a + b(Y - Tx) + b'Tr + I + G + F.$
2. $Y = \$10 + .60(Y - \$50) + .80(\$50) + \$80 + \$20 + \$10.$
3. $Y = .60Y + \$130.$
4. $.40Y = \$130.$
5. $Y = \$325.$

Tax multiplier. The addition of $50 billion in taxes causes this example economy's equilibrium level of income to fall by $75 billion. This decrease has two sources. First is the initial decline in consumption purchasing that results from the economy's disposable income being initially lower by the amount of the taxes. Second is the subsequent additional decline in consumption purchasing caused by the even lower disposable incomes resulting from the initial and subsequent declines in the level of consumption purchasing. The degree of change in an economy's equilibrium level of income which a given amount of taxes will cause is called the "tax multiplier." It is computed by the following formula whenever consumption is the only purchasing component whose size increases as the level of income increases:

$$\text{Tax multiplier} = \frac{-\text{MPC}}{1 - \text{MPC}} = \frac{-b}{1 - b}$$

Thus, where the MPC is 60 percent,

$$\text{Tax multiplier} = \frac{-.60}{1 - .60} = -1\tfrac{1}{2}$$

This multiplier tells us that the imposition of a tax will decrease the equilibrium level of income in the example economy by $1\tfrac{1}{2}$ times the initial change in taxes. Thus, raising the economy's taxes by $10 billion will cut its level of income by $15 billion; raising them by $40 billion will cut its level of income by $60 billion; cutting its taxes by $20 billion will raise its level of income by $30 billion.

The formula for an economy's tax multiplier can be derived from the basic equilibrium income-estimating equation in the following manner when the economy's disposable income is equal to total purchasing minus government taxes, and the MPC is represented by b:

1. $Y = a + b(Y - Tx) + I + G + F.$
2. $Y - bY = a - bTx + I + G + F.$
3. $Y(1 - b) = a - bTx + I + G + F.$

4. $Y = \dfrac{1}{1 - b} (a - bTx + I + G + F).$

Since total purchasing will change by some amount (ΔY) if more taxes (ΔTx) occur:

5. $Y + \Delta Y = \dfrac{1}{1 - b} (a - bTx + I + G + F - b\Delta Tx).$

Removing the original amount of Y from both sides of the equation (by subtracting Y itself from the left side and the components of Y from the right side) leaves only the change in total purchasing and the way it is caused:

6. $\Delta Y = \dfrac{1}{1 - b} (-b\Delta Tx).$

7. Or $\Delta Y = \dfrac{(-b\Delta Tx)}{1 - b}.$

8. Or $\Delta Y = \dfrac{-b}{1 - b} (\Delta Tx)$

↗	↑	↖
Total pur- chasing will change by	this multiple	of a change in the level of government taxes

Thus $\dfrac{-b}{1 - b}$ is the value of the tax multiplier.

Graphic effect of taxes. The initial effect of taxes is that the amount of income available to be saved by businesses and persons decreases by the amount of the tax. Thus, if taxes are levied in an economy, the same level of business and personal savings would tend to occur only if the economy's equilibrium level of income is higher by the amount of the taxes. Furthermore, taxes themselves are a form of savings, even though involuntary or forced in nature; that portion of each level of income used to pay taxes, like income voluntarily saved by persons and businsses, is not used to purchase newly constructed goods and services. Thus the total of the amount of income saved (that which cannot or will not be used for consumption purchasing) at each level of income can be found by adding the amount of taxes to the after-tax voluntary business and personal savings associated with each level of income.

The two-phase procedure for graphically determining the total amount of savings that will occur in an economy at each level of income is depicted in Figure 7-4. First, the savings function representing the voluntary savings of businesses and persons (Sv) is shifted horizontally to the right by the amount of the taxes; this move occurs because the same amounts of business and personal savings at each pretax level of income will tend to occur only at income levels that are higher by the amount of the taxes (so that an amount equivalent to the original level of income is available to be saved by businesses and persons in the economy). Then the savings function is shifted vertically upward from the new Sv curve by the amount of the taxes in order to add the forced savings to the voluntary business and personal savings and thus get the total amount of savings that will occur in the economy at each level of income. The result is a new savings function S = Sv + Tx.

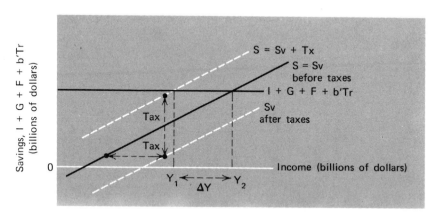

FIGURE 7-4
Taxes and the equilibrium level of income.

Figure 7-4 shows that a tax of the size depicted will drive the example economy's equilibrium level of income from Y_2 down to Y_1. The analysis in this figure is based on the premise that the amount of voluntary savings remains the same at levels of Y that are higher by the amount of the tax. Such an approach is traditional but it may be most unrealistic. After all, business savings may be affected by both the level of Y and the level of taxes. And if the amount of business savings is larger at the higher levels of Y, more savings will tend to occur at each Y than just the sum of the taxes and the pretax level of voluntary savings.

Taxes and the commodity market. Taxes tend to decrease the equilibrium level of income at each level of interest rates because they cut the consumption purchasing that is added to the investment and other purchasing that also occur at each interest rate level. Their effect is depicted in Figure 7-5. Basically, the total amount of savings at each level of income has increased and the economy's IS curve shifts to the left to depict the decline in purchasing caused by the increase in savings.

Net taxes. The taxes and transfers in the foregoing examples had exactly the opposite effects on the equilibrium level of income when the individuals who earn their disposable incomes in the production process and transfer recipients had identical marginal propensities to consume. Since they have counteracting effects, it is possible to simplify the process of graphing their effects by combining the two and graphing only the net difference. Thus, with taxes of $20 billion and transfers of $5 billion, the net effect is a tax of $15 billion. Many analysts combine the two, and usually there is a net tax to add to the other savings since taxes generally are used for much more than just to provide the revenues needed to finance transfer payments.

Nevertheless, despite the common tendency to combine them, taxes and transfers are better analyzed separately with taxes being included with the other forms of savings, and transfers being considered separately as having the same type of expansionary effect on the level of income as investment and foreign purchasing. This is desirable because, as we have seen, the recipients of transfers reasonably may be expected to have higher marginal propensities to consume than the other recipients of disposable income.

GOVERNMENT BORROWING

Governments may either deliberately or accidentally spend more money for purchasing or transfers than they receive in taxes. Such differences

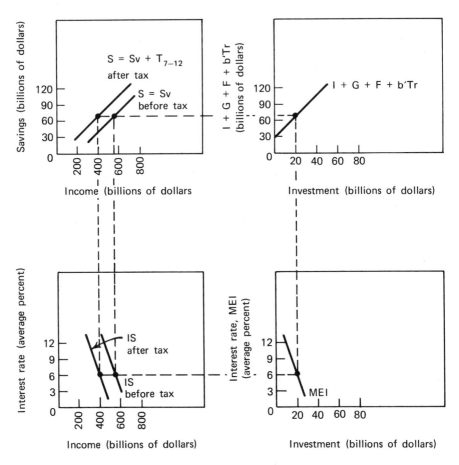

FIGURE 7-5
Taxes and the commodity market.

typically are referred to as "deficits" as opposed to the "surpluses" that exist when governmental tax revenues exceed governmental outlays. Why deficits and surpluses occur will be discussed later, but, whatever the cause, a government facing a deficit must obtain the money to cover it if it is to have the financial ability to make the purchases and transfers that its population desires.

Several sources of funds are potentially available to finance a deficit: the government may have accumulated a surplus during preceding periods of time when its tax revenues exceeded its outlays; it may print or coin the money it needs; it may "borrow" the money by offering repayment plus interest to potential lenders; or it may "borrow" the money from its own central bank which can create it to meet the government's needs.

Two Basic Types of Borrowing

The governments of an economy may engage in two basic types of borrowing. The more easily accomplished and apparently more often used type involves borrowing from certain financial institutions that literally can create new money for a government to borrow. The way such new money is created and certain of the advantages and disadvantages of such activities are the subject of subsequent chapters which deal with money and its influence on the equilibrium level of income. The second type of borrowing is less often used and differs fundamentally from the first in that it tends to reduce an economy's equilibrium level of income; it involves the governments' borrowing from individuals and businesses.

Borrowing from individuals. The possibility of individuals in an economy lending money to governments means that they have another alternative use for their disposable incomes. If the individuals are to make such loans, they will have to either reduce their consumption purchases or devote less of their disposable incomes to other forms of savings. If government borrowing causes people to reduce their consumption purchasing by some amount, the initial decline in total purchasing then will be followed by further declines as the reduced purchasing causes disposable income to fall. Such reductions in the level of total purchasing will continue, of course, until a new and lower equilibrium level of income is reached. Consider a situation in which an economy's level of income initially is $325 billion because a = $10 billion, b = .60, G = $20 billion, BS = $0, Tr = $50 billion, b' = .80, I = $80 billion, F = $10 billion, Tx = $50 billion, and the economy's governments do not finance their $20 billion deficits (they take in $50 billion of taxes and spend $70 billion for purchases and transfers) by borrowing from individuals or business firms. Now assume that the economy's governments change their method of financing deficits so that government bonds become available in the economy and that the desire of some consumers to buy these bonds rather than commodities causes the average and marginal propensities to consume disposable income from sources other than transfers to fall to 58 percent. If this occurs, the economy's equilibrium level of income will decline to $311.9 billion.

1. $Y = a + b(Y - Tx) + b'Tr + I + G + F.$
2. $Y = \$10 + .58(Y - \$50) + .80(\$50) + \$80 + \$20 + \$10.$
3. $Y = .58Y + \$131.$
4. $.42Y = \$131.$
5. $Y = \$311.9.$

Borrowing from business. Governments' borrowing from business also tends to reduce an economy's equilibrium level of income. This occurs if businesses increase their savings in order to buy government IOU's and in so doing reduce the level of disposable income and thus the level of consumption purchasing. Of course, business loans do not necessarily have such an effect. Instead, businesses may lend money to governments without directly affecting the level of disposable income if they simultaneously make offsetting reductions in other types of savings.

How business loans can affect the equilibrium level of income may be seen in the economy whose level of income is $311.9 billion because government bonds are available for its consumers to purchase. Now add the possibility that such bonds are also available for the economy's businesses to buy and as a result net business savings rises from zero to 2 percent of Y. In other words, because they now have another use for their receipts, the businesses in the economy will no longer be passing all of them on to be part of the economy's personal and disposable income. If this occurs, the economy's equilibrium level of income will decline to $303.52 billion:

1. $Y = a + b(Y - BS - Tx) + b'Tr + I + G + F.$
2. $Y = \$10 + .58(Y - .02Y - \$50) + .80(\$50) + \$80 + \$20 + \$10.$
3. $Y = .5684Y + \$131.$
4. $Y = \$303.52$

GOVERNMENT BUDGETS AND THE LEVEL OF INCOME

"Budget" is the term used to describe the combination of fiscal activities in which a government engages during a specific period of time. When a government's outlays are exactly equal to its tax receipts, the government's budget is said to be "balanced"; when the outlays differ so that surpluses or deficits exist, the budget is said to be "unbalanced." Whatever happens, the net effect on the equilibrium level of income of a budget containing specific amounts of each type of fiscal activity can be determined by combining the effects of the individual fiscal components. Various types of budgets and their net effects follow.

Balanced Budgets: Taxes Finance Government Purchasing

An increase in the amount of government purchasing financed by an equal amount of additional taxes (a balanced budget) may cause an increase in an economy's equilibrium level of income. The basis for the expansionary effect of this kind of balanced budget is that a tax merely tends to reduce the level of disposable income. Therefore, when only a portion of an economy's disposable income is used for consumption purposes, the economy's consumption purchasing will not fall by the full amount of the tax. On the other hand, government purchasing increases by the full amount of the tax. Thus government purchasing rises more than consumption purchasing falls and there is a net increase in the level of purchasing in the economy. Once such a net increase occurs, total purchasing expands further as the initial increase in purchasing causes higher levels of disposable income and thus additional consumption purchasing.

How much of an increase in the level of an economy's income will occur when there are equal amounts of government taxes and purchases can be determined by comparing the tax and the purchasing multipliers. For instance, in one of the economies described earlier the purchasing multiplier was $2\frac{1}{2}$ and the tax multiplier $-1\frac{1}{2}$. The difference means that equal amounts of government taxes and government purchases will not exactly offset each other in terms of their effect on total purchasing; instead there will be a net multiplier effect of 1 on the economy's level of income. The existence of such a "balanced budget multiplier" means that an increase in government purchasing financed by an equal increase in taxes will cause the equilibrium level of income in an economy to increase by the amount of its additional government purchasing.

The complete effect of such a balanced budget may be seen in the economy in which the level of income is $250 billion because a = $10 billion, b = 60 percent, I = $80 billion, Tr = $0, and F = $10 billion. If the governments in this economy collect $20 billion of taxes and use the receipts to purchase newly constructed goods and services, the economy's equilibrium level of income will rise (by the balanced budget multiplier of one times the $20 billion change in the level of government activity) to $270 billion:

1. $Y = a + b(Y - Tx) + b'Tr + I + G + F.$
2. $Y = \$10 + .60Y - .60(\$20) + \$0 + \$80 + \$20 + \$10.$
3. $.40Y = \$108.$
4. $Y = \$270.$

Thus *increases in the level of government purchasing tend to expand the equilibrium level of purchasing in an economy even when they are accompanied by an equal increase in the amount of taxes.*

The increase in the equilibrium level of income associated with such a balanced budget also can be depicted graphically by starting with an equilibrium level of income and then introducing a balanced budget involving equal amounts of taxes and purchasing. Example results for one situation are presented in Figure 7-6; they show that the equilibrium level of income increases by the amount of the increase in purchasing and taxes. These results are derived in the following manner. First, the initial equilibrium level of income (Y_1) in an economy without government purchasing or taxes is identified by the intersection of the economy's savings function and the curve representing the amounts of I and F that will occur in the economy at each level of income. Second, the effect on the level of savings of a given amount of taxes is determined; this involves shifting the initial savings function to the right by the amount of the tax in order to reach the higher level of Y needed to yield the same level of disposable income and voluntary savings, and then adding the taxes to the initial savings to get the total amount of savings that will occur at each level of income. Third, an amount of government purchasing equal in size to the amount of taxes is added to the existing investment and foreign purchasing, and a new curve, $I + F + b'Tr + G$ is formed to represent the new total level of investment, foreign, and government purchasing that will occur in the economy at each

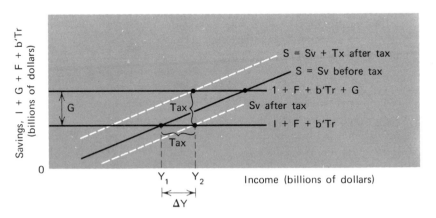

FIGURE 7-6
A balanced budget.

level of income. Finally, the new equilibrium level of income (Y_2) is identified by the intersection of the lines representing the economy's new savings function and its new $I + F + b'Tr + G$ curve.

Balanced Budgets: Taxes Finance Government Transfers

Transfers increase and taxes decrease the level of income by some multiple. When transfer recipients and taxpayers have the same propensities to consume, the multipliers will be of equal size. Thus a balanced budget of taxes being used to finance transfer payments neither expands the level of purchasing nor contracts it; it merely redistributes the disposable income, and thus the commodities being purchased, away from the taxpayers and to the transfer recipients.

This lack of effect can be demonstrated by simultaneously adding taxes and transfers of $50 billion each to the example economy whose equilibrium level of income was initially $250 billion:

1. $Y = a + b(Y - Tx + Tr) + I + G + F.$
2. $Y = \$10 + .60Y - .60(\$50) + .60(\$50) + \$80 + \$0 + \$10.$
3. $Y = .60Y + \$100.$
4. $Y = \$250.$

On the other hand, if the transfer recipients' propensity to consume is larger than that of the taxpayers, this form of balanced budget will be expansionary because the decrease in purchasing caused by removing some disposable income from the economy's taxpayers will be more than offset by the increased purchases of those who receive the transfers. Such an expansionary effect on total purchasing can be demonstrated with the same data previously used except that transfer recipients are now assumed to spend 80 percent of their transfer receipts. The equilibrium level of income in the example economy will rise to $275 billion:

1. $Y = a + b(Y - Tx) + b'Tr + I + G + F.$
2. $Y = \$10 + .60Y - .60(\$50) + .80(\$50) + \$80 + \$0 + \$10.$
3. $Y = .60Y + \$110.$
4. $Y = \$275.$

THE EFFECT OF CHANGES IN THE LEVEL OF INCOME

The foregoing discussion of the effects of governmental fiscal activities has proceeded as if the purchasing, taxes, and transfers of governments were autonomous of the level of income. Nevertheless, some of the fiscal activities of the governments in an economy may be affected by its level of income.

Taxes

Certain taxes are "autonomous taxes" (Tx_a) in the sense that their sizes are not affected by changes in the level of income. For instance, property taxes are autonomous because the amount of money collected from them does not go up or down if the level of income changes; a government using such taxes decides upon a fixed amount of tax revenues which it desires to obtain from property taxes and then, basically, requires each property owner to pay a share proportional to his share of the total assessed value of taxable property under the government's jurisdiction. Each individual property owner must pay his fixed amount of tax no matter what happens to his income or the total level of income in the economy.

Such taxes differ fundamentally from "induced taxes" (Tx_i) whose sizes relate directly to the level of income so that changes in the amounts of these taxes result from changes in the level of income. For example, personal income taxes are collected on the basis of how much income is received by individuals so that if an individual's income rises, so do the taxes he must pay. Furthermore, should there be an increase in an economy's level of income, it is reasonable to expect that income tax collections will rise as individuals in the economy receive higher personal incomes. The same effect occurs when incomes rise or fall and the individuals and businesses that receive the higher or lower levels of income purchase more or fewer commodities covered by excise and sales taxes.

The amount of induced taxes usually is presented as being equal to some proportion (t) of the level of income (Y) so that tax collections rise if the level of income rises; thus the amount of induced taxes is equal to tY. For example, if the t of an economy is 20 percent (20 percent of its Y is taken in taxes), its induced taxes will yield $40 billion when the economy's Y is $200 billion, $60 billion when it is $300 billion, and $80 billion when it is $400 billion. Furthermore, induced taxes may be "progressive" in that progressively higher proportions of each increment of income must be paid in taxes. In the United States, for example, the personal income rate of taxation runs from zero percent for individuals with low personal incomes to 70 percent of each additional amount of income for individuals with high incomes; thus, to the extent that higher and higher equilibrium levels of income mean that individuals in the economy have higher and higher personal incomes and reach income levels where greater proportions of each increment are taken in taxes, the proportion of each increment of the economy's income taken in taxes will rise as the level of its income rises.

The total amount of taxes collected in an economy is equal to the sum of the economy's induced and autonomous taxes: $Tx = Tx_a + Tx_i$; or, with the more complex description of induced taxes, $Tx = Tx_a + tY$. Thus, if an economy's autonomous taxes are $50 billion and if 20 percent of each level of the economy's income is taken as induced taxes, total tax collections will be $70 billion if the economy's Y is $100 billion, $90 billion if its Y is $200 billion, and $110 billion if its Y is $300 billion.

Transfers

"Autonomous transfers" (Tr_a) are those which the governments in an economy will provide no matter what happens to the level of income in the economy. For instance, even if the level of income in an economy is very high, there may still be those individuals such as the aged or the very young who will not be able to earn incomes in the productive process. On the other hand, "induced transfers" (Tr_i) are related to the level of income in the economy. For example, individuals with low personal incomes resulting from unemployment caused by low levels of total purchasing may receive unemployment compensation. Then, as the level of income increases in the economy, more and more individuals will be able to earn enough in the production process that they will no longer be eligible for transfers. At some level no such induced transfers will be given; all individuals who can earn incomes will be able to earn enough so that they cannot meet the government's eligibility requirements.

Since the level of induced transfers declines as income rises, it is possible to depict them as being equal to some amount that would occur if there were no income (Tr_{ii}) minus the reduction in transfers caused by the presence of a level of income which reduces the need for transfers. The reduction in induced transfers can be presented as being some proportion (z) of the level of Y so that the net amount of induced transfers gets smaller and smaller as the level of income in an economy grows. The level of induced transfers is thus $Tr_{ii} - zY$ except that it cannot be negative, and the total amount of transfers becomes $Tr_a + (Tr_{ii} - zY)$. For example, if an economy's Tr_{ii} is $100 billion and its z is 20 percent, the economy's induced transfers will be $80 billion when Y is $100 billion, $40 billion when Y is $300 billion, and zero when Y is $500 billion or larger. And if autonomous transfers are $50 billion no matter what the level of income, total transfers will be $130 billion when Y is $100 billion, $90 billion when Y is $300 billion, and $50 billion when Y is $600 billion.

Government Purchasing

The purchasing by governments is generally accepted to be of independently determined amounts whose sizes do not change with the level of income. This inflexibility is accepted on the premise that the level of government purchasing is based primarily on an economy's need for certain public goods and services, needs that do not change as the economy's level of total purchasing changes. Nevertheless, the level of government purchasing may be affected by the size of the equilibrium level of income so that government purchasing, like government transfers, will be higher at relatively low levels of income and decline in size at higher levels of income. For instance, it might be suggested that in the United States the administrators of some of the government purchasing programs deliberately speed up the amount of purchasing when the level of income in the economy is low and go slowly when it is so high that most of the economy's factors of production are already employed producing commodities. Why the administrators might do this is discussed in later chapters, but, if they do, it means that the level of government purchasing in an economy varies as the economy's level of income varies.

The total amount of government purchasing in an economy can be broken into those purchases whose size is autonomous of the level of income (G_a), and those purchases whose size depends on (is induced by) the level of income (G_i). The level of induced government purchasing can be presented as the amount that occurs if there is no income (G_{ii}) minus some proportion (g) of the level of income. Thus $G_i = G_{ii} - gY$ except that the level of induced purchasing in an economy cannot continue to fall once it reaches zero. For example, if an economy's G_{ii} is $60 billion and its g is 10 percent, the economy's induced government purchasing would be $50 billion when Y is $100 billion and $30 billion when its Y is $300 billion. Then, if autonomous government purchasing in the economy is an additional $80 billion, total government purchasing would be $120 billion if the economy's Y is $200 billion, $110 billion if its Y is $300 billion, and $90 billion if its Y is $500 billion.

The Net Effect of Autonomous and Induced Fiscal Activities

The net effect of the various autonomous and induced fiscal activities can be determined by solving for the equilibrium level of income that would occur in an economy having such activities and comparing it to the level that would exist in the economy if there were no government fiscal activity. For example, begin with an economy with the capacity to produce $500 billion of commodities but initially no fiscal activities so that the level of income is $163.16 billion because a = $10 billion, b = 60 percent, BS = .10Y, I_a = $18 billion, I_r = .22Y, F_a = $5 billion, and F_i = .05Y. Now add the following fiscal activities on the part of the economy's governments: autonomous taxes of $20 billion, induced taxes of 30 percent of Y, autonomous transfers of $20 billion, induced transfers of $175 billion minus 35 percent of Y, autonomous government purchasing of $85 billion, induced government purchasing of $9 billion minus 3 percent of Y, and a marginal propensity to consume transfers of 80 percent. The new equilibrium level of income with such government activity will be $400.0 billion.

The steps required to obtain this result follow. Notice that the induced government purchasing and induced transfers have been placed at the end of the equation. This facilitates their exclusion if the level of income is high enough to warrant it. Also notice the preliminary calculation of the level of income that excluded the induced transfers and purchasing. This has been done to determine whether these items should be excluded:

1. $Y = a + b(Y - BS - Tx_a - Tx_i) + b'Tr_a + I_a + I_r + G_a + F_a + F_i +$ (potentially excluded items $b'Tr_i + G_i$).
2. $Y = $10 + .60(Y - .10Y - $20 - .30Y) + .80($20) + $16 + .22Y + $85 + $5 + .05Y +$ [potentially excluded $.80($175 - .35Y) + ($12 - .03Y)$].
3. $Y = $120 + .63Y +$ [potentially excluded $.80($175 - .35Y) + ($9 - .03Y)$].

Then solving for Y without the potentially excluded items:

4. $Y = $324.32

Since the economy's level of income will exceed $300 billion, there will be no induced government purchasing. But there will be induced transfers because the economy's level of income is less than the $500 billion needed to eliminate them. So, adding these transfers:

5. $Y = $120 + .63Y + .80($175 - .35Y)$.
6. $Y = $260 + .35Y$.
7. $Y = 400.0.

Fiscal Drag

The economy with the $400 billion level of income has a balanced budget with $140 billion of tax collections and $140 billion of government purchasing and transfers. But $500 billion is the level of purchasing needed to fully employ the economy's factors of production. Thus, so long as only $400 billion of purchasing occurs, some of the economy's factors of production, those required to build the additional $100 billion of goods and services, will be unemployed and will receive unemployment transfers. But their transfer incomes will only average 35 percent of the value of their potential $100 billion contributions to production. However, if the economy did move to a $500 billion level of income with its present fiscal structure intact, it would generate a budgetary surplus of $65 billion: the economy's tax revenues would rise $30 billion as the existing 30 percent tax rate is levied on the $100 billion higher level of income and the government expenditures for transfers would fall $35 billion since the higher levels of production caused by the increased purchasing would take factor owners off the economy's welfare rolls and put them to work as commodity producers and taxpayers.

The $65 billion tax surplus at full employment is a measure of the degree of "fiscal drag" on the economy's total purchasing that is imposed by the economy's fiscal structure and that tends to keep the economy from reaching full employment levels of purchasing. But mere removal of such a fiscal drag in order to provide a budget that is balanced at full employment may not be sufficient to ensure either adequate levels of purchasing or the attainment of a balanced budget. For example, the fiscal drag associated with the example economy's $65 billion "full employment surplus" could be eliminated if the economy's tax rate was reduced from 30 percent to 17 percent. Then the economy's tax structure would yield $65 billion less of tax revenues when the economy's level of income is at $500 billion. But such a tax cut would only cause purchasing in the economy to rise to $454.54 billion. And at that level of total purchasing there would be a budgetary deficit of almost $30 billion since tax collections and transfer payments would be adversely affected by the economy's being $45.45 billion short of its full employment level of production. To get both $500 billion of total purchasing and a balanced budget under such circumstances requires both the elimination of the fiscal drag and additional changes that result in increases totalling $26 billion in one or more of the nongovernment components of purchasing.

Automatic Stabilizers

A change in one component that affects the level of income in an economy may not have a full multiplier effect on the economy's equilibrium level of income because of the offsetting changes induced in the other components when the level of income in the economy begins to change. For example, consider the effect of an increase in autonomous investment purchasing in the foregoing economy in which the equilibrium level of income is initially $400.0 billion. There will be an increase in the equilibrium level of income, but there also will be an increase in both taxes and business savings, and a decrease in the level of transfers. Because these changes tend to reduce the equilibrium level of income, they will dampen the expansionary effects of the initial change in investment. If autonomous investment increases by $10 billion, for example, the level of income will rise from $400.0 billion to $476.92 billion if there is no change in the level of business savings, transfers, taxes, or government purchasing. But if these items are allowed to change in the manner specified, the level of income in the economy will rise only by a multiple of about 1.538 to $415.38 billion.

Since these subsequent changes occur automatically and tend to keep an economy's level of income stabilized near its original level by offsetting the effect of any initial change, they often are referred to as "automatic stabilizers." The term is applied particularly to the government fiscal activities of induced taxes and induced transfers and is used to distinguish between fiscal changes that are induced automatically by changes in the level of income and those that are not made automatically but occur only at the discretion of the economy's governments (the effects of discretionary fiscal policies). For example, the decline in tax receipts induced by a fall in the level of income resulting from the existing tax rates' being applied to a lower level of income is part of automatic stabilization. The decline in tax receipts that occurs if the economy's governments decide to cut their tax rates or reduce autonomous taxes is the result of implementing discretionary fiscal policies.

A complete multiplier. The effect of a given change in one of an economy's income-determining components depends, of course, on the nature of the various components and whether induced transfers and government purchasing are in effect. The formula for a "complete multiplier" that takes all the various components into consideration can be computed in the following manner from the basic income-estimating formula:

1. $Y = a + b(Y - BS - Tx_a - Tx_i) + b'Tr_a + I_a + I_r + G_a + F_a + F_i + b'Tr_i + G_i.$

2. $Y = a + b(Y - eY - Tx_a - tY) + b'Tr_a + I_a + vY + G_a + F_a + xY + b'(Tr_{ii} - zY) + (G_{ii} - gY).$

3. $Y = a + bY - b \cdot eY - bTx_a - b \cdot tY + b'Tr_a + I_a + vY + G_a + F_a + xY + b'Tr_{ii} - b' \cdot zY + G_{ii} - gY.$

4. $Y - bY + b \cdot eY + b \cdot tY - vY - xY + b' \cdot zY + gY = a - bTx_a + b'Tr_a + I_a + G_a + F_a + b'Tr_{ii} + G_{ii}$

5. $Y(1 - b + b \cdot e + b \cdot t - v - x + b' \cdot z + g) = a - bTx_a + b'Tr_a + I_a + G_a + F_a + b'Tr_{ii} + G_{ii}$

6. $Y = \dfrac{1(a - bTx_a + b'Tr_a + I_a + G_a + F_a + b'Tr_{ii} + G_{ii})}{1 - b + b \cdot e + b \cdot t - v - x + b' \cdot z + g}$

Since total purchasing will change by some amount (ΔY) if more investment purchasing (ΔI_a) occurs:

7. $Y + \Delta Y = \dfrac{1(a - bTx_a + b'Tr_a + I_a + G_a + F_a + b'Tr_{ii} + G_{ii} + \Delta I_a)}{1 - b + b \cdot e + b \cdot t - v - x + b' \cdot z + g}$

Removing the original level of income from both sides of the equation:

8. $\Delta Y = \dfrac{1}{1 - b + b \cdot e + b \cdot t - v - x + b' \cdot z + g} (\Delta I_a)$

Total purchasing will change by

this multiple

of a change in the level of autonomous investment (or F_a or G_a or b $'Tr_a$ or a)

For instance, using the values from the example economy whose equilibrium level of income was initially \$400.00 billion so that induced government purchasing is excluded, the complete multiplier is:

$$\dfrac{1}{1 - .60 + .60(.10) + .60(.30) - .22 - .05 + .80(.35)} = 1.538$$

Automatic stabilizers and multiplier values. Automatic stabilizers and their effects can be depicted both algebraically and graphically. The higher level of taxes at higher levels of income can be depicted with a savings function that represents the total of each income level's taxes and other savings and the different amounts of government transfers and purchases with different injection curves representing the total nonconsumption purchasing at each level of income. Needless to say, once the conditions in the economy are so depicted, an IS curve can be devised to derive the levels of total purchasing that would occur at each rate of interest before and after a particular change takes place. But no matter what type of model is used as a framework of analysis, care must be taken to ensure that the model does not uniformly treat two seemingly identical changes in governmental or other variables that may have substantially different effects. For example, the propensities to consume of recipients of transfers in the form of interest may differ from those of individuals receiving welfare; a surtax deemed temporary may have a different effect than a tax change that is deemed permanent; and changes in the purchasing of different types of government commodities may have different effects if their producers have different income levels and propensities to consume.

● REFERENCES

Arrow, K. and M. Kurz, "Optimal Public Investment Policy and Controllability with Fixed Private Savings Ratio," *Journal of Economic Theory*, **I**, pp. 141–177 (Aug. 1969).

Baumol, W. J., and M. H. Peston, "More on the Multiplier Effects of a Balanced Budget," *American Economic Review*, **XLV**, pp. 140–148 (1955).

Boyle, G., "The Anatomy of Fiscal Imbalance," *National Tax Journal*, **XXI**, pp. 412–424 (Dec. 1968).

Christ, C., "A Simple Macroeconomic Model with a Government Budget Restraint," *Journal of Political Economy*, **LXXVI**, pp. 53–67 (Jan.–Feb. 1968).

Council of Economic Advisers, "Tax Revision: Impact on Output and Employment," *1963 Annual Report of the Council of Economic Advisers* (Washington, D.C.: U.S. Government Printing Office, 1963), pp. 45–51.

Eilbott, P., "The Effectiveness of Automatic Stabilizers," *American Economic Review*, **LVI**, pp. 450–465 (1966).

Haavelmo, T., "Multiplier Effects of a Balanced Budget," *Econometrica*, **XIII**, pp. 311–318 (1945).

Keiser, N., "The Development of the Concept of 'Automatic Stabilizers,'" *Journal of Finance*, **XI**, pp. 422–441 (1956).

Legler, J. and P. Shapiro, "The Responsiveness of State Tax Revenue to Economic Growth," *National Tax Journal*, **XXI**, pp. 46–56 (March 1968).

Lindauer, J. and S. Singh, "Effects of the Punjab Land Tax," *National Tax Journal*, **XIX**, pp. 427–433 (Dec. 1966).

Musgrave, R., and M. Miller, "Built-in Flexibility," *American Economic Review*, **XXXVIII**, pp. 122–128 (1948).

Smithies, A., "The Balanced Budget," *American Economic Review*: Papers and Proceedings, **L**, pp. 301–309 (1960).

Smyth, D. J., "Built-in Flexibility of Taxation and Automatic Stabilization," *Journal of Political Economy*, **LXXIV**, pp. 396–400 (1966).

_____, "Can Automatic Stabilizers Be Destabilizing?" *Public Finance*, **XVIII**, pp. 357–364 (1963).

Money, Interest, and Intermediation

8

Interest is the payment that possessors of money can earn by lending their money to those who want to borrow it. It is the price of using or holding borrowed money, since those who want this money must pay something for the privilege of borrowing it. For example, if an investor wants to purchase a new machine but does not immediately have all the money needed to complete the purchase, he may be able to induce one of the possessors of money to lend him the amount he requires to make the purchase. But can he induce any of the possessors to let him have the amount he wants merely by offering to repay the money at some future date? No. The possessors of money would gain nothing by letting the investor use their money on these terms. The investor therefore must agree to pay an additional amount (interest) that is high enough to induce the possessors of money to temporarily forego possessing it. Furthermore, interest is not just the cost of obtaining someone else's money to use or hold; there is also an interest cost inherent in possessing or using one's own money. For instance, the aforementioned investor will still, in effect, pay the interest price even if he uses or holds his own money, because his possession of it causes him to lose the interest income he would earn if instead he lent his money to a borrower. Thus all holders and users of money directly or indirectly pay an interest price for any money they hold or use, whether it is their own or someone else's.

The interest price of money for a given period of time typically is expressed as a percentage. For example, if one borrows $100 and has to pay back the original $100 plus $5 interest at the end of one year, the price of money for one year is 5 percent of the amount borrowed. This percentage price is the "rate of interest" (i). The advantage of using interest rates when discussing the interest price of money is that it is possible to compare the interest prices of different quantities of money. For example, an interest payment of $5 to obtain the use of $50 for one year means an interest price of 10 percent; this is double the 5 percent price paid when $20 of interest is paid to obtain the use of $400 for one year.

The basic level of interest-rate money prices in an economy is set by the demand for money in the economy and the supply. Money demand refers to the amounts of money desired for various reasons at each price (rate of interest) of money. Money supply is the amount of money available at each level of interest-rate prices. The supply and demand of money, and how they determine the level of interest rates in an economy, are examined in subsequent sections of this chapter and in the next two chapters. They are examined because the level of interest rates in an economy is important; it affects certain types of purchasing and thus the equilibrium level of income.

MONEY

Money is anything that generally can be used to purchase commodities. Typically the money supply (Ms) of a modern economy consists of the coins, currency, and demand deposits owned by the economy's nonbank public. The term "demand deposit" comes from the fact that money deposited in checking accounts is obtainable immediately on the demand of the depositors. The depositors make such demands by writing checks, which are simply their instructions to the bank regarding the disposition of the deposits that are available to them upon their demand. The money supply includes demand deposits because checks make the deposits instantly available for use in purchasing and because checks representing the ownership of these deposits generally are accepted in payment for commodities.

Other things are not included in the money supply because they generally cannot be used to purchase commodities. For instance, books, jewels, cigarettes, and houses are not included in the money supply of the United States because few sellers of commodities are willing to take them in payment for commodities. Savings deposits in financial institutions such as banks or savings and loan companies also are excluded as part of the money supply; unlike demand deposits, they cannot be used to make purchases because they cannot be transferred to new owners at the order (by check) of the old owners. Additionally excluded from the money supply are any coins, currency, or demand deposits that are not available for the nonbanking public to use in making purchases in the economy. Thus, coins and currency are not part of the money supply when they are outside the economy or merely being accumulated in government warehouses so that they will be readily available if they are ever needed.

The Amount of Coins and Currency

The total amount of coins in an economy tends to expand whenever new coins are minted; it tends to decline whenever coins are lost, melted down, placed in coin collections, or sent to other economies. But whether the amount of coins actually available for use, and thus in the money supply, grows or declines usually depends on the users of the coins; it is the general policy of the monetary authorities of most economies to add coins to their money supplies whenever potential users are willing to exchange other types of money for the coins.

The total amount of currency in an economy's money supply is affected by the same basic considerations that affect the amount of coins; new currency generally is added to an economy's money supply whenever potential users are willing to exchange other types of money for the currency. The only exception to the users' determination of the amount of currency in the money supply occurs when the amount of currency available for inclusion in the money supply is limited. Such limits involve either the physical requirements of printing or, perhaps more importantly in the United States since it seems to have enough printing presses, the lack of acceptable assets with which to back the currency. Most countries require that certain types of assets stand behind each amount of their currency. The monetary authorities of the United States, for instance, are supposed to have 100 cents worth of government bonds or other assets for every dollar's worth of the major type of currency in the United States' money supply. Until a few years ago, the United States' authorities were required to have gold certificates, representing gold in the possession of the treasury, equal to some portions of the value of the currency in circulation.

The Amount of Demand Deposits

The amount of demand deposit money in an economy such as that of the United States is affected by the actions of its commercial banks and their clients and the regulations governing bank operations. How these actions and regulations influence the size of an economy's money supply can be examined by tracing the effect of someone's depositing $100 of currency into a bank checking account.

The initial deposit means that the bank owes $100 to its depositors and that it has $100 more in "reserves" which are immediately available to be paid to the bank's depositors any time they want to withdraw their deposits. But the bank is not required to hold all of the $100 in the form of immediately available reserves since all of its deposits probably will not be withdrawn at one time and since it is expected to receive deposits as well as have them withdrawn; thus the bank is only required to have immediately available reserves sufficient to cover some proportion of its total demand deposits. The balance of the initial deposit thus is available for the bank to lend to borrowers. For example, suppose all the banks are required to hold immediately available reserves equal to 20 percent of their demand deposits: in the foregoing situation, "required reserves" of $20 will be needed by the bank in which the $100 is deposited, but at the same time the bank will have $80 in "excess reserves" available to lend to borrowers.

Even though reserves lent to borrowers no longer will be immediately available for depositor withdrawals, the bank probably will attempt to lend the $80 in excess reserves in order to earn the interest that borrowers might pay. The lending of these excess reserves has the effect of turning the original $100 into $180: the borrower will now have $80, and the original depositor will still have his $100. Furthermore, the borrower might either deposit his $80 in his bank account before using it or dispose of it to someone else who will make such a deposit. Should this occur, the bank obtaining the deposit will be required to hold an additional $16 in immediately available reserves (20 percent of the $80 deposited) and thus will have $64 in excess reserves to lend to another borrower. When the bank receiving the $80 lends this $64, the money supply rises even higher; the original depositor has $100 in demand deposits, the first borrower has $80, and the second borrower has $64. This cycle of expanding demand deposits could continue through subsequent loans and deposits until the total amount of demand deposits, and thus the supply of money in the economy, has expanded by some multiple of the original deposit. Specifically, the economy's money supply can be expanded until an amount equal to the original deposit ($100) has to be held as required reserves somewhere in the banking system. Thus, with an initial deposit of $100 and reserve requirements of 20 percent, total demand deposits in the economy can rise by as much as $500.

FINANCIAL INTERMEDIARIES

Not all savings are deposited in banks and not all borrowers turn to banks for money and credit. There are, in fact, many different forms of financial intermediaries that stand between borrowers and savers. The intermediaries are alike in that they each create their own form of "intermediate financial assets" and offer them to savers in exchange for the savers' monetary assets in the form of coins, currency, and demand deposits. The intermediaries, in turn, use the funds they obtain to acquire "primary financial assets" from borrowers. For example, a savings and loan association creates secondary assets in the form of deposits for its savers and then uses the money it receives to buy real estate mortgages from economic units that offer such primary financial assets in exchange for the funds they require for the purchases they desire to make.

Financial intermediaries exist when an economy has deficit sectors which desire to spend in excess of their incomes and surplus sectors with both incomes in excess of their expenditure desires and a willingness to exchange their monetary surpluses for nonmonetary assets. The financial intermediaries stand between the ultimate borrowers with their deficits and the ultimate lenders with their surpluses and earn an interest differential by reducing the risk of nonrepayment to the lenders; they, in effect, add their guarantees to the primary financial assets that the borrowers put up in order to obtain the surplus money of the savers. The size of the interest differential depends on the degrees of risk and the administrative costs involved in the primary and intermediate assets.

Financial intermediaries include savings and loan associations, insurance companies, pension funds, investment companies, government lending agencies, and commercial banks. Commercial banks, for example, are included because they accept money and, in exchange, issue intermediate financial assets in the form of demand deposits, savings deposits, or certificates of deposit. The banks then use whatever portion of the funds that do not have to be held as reserves to make loans to borrowers in exchange for primary financial assets such as the notes, mortgages, and other forms of securities that might be issued by ultimate borrowers.

Intermediaries and the Supply of
Financial Assets and Credit

The trend in the United States has been for a constant percentage of total private expenditure to be financed with primary debt instruments such as notes and mortgages. But the percentage of private deficits financed by commercial banks has been declining for decades. Thus, since the nonbank intermediaries tend to both have lower reserve requirements than banks and tend to hold the reserves in the form of other intermediate financial assets instead of monetary assets, there has been an increase in the level of money and credit that could be supported by a given amount of monetary assets before the assets are all held as reserves by the financial intermediaries. We have already seen that an initial $100 deposit could expand the value of an economy's financial assets to $500. But the value of the increase in financial assets that an initial $100 would support is increased if financial intermediaries exist with lower reserve requirements. For example, $80 of the initial $100 deposit could be loaned out by a bank receiving the deposit if the reserve requirement of the bank were 20 percent. The borrower receiving the $80 loan would create a primary financial asset (his I.O.U.) and exchange it for the $80. If the borrower uses the $80 to purchase an item and the seller of the item accepts the money and then redeposits it into a bank in exchange for an intermediate financial asset created by the bank (a deposit), the bank would be required to hold $16 and could loan out $64. But if the intermediate assets created by another form of financial intermediary such as savings and loan (deposit) or insurance company (policy) appeal to the seller more than do the intermediate assets created by the bank in return for the seller's money (deposit), the seller may choose to exchange his $80 for the nonbank intermediaries' financial assets. If the seller chooses the insurance company and the insurance company holds 10 percent reserves to back the intermediate assets that it creates, then the insurance company might loan out $72 to another borrower and deposit the $8 it is holding in reserve into a savings and loan which would, in turn, lend almost all of the $8 to its own borrowers. Contrast this expansion of financial assets and loans to borrowers to that which occurs when only banks create intermediate assets and make loans.

Since the trend in the United States has been to move away from the acquisition of the relatively high reserve, intermediate financial assets created by banks to the lower reserve assets of other intermediaries, there has constantly tended to be an increase in the amount of money available in the economy to acquire primary securities. Under these circumstances, if an economy's banking authorities desire to keep the economy's stock of financial assets and credit stable, they will be forced to contract the ability of the commercial banks to engage in lending operations and the creation of monetary assets.

THE SUPPLY OF MONEY AND CREDIT

The key to how much an economy's supply of money and credit can expand with a given structure of financial intermediaries is the percentage of each bank deposit and other financial assets that must be held as required reserves and the preference of the economy's participants for the various forms of intermediate assets that can be created for them. The smaller the proportion of the value of the intermediate assets that must be held in reserve by their issuers, the larger the excess reserves that can be loaned out to expand the economy's supply of money and credit. Various state and national regulatory bodies determine the reserve requirements of the United States' financial intermediaries. But the percentage of each bank deposit which must be held is determined primarily by the Federal Reserve System from a range of possible percentages approved by the Congress.[1] Even though it is technically owned by the commercial banks that participate in its program, the Federal Reserve System is much more than a servant of the banks. Its policy-making officials (governors) are appointed by the President of the United States, and its primary function is to act as the nation's chief monetary authority and provide what the governors consider to be the most desirable supply of money. To fulfill this function, it engages in various activities that tend to affect the reserves of the nation's commercial banks. The major activities that the Federal Reserve uses to affect the size of the money supply are discussed in the following sections along with other determinants of an economy's supply of money and credit. The Federal Reserve is emphasized because it is the regulatory body responsible for the supply of money and credit in the United States; thus it must act to offset the effect of any changes caused by the activities of the other regulatory bodies.

Changes in Reserve Requirements

A change in the percentage of deposits that an economy's banks hold in the

[1] Banks with about 85 percent of the nation's demand deposits participate in the Federal Reserve program. One of the Federal Reserve's functions is to hold the immediately available reserves of the commercial banks. Commercial banks may deposit such reserves at the "Fed" if they do not want to keep them in their own vaults. These deposits are available for the commercial banks to use whenever they need to cover their own depositors' withdrawals.

form of immediately available reserves affects the economy's money supply by affecting the amount of excess reserves that its banks have available to lend. Consider a situation in the United States' economy in which the banks have $500 billion in demand deposits and $100 billion in immediately available reserves, with the requirement being that they have such reserves equal to 20 percent of their demand deposits. Under these conditions, all the immediately available bank reserves are required reserves, and the banks have no excess reserves that can be lent to increase the supply of money. But what if the Federal Reserve lowers the reserve requirements to 15 percent of the demand deposits? The banks then will be required to hold only $75 billion in immediately available reserves; by its decree the Federal Reserve has given the banks $25 billion in excess reserves. Then, so long as the banks do not feel that they must continue to maintain immediately available reserves equal to 20 percent of their demand deposits in case deposit withdrawals occur, the resulting bank activity of lending new excess reserves to borrowers will cause the economy's money supply to expand.

An increase in reserve requirements tends to have an opposite effect. For example, begin with an economy in which initially there are $500 billion of demand deposits, $100 billion of immediately available reserves, and a reserve requirement of 20 percent so that all the reserves are required reserves. Now assume that the Federal Reserve increases the reserve requirement to 25 percent. If this occurs, the additional reserves which the banks obtain as their loans are repaid by check will tend not to be lent again because the banks will not have excess reserves. In this case, the reduction in demand deposits as borrowers pay their debts by check will continue until the amount of demand deposits in the economy is reduced to the $400 billion level which can exist with $100 billion in immediately available reserves and a reserve requirement of 25 percent. Of course, a reduction of such magnitude will not occur if some of the loans are repaid with coin or currency since this money would expand the size of the banks' reserves. For example, if $10 billion of loans are repaid with coin or currency, the commercial banks in the economy will have $110 billion in immediately available reserves and thus will be able to support $440 billion of demand deposits.

Open Market Operations

The Federal Reserve's purchases and sales of government bonds and other government debt instruments are known as "open market operations." Such operations affect the size of the supply of money by affecting the size of the bank reserves. To increase the money supply, the Federal Reserve buys government bonds by offering a good price for them in the markets where such bonds are bought and sold. Then, as the banks holding government bonds sell them to the Federal Reserve, they receive a payment that increases their reserves. Since the banks' demand deposits are not affected by such transactions, all these additional reserves are excess reserves which the banks can lend, thus causing the United States' money supply to begin to increase. Exactly opposite effects occur when the Federal Reserve sells government bonds in the market at prices that induce the banks to use their excess reserves to purchase the bonds; if banks use their excess reserves to purchase the bonds, they have fewer reserves with which to make loans that would tend to expand the money supply.

Similar effects occur when the Federal Reserve deals with bank depositors rather than the banks themselves. For instance, suppose the Federal Reserve spends $100 to buy a bond from a seller other than a bank. If the seller either deposits the money he receives in bank checking accounts or disposes of it to someone else who so deposits it, the amount of demand deposits and bank reserves in the economy will rise by $100. Though the banks receiving the deposit must hold an additional $10 in immediately available reserves if the reserve requirement is 10 percent, they have an additional $90 in excess reserves with which to make loans and thus cause the economy's money supply to increase. On the other hand, the situation is reversed when bank depositors use $100 of their demand deposits to purchase bonds from the Federal Reserve. If the reserve requirement is 10 percent, excess reserves in the economy will decline by $90; the banks' immediately available reserves will decline by the $100 that is withdrawn and paid to the Federal Reserve while the amount of reserves the banks are required to have immediately available will decline by $10 as a result of the lower level of demand deposits.

Rediscounting

"Rediscounting" is a process wherein the banks of an economy obtain additional reserves by borrowing them from the economy's monetary authority. It involves the banks' lending their excess reserves and then using the promises of repayment which they receive from their customers as collateral for their own borrowing from the monetary authorities. In economies other than the United States, banks may borrow reserves from their monetary authorities and then use them as the basis for making additional loans to their own borrowers. Of course, banks take such action only when the difference between the interest rates that their own borrowers will pay and those that they must pay to the monetary authorities is more than enough to cover any additional administrative costs that might be associated with the loans. In such economies, the rate of interest at which banks must borrow, the rediscount rate, is set high when the monetary authorities do not want the banks to borrow reserves and make loans and low when they want the banks to borrow reserves and make loans.[1]

In the United States the banks traditionally borrow only those reserves that are needed temporarily to satisfy existing reserve requirements; the banks do not borrow to obtain excess reserves so that they will have the capacity to make larger amounts of loans to their customers. As a result, rediscounting occurs under such circumstances as when banks have had unexpectedly high levels of deposit withdrawals which reduce their immediately available reserves below the required minimum or when the banks have experienced a shortage of immediately available reserves while adjusting to new and higher reserve requirements. The tradition is enforced by the Federal Reserve; it reviews the requests it receives for loans and does not have to lend money to a bank if it feels that the bank is trying to obtain excess reserves with which to make loans. Thus the Fed prevents the rediscount rate from becoming the "wholesale" price of money that is obtained by banks and loaned to borrowers. Instead, the rediscount rate is the penalty rate that the banks must pay with the permission of the Federal Reserve when the banks do not have adequate reserves to cover the Fed's requirements.

The most important role of the United States' rediscount rate is informational. There are many thousands of banks, and the rediscount rate is used to inform them of the Federal Reserve's intentions regarding the monetary

---

[1] The terms "rediscounting" and "rediscount rate" arise from the way in which banks typically lend and borrow. The interest expenses that banks charge their own customers often are computed on a discount basis. A borrower who obtains $96 from a bank in return for his promise to pay $100 in one year is being charged interest at the rate of 4 percent per year of the amount he has promised to repay. Of course, the borrower actually is paying more than a 4 percent rate of interest; he is paying $4 to borrow $96 for a rate of 4/96. In any event, such a borrower in effect is selling or discounting his $100 note to the bank for $96. The bank may then rediscount (in effect resell) the borrower's note to the monetary authority. If, for example, the monetary authority's rediscount rate is 3 percent, the bank will be able to get $97 for the customer's $100 note which it paid $96 to obtain. Under these circumstances, banks may find it profitable to expand the money supply continually by making loans and then using the notes they receive to get the reserves they need to make additional loans. Furthermore, when banks make such loans and borrowers either deposit their new funds in demand deposits or dispose of them to others who will make such deposits, there will be a tendency toward further increases in the money supply; the banks will only need to hold some proportion of the additional deposits in reserve and the rest will be excess reserves available for the banks to lend.

future of the economy. Thus the Federal Reserve raises the rediscount rate when it believes that there will be a need for greater future restrictions on the availability of money and credit and wants the banks to begin being more cautious in their lending policies. On the other hand, the Fed lowers the rediscount rate when it anticipates an increased availability of money and credit and wants the banks to begin easing their requirements for bank borrowers. The banks respond because they know from tradition that changes in rediscount rates mean that the Federal Reserve envisions monetary conditions associated with the direction and degree of the rediscount rate change.

Involuntary Federal Reserve Purchases That Create Monetary Assets

No matter what its desires and intentions, the Federal Reserve may be involuntarily committed by law or agreement to engage in operations that tend to expand the United States' stock of monetary assets and thus the level of financial assets and credit that can occur in the economy. For example, the United States' government is committed to issue gold certificates to pay a fixed price for all gold offered to it. The Treasury issues gold certificates with which to make such payments. Furthermore, the Federal Reserve is committed to create other monetary assets and exchange them for the certificates. These assets are then available to be held as reserves by the economy's financial intermediaries. Thus, the stock of money and credit in the economy tends to expand whenever gold flows into the United States.

The same type of effect exists whenever the Federal Reserve is required by law or agreement to finance government deficits by buying the government I.O.U.'s for the differences between tax revenues and expenditures. Under such circumstances, the economy's stock of monetary assets would tend to rise whenever the government runs a deficit. Such a situation existed during and after World War II when the Federal Reserve obligated itself to purchase at fixed prices all government securities offered to it. The securities were patriotically purchased during the war by the surplus sectors despite their relatively low yields. After the war, however, their holders sold them in great numbers in order to get funds to loan to private borrowers at higher rates of interest. Thus, at a time when the economy's money supply may have already been too high, the Federal Reserve was obligated to buy these financial assets in the open market and thus further expand the economy's money supply.

INTEREST RATES AND THE SUPPLY OF
MONETARY ASSETS AND CREDIT

The size of the supply of monetary assets in an economy such as the United·
States, and thus the total amount of financial assets and the level of credit
that can be generated by the economy's financial intermediaries, is determined primarily by the reserve-influencing activities and regulations of the
monetary authorities; it is not affected by the interest-rate price of money
due to the absence of rediscounting for the purpose of obtaining excess
reserves. Thus a curve representing the supply of money that would exist
in an economy at each level of interest rates might indicate no difference
in the economy's money supply from one level of interest rates to the next.
An example of such a money supply curve, Ms_1, appears in Figure 8-1 in
which the general level of interest rates in an economy is measured on the
vertical axis and the size of the economy's money supply on the horizontal
axis. The curve is perfectly vertical to represent the constant size of the
money supply at every level of interest rates.

Of course, the relationship described in Figure 8-1 between the supply of

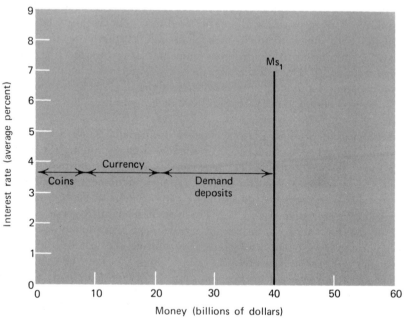

FIGURE 8-1
A money supply curve.

money and the level of interest rates might not exist in an economy in which rediscounting can be used to increase the amount of excess reserves and thus the money supply; at interest rates above the rediscount rate, the banks will be willing to engage in borrowing and lending activities that tend to increase the supply of money in the economy. It is reasonable, however, to expect the monetary authorities to set the rediscount rate low enough to cause rediscounting only if they desire an increase in the size of the economy's money supply. Thus, in the absence of such intentions, the rediscount rate will be kept high enough so that the economy's money supply is not affected by any changes in the general level of the interest rates paid by its borrowers.

Foreign Holdings of Monetary Assets

The level of interest rates in an economy may affect the economy's stock of financial assets and credit if the level influences foreign holdings of the economy's monetary assets. For example, United States' monetary assets being held abroad for use in financing international trade might be returned to the United States if the interest rates that the assets could earn would be high enough to make it worthwhile to use some other economy's money to finance trade. Figure 8-2 depicts such a situation. It indicates that $10 billion of foreign-held monetary assets will return to the economy's money supply at an interest rate level averaging 6 percent. Furthermore, it is also possible that the monetary assets of other economies may be acceptable for certain types of purchases. Thus, when the level of interest rates that an economy's borrowers are willing to pay to acquire monetary assets exceeds the levels of other economies, the borrowers may expand the economy's stock of monetary assets as they exchange their primary and intermediate financial assets for foreign monetary assets that also can be used to make some purchases in the economy. Figure 8-2 suggests that increasingly larger amounts of foreign monetary assets will come into the example economy to expand its money supply at interest rate levels above 6 percent.

The Money-Credit Relationship and the Rate of Interest

In addition to the possible development of new forms of financial inter-mediaries with lower reserve requirements and the possibility that interest rates will be high enough relative to those abroad to attract foreign monetary assets and foreign holdings of an economy's monetary assets, higher interest rates could also result in an expansion of an economy's supply of money and credit if there are restrictions on the level of interest rates that can be paid by certain intermediaries and not by others.

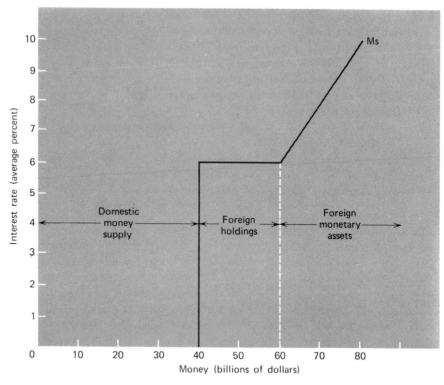

FIGURE 8-2
The supply of monetary assets in an open economy.

The interest differential earned by intermediaries depends on the rates they can charge to primary borrowers and the rates they must pay to obtain monetary assets from the surplus sectors. The intermediaries are, however, in competition with each other for the business of both the lenders with surpluses and the borrowers with deficits. Thus the interest rates they charge and the interest rates they pay tend to go up and down together. But some intermediaries such as commercial banks and savings and loan associations are restricted in terms of the level of the interest rates they can pay for monetary assets while other intermediaries are not. Thus, if interest rates that can be charged on loans to deficit sectors in an economy are high enough, certain intermediaries in the economy may be willing and able to pay rates to the surplus sectors in excess of the rates that other intermediaries are allowed to pay. In this case, there would be a move of the surpluses to the intermediaries that can pay the higher rates. In the United States, the commercial banks tend to have the highest reserve requirements and when the rates in the economy rise above a certain critical level, there tends to be a shift to nonbank intermediaries with lower reserve requirements that can pay higher rates of interest. Thus once the critical level of interest rates is reached, there can be an increase in the economy's supply of money and credit without an increase in the amount of monetary assets available to be held as reserves. If such a critical rate level exists, and it seems to, the supply of money and credit in the economy could be higher at rates above the critical level than it would otherwise be. In a later chapter we shall discuss the critical rate concept in terms of its monetary policy implication and the experiences of the United States.

● REFERENCES

Benavie, A., "Intermediaries in a Macroeconomic Model," *Journal of Finance*, **XXII**, pp. 441–453 (Sept. 1967).

Board of Governors of the Federal Reserve System, *The Federal Reserve System: Purposes and Functions*.

Chetty, V. K., "On Measuring the Nearness of Near-Moneys," *American Economic Review*, **LIX**, pp. 270–281 (June 1969).

Friedman, M. and A. J. Schwartz, "The Definition of Money: Net Wealth and Neutrality as Criteria," *Journal of Money, Credit and Banking*, **I**, pp. 1–14 (Feb. 1969).

Gurley, J. and E. Shaw, "Financial Intermediaries and the Savings-Investment Process," *Journal of Finance*, **II**, pp. 257–276 (May 1956).

Johnson, H. G., "Inside Money, Outside Money, Income, Wealth and Welfare in Monetary Theory," *Journal of Money, Credit and Banking*, **I**, pp. 30–45 (Feb. 1969).

Kaufman, G. G., "More on an Empirical Definition of Money," *American Economic Review*, **LIX**, pp. 78–87 (March 1969).

Malkiel, B., "The Term Structure of Interest Rates," *American Economic Review*, **LIV**, pp. 532–543 (May 1964).

Meltzer, A., "Money Supply Revisited: A Review Article," *Journal of Political Economy*, **LXXV**, pp. 169–182 (April 1967).

Patinkin, D., "Money and Wealth: A Review Article," *Journal of Economics and Law*, pp. 1140–1160 (Dec. 1969).

Ranlett, J., *Money and Banking* (John Wiley, 1965).

Roosa, R., "Interest Rates and the Central Bank" in *Money, Trade and Economic Growth* (Macmillan, 1951).

Smith, W., "The Instruments of General Monetary Control," *National Banking Review*, **I**, pp. 47–76 (Sept. 1963).

Subcommittee on Domestic Finance, Committee on Banking and Currency, House of Representatives 88th Congress, 2nd Session, "The Federal Reserve's Attachment to the Free Reserve Concept: A Staff Analysis," 1964.

Tobin, J., "Commercial Banks as Creators of Money" in *Banking and Monetary Studies*, D. Carson, Ed. (Richard D. Irwin, Inc., 1963).

Tolley, G., "Providing for Growth of the Money Supply," *Journal of Political Economy*, **LXV**, pp. 465–485 (Dec. 1957).

The Demand for Money

9

There are three basic uses of money, suggested John Maynard Keynes,[1] that cause individuals and businesses in an economy to prefer to hold their wealth in the form of money balances in spite of the interest expense involved in possessing money. These are the so-called transaction, speculation, and precautionary uses of money holdings. The total demand for money holdings in an economy is the sum of the amount of money desired for each of these purposes.

TRANSACTIONS DEMAND

The transactions demand for money refers to the money that must be held in wallets, checking accounts, and cash registers so that money outlays anticipated in the future can actually be made. Money is held for such

[1] J. M. Keynes, *The General Theory of Employment, Interest and Money* (Harcourt, Brace, 1936), pp. 194–209.

201

purposes primarily because there may be a lack of correspondence between money inflows and money outflows. Many households tend to receive money on periodic paydays, for example, but they may make their outlays such as house and food purchases on other days. Obviously, when such differences occur, these households need to hold certain sums of money in wallets and checking accounts for a period of time after payday. Similar circumstances exist for businesses. They may not receive payments for their products at exactly the same time that they must pay their own bills. Furthermore, they may not receive payments in exact amounts and must hold a supply of money in their cash registers in order to make change.

How much money is desired for transactions purposes depends, of course, on the number and size of the transactions occurring in the economy and the amount of time elapsing between subsequent money inflows. The latter is important since the more time between inflows, the greater the tendency for transactions involving money outlays to fall between them, thus increasing the amount of money desired for transactions purposes.

The money holdings required for transactions in an economy tend to be larger when income is at higher levels. This is because the higher levels of income tend to mean an increase in the number and size of transactions occurring in the economy. Thus the amount of money demanded for transactions purposes in an economy (M_1) depends on (f) the level of income in the economy (Y), or $M_1 = f(Y)$. It is possible, of course, to relate the amount of money demanded for this purpose more specifically to an economy's level of income. For example, if the households and businesses in an economy tend to hold for transactions purposes the amount of money needed to make 10 percent of the economy's total commodity purchases, they will want to hold $2 billion if the economy's Y is $20 billion, and $10 billion if it is $100 billion.

Factors other than income that affect transactions demand. The proportion of each level of income that householders and businesses desire to hold in the form of money for transactions depends on more than just the amount of time between subsequent inflows and outflows and the amount of money outlays involved. Among the other influences might be suggested:

1. *Vertical integration:* Business firms that are vertically integrated have fewer buying and selling transactions and thus need less money for transactions than unintegrated firms. Business firms are integrated vertically when they perform the subsequent steps required in the production of a commodity, whereas those producing at only one stage

of production are not. For instance, a steel firm is not vertically integrated when it buys iron and coal from other firms to produce steel and then sells that steel to other users; it is integrated if it mines and processes its own coal and iron, uses the coal and iron to make steel, and then uses the steel to produce finished products which it sells. The point is that the integrated firm does not need to engage in any money-requiring transactions to buy coal and iron or to sell steel, whereas the unintegrated firm does.

2. *Use of credit:* Credit reduces the amount of money needed for transactions at every level of income. It allows the payments associated with transactions occurring between money inflows to be delayed until the money inflows take place. When such delays are possible there is no need to hold money from earlier inflows to make payments when the transactions occur. For example, the use of credit cards and time-payment plans in the United States has virtually eliminated the need for certain individuals to accumulate and hold money in order to make purchases of meals, travel, and shelter.

3. *Sales of used goods or financial assets:* Money also has to be held so that it will be available for use in transactions involving used goods or financial assets such as stocks and bonds. Thus the more used goods and financial assets being sold, the larger will be the proportion of the amount of total purchasing for new commodities that is needed for transactions.

4. *Barter:* Barter involves the exchange of one commodity for another; it does not involve the use of money. Thus the greater the amount of bartering in an economy, the smaller will be the amount of money held for transactions.

5. *Rate of interest:* There is an interest expense in holding money for transactions and other purposes. And it may be that higher rates of interest tend to cause holders of money to avoid transactions that require their holding money balances. Nevertheless, the rate of interest is probably of relatively little importance in influencing the amount of money desired for transactions. After all, at every rate of interest, rational holders of money for transactions will already be making all possible efforts to avoid transactions requiring their holding money balances; they will always hold the minimum amount in order to keep their interest expenses as low as possible so that they will have maximum amounts of money available for other uses. There are, however, several exceptions which lead to less money being held for transactions at higher rates of interest. One occurs when the interest costs of holding the money required for transactions are higher than the additional costs of avoiding such trans-

actions through barter, vertical integration, and the use of credit; at higher interest rates transactions might be handled through those channels in order to avoid the higher interest costs. Another occurs when the interest that could be earned by lending the money during the interim period of time before it is needed is higher than the administrative cost associated with such lending; since the amount of interest earned will tend to be higher than such costs at higher rates of interest, less money may be held for transactions purposes at higher rates of interest.

Transactions demand curve. A transaction demand curve depicts the amount of money that will be desired for transactions purposes in an economy at each level of income. How much is actually desired at each level of income is determined, of course, by the factors just listed. Figure 9-1 presents such a curve. The level of income is measured on the horizontal axis and the amount of money is measured vertically. The curve rises to the right in order to depict the additional need for money for transactions at the higher levels of income where there are more transactions. It indicates, for instance, that $55 billion will be demanded for transaction purposes when the level of income in the economy is $300 billion.

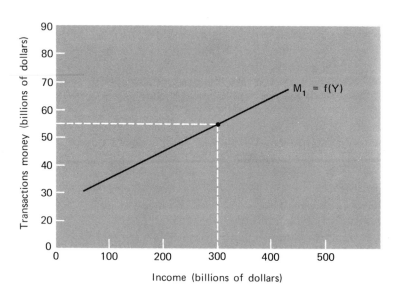

FIGURE 9-1
Transactions demand for money.

SPECULATIVE DEMAND

The speculative demand to hold money is based on the desire of speculators to make capital gains by buying assets when their prices are low and selling them when their prices rise. Any owner of wealth is considered to be a speculator if he foregoes earning a rate of return by holding any portion of his wealth in the form of money for other than transactions and precautions purposes. Fundamentally, speculators desire to hold more of their wealth in the form of money when the prices of other assets are relatively high because they expect such prices to fall, and they want to have money available to buy the assets at the lower prices. Also they want their wealth in the form of money when the prices of other assets are relatively high because they do not want their wealth to be in the form of assets that they expect to be declining in value. On the other hand, the owners of wealth do not want to hold money when the prices of nonmonetary assets are so low that they are expected to rise. Instead, when such low prices exist, the owners of wealth use any wealth that they had been holding in the form of money to buy these low-priced assets so they can resell them at a profit when the expected increase in prices occurs.

The type of assets. Interest-earning financial assets such as bonds usually are emphasized in most discussions of the speculative demand for money. This is valid since the owners of wealth will not desire to hold their wealth in the form of money when the prices of bonds and other interest-earning assets are so low that they are expected to rise; on the other hand, they will tend to hold their wealth in the form of money when the prices of such assets are so high that they are expected to fall. Speculation, however, does not involve only bonds and other financial assets; it involves all assets. When the prices of assets are so high that the owners of wealth expect them to fall, they want to hold their wealth in the form of money rather than assets which they expect to decline in value. Conversely, when the prices of nonmonetary assets are expected to rise, they will not want to hold their wealth in the form of money. Instead, they will want their wealth in the form of assets which can be sold for a profit when their price rises.

Asset prices and the rate of interest. There is a relationship between interest rates and asset prices: the prices of assets are high when interest rates are low and low when interest rates are high. For example, consider a government bond or other nonmonetary asset that is expected to continuously pay an annual interest sum of $5. If the annual interest rate is 10 percent, the price of the asset will be $50. (An outlay of $50 for the asset earns $5 per year: a 10 percent return.) Higher prices for the asset mean a lower interest rate. For example, if someone paid $100 for a bond in order to get $5, he will be receiving only a 5 percent return. On the other hand, lower prices for the bond would mean a higher rate of interest; a buyer would receive 20 percent if he could buy such a bond for only $25.

The Amount of Money Demanded at Each Level of Interest Rates

How much money the owners of an economy's wealth normally want to hold as an asset at any one point in time when there is no reason to believe that the general level of prices of nonmonetary assets in the economy will rise or fall depends upon the magnitude of their wealth and the level of interest rates in the economy. They can hold their wealth in various portfolios of wealth forms including money, bonds, and real property. The loss of the rate of return on bonds and other nonmonetary assets is the price paid for holding wealth in the form of money. The lower the level of the interest rate price of money in an economy, the more that the owners of wealth in the economy will substitute money holdings for other forms of wealth in their portfolios. More specifically, they will move wealth into nonmonetary assets until the potential gains from the rates of return on the nonmonetary assets and their possible increases in price are offset by both the brokerage fee costs associated with getting wealth into and out of non-monetary assets and the implicit costs of the risk and uncertainty of net capital losses from possible reductions in asset prices.[1] The lower the level of interest rates in an economy, the more money that will be held as assets in the economy because of the lower net gains associated with the holdings of wealth in other forms. Finally, at some low level of interest rates, an infinite amount of money will be held by the possessors of wealth. This occurs, even if there is no risk and uncertainty regarding changes in asset prices, because the rate of return on nonmonetary assets—the alternative form of wealth—will be so low that it would not cover the brokerage fee costs of moving into the nonmonetary assets. And if no additional money is used to purchase such assets, their prices will not be bid higher and the level of interest rates in the economy will not fall lower.

Speculative demand curve. A graphic example of an economy's speculative or wealth-holding demand for money is presented

---

[1] The implicit costs are the prices that the owners of wealth would pay to avoid the risk and uncertainty of possible net capital losses caused by holding wealth in the form of nonmonetary assets.

in Figure 9-2. The curve in the figure indicates that holdings of $50 billion will be desired by the owners of wealth when the level of interest rates in the economy averages 4 percent. Notice that no money is demanded for speculative purposes when the interest rates in the economy average 8 percent or higher. This occurs because the owners of the economy's wealth want to hold all their wealth in the form of assets other than money at the low asset prices associated with that level of interest rates. The curve slopes down to the right from 8 percent to indicate that the owners of the economy's wealth will want to hold more and more of their wealth in the form of money at lower and lower rates of interest. In the example economy, the curve becomes perfectly elastic at a minimum interest rate level of 2 percent because at such a low rate all the owners of wealth in the economy will desire to hold any money they might acquire rather than bear the risks and the transaction costs associated with the high asset prices that exist at that low level of rates. Since there are no buyers, the prices of nonmonetary assets will not be bid up and the level of interest rates in the economy will not decline further. Thus, even if additional money is subsequently made available to be either held or used to buy nonmonetary assets, it all will be

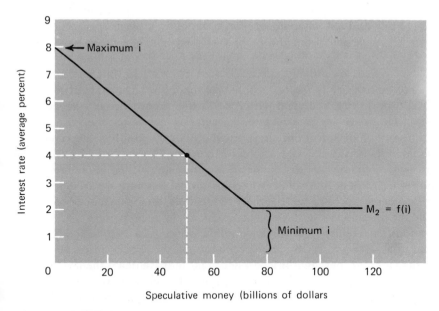

FIGURE 9-2
Speculative demand for money.

held because of the low level of rates of return and the existence of transaction costs.

Deviations from the Normal Level of Interest Rates

In an economy at any point in time there is a normal level of interest rates at which the entire amount of money available to hold as wealth is equal to the amount of money that the owners of wealth desire to hold. When such a normal level of rates exists there is no shortage or surplus of monetary assets to cause the level of interest rates to be bid up or down by wealth-owners seeking to obtain the amount of money that they desire to hold. Furthermore, when such a normal level of interest rates exists, there tends to be no net buying or selling of nonmonetary assets to drive the general level of interest rates down or up since for every speculative buyer of assets who thinks that their prices will go up and is willing to change his wealth from money to nonmonetary assets there is a seller who thinks that their prices will go down and is willing to exchange his nonmonetary assets for money.

Any move away from the normal rate tends to be offset by the speculative activities of the economy's wealth-holders. They maintain it with the willingness to buy and sell nonmonetary assets out of their portfolios whenever the asset prices deviate from the level associated with the economy's normal rate of interest. The speculative actions of buying and selling by wealth-holders are based on their experiences and expectations. But wealth-holders are not automatically perfect prophets of the future. Thus they tend to rely on historical price and yield patterns and their knowledge of current situations. The more sophisticated the speculators, the faster they react when interest rates deviate from the normal rates, and the less the economy's actual interest rates deviate from their normal levels. Specifically, if the prices of nonmonetary assets rise in an economy so that its interest rates and other rates of return fall below the normal level of rates, the owners of the economy's wealth will tend to redistribute their inventories of wealth holdings by selling their assets for profits at the higher prices and holding the additional money they receive until the prices of such assets again decline. The sale of the assets by the speculators at the higher prices and their tendency to not buy high-priced assets tend to drive down the level of asset prices in the economy and restore the normal level of interest rates. On the other hand, any move for asset prices to fall and the economy's level of interest rates to rise above the normal rate also tends to be offset by the speculative reaction of the wealth-holders since the lower prices induce them to use their existing money holdings to buy the assets that have relatively low prices and yield interest rates that are above the normal level. The wealth-holders' acts of buying the nonmonetary assets tend to cause their prices to be restored to the levels associated with the normal level of interest rates.

Since the prices of interest-earning financial assets and other nonmonetary assets tend to go up and down together as the owners of wealth buy and sell assets in response to their expectations about future asset prices, the amount of money desired for speculative purposes tends to be larger when interest rates are low and smaller when interest rates are high. Reinforcing the wealth-holders' willingness to hold less money at relatively high rates of interest is the interest income the assets provide. This income is lost when money is held rather than assets, and the losses are greater when interest rates are higher than when they are lower. For these reasons, the amount of money demanded in an economy for speculative purposes (M_2) can be related to the level of the economy's interest rates (i) and is expected to vary inversely as the economy's interest rate levels vary.

Minimum and maximum levels of interest rates. An economy's level of interest rates can fluctuate around its normal level of rates. But the actual level of rates can only rise to some maximum level above the normal level or fall to some minimum level below it. For when the prices of the interest-earning and other assets rise so that this minimum level is reached, the owners of wealth in the economy will believe that the only way asset prices can go is down and thus that there is no chance of making a profit on any nonmonetary assets they might subsequently purchase. Once the prices of such assets rise so high in an economy that the interest-earning assets yield this level of rates, the price expectations of the economy's speculators will cause enough of them to hold the wealth that they have available for speculation in the form of money while they wait for asset prices to fall. The fact that they are holding this wealth in the form of money and not using it to purchase assets tends to mean the level of interest rates in the economy will not fall further because these buyers will not be bidding up the prices of the interest-earning assets. The same type of reasoning applies to a maximum level of interest rates at which no money is demanded for speculative purposes. Specifically, asset prices may become so low in an economy, and thus interest rates so high, that no owner of wealth will want to hold money for speculative purposes; they will hold all of their wealth in the form of nonmonetary assets since they expect the prices of such assets to rise.

PRECAUTIONARY DEMAND

Money is held for precautionary purposes so that anticipated outlays can continue despite the arrival of unexpected circumstances that require additional outlays or cause reduced incomes. Examples of such unexpected circumstances include the loss of money inflows owing to illness or unemployment or the need for additional outlays caused by accidental damage to a person or machine.

Precautionary demand influences. The amount of money demanded for precautionary purposes in an economy is related to the confidence that the economy's producers, financial institutions, and individuals have in their ability to make all the outlays of money that they may desire; the less confidence they have in their ability, the more money they will wish to hold for precautionary purposes. Various things can influence the level of confidence. For instance, the availability of credit tends to mean that unexpected additional outlays or reductions in income can be temporarily covered without having precautionary money holdings available.

Another factor that may affect the level of confidence, and thus the amount of money desired for precautionary purposes, is the level of income in an economy. At relatively high levels of income, individuals and businesses might receive more money and thus be better able to meet unexpected situations without having to use previously accumulated holdings. Furthermore, with high incomes, they may have better chances of obtaining credit when the need arises because of their ability to repay debts.

Since the amount of money desired for precautionary purposes in an economy may be related to the economy's level of income and the level of confidence existing at each income level, the amount of money demanded for such purposes in an economy (M_3) can be presented algebraically as depending on the economy's level of income: $M_3 = f(Y)$. And this relationship exists even though the amount of money actually desired for precautionary purposes at each level of income also depends on factors that do not affect the degree of confidence at each level of income. For instance, the rates of interest in an economy might and can affect the amount of money held for precautionary purposes. After all, higher rates of interest tend to cause less money to be held for precautionary purposes when the holders of such money do not value their ability to meet unexpected situations as highly as the interest they lose by holding the money.

Precautionary demand curve. A curve depicting the amount of money desired for precautionary purposes in an economy at each level of income is presented in Figure 9-3. The amount of money is measured on the vertical axis and the level of income on the horizontal axis. Notice that the curve slopes downward to the right to indicate that less money will be held for precautionary purposes at higher levels of income. This will be the case if higher incomes increase the level of confidence in the economy. The particular curve depicted in the figure indicates, for instance, that holdings of $30 billion will be desired for precautionary purposes when the level of income in the economy is $500 billion.

TOTAL MONEY DEMAND

The total amount of money holdings that will be desired in an economy at each level of interest rates (Md) is the sum of the amounts desired for transactions, speculation, and precautionary purposes: $Md = M_1 + M_2 + M_3$. A money demand curve showing the amount of money holdings desired at each general level of interest rates in an economy with a given combination of income and wealth may be seen in Figure 9-4. The curve slopes downward to the right to indicate that the participants in the economy will desire to

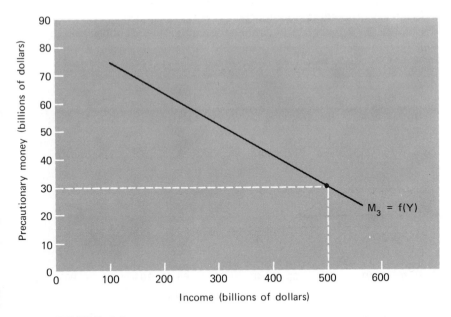

FIGURE 9-3
A precautionary demand curve.

hold more money at lower rates of interest. More money is desired there primarily because lower interest rates are associated with an increased willingness on the part of the owners of wealth to hold their wealth in the form of money; the amount of money demanded for transactions and precautions purposes is determined basically by the level of income in the economy and is relatively unaffected by the rate of interest. Notice that the money demand curve appears to have three distinct portions. Above an interest rate level of 10 percent the curve becomes almost perfectly inelastic. This occurs because no money holdings are desired by the owners of the economy's wealth when the level of interest rates in the economy is this high or higher and because the money holdings desired for transactions and precautions purposes decline little as interest rates in the economy increase. The total amount of money holdings desired increases at interest rate levels below 10 percent mainly because more and more owners of wealth desire to hold their wealth in the form of money at lower levels of interest rates. Finally, at an interest rate level of 4 percent, the economy's demand curve becomes perfectly elastic because at such low interest rates and high asset prices the economy's wealth owners are willing to hold infinitely large amounts of money rather than bear the risks and pay the brokerage fees associated with holding nonmonetary assets.

Complicating any analysis of money demand is the likelihood that different amounts of money will be demanded for transactions and precautions

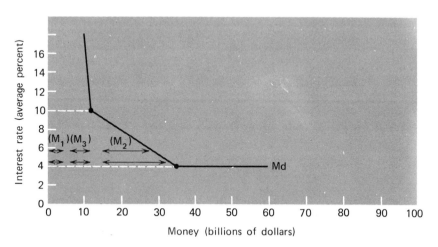

FIGURE 9-4
A money demand curve.

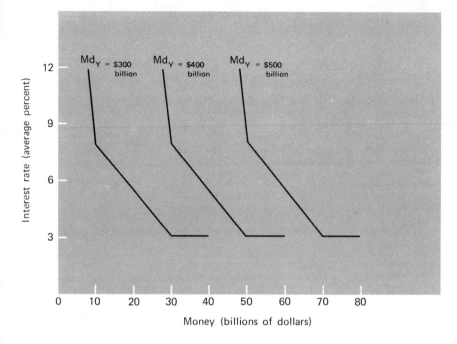

FIGURE 9-5
Money demand curves.

purposes at different levels of income and wealth. Thus the total amount of money demanded at each interest rate will differ from one income and wealth level to the next. This means that a complete graphic description of an economy's demand for money requires a different money demand curve for each level of income and wealth. Figure 9-5 presents an example of such different money demand curves. The implications of having different demands for money at different levels of income and wealth will be discussed in the next chapter.

● REFERENCES

Baumol, W., "TheTransactions Demand for Cash: An Inventory Theoretic Approach," *Quarterly Journal of Economics*, **LXVI**, pp. 545–556 (1952).

Bronfenbrenner, M., and T. Mayer, "Liquidity Functions in the American Economy," *Econometrica*, **XXVIII**, pp. 810–834 (1960).

Brunner, K. and A. Meltzer, "Economics of Scale in Cash Balances Reconsidered," *Quarterly Journal of Economics*, **LXXXI**, pp. 422–436 (Aug. 1967).

———, "Liquidity Traps for Money, Bank Credit, and Interest Rates," *Journal of Political Economy*, **LXXVI**, pp. 1–37 (Jan.–Feb. 1968).

Canterbery, E. R., "A Note on Recent Money Supply Behavior," *Western Economic Journal*, **IV**, pp. 91–98 (1966).

Chow, G., "On the Long-run and Short-run Demand for Money," *Journal of Political Economy*, **LXVII**, pp. 327–351 (June 1959).

Courchene, T. J., and H. T. Shapiro, "The Demand for Money: A Note from the Time Series," *Journal of Political Economy*, **LXXII**, pp. 498–503 (1964).

Friedman, M., "The Demand for Money—Some Theoretical and Empirical Results" *Journal of Political Economy*, **LXVII**, pp. 327–351 (Aug. 1959).

Johnson, H., "Monetary Theory and Policy," *American Economic Review*, **LII**, pp. 335–384 (1962).

Keynes, J. M., *The General Theory of Employment, Interest and Money* (New York: Harcourt, Brace, 1936), pp. 165–174, 194–208.

Laidler, D., *The Demand For Money: Theories and Evidence* (International Textbook Company, 1969).

Lee, T., "Alternative Interest Rates and the Demand for Money: the Empirical Evidence" *American Economic Review*, pp. 1168–1181 (Dec. 1967).

Lydall, H., "Income, Assets, and the Demand for Money," *Review of Economics and Statistics*, **XL**, pp. 1–14 (1958).

Meltzer, Allan H., "The Demand for Money: The Evidence from the Time Series," *Journal of Political Economy*, **LXXI**, pp. 219–246 (1963).

Miller, L. L., Jr., "On Liquidity and Transactions Costs," *Southern Economic Journal*, **XXXII**, pp. 43–48 (1965).

Ranlett, J., *Money and Banking: An Introduction to Analysis and Policy* (John Wiley, 1965), pp. 263–269.

Spenkle, C. M., "Large Economic Units, Banks and the Transactions Demand for Money," *Quarterly Journal of Economics*, **LXXX**, pp. 436–442 (1966).

Tobin, J., "The Interest Elasticity of the Transactions Demand for Cash," *Review of Economics and Statistics*, **XXXVIII**, pp. 241–247 (1956).

———, "Liquidity Preference as Behavior Toward Risk," *Review of*

Economic Studies, **XXV**, pp. 65–68 (1958).

————, "A General Equilibrium Approach to Monetary Theory," *Journal of Money, Credit, and Banking*, **I**, pp. 15–29 (Feb. 1969).

Tsiang, S. C., "The Precautionary Demand for Money: An Inventory Theoretical Analysis," *Journal of Political Economy*, **LXXVII**, pp. 99–117 (Jan.–Feb. 1969).

Walters, A., "The Demand for Money—the Dynamic Properties of the Multiplier," *Journal of Political Economy*, **LXXV**, pp. 293–298 (June 1967).

Whalen, E., "A Rationalization of the Precautionary Demand for Cash," *Quarterly Journal of Economics*, **LXX**, pp. 314–324 (May 1966).

Wicker, E. R., "The Behavior of the Consumer Money Supply Since World War II," *Journal of Political Economy*, **LXIX**, pp. 437–446 (Oct. 1961).

Equilibrium Level
of Interest Rates

10

An economy's equilibrium level of interest rates is that level which causes the amount of money demanded in the economy to equal the amount of money supplied. This contrasts with the differences that will exist between the amounts supplied and demanded at all other levels of interest rates. Such differences will exist because, as discussed in Chapter 9, the amount of money demanded in an economy tends to decline at higher and higher rates of interest whereas the supply of money tends to either remain unchanged or increase. Consequently, since the amount of money demanded at the equilibrium level equals the amount supplied, less money will be demanded than will be supplied at higher levels of interest rates and more money will be demanded than will be supplied at lower levels.

The differences between the amounts of money demanded and supplied at other levels of interest rates ensures that such rates can exist only temporarily while the economy is moving to the equilibrium level. For instance, interest rates in an economy cannot be maintained at levels higher than the equilibrium level because less money would be demanded in the economy than would be supplied. In other words, there will be a surplus of undemanded money at the higher levels of rates. Then, since the possessors of this surplus have some of their wealth in a form that they do not desire, they might exchange their surplus money for other assets such as bonds by using it to purchase them. (Of course, they also could give away the surplus money or use it to buy commodities.) Such purchases tend to bid up asset prices. Then, as asset prices rise and the level of interest rates declines, more and more money will be demanded. The lower rates of interest associated with the higher prices of interest-earning financial assets reduce the cost of holding money so that more holders of wealth will reach the interest rate minimums at which they would prefer to hold money rather than bear the brokerage fees and the cost of risk associated with nonmonetary assets. In addition, both the lower interest rates and the use of surplus money to buy goods and services may cause an increase in total purchasing and thus result in larger amounts of money being desired for transaction purposes. Asset prices will continue to rise until the level of interest rates is reduced to a level (the equilibrium level of interest rates) that causes the amount of money demanded in the economy to be equal to the amount of money supplied so that there is no longer a surplus to cause further changes.

Conversely, if an economy's level of interest rates is below the equilibrium level, more money will be demanded in the economy than will be available to be held. The difference between the amount of money available and the larger amount demanded is eliminated, however, by the efforts of those who desire to have more of their wealth in the form of money but who cannot obtain all the money they want: they cause asset prices to be bid down as they attempt to sell some of their assets in order to obtain the additional money desired. The decline in asset prices and the higher interest rates that accompany the lower prices of financial assets cause smaller and smaller quantities of money to be demanded. The sale of assets and the decline in their prices will continue until some level of interest rates (the equilibrium level) is reached at which the total amount of money demanded in the economy is reduced to the size of the money supply available to be held. Then there is no longer a money shortage, and no more assets are sold to cause the economy's interest rates to increase further.

A graph containing curves that represent an economy's money demand and money supply can be used to depict the equilibrium level of interest rates in the economy. The curves reflect the conditions in the economy's money market where the foregoing monetary transactions occur. Figure 10-1 contains an example of such a graph. It measures the level of interest

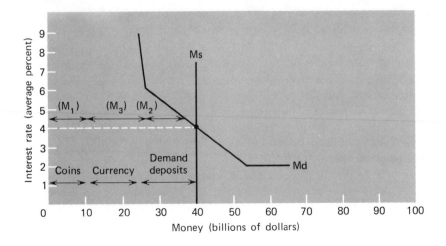

FIGURE 10-1
An equilibrium level of interest rates.

rates on the vertical axis and the quantity of money on the horizontal axis. The equilibrium level of interest rates in the Figure 10-1 economy averages 4 percent; it is the only level at which the amount of money demanded in the economy is equal to the amount supplied.

Changes in the Equilibrium Level of Interest Rates

Changes in an economy's equilibrium level of interest rates may be caused by changes in either the demand or supply of money. For example, the monetary authorities of an economy might increase its supply of money through the use of one of the money-expanding techniques described in Chapter 8. The supply of money available to be held at the original equilibrium level of rates then will exceed the amount of money desired at that level. Since no one wants to hold the additional money, it is surplus and may be used to either purchase newly produced goods and services or other existing forms of wealth. The latter purchases will drive asset prices up and interest rates down until some new and lower equilibrium level of interest rates is reached where the amount of money demanded has increased so that there is no longer a surplus. A similar effect will occur if there is a decrease in the amount of money demanded. For instance, suppose the amount of money needed for transactions purposes is reduced by the use of credit. The result will be less money demanded than is available at the original level of interest rates. Holders of the surplus of money that results then may switch this portion of their wealth to other assets by purchasing these assets with their surplus money. This will cause the price of these assets to be bid up and the interest rates to fall. Asset prices will rise and the level of interest rates in the economy will fall until enough additional money is demanded to eliminate the surplus.

Figure 10-2 portrays these situations. Figure 10-2a depicts the effect of an increase in the supply of money. It shows an economy's money supply rising from $40 billion to $60 billion and the resulting decline in its equilibrium level of interest rates from i_2 to i_1. Figure 10-2b depicts the similar effect of a decline in the economy's demand for money from Md_1 to Md_2. Such a decline in demand, for instance, could be caused by a reduction in the level of income in an economy so that less money is needed for transactions purposes. The same effect would tend to occur if new credit arrangements, such as credit cards, are implemented.

Investment Purchasing and the Rate of Interest

Investment purchasing occurs whenever the marginal efficiency of a potential new capital asset exceeds the interest rate price required to finance the asset's purchase. Thus the amount of investment purchasing in an economy is related to the conditions in its money market where the interest rates of the economy are determined by the amount of money supplied and demanded. The relationship between an economy's money market and its level of investment purchasing can be shown with a two-diagram figure like that in Figure 10-3. The left graph represents the money market, the right

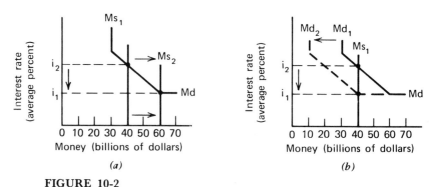

FIGURE 10-2

(a) The effect of an increase in the supply of money. (b) The effect of a decrease in the demand for money.

graph the demand for the investment purchasing. Basically, the figure shows the example economy's equilibrium level of interest rates (4 percent) being determined by the conditions that exist in the economy's money market, and then the amount of investment purchasing at that level ($20 billion) being determined by the demand for investment purchasing that exists in the economy at each level of interest rates.

The way in which the level of investment purchasing is affected by a change in the money market also can be depicted graphically. For instance, in the economy represented by Figure 10-4, the money supply increases by $20 billion from an original money supply of $30 billion to a new money supply of $50 billion. As a result, the economy's equilibrium level of interest rates declines from an average of 4 percent to a new and lower level averaging 2 percent and causes an increase in the level of investment purchasing from $15 billion to a new and higher level of $25 billion.

The Liquidity Trap

Would an even greater supply of money in the Figure 10-4 economy encourage even more investment purchasing if it were needed to achieve an adequate level of total purchasing? No. The minimum level of interest rates has been reached, and any further additions to the supply of money will merely be held by speculators. In any event, since no money is used to purchase nonmonetary assets, their prices do not rise despite the increase in the supply of money. Thus the general level of interest rates in the economy does not fall and the level of total purchasing tends not to rise.

The willingness of the owners of an economy's wealth to hold infinite amounts of money at the minimum level of interest rates (represented

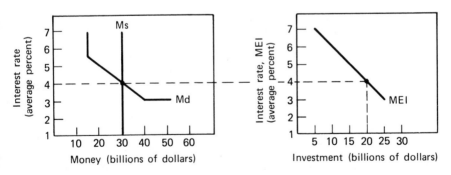

FIGURE 10-3
The level of interest rates and the level of investment.

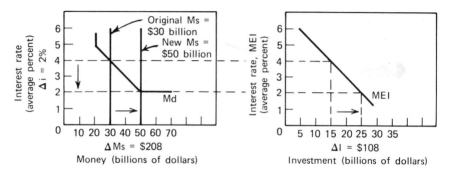

FIGURE 10-4

Changes in the level of interest rates and changes in the level of investment.

graphically by the perfectly horizontal portion of the money demand curve) is known as the *liquidity trap*. Once the minimum level is reached, expanding the money supply ceases to be a method of obtaining more investment and other types of purchasing through lower interest rates; rather than being used to buy assets, any increase in the supply of money is "trapped" by the possessors of these monetary assets who hold them instead of using them to buy monetary assets.

The existence of a minimum level of interest rates, however, does not mean that further increases in the money supply will have no effect on the level of purchasing. After all, since liquid assets such as money are among the things that influence consumption, an increase in the amount of such assets may result in increased consumption purchasing. If this occurs, both total purchasing and the amount of money desired for transactions purposes will tend to rise when the supply of money increases.

The Effect of Changes in the Level of Income

When an economy is not in the liquidity trap, the primary effect of an increased money supply or lower money demand is a lower level of interest rates and an increase in the level of total purchasing. There is a secondary effect, however, that simultaneously tends to offset the way initial changes in money demand or money supply affect the amount of purchasing. The secondary effect occurs because the changes in the level of total purchasing tend to change the amount of money demanded for transactions and precautions purposes. On balance, the amount of money demanded for these purposes in an economy tends to rise in response to increases in the level of the economy's total purchasing. Thus the decline in interest rates, which an

---

222   EQUILIBRIUM LEVEL OF INTEREST RATES

increased money supply causes, tends to be at least partially offset by the resulting increases in the demand for money caused by the higher levels of income that result from the lower levels of interest rates. This means that if the money supply of an economy is increased, the economy's rates of interest tend not to decline as far as they would in the absence of the offsetting secondary effects, and that the level of purchasing in the economy will not increase as much.

Figure 10-5 contains an example of the secondary effect. It represents the same economic circumstances depicted by Figure 10-4 plus an increased demand for money such as might result from an increase in the level of total purchasing. The result is a slightly higher level of interest rates and lower level of investment purchasing than would occur in the absence of the secondary effect.

MONEY MARKET EQUILIBRIUM

Since the demand for money in an economy is affected by the level of income, an economy's equilibrium level of interest rates cannot be determined until its level of income is known. A problem arises at this point since an economy's interest rates not only depend on the level of income in the economy but also influence its size by affecting the levels of investment and other purchasing. Even though it is not possible to determine an economy's equilibrium level of interest rates until the economy's level of income is known, it is possible to determine the various interest rate levels that would provide enough money demand at each level of income so that the economy's money market would be in equilibrium with the amount of money demanded exactly equal to the amount supplied. A curve representing

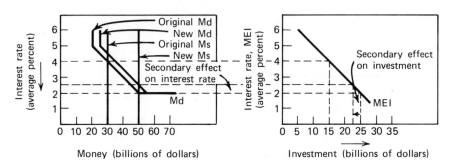

Money (billions of dollars)   Investment (billions of dollars)

FIGURE 10-5
The secondary effect.

such equilibrium interest rate levels is a "money market equilibrium curve." Commonly designated as the LM curve, this curve represents the various combinations of interest rate levels and income that would result in an economy's demand for liquid assets—money—equaling its money supply. No other combinations can exist, except in passing, because they would not result in equilibrium in the economy's money market; they would cause the economy's level of interest rates to change, in turn causing changes in the economy's level of income, until an equilibrium combination is reached.

Money Market Equilibrium Curves

Figure 10-6 presents a money market equilibrium curve. Notice that the curve depicts an economy in which the level of interest rates will be very low at low levels of income. This occurs because the total quantity of money demanded for transactions purposes and precautions purposes is low at low levels of income; any tendency for the amount of money demanded for precautionary purposes to be high at such low income levels is more than offset by the reduced need for money for transactions purposes so that a relatively large supply of money is available for the economy's speculators to hold. Notice further that the level of interest rates in the example economy is constant at an average of 4 percent for all income levels below $250

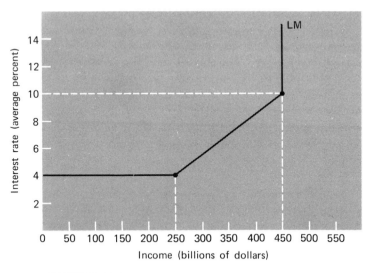

FIGURE 10-6
Money market equilibrium curve.

billion. Four percent is the minimum level of interest rates in this economy, and there is a sufficient amount of money available to be held for speculative purposes when the level of income in the economy is below $250 billion to cause it to be reached.

The economy's LM curve indicates that, if the level of income in the economy is $250 billion or higher, the money held for transactions and precautions purposes will reduce the amount of money available for the owners of the economy's wealth to hold to such an extent that the economy's equilibrium level of interest rates will be above the minimum level. The equilibrium level of interest rates is higher and higher for each subsequent higher level of income until an income of $450 billion is reached at an average interest rate of 10 percent: this is the maximum level of income that can exist in the economy. It is reached when interest rates are high enough so that no money is being held for speculative purposes, all foreign money holdings have returned, all interest related changes in the nature of intermediaries have occurred, and all possible degrees of barter transactions and uses of foreign monies and money substitutes have been attained. When it is reached, the economy's money market cannot be in equilibrium at higher levels of income since more money would be required for transactions and precautions purposes than would be supplied. Under these conditions, any tendency to move past $450 billion to a higher level of income will only cause the level of interest rates in the economy to rise as nonmonetary assets are sold by wealth-owners to obtain the additional money required for transactions purposes. The level of interest rates will continue to rise until the level of income in the economy is cut back to $450 billion where the amount of money demanded in the economy will again equal the amount of money supplied. It is, of course, also possible that less and less money will be demanded for precautions and transactions purposes at higher levels of interest rates. If this occurs, the existing supply of money in the economy will permit higher levels of income to occur at higher rates of interest. In this case, the economy's LM curve would no longer be perfectly inelastic at some relatively high level of interest rates.

Developing Money Market Equilibrium Curves

An economy's money market equilibrium curve can be derived by starting with a given level of income and finding the amount of money required to support the transactions associated with that level of income. The difference between the amount of money demanded for transactions purposes in an economy and the economy's money supply is the amount of money that is available for speculative and precautionary purposes. Subtracting the money required for precautionary purposes leaves an amount that is available for the economy's speculators to hold. The level of interest rates at which such owners of wealth desire to hold all the available money is the equilibrium level. This level and the accompanying level of income is a combination that would put the economy's money market in equilibrium. The combination is represented by one point on the economy's money market equilibrium (LM) curve. Subsequent points can be found for other levels of income by repeating the process.

An LM curve can be constructed graphically with this approach using curves that represent the conditions in an economy's money market. The curves are the "transactions-precautions curve," the "money supply curve," and the "speculative demand curve." The first of these curves shows how much money will be desired in an economy for transactions and precautions purposes at each level of income. The money supply curve represents the total amount of money in an economy. The speculative demand curve, as we have seen, shows how much money will be demanded in an economy for wealth-holding purposes at each level of interest rates.

An example of the transactions-precautions curve appears in Figure 10-7. The level of income in the economy is measured on the horizontal axis, and the amount of money demanded for these purposes at each level of income is measured on the vertical axis. The position and shape of the curve are obtained by vertically adding the curve representing precautionary demand for money holdings in the economy at each level of income to the curve representing the amounts of money that would be held in the economy for transactions at each level of income. The example curve indicates, for instance, that $35 billion of money holdings would be desired for transactions and precautions purposes when the level of income in the economy is $400 billion. The curve slopes upward and to the right to indicate that the increases in the amounts of money demanded for transactions purposes at higher levels of income more than offset any decreases in the amounts of money demanded for precautionary purposes at the higher levels of income.

A curve that represents an economy's supply of money is presented in Figure 10-8. The curve itself is a straight line joining the points on the axis which represent the total size of an economy's supply of money. The straight line ensures that when the amount of money going to one use is measured on the vertical axis, the amount of money remaining for other purposes can be identified on the horizontal axis. Such identification is accomplished by moving from the vertical axis straight over to the money supply curve

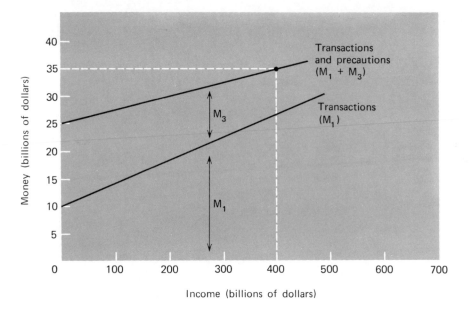

FIGURE 10-7
Transactions-precautions curve.

and then straight down to the horizontal axis. For instance, the curve in Figure 10-8 shows that when the supply of money in an economy is $90 billion and $60 billion of it is allocated to transactions and precautions uses, $30 billion will be available for speculative uses.

It is possible to combine the three curves representing the conditions in an economy's money market in such a way as to specify the shape and position of the economy's LM curve. This is done in Figure 10-9 using the procedure described above to derive points on the example economy's LM curve.[1]

---

[1] Several procedures may be used to simplify the process of identifying the shape of an economy's LM curve. First, find the initial level of income where the LM curve is no longer perfectly elastic. This is located by working the process backward from point (a) on the speculative demand curve where the liquidity trap begins. Then work clockwise from point (b) to find the lowest level of income at which there will be no money available for speculative purposes. The latter procedure generates the level of income ($500 billion) and the level of interest rates (an average of 7 percent) where the LM curve must become perfectly inelastic because all of the money in the economy will be used for transactions and precautions purposes.

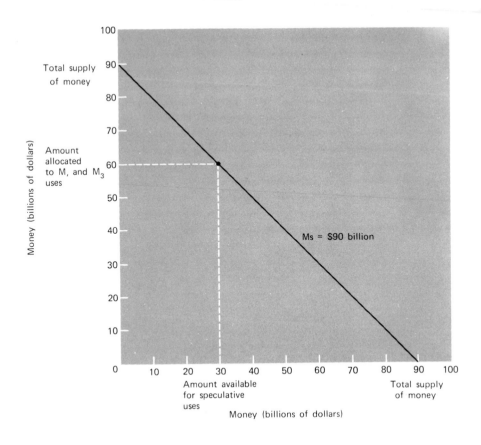

FIGURE 10-8
A money supply curve.

LM Curves When Interest Rates Affect M_1 and M_3

The transactions and precautions demands for money presented in Figures
10-7 and 10-9 provide for no differences in the amounts of money demanded
for these purposes at different levels of interest rates. Thus the maximum
level of income in the Figure 10-9 economy is reached at the level of interest
rates that is high enough to eliminate speculative holding so that all the
money in the economy is available for transactions and precautions uses.
But, for reasons already considered, the level of interest rates in an economy
also may affect the amounts of money demanded in the economy for these

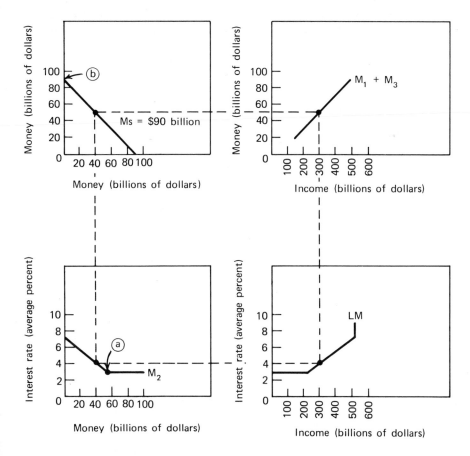

FIGURE 10-9
The money market.

purposes; higher rates may reduce the amount of money demanded at each level of income. Thus it is possible that the money supply in an economy could support more transactions and the level of income could increase even if the general level of interest rates in the economy were so high that all speculative holdings had already been eliminated.

The effect of different rates of interest on the transactions and precautions demands can be depicted graphically with the use of different transactions-precautions curves to represent the different amounts of money that will be demanded for these purposes at each level of interest rates. For example,

Figure 10-10 reflects the money market conditions of an economy in which smaller amounts of money are demanded for transactions and precautions purposes at higher rates of interest. Specifically, the figure represents an economy in which less and less money is demanded for these purposes until an interest rate level averaging 5 percent is reached. Such an economy's LM curve can be derived by beginning with a level of interest rates and then identifying the level of income that will provide enough transactions and precautions demand at those rates to put the money market in equilibrium. This involves arbitrarily selecting an interest rate level, then determining

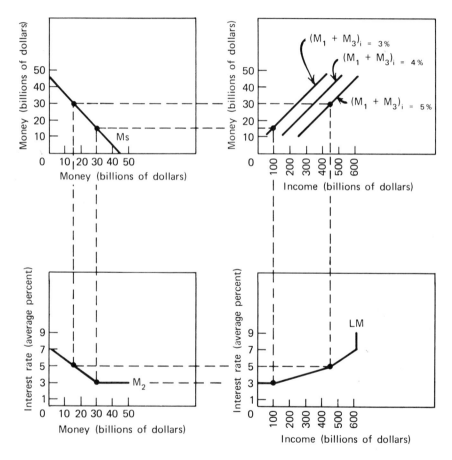

FIGURE 10-10
An LM curve when interest rates affect M_1 and M_3.

how much money will be held for speculative purposes at this level and thus how much will be available for M_1 and M_3 uses and the level of income that will use the available amount.

Shifts in Money Market Equilibrium Curves

Anything that changes the conditions in an economy's money market may change the nature of equilibrium in that market and thus affect the relationships depicted by the economy's LM curve. For instance, an increase in an economy's supply of money has effects which are represented by shifting the economy's LM curve to the right. Such a shift is demonstrated in Figure 10-11 where, for the sake of exposition, the level of the economy's interest rates is assumed to have no effect on the amount of money demanded for transactions and precautions purposes. The LM curve moves from LM_1 to LM_2 as a result of a rise in the economy's money supply from $50 billion to $70 billion. The shift is caused by the increase in the amount of money available to be held at every level of interest rates; the economy's money market can be in equilibrium at each of the original levels of interest rates only if the level of income associated with each interest rate level is higher so that all the additional money is demanded for transactions and precautions purposes.

EQUILIBRIUM LEVELS OF INTEREST AND INCOME

Various combinations of interest rate levels and incomes that will meet the equilibrium conditions for an economy's money market (money supplied equals money demanded) and its commodity market (total savings equals $I + G + F + b'Tr$) are depicted by LM and IS curves. There is, however, only one level of interest rates and one level of income that will result in equilibrium occurring simultaneously in both of an economy's markets. Graphically, this equilibrium combination occurs at the intersection of the LM and IS curves. In the economy represented by Figure 10-12, the equilibrium level of interest rates averages 5 percent and the equilibrium level of income is $450 billion.

Nonequilibrium combinations of interest rate levels and levels of income can exist only temporarily in an economy because any departure from the equilibrium combination sets up forces in one or both of its money and commodity markets that will automatically move the economy back toward the equilibrium levels.

For example, assume that both the level of interest rates and the level of income in an economy are higher than the equilibrium combination.

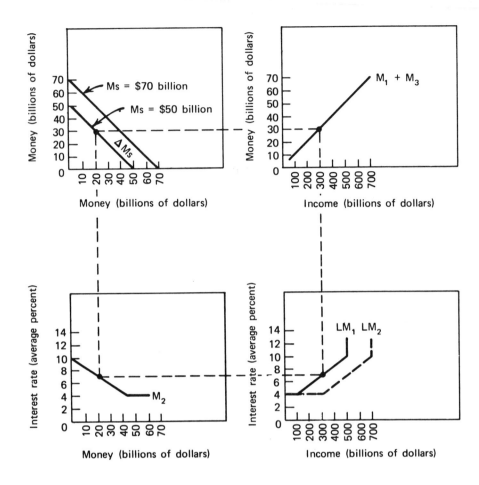

FIGURE 10-11
Shifts in an LM curve.

Such a condition is shown in Figure 10-12 by point 1 which represents an interest level averaging 7 percent and a level of income of $600 billion. Since the point lies on the LM curve, the economy's money market is in equilibrium and there is no reason for its level of interest rates to change. But the level of income is too high for the economy's commodity market to be in equilibrium; the IS curve shows that an interest rate level averaging 7 percent can only cause enough investment and other purchasing for the economy's level of income to be maintained at $350 billion. Thus the level of income in the economy will fall. Then, as the level of income in the economy declines, the amount of money demanded for transactions and precautions purposes falls and this releases additional money to satisfy the speculative demand for money and cause the economy's rates of interest to decline. Both the level of income and the level of interest rates will decline until they reach $450 billion and an average of 5 percent; this is the combination of income and interest at which the level of income generates enough transactions and precautions demand for money to keep the economy's level of interest rates from falling and at which the level of interest rates induces enough investment and other purchasing to keep the economy's level of income from falling. In other words, the levels of income and interest in an economy will change until both of the economy's markets are simultaneously in equilibrium so that no forces exist to cause further changes. Similar circumstances will occur if the levels of interest and income in an economy are at the levels depicted by point 2 in Figure 10-12. Under these circumstances, the investment and other purchasing that would occur at such an interest rate level will tend to drive the economy's income to higher levels. Additionally, the shortage of money associated with interest rate levels that are below equilibrium, plus the additional demand for money that develops as the level of income rises, will cause the economy's level of interest rates to rise. The levels of income and interest will rise until both of the economy's markets are in equilibrium. Then the interest rate

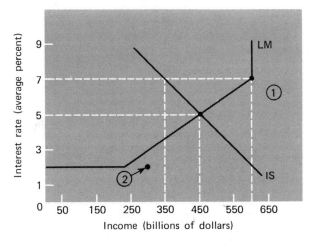

FIGURE 10-12
The equilibrium combination of income and interest.

level will be high enough (an average of 5 percent) to keep purchasing from rising and pushing the level of income up, and the level of income in the economy will be high enough ($450 billion) to provide the demand for money needed to keep the economy's level of interest rates from falling and causing more purchasing.

THE COMBINED MARKETS

Figure 10-13 shows how the various conditions in an economy's money market and commodity market can be brought together graphically to provide the LM and IS curves needed to depict the equilibrium levels of interest and purchasing in the economy. Notice the uniformity of what is

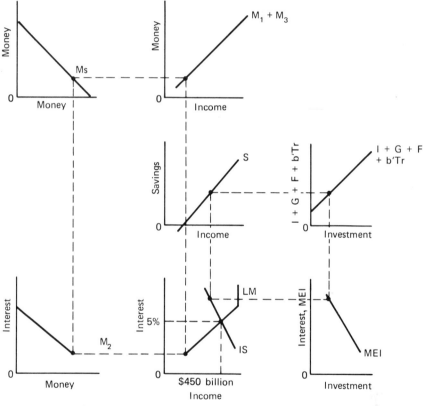

FIGURE 10-13
The combined markets.

being measured on the axes of the various graphs. Also notice that the basic relationships between the curves depicting the circumstances in each market have been retained from the earlier discussions of each market. The only difference is that the graph containing the economy's savings function has been inserted between the graphs representing the economy's money market.

The Effects of Shifts in the IS Curve

Changes in the size of one or more of the purchasing components may affect both the equilibrium level of interest rates and the level of income if they have effects that are depicted by shifts in an economy's IS curve. Thus, if expectations of future profits rise in an economy so that its demand for investment commodities is higher at every level of interest rates, the economy's IS curve will shift to the right to indicate that a higher level of income would exist in the economy at every level of interest rates. Figure 10-14 depicts such a situation; the example economy's IS curve moves from IS_1 to IS_2.

If there is no change in the example economy's level of interest rates, the initial increase in purchasing will drive the economy's equilibrium level of income from $500 billion to $650 billion. Under the conditions depicted in Figure 10-14, however, there will be offsetting effects that preclude a

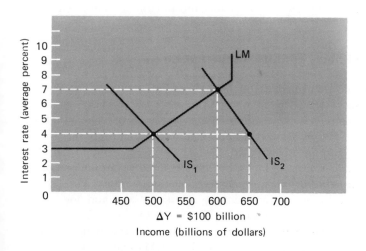

FIGURE 10-14
The effects of a change in the commodity market.

complete multiple expansion of the level of income: the increased amount of money demanded for transactions and precautions purposes at the higher levels of income will drive up the level of interest rates in the economy from an average of 4 percent to an average of 7 percent and thus tend to limit the expansion of the equilibrium level of income. The expansionary effect of the initial increase on total purchasing thus will be dampened, and income in the economy will rise by less than the full multiplier—from $500 billion to $600 billion rather than $500 billion to $650 billion.

The full multiplier effect will occur, of course, if the changes in the commodity market just described take place under the money market conditions represented by the perfectly horizontal portion of the LM curve: the increased demand for money caused by the economy's move to a higher level of income would not be enough to raise the level of interest rates in the economy. On the other hand, no increase in the level of income will occur if the changes that result in the IS curve's shifting take place under the conditions portrayed by the perfectly vertical section of the LM curve; the initial increase in income and money demand would increase only the interest rate level until the amounts of investment and other purchasing are reduced enough so that income in the economy returns to the level that the available money can handle. This occurs because the initial change in purchasing would take place when all the money in the economy is already being used for transactions and precautions purposes and because higher levels of interest rates will not reduce the amount of money demanded for these purposes.

The Effects of Shifts in the LM Curve

Changes in an economy's demand for money or supply of money will cause the conditions represented by the economy's LM curve to change if they change the combinations of interest rates and levels of income that will put the economy's money market into equilibrium. For instance, if an economy's money supply is increased, its LM curve will shift to the right to indicate that higher levels of income will be required to put the economy's money market in equilibrium at each level of interest rates. The level of income has to be higher to provide the additional demand for money needed to offset the additional supply. Figure 10-15 shows the effects of such an occurrence on an economy's equilibrium combination of income and interest: the LM curve shifts from LM_1 to LM_2 and, as a result, the equilibrium level of interest rates declines from 6 percent to 3 percent, whereas the equilibrium level of income in the economy increases from $400 billion to $500 billion.

The increased money supply, in this case, causes the equilibrium level of interest rates in the economy to fall and the equilibrium level of income to rise. Hopes of duplicating such a result may lead the monetary authorities to increase the supply of money again, thus changing the example economy's money market equilibrium conditions to those depicted by LM_3. But this time such an action will not change the equilibrium levels of interest and income. Instead, the additional money will be held by the owners of the economy's wealth rather than being used by them to buy financial assets. Thus the economy's level of interest rates will not be driven down, and there will be no change in the level of investment purchasing to cause a change in the economy's equilibrium level of income. The economy is in the liquidity trap.

DIFFERENT RATES OF INTEREST

The foregoing discussion of interest rates is in terms of the general level of interest rates that might exist in an economy at any one point in time. This is, of course, a form of oversimplification since in most economies money is simultaneously being borrowed and held at various different rates of interest. For example, some loans to purchase houses in the United States have interest rates of 6 percent, whereas others being made on the same day for the purchase of automobiles may have rates of 10, 15, and even 20 percent.

Nevertheless, an analysis based on an economy's general level of interest rates is not adversely affected by the existence of various different rates.

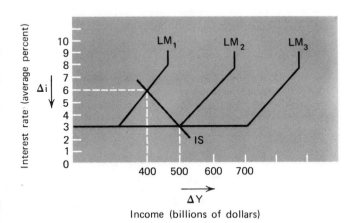

FIGURE 10-15
The effects of a change in the money market.

Indeed, the forces that tend to cause changes in the level of an economy's interest rates exert their influence through their effect on the various different rates. For example, when there is a money surplus in an economy, such as tends to occur when the economy's money supply increases, all the different interest rates in the economy would tend to fall as the surplus money is spent and the prices of the different interest-earning assets in the economy are bid up; the ensuing general decline in the different interest rates means that the whole pattern of interest rates in the economy has fallen.

Why a combination of different interest rates exists in an economy instead of one rate of interest relates to the degree of certainty that the loans and interest actually will be repaid. Specific interest rates tend to be higher, for instance, when the term of the loan is longer so that more things can happen during the time to prevent repayment; when the money is to be used for relatively unproved or haphazardly conceived projects that may not generate the funds needed for repayment; when the value of the assets pledged as collateral (assets reverting to the lender or to be sold in case of nonpayment) is low or nonexistent; when the borrower's promise to repay is not very marketable or has to be held to maturity; and when the distance between the lender and borrower is greater, because distance may make collections more difficult or provide the basis for concealing knowledge of relevant factors.

● REFERENCES

Ackley, G., "Liquidity Preference and Loanable Fund Theories of Interest," *American Economic Review*, **XLVII**, pp. 662–673 (1957).

Brunner, K. and A. Metzler, "A Liquidity Trap for Money, Bank Credit, and Interest Rates," *Journal of Political Economy*, **LXXVI**, pp. 1–37 (Jan.–Feb. 1968).

Cagan, P., "The Non-Neutrality of Money in the Long Run: A Discussion of the Critical Assumption and Some Evidence," *Journal of Money, Credit, and Banking*, **I**, pp. 207–227 (May 1969).

Clower, R. A., "A Reconsideration of the Microfoundations of Monetary Theory," *Western Economic Journal*, **VI**, pp. 1–8 (Dec. 1967).

————, "What Traditional Monetary Theory Really Wasn't," *Canadian Journal of Economics*, **II**, pp. 299–302 (May 1969).

Edwards, E., "The Interest Rate in Disequilibrium," *Southern Economic Journal*, **XXXII**, pp. 49–57 (July 1966).

Floyd, J. E., "International Capital Movements and Monetary Equilibrium," *American Economic Review*, pp. 472–492 (Sept. 1969).

Friedman, M., "The Present State of Monetary Theory," *Economic Studies Quarterly*, **XIV**, pp. 1–15 (Sept. 1963).

Gibson, W. E. and G. G. Kaufman, "The Sensitivity of Interest Rates to Changes in Money and Income," *Journal of Political Economy*, **LXXVI**, pp. 472–478 (May–June 1968).

Hansen, A., *A Guide to Keynes* (McGraw-Hill, 1953), pp. 143–146.

Hicks, J., "Mr. Keynes and the 'Classics'; a Suggested Interpretation," *Econometrica*, **V**, pp. 147–159 (1937).

————, "Monetary Theory and History—An Attempt at Perspective" in *Critical Essays in Monetary Theory* (Oxford University Press, 1967), pp. 155–173.

Horwich, G., "Real Assets and the Theory of Interest," *Journal of Political Economy*, **LXX**, pp. 157–169 (1962).

Johnson, H. G., "Monetary Theory and Policy," *American Economic Review*, **LII**, pp. 335–384 (June 1962).

Malkiel, B. G., "Expectations, Bond Prices, and the Term Structure of Interest Rates," *Quarterly Journal of Economics*, **LXXVI**, pp. 197–218 (1962).

Ruffin, R. J., "The Equivalence of Liquidity Preference and Loanable Funds Theories in Stocks-Flow Economies: A Comment," *Review of Economic Studies*, pp. 420–421 (Oct. 1967).

Samuelson, P. A., "What Classical and Neoclassical Monetary Theory Really Was," *Canadian Journal of Economics*, **I** pp. 1–15 (Feb. 1968).

Scott, R. H., "Liquidity and the Term Structure of Interest Rates," *Quarterly Journal of Economics*, **LXXIX**, pp. 135–145 (1965).

Shackle, G., "Recent Theories Concerning the Nature and Role of Interest," *Economic Journal*, **LXXI**, pp. 209–254 (1961).

Smith, W., "Monetary Theories of the Rate of Interest: A Dynamic Analysis," *Review of Economics and Statistics*, **XL**, pp. 15–21 (1958).

Tsiang, S. C., "Liquidity Preference and Loanable Funds Theories, Multiplier and Velocity Analysis: A Synthesis," *American Economic Review*, **XLVI**, pp. 539–564 (1956).

Van Horne, J., "Interest-Rate Risk and the Term Structure of Interest Rates," *Journal of Political Economy*, **LXXIII**, pp. 344–351 (1965).

Wright, A., "The Rate of Interest in a Dynamic Model," *Quarterly Journal of Economics*, **LXXII**, pp. 327–350 (Aug. 1958).

Aggregate Demand

11

The real income of an economy is the commodities produced and distributed in it. Production requires purchasing, and the total or aggregate amount of commodities purchased in an economy depends on the level of money expenditures and the prices of the economy's commodities. For instance, if the average price of each commodity produced in an economy is $200 and the total or aggregate demand for commodities in the economy is such that $600 billion of purchasing occurs, then three billion commodities will be purchased. But what if the economy's business firms are capable of producing a real income of four billion commodities and are willing to do so if they can sell them for an average of $200? Production capacity and a willingness to supply goods and services does not matter. No businessman is going to produce more commodities than he can sell. Therefore only the three billion commodities that can be sold will be produced. Thus, owing to a lack of purchasing, the economy's labor, capital, and other materials that are available to produce the fourth billion will not be employed, and the economy will be without one billion commodities which it might otherwise have enjoyed.

One possible answer for such a situation is to increase the level of money expenditures. For example, expenditures of $800 billion would result in all four billion of the potentially available commodities being purchased if the average price of the commodities remained $200. This higher level of total purchasing could be attained through various changes in the economy's money or commodity markets. Under certain circumstances, for instance, it could be accomplished through lower interest rates and taxes or higher levels of foreign and government purchasing.

It may not be necessary, however, for an economy with unpurchased commodities to obtain an increase in its level of monetary expenditures. Instead, the prices of the various commodities may decline so that the level of purchasing in the economy is sufficient to acquire all the commodities that its businessmen are willing to produce. For instance, all of the potentially producible four billion commodities in the example economy could be purchased with money outlays of $600 billion if prices in the economy generally decline by 25 percent so that the average commodity price is $150. On the other hand, a general reduction in the level of the economy's commodity prices to an average of $150, accompanied by a reduction in total purchasing to $450 billion, would have no effect on the amount of commodities purchased. But will an economy's commodity prices fall when there are less than maximum levels of production and, if they do, will the amount of commodities purchased increase? If these questions are answered in the affirmative, lower prices—deflation—can be accepted as a possible remedy for situations in which the equilibrium levels of money outlays in an economy are inadequate to purchase all the commodities that can be produced.

AGGREGATE DEMAND CURVES

Aggregate demand curves depict the total amount of commodities that would be purchased in an economy at each level of commodity prices. Economists disagree on the shape of such curves because they cannot agree on whether more will be purchased in an economy at lower levels of prices. As we shall see later in this chapter, the disagreement is based on the effects that lower prices will have on the commodity and money market determinants of the amount of commodities that would be purchased.

Real Income Instead of Money Income

Up to this point, the circumstances in an economy's money and commodity markets have been discussed in terms of money. For example, these markets have been discussed in terms of the amount of money demanded by speculators or the amount of money spent by foreigners. Before using these markets, however, to analyze how many commodities will be purchased in an economy at each price level, it is desirable to convert them so that they represent commodities rather than money—so that they are in real terms rather than money terms. This can be accomplished by dividing the money amounts of each market component by the average level of commodity prices.

Consider an economy in which the general level of commodity prices is such that the average price paid for commodities is $200. Now, for example, rather than showing that $200 billion in consumption purchasing will occur when the level of income is $300 billion, the curve representing the economy's consumption function will show that one billion commodities will be purchased when the economy's real income, the total amount of commodities being purchased and produced, is $1\frac{1}{2}$ billion commodities. And rather than showing that $20 billion of investment purchasing will occur at a certain interest rate, the curve representing the investment demand will indicate that 100 million commodities will be purchased by investors at that rate. With such changes from amounts of money to amounts of commodities, there are no changes in either the nature of the components that affect these markets or the nature of the curves that depict them. The advantage of describing the market components and the resulting levels of real income in such terms is that it is possible to identify the way that the changes in the level of prices affect the amount of commodities purchased. After all, if lower prices are to cause an increase in the number of commodities purchased, they must cause one or more of the different types of purchasers to buy more commodities.

Deriving Aggregate Demand Curves

A graphical representation of the conditions existing in an economy's money and commodity markets can be used to construct an aggregate demand curve showing the amount of commodities—the level of real income—that will be purchased in the economy at each level of prices. An example of such a representation is presented in Figure 11-1 for an economy in which only the propensity to save is affected by changes in the price level. Some of the components of the example economy's two markets have "r" superscripts. This denotes that they are depicting the economy's macroeconomic market relationships in real terms.

The basic procedure for constructing an economy's aggregate demand curve involves determining the economy's equilibrium level of real income at one level of prices and then repeating the income-determining procedure

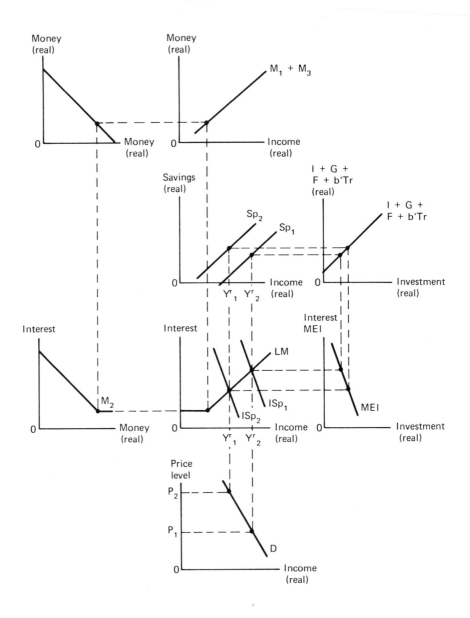

FIGURE 11-1
An aggregate demand curve.

for other price levels. Thus it requires the arbitrary selection of a level of prices and then the use of the commodity and money market curves that represent the conditions which will exist in the economy at this price level. For instance, notice that one of the total savings functions in the Figure 11-1 economy has the subscript P_2 to identify it as depicting the propensity to save that occurs in the economy when price level P_2 exists. Examination of the IS and LM curves which result from using that savings function indicate that, when price level P_2 exists, both markets will simultaneously be in equilibrium at an income level of Y^r_1. The combination of price and real income (P_2 and Y^r_1) thus represents one point on the economy's aggregate demand curve.

Other points on the economy's aggregate demand curve are obtained for different levels of prices by recomputing the equilibrium level of commodity purchasing based on the conditions that would exist in the economy's money and commodity markets at the other price levels. For instance, consider a lower price level such as P_1 which has no effect on any aspect of the two markets except that the lower prices cause the amount of goods and services purchased in the economy by consumers to rise at every level of real income. This increase is depicted with a new total savings curve, S_{P_1}; it lies below the original S_{P_2}, since more real consumption, and thus less real savings, occurs at the wage level and income distribution associated with every level of real income as a result of the lower level of prices. The new savings function for the lower price level means that at the lower level of prices there also will be a new IS curve (IS_{P_1}) and an increase in the economy's equilibrium level of real income to Y^r_2. Thus another possible combination of prices and equilibrium amounts of commodity purchasing is P_1 and Y^r_2. Other levels of prices yield other levels of real income. When the points representing each combination are joined, they form an aggregate demand curve like that in Figure 11-1. Each point on the curve represents the amount of commodities that will be purchased at a particular level of prices. The aggregate demand curve for the economy reflected in Figure 11-1 slopes down and to the right; more commodities will be purchased in this economy at lower levels of commodity prices.

THE SHAPE OF AGGREGATE DEMAND CURVES

Several theories have been advanced to describe the effect of the level of prices on the number of commodities purchased. The two most important, those of Keynes and Pigou, follow.

Keynes and the Effect of Price Changes

John Maynard Keynes considered the possibility that unemployed workers could find jobs producing commodities if they would accept lower money wages.[1] First, he acknowledged that lower wage costs might cause businessmen to be willing to produce and sell commodities at lower prices. Then he attempted to determine whether lower wages and prices would increase the amount of commodities purchased in an economy and thus increase the number of jobs available for the economy's workers. Basically, he examined each of the components of the money and commodity markets to see if it would be affected by lower prices and money wages. The only influence he found that might definitely tend to expand the level of commodity purchasing (when his reasoning is put in real terms) is that a decline in the level of wages and prices in an economy has the effect of increasing the real size of the economy's supply of money.

An economy's real supply of money increases when wages and prices fall because the existing amount of money in the economy can handle a greater amount of transactions. This is important, as Keynes noted, because the transactions associated with the purchasing of a given amount of commodities will no longer require so many of the economy's monetary assets. Consequently, there would tend to be a surplus of money as prices fell which could be used to bid up the price of the economy's financial assets and thus reduce the level of interest rates in the economy and cause more commodities to be purchased. How much the economy's level of real income would rise as the result of such a "general deflation" depends upon such things as the interest elasticity of investment demand and the multiplier effect of any initial increase that occurs in the level of income.

Keynes saw wage and price declines as causing no definite changes in any of the other determinants of the equilibrium amount of commodity purchasing such as the real consumption function, the real MEI, or the real level of government purchasing and transfers. According to him, and the economists who subsequently refined his position, there is nothing inherent in generally lower prices that would cause the consumers in an economy to change the proportion of each level of real income they are willing to allocate to consumption purchasing; the governments still would need and thus purchase the same number of commodities such as planes and roads as before; and investors would not change their willingness to make com-

[1] J. M. Keynes, *The General Theory of Employment, Interest and Money* (Harcourt, Brace, 1936), pp. 257–279.

modity purchases at each rate of interest because the percentage return to each potential new capital investment would remain the same since supply prices and expected costs and revenues would all tend to decline together in the general deflation.

Keynes did acknowledge, however, that there were other possible effects of a general wage and price deflation which might occur under certain circumstances and influence the level of commodity purchasing. Some of these are:

1. *Redistribution of income:* Money wages are only one of the costs of production that must be covered by the prices of commodities before business firms will actually be willing to produce goods and services. Thus, to lower the cost of producing commodities enough so that the businessmen will be willing to produce them at lower levels of prices, money wages might have to fall proportionally more than any decline in commodity prices. But a decline in money wages in excess of the decline in commodity prices means a decline in the real income being distributed to each worker and thus an increase in the levels of income going to non-workers. This may mean that real income is being redistributed from the workers, with their relatively high propensities to consume, to other individuals with relatively low propensities to consume.

   The possibility of such a redistribution occurring will be discussed in a later chapter. But should such redistribution occur when there is price deflation, there will be a decline in the proportion of each level of real income that will be used for consumption purchasing and thus a tendency for the money and commodity markets to be in equilibrium at lower levels of prices with even smaller total amounts of commodities being purchased. On the other hand, reductions in money wages could have just the opposite effect. This would occur if a reduction in wages results in the now cheaper labor replacing other factors in the productive process so that a proportionally greater number of workers are employed. Then a larger proportion of the economy's real income would be going to individuals with relatively high propensities to consume and the level of commodity purchasing in the economy might rise.

2. *Foreign purchasing:* A decline in prices in the economy relative to those in other economies may lead foreigners to increase the number of commodities they purchase. Whether this actually will occur is not certain. It depends on whether exchange rates change or the foreign economies retaliate against the possibility of losing sales by imposing tariffs or

quotas in order to prevent their buyers from switching to the economy with relatively lower prices.

3. *Expected future prices and wages:* Both the consumption function and the MEI of an economy may be affected if a wage and price decline is not expected to be permanent. Prices and wages that are thought to be temporarily low may cause the proportion of the economy's income devoted to consumption purchasing to rise as consumers act to take advantage of temporarily low prices in order to avoid making purchases later when prices are expected to be higher. Investment purchasing also may increase as investors take advantage of temporarily low supply prices in light of their thoughts that the sales prices of the goods and services produced by the acquired capital assets will be restored in the future. The reverse is true if wages and prices are expected to fall further in the future; consumers will tend to save more from their present incomes in order to buy later when prices are lower, and investors will not purchase as many new commodities because those they obtain will have to compete with similar assets that will not have to earn as much to cover their supply prices.

The Keynes effect of lower prices causing changes in the real size of an economy's money supply is presented graphically in Figure 11-2. The figure depicts the effects of the larger real supply of money that would exist in an economy when its prices are lower; it indicates that an economy's LM curve is shifted to the right by lower levels of prices and that its equilibrium level of real income is higher for each subsequent lower level of prices. But the equilibrium level of real income in the Figure 11-2 economy continues to rise only until the price level P_3 and the real income level Y^r_{200} are reached. Then any further decline in the level of the economy's prices, such as to P_2, merely increases the real supply of money in the economy and shifts its LM curve further to the right but does not lower the level of interest rates in the economy to cause more commodities to be purchased. There is no increase in the level of purchasing in the economy because all the additional real money caused by commodity prices below P_3 will be held by the owners of the economy's wealth. Since they hold the additional money rather than use it to buy financial assets, the economy's level of interest rates does not decline and no additional increments of purchasing occur to have a multiplier effect on the economy's equilibrium level of income. This is the essence of Keynes' thoughts regarding deflation: the liquidity trap means that there is some upper limit to the effects of a general wage and price deflation in terms of increasing the amount of commodities purchased in an economy.

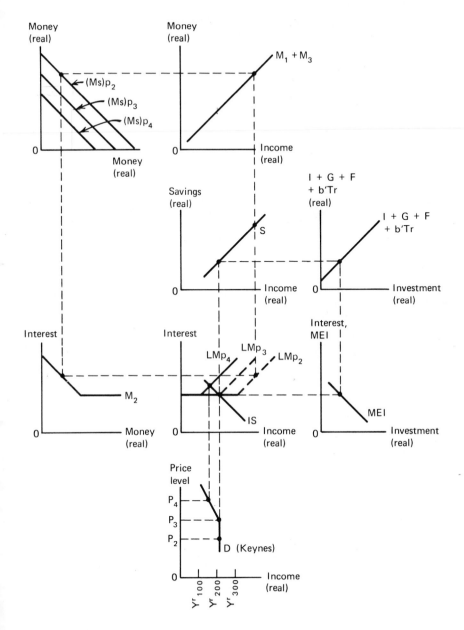

FIGURE 11-2
The Keynes effect.

Pigou and the Real-Balance Effect of Deflation

A. C. Pigou[1] and subsequent economists have rejected Keynes' notion that the impact of a decline in the level of an economy's money wages and prices was equivalent only to a change in the supply of money. They note that when commodity prices are lower, the savings that individuals have accumulated in the form of financial assets with fixed money values (debt instruments, fixed income streams such as pensions, and money assets such as coins, currency, and demand deposits) will have higher real values since they can be used to purchase more commodities. For example, if commodity prices are cut in half, each dollar's real value will be doubled because it can purchase twice as many commodities. Furthermore, the higher real value of financial assets which occurs when commodity prices are lower means that the owners of such assets will not have to save as much of their real incomes in the future to attain their savings goals. Therefore, Pigou and the others reason, when commodity prices fall and the pressures to save are reduced accordingly, more commodities will be purchased for consumption purposes at every level of real income. This means that lower prices will increase the number of commodities purchased in an economy by changing the economy's propensity to consume as well as by changing its supply of money and affecting its interest rates.

The effect of price changes that change both the real money supply and the propensity to consume is depicted in Figure 11-3. Notice that the economy's aggregate demand curve no longer becomes perfectly inelastic at some low level of prices as it does when only the Keynes effect is considered. Instead, more and more commodities will be purchased at lower and lower levels of prices. It is the increase in the proportion of income devoted to consumption, the shift in the consumption function, resulting from deflation that is the essence of Pigou's rejection of Keynes' conclusion that there is an upper limit to the increase in commodity purchasing that deflation can cause. This assumes, of course, that the Keynes and real-balance effects on commodity purchasing both exist in response to price reductions and are not offset by the effects of any income redistribution caused by the deflation or the effects of expected further wage and price reductions. More will be said in later chapters about the Keynes and real-balance effects and their relevance during periods of recession and depression when purchasing in an economy is too low so that production and employment in the economy is either receding or depressed below the levels which the economy is capable of providing.

[1] A. C. Pigou, "The Classical Stationary State," *Economic Journal*, **LIII**, pp. 343–351 (1943).

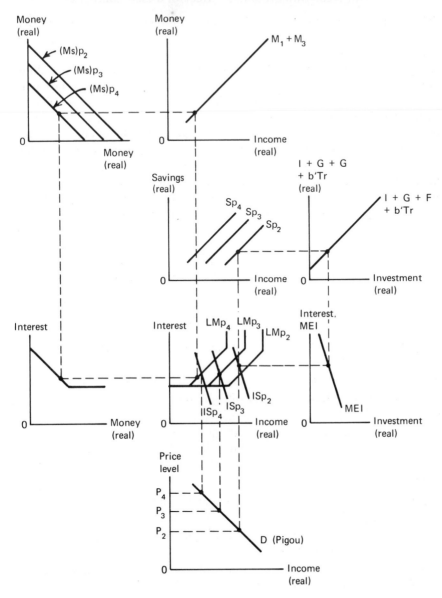

FIGURE 11-3
The Pigou effect.

The Real-Indebtedness Effect of Price Changes

The expansionary effect of price deflation through increases in the real value of assets with fixed money values may be partially offset by the effect of the lower prices on the level of real indebtedness. The basis for this effect is that smaller money incomes will be received when commodities are sold at lower levels of prices. Thus those who have obligations specifying fixed amounts of money payments will have to save larger proportions of their smaller money incomes in order to pay their obligations as they come due. The only financial obligations that do not have such an effect are those owed by governments that can create money; if they will create the necessary money, their obligations can be paid without forcing taxpayers to make additional savings out of their smaller money incomes. In any event, since the increased propensity to consume on the part of the holders of private and public debt instruments and recipients of fixed money incomes may be offset by the reduced propensities to consume of those who owe those obligations, the positive real-balance aspects of deflation tend to be limited to assets in the form of government liabilities such as money and debt and pensions that do not require additional savings in order that they be paid.

● REFERENCES

Ackley, G., "The Wealth-Saving Relationship," *Journal of Political Economy*, **LIX**, pp. 154–161 (1951).

Bowen, H., "Technological Change and Aggregate Demand," *American Economic Review*, **XLIV**, pp. 917–921 (1954).

Davidson, P., "A Keynesian View of Patinkin's Theory of Employment," *Economic Journal*, **LXXVII**, pp. 559–594 (Sept. 1967).

————, "A Keynesian View of the Relationship Between Accumulation, Money and the Money Wage Rate, *Economic Journal*, **LXXIX**, pp. 300–323 (June 1969).

Gallaway, L., and P. Smith, "Real Balances and the Permanent Income Hypothesis," *Quarterly Journal of Economics*, **LXXV**, pp. 302–313 (1961).

Glustoff, E., "On the Existence of a Keynesian Equilibrium, *"Review of Economic Studies*, **XXXV**, pp. 327–334 (July 1968).

Haberler, G., "The Pigou Effect Once More," *Journal of Political Economy*, **LX**, pp. 240–246 (1952).

Hansen, A., "The Pigouvian Effect," *Journal of Political Economy*, **LIX**, pp. 535–536 (1951).

Kalecki, M., "Professor Pigou and the 'Classical Stationary State' a Comment," *Economic Journal*, **LIV**, pp. 577–587 (1944).

Kessel, R., and A. Alchian, "Effects of Inflation," *Journal of Political Economy*, **LXX**, pp. 521–553 (1962).

Keynes, J. M., *The General Theory of Employment, Interest and Money* (Harcourt, Brace, 1936), Chapter 19.

Klein, L., "Theories of Effective Demand and Employment," *Journal of Political Economy*, **LV**, pp. 108–131 (1947).

Mayer, T., "The Empirical Significance of the Real Balance Effect," *Quarterly Journal of Economics*, **LXXIII**, pp. 275–291 (1959).

Melitz, J., "Pigou and the 'Pigou Effect': Rendez-vous with the Author," *Southern Economic Journal*, **XXXIV**, pp. 268–279 (Oct. 1967).

Peltzman, S., "The Structure of the Money Expenditures Relationship," *American Economic Review*, **LIX**, pp. 129–137 (March 1969).

Phelps, E., "Anticipated Inflation and Economic Welfare," *Journal of Political Economy*, **LXXIII**, pp. 1–17 (1965).

Pigou, A., "Economic Progress in a Stable Environment," *Economica*, **XIV**, pp. 180–188 (1947).

Power, J., "Price Expectation, Money Illusion and the Real Balance Effect," *Journal of Political Economy*, **LXVII**, pp. 131–143 (1959).

Thompson, E., "Debt Instruments in Both Macroeconomic Theory and Capital Theory," *American Economic Review*, **LVII**, pp. 1196–1210 (Dec. 1967).

Tobin, J., "Money Wage Rates and Employment" in *The New Economics*, Seymour Harris, Ed. (Knopf, 1947), pp. 572–587.

Aggregate Supply

12

The amount of commodities an economy can produce to be the real income of the economy's participants depends on the amount of labor employed by the economy's firms and the productivity of that labor. To the extent that they attempt to maximize profits and are free to employ as much labor as they desire, the firms of an economy employ only workers who add commodities to the firms' total production that are salable for at least enough to pay for the workers' services and for any other additional costs of production. For instance, a firm probably would be willing to hire a worker for $20 per day whose employment would raise its production by ten commodities of a type always salable at $4 each and would not cause the firm to bear any additional costs; even though the worker costs the firm an additional $20, he adds $40 in revenues. This is the same as saying that the firm hires the worker because he can produce ten additional commodities but only has to be paid wages that are equivalent to five of them.

Complicating the determination of how many workers a firm will be willing to hire is the possibility that, at some point, each subsequent worker may begin to add fewer and fewer commodities to the firm's total amount of production. Take, for example, a plant that could be operated by a firm except that there are no workers in it. Now picture a line of potential new workers walking into the plant. At first, each subsequent worker takes his place by an idle machine and commences producing so that the machine is no longer idle. But after a while, all the machines are busy. New workers then may assist the already employed workers and relieve them so that production can continue when they take breaks. Sooner or later, however, a new worker is going to walk in whose presence does not add anything at all to the total production coming from the plant; every machine will already be getting all the labor it can use.

In any case, the aforementioned firm will not be willing to keep hiring workers until it comes to that one who adds no additional production. Instead, it will add workers only until it reaches the last worker whose efforts will raise its total output by five commodities since the sale of these commodities for $4 each will only provide enough money to pay for his money wage of $20. The firm will not attempt to hire subsequent workers who add fewer than five commodities because the sale of these commodities would not bring in enough money to cover the costs of employing them. For instance, the firm would not hire a worker for $20 if he added only four commodities that could be sold for $4 each. His employment would increase the firm's costs more than its revenues.

It is also possible that the firm will not be able to hire all the workers it would like to employ. In this case, the amount of commodities produced would be determined by the number of workers willing to work and their productivity. Still another possibility to consider is that subsequent workers would not be employed because the additional commodities they produce could not be sold. These possibilities and their effect will be examined in subsequent sections of the book.

AGGREGATE SUPPLY CURVES

An aggregate supply curve represents the levels of real income that can occur in an economy at different price levels if there is a sufficient level of purchasing. This curve depicts the maximum amount of commodities which an economy's business firms would be willing and able to produce at each level of commodity prices that might exist in the economy. The maximum amounts may differ at different price levels because higher or lower commodity prices may cause more or fewer workers to be employed, and thus more or fewer commodities to be produced. For instance, an additional worker will not be employed in an economy in which workers are being paid $20 if he would add only four commodities that could be sold for $4 each. But will an additional worker be employed and the extra commodities produced if commodity prices are 50 percent higher so that the additional commodities can be sold for a total of $24? He will be hired if additional workers are available for a rate of pay of $24 or less. He will not be hired, however, if there are no more workers who will work at those wages. Thus the key to what happens to the aggregate supply of goods and services that could be produced at different levels of commodity prices depends on the availability of labor in the economy, the productivity of the workers, and the general level of wages that workers are paid. Whether all the goods and services that firms are willing to supply are actually produced at a given price level depends upon whether aggregate demand is high enough. Regardless of prices or productive capacity, businesses only produce what they can sell.

Labor Productivity

The total amount of goods and services produced and distributed in an economy, the real income of the economy's participants, depends on the number of workers employed, their skills and habits, the quantity and quality of the capital and other materials that they use, and the level of technology with which they work. A curve depicting the different levels of commodity production that would occur in an economy if different numbers of workers produce with the economy's capital and other productive materials is often referred to as an economy's "production function" since the level of production that can occur in an economy is a function of the number of workers employed in it.

Figure 12-1 presents an example of an economy's production function. The amount of commodities (Y^r) produced and distributed in the economy is measured on the vertical axis, and the number of workers (N) that are employed to produce the commodities is measured on the horizontal axis. For example, the employment of N_6 workers means the production of Y^r_{35} commodities. Also notice the shape of the production function in the figure: Because there is a limited amount of capital and other productive materials in the economy, additional workers add increasingly smaller amounts of additional commodities to the level of total production until worker N_9 is reached whose employment would result in no additional production; just as a line of workers filed into one plant and added diminishing amounts of additional commodities until one further worker's presence resulted in no

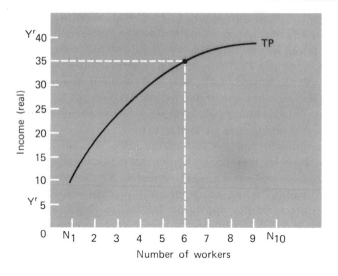

FIGURE 12-1
A production function.

additional production, so additional workers can be added to the other factors and materials possessed by all the firms in the economy until a worker is reached at N_9 whose employment would result in no additional commodities being produced no matter how he is employed.

Money Wages

Workers ordinarily are compensated for their services with monetary payment in the form of wages, salaries, or commissions. The payments usually are lumped together and discussed as "money wages" (Wm). It is also possible to convert such monetary payments into "real wages" (W^r), which represent the amounts of commodities that can be purchased with money wages. Firms, in essence, pay real wages because their money wages represent commodities that the firms must produce and give up to purchasers in order to raise enough money to pay the workers' money wages. And workers receive real wages because their money wages can be used to purchase commodities; in essence, money wages represent the amount of commodities that workers can receive when they provide their labor to the firms.

The level of real wages can be computed by dividing money wages by the price level. For instance, if the average level of money wages in an economy is $5,000 per year and the average level of commodity prices is $25, then the average real wage of the workers is equivalent to 200 commodities per year. Alternatively, money wages can be converted into real wages that represent relative purchasing power. For instance, if the level of money wages remains at $5,000 and the price level doubles, the number of commodities the firm must sell over and above the amount needed to cover the other costs of production so that workers can be paid, will be cut in half to the equivalent of those that could have been purchased for $2,500 at the original prices.

Each level of money wages in an economy can be represented by a curve that allows the level of money wages paid for the use of labor to be converted into the different levels of real wages occurring with each price level. Such a curve representing a specific level of money wages, a "money wage curve," is set on a graph measuring the various possible levels of commodity prices on the vertical axis and the various possible real wages on the horizontal axis; the curve is a rectangular hyperbola sloping downward to the right so that a change in the level of prices is associated with a proportional change in the level of real wages. An example of such a curve is presented in Figure 12-2 for an economy with a general level of money wages of $5,000.

It shows, for example, that if the general level of commodity prices in the economy is halved (to P_2), the number of commodities the firm must sell and the worker can obtain will be doubled.

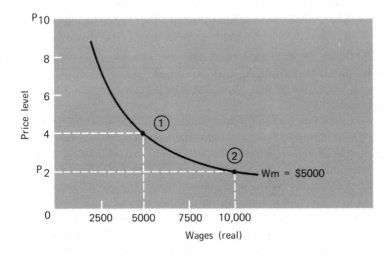

FIGURE 12-2
A money wage curve.

Individual wage differences. There is no conflict between the emphasis on the existence of a single level of wages and the obvious fact that workers may receive different sizes or types of wages for their services. What is being considered here is the general level of wages that an economy's labor force receives. There is no conflict because these general levels are based on, and determined by, the diverse wages of the individuals who compose an economy's labor force. Thus, just as one level of interest rates is used to represent the various different rates of interest that exist in an economy, and a single level of commodity prices is used to represent the general level of all the different commodity prices, so each level of wages represents the general level of the various wages received in an economy for all the different types of employment.

Labor Supply and Demand

An economy's firms employ workers to produce commodities when the commodities can be sold for at least enough to cover all the firms' costs of production. In other words, firms will desire to employ additional workers as long as they produce enough additional commodities to cover any other costs associated with their employment plus enough commodities to cover the real wages that must be paid to obtain their services. For example, if the employment of an additional worker would result in ten additional commodities being produced and additional capital and other costs equivalent to four commodities, a firm would be willing to hire another employee so long as his employment increased the real wages paid by the firm by six commodities or less.

The nature of the demand for labor. A curve depicting the production in excess of additional costs that will be caused in an economy by the employment of each subsequent worker represents the demand for labor in the economy when the commodities produced by the labor can be sold; it shows the maximum amount of labor that the economy's firms will be willing to employ at each level of real wages. Such a curve for most economies will slope downward and to the right to indicate that more labor will be demanded in an economy when the general level of real wages in the economy is lower. More labor tends to be demanded when real wages are lower because the lower wages result in labor being substituted for other factors of production in the economy's production process. Thus, the amount of labor that will be demanded at each wage level is influenced by the degree to which it is technically possible to substitute labor for the other factors and the response of the prices of the other factors to the tendency to adopt production techniques that employ more labor. Additionally, the elasticity of the demand for labor, as with the demand for capital, is affected to whatever extent the employment of additional labor results in additional production that drives down commodity prices. The demand for labor is also affected by the extent to which diminishing marginal productivity and increased nonlabor costs cause the additional workers to produce fewer and fewer commodities in excess of the nonlabor costs that result from their employment.

An example of a "labor demand curve" (Nd) is presented in Figure 12-3. It shows, for example, that employment of a maximum of N_6 workers will be desired by firms when the general level of money wages paid to the workers is the money equivalent of W^r_{15} in commodities. Even if more commodities could be sold, no more workers will be employed because profit-maximizing business firms will not pay more for additional workers than such workers contribute. On the other hand, the level of employment will not be lower under such circumstances because it would mean business firms generally were foregoing the employment of workers who would contribute more commodities than they would be given as wages.

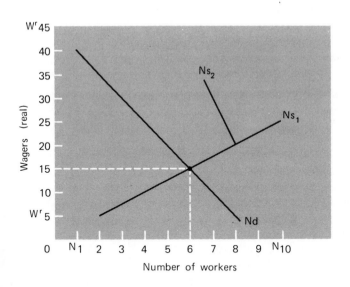

FIGURE 12-3
Labor supply and demand.

Purchasing and the demand for labor. It is important to note, however, that the actual amounts of workers that an economy's firms will desire to employ at each level of real wages can be below the levels represented by such a labor demand curve. This occurs because no firm will employ workers to produce commodities that it cannot sell. If the firms in the economy depicted by Figure 12-3, for example, are unable to sell more commodities than those produced by N_3 workers, they will hire no more workers at real wage level W^r_{15} even though they would be willing to hire as many as N_6 workers if they could sell the commodities. In other words, labor demand curves of the type described merely represent the maximum number of workers that will be demanded in an economy at each level of real wages when the production of those workers can be sold. The curves do not necessarily depict the actual number of workers that the firms in an economy will desire to employ.

Labor supply. The supply of labor in an economy (Ns) depends on the size of the working-age population and the degree to which such individuals can be induced to produce commodities instead of remaining at leisure. It is usually accepted that the more goods and services an economy's workers are able to purchase with the money wages they receive for their services, the more that the economy's labor force will be willing to give up its leisure and, instead, work. Curve Ns_1 depicts this situation in Figure 12-3; it shows more and more labor being supplied in an economy at higher levels of real wages.

Another possibility is that as real wages get higher, workers will begin to desire more and more leisure because they feel that they will be able to obtain enough goods and services with less work. In such circumstances, the quantity of labor supplied in an economy will fall if the economy's real wages rise past the amounts needed to obtain some desired level of commodities. This possibility is depicted in Figure 12-3 by labor supply curve Ns_2. It shows that the amount of labor supplied will fall if the economy's general level of real wages exceeds Wr_{20}. Alternately, less labor may be supplied at higher wage levels because married women may get out of the labor force if their husbands' incomes are high enough to support the family.

Further complicating the situation is the possibility that less labor will be supplied when there are higher levels of unemployment in an economy since some unemployed individuals may not even bother to offer to supply their labor when such circumstances exist if they feel that discrimination on the basis of such factors as education, age, and race will mean that they will not be able to obtain or retain employment until other more qualified or preferred individuals are employed. In any event, the latter situation does not affect what we represent with labor supply curves such as Ns_1 and Ns_2; such curves represent the amount of labor that will be supplied at each level of real wages if employment is available.

CONSTRUCTING AGGREGATE SUPPLY CURVES

The maximum amount of commodities that will be supplied in an economy at each level of commodity prices can be determined in the following fashion. First, the general level of commodity prices and the general level of money wages determine the level of real wages. Then the number of workers who will be employed at this level of real wages is determined by the demand for labor and the supply of labor; it is the smaller of either the number of workers willing to work at these real wages, or the number of workers desired by business at that level of real wages. It must be the smaller amount because employers will not hire workers just because the workers need jobs, and workers will not work in excess of the amount they want to work just because job vacancies exist. Finally, the total output which this number of workers will produce is determined by the nature of the economy's production function. The resulting output is the maximum amount of commodities that will be supplied at that price level; the combination of that price level and the resulting production of commodities is represented by one point on the economy's aggregate supply curve. Subsequent points represent the levels of production that will occur at other price levels if there is sufficient purchasing.

An economy's aggregate supply curve can be obtained graphically with the aforementioned procedure by placing the graphs containing the four curves in the particular relationship depicted in Figure 12-4 and proceeding in the manner described above.

The aggregate supply curve in this particular figure is designated S_{nc} to indicate that it is for an economy in which money wages do not change when there are different levels of commodity prices and real wages.

THE SHAPE OF THE AGGREGATE SUPPLY CURVE

The supply and demand components of its labor market determine the shape of an economy's aggregate supply curve because they determine the maximum level of employment that can occur at each level of real wages. Three possible situations relating to the flexibility of money wages can exist in the

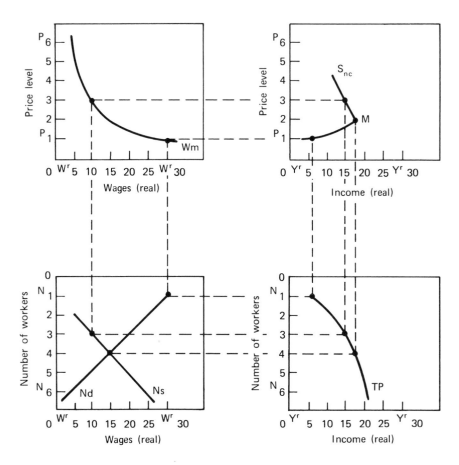

FIGURE 12-4
An aggregate supply curve.

labor market; each results in an aggregate supply curve with a different shape.

Flexible Wages

Economies with money wages that rise when there is a shortage of workers or fall when there is a surplus have aggregate supply curves like the one shown in Figure 12-5. For example, if the level of real wages in the economy depicted by Figure 12-5 is W^r_{30} because the level of commodity prices is

P_1 and the level of money wages is Wm_2, less labor will be demanded by firms in the economy than the economy's workers are willing to provide. However, since money wages are flexible, the unemployed workers will compete for jobs by offering to work for money wages lower than Wm_2. Money wages will fall until they reach the level of Wm_1 which yields a full-employment level of real wages (W^r_{15}) when the price level is P_1 so that there is no longer either a labor surplus or labor shortage in the economy. It is important to note that such a "full employment" level of real wages does

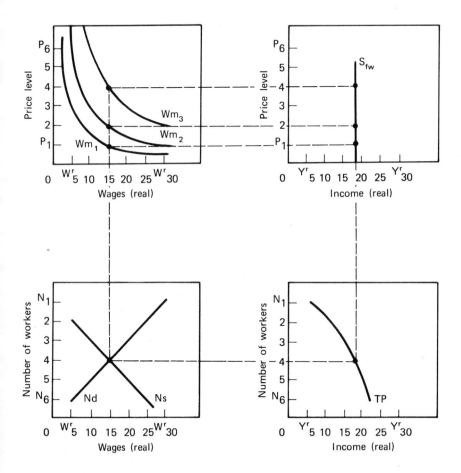

FIGURE 12-5
Aggregate supply with flexible wages.

not mean that everyone in the economy's labor force will be employed if there is enough purchasing; it means that everyone is employed except individuals in the process of normally moving between jobs and individuals who, though willing to work, are not able to work due to reasons of health, location, or ability. Thus N_4 workers will be employed at the price level of P_1 and they will produce Y^r_{18} commodities which is the full-employment level of production in the example economy. One point on the economy's aggregate supply curve, therefore, represents the combination P_1, Y^r_{18}, and it is attained by a decline in the level of money wages in the economy.

On the other hand, when prices are higher (P_4) so that the level of real wages in the economy is lower than W^r_{15} at the initial money wage of Wm_2, more workers will be demanded at the lower real wages than are willing to work. The shortage of workers at these price and money wage levels then will cause the economy's employers to bid for the available supply by offering higher money wages. Money wages and thus real wages will rise until a real wage level of W^r_{15} is reached. This requires a money wage level of Wm_3. When Wm_3 is reached, N_4 workers will be employed and they will produce Y^r_{18} commodities. Thus P_4, Y^r_{18} is another point on the economy's aggregate supply curve. Subsequent combinations of price and output will all fall onto a perfectly inelastic aggregate supply curve as is depicted in Figure 12-5. It is designated S_{fw} to note that it is for an economy in which there are flexible wages.

Wages Flexible Upward and Inflexible Downward

It is realistic to expect that a shortage of workers will lead the employers of an economy to offer, and the workers to accept, higher money wages. On the other hand, it is also possible that money wages are somewhat inflexible downward because of such things as the legal restrictions imposed by minimum wage laws and long-term labor contracts calling for the maintenance of specific rates of pay. An example of the effects of this situation on an economy's aggregate supply curve appears in Figure 12-6 for an economy which initially has a general level of money wages of Wm_2.

With money wages of Wm_2, price levels below P_2 will mean real wages high enough to entice more workers to offer their services than are demanded. And yet money wages in the economy will not fall to lower the level of real wages and eliminate the surplus of unemployed workers. The aggregate supply curve that results from such money wage inflexibility can be derived in the following manner. First, move from the price level to the money wage

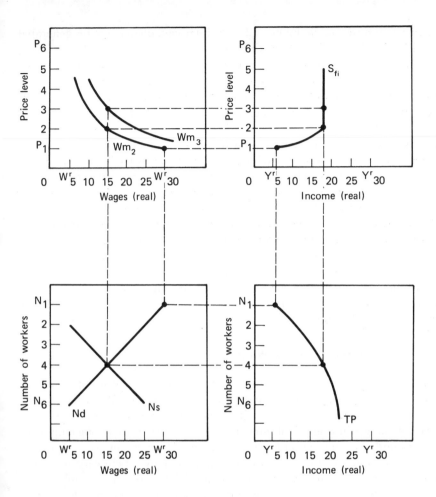

FIGURE 12-6
Aggregate supply with money wages flexible upward and inflexible downward.

curve in order to identify the general level of real wages in the economy and then down to the labor demand curve to determine how many workers will be employed at that level of real wages. Next, find the level of output associated with the workers who will be employed by moving to the production function. Finally, move from the level of total production up into the aggregate supply graph to a point opposite the price level. An example of this process is traced out in Figure 12-6. Subsequent points can be generated for all prices below P_2 by repeating the process.

Prices above P_2 (such as P_3) mean that the real wages associated with the initial money wage level of Wm_2 are so low that there is a shortage of workers. Employers will then offer, and workers accept, higher money wages. Thus, even though the level of real wages initially causes a shortage of workers at price level P_3 when the general level of money wages in the example economy is Wm_2, the level of money wages will rise until a real wage level of W^r_{15} is reached. Wm_3 represents the level of money wages needed to attain W^r_{15} when prices are at P_3. The aggregate supply at the price level P_3 then can be found by moving from P_3 to the new money wage curve (Wm_3) and then into the economy's labor market at W^r_{15}. At this level of real wages, N_4 workers will be hired, and the production function indicates that they can produce Y^r_{18} commodities. This is the amount of commodities that the economy's producers will supply at price level P_3 if the commodities can be sold. Subsequent points can be generated for other price levels above P_2. The result is an aggregate supply curve for the Figure 12-6 economy. It is designated S_{fi} to indicate that money wages in the economy are flexible upward and inflexible downward.

Inflexible Money Wages

The aggregate supply curve of an economy with money wages that neither rise nor fall in response to labor shortages and surpluses has already been considered in Figure 12-4. Such a situation can exist only if legal restrictions prevent changes in wages or if some form of collusion exists among employers to eliminate the competition for labor which leads to money wage increases, or among employees to prevent competition for jobs which leads to money wage decreases. Point M on the Figure 12-4 aggregate supply curve represents the highest level of production that can occur in the example economy. It occurs at price level P_2 because that is the only price level which will yield the economy's full employment level of real wages with the economy's existing level of money wages. All of the other price levels cause less than N_4 workers to be either demanded or supplied. Thus the economy's employers will employ only N_1 workers when the level of commodity prices in the economy is P_1. There are more workers willing to work than are demanded, but they are surplus or unemployed at that relatively high level of real wages. And they will remain unemployed because they cannot compete to drive down the level of money wages in the economy so that it will have a level of real wages (W^r_{15} for the Figure 12-4 economy) low enough to provide employment for all the workers in the economy who desire to work.

On the other hand, when real wages are below W^r_{15} because the level of commodity prices in the economy is higher than P_2, the opposite is true: there is a shortage of workers as fewer are supplied than are demanded at those relatively low real wages. Thus, at price level P_3 the economy's employers want to employ N_5 workers but only N_3 workers will work. There is a shortage because money wages are inflexible so that employers cannot increase the workers' real wages in order to get more of them to work.

● REFERENCES

Alchian, A., "Information Costs, Pricing, and Resource Unemployment," *Western Economic Journal*, pp. 109–128 (June 1969).

Bronfenbrenner, M., "A Contribution to the Aggregative Theory of Wages," *Journal of Political Economy*, **LXIV**, pp. 459–469 (1956).

Gallaway, L., "A Note on the Incidence of Hidden Unemployment in the United States," *Western Economic Journal*, pp. 71–83 (March 1969).

Hansen, W., "The Cyclical Sensitivity of the Labor Supply," *American Economic Review*, **LI**, pp. 299–309 (1961).

Keynes, J., *The General Theory of Employment, Interest and Money* (Harcourt, Brace, 1936), Chapter 20.

Kuh, E., "Measurement of Potential Output," *American Economic Review*, **LVI**, pp. 758–776 (1966).

Lucas, R. and L. Rapping, "Real Wages, Employment and Inflation," *Journal of Political Economy*, **LXXVII**, pp. 721–754 (Sept.–Oct. 1969).

Mishan, E. J., "The Demand for Labor in a Classical and Keynesian Framework," *Journal of Political Economy*, **LXXII**, pp. 610–616 (1964).

Robinson, J., "The Production Function and the Theory of Capital," *Review of Economic Studies*, **XXI**, pp. 81–106 (1953–54).

Tella, A., "The Relation of Labor Force to Employment," *Industrial and Labor Relations Review*, **XVII**, pp. 454–469 (1964).

Weintraub, S., "A Macroeconomic Theory of Wages," *Amercian Economic Review*, **XLVI**, pp. 835–856 (1956).

Macroeconomic Equilibrium

13

It was suggested in previous chapters that different levels of goods and services may be supplied or demanded in an economy at different levels of commodity prices. At any particular point in time, however, there can be only one level of prices, and it is important because it determines the level of output that will actually occur in the economy. That price level, in economies where prices are free to rise and fall, tends to be the one that causes the total amount of commodities supplied to equal the amount of commodities demanded. For example, in the economy depicted in Figure 13-1 the level of commodity prices will be P_6 if the economy's prices are free to rise and fall. The amount of commodities purchased and produced at that price level, the economy's level of real income, will be Y^r_{30}.

P_6 and Y^r_{30} are the equilibrium price and real income levels for the example economy. Any other levels result in pressures that will move the economy back to P_6 and Y^r_{30}. For instance, at a lower level of commodity prices such as P_3, more commodities will be demanded by purchasers than supplied by the economy's producers. This shortage will cause purchasers

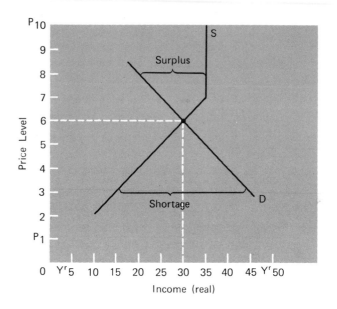

FIGURE 13-1
An equilibrium level of prices.

to compete for the smaller amount of available commodities by bidding up the price of the commodities. The shortage will continue and the price level will rise until prices are high enough (P_6) to induce enough additional production to eliminate the shortage. On the other hand, the level of prices in such an economy cannot permanently be higher than P_6, such as P_8, because the higher prices will cause the firms in the economy to be willing to supply more commodities than the various types of buyers are willing to purchase. This surplus leads to price cutting among the producers as they attempt to sell all they are willing to produce by offering their products to the purchasers at lower prices. Prices will fall until surpluses no longer exist. In the Figure 13-1 economy, that occurs at price level P_6.

AN ECONOMY IN EQUILIBRIUM

Simultaneously occurring with the determination of an economy's equilibrium levels of real income and commodity prices is the determination of the equilibrium amounts of its money market, commodity market, and labor market components. For instance, the determination of an economy's equilibrium level of income means the determination of the amount of money that will be used in the economy for transactions and precautions purposes, as well as the levels of interest rates, consumption, investment, taxes, and transfers that will occur in the economy.

By bringing together the various markets that exist in an economy, it is possible to construct a complete graphic model which can be used to identify the economy's equilibrium price level as well as its equilibrium level of real income and the value of each of its market components. Figure 13-2 presents an example of such a model for an economy in which prices are flexible, money wages are flexible above the Wm level depicted in the figure and inflexible below it, and price changes cause both a Keynes effect in the money market and a Pigou effect in the commodity market. The economy is in equilibrium at price level P_2 and real income level Y_e^r.

The equilibrium amounts of some of the market components that will occur in the economy have been identified with the subscript "e" to facilitate recognition. The figure indicates, for example, that the general level of interest rates in the economy will be i_e and the level of investment purchasing will be I_e. Graphically the amount of each component can be identified by working back from the equilibrium level of commodities and commodity prices as demonstrated by the broken line in the figure. The relevant consumption function and money supply curve are those for price level P_2.

THE NATURE OF MACROECONOMIC EQUILIBRIUM

Macroeconomic equilibrium exists when all of the markets of an economy are in equilibrium. In other words, it exists when the whole economy is in equilibrium. When commodity prices are flexible, all the markets will be in equilibrium when the amount of commodities demanded equals the amount of commodities supplied. If they were not equal the accompanying surplus or shortage of commodities would cause the price level to change, which might affect conditions in one or more of the markets. But will such a macroeconomic equilibrium ever occur in an economy and, if it does, will it always occur at the full employment level of production? Various aggregate demand and aggregate supply situations are considered below in an attempt to determine the conditions under which maximum levels of production will and will not occur in market economies such as the United States.

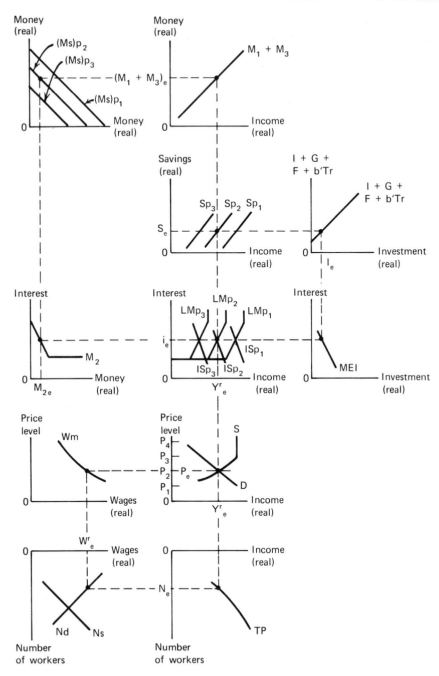

FIGURE 13-2
A complete macroeconomic model.

Flexible Prices with Money Wages Inflexible Downward

Even though prices are flexible and lower prices result in more commodities being purchased by causing Keynes or Pigou effects, inadequate aggregate demand (not enough commodities being purchased) can result in an economy's being in equilibrium with unemployment and less than maximum levels of production when money wages are inflexible downward. Such a situation is shown in Figure 13-3 for an economy whose aggregate demand

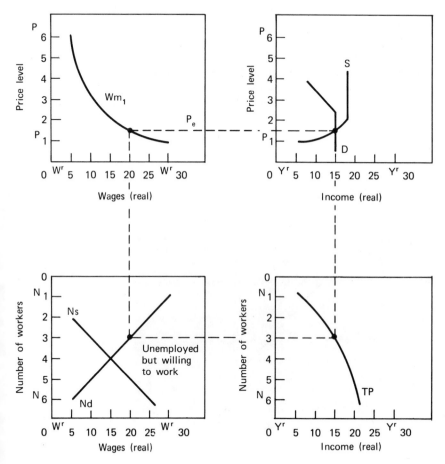

FIGURE 13-3
Unemployment equilibrium with the Keynes effect and money wages inflexible downward.

at different levels of commodity prices is based on the Keynes effect and whose aggregate supply is affected by money wages that are inflexible downward from their initial level of Wm_1. In this economy, the amounts of commodities purchased and produced are equal so that no further price declines occur at a level (Y^r_{15}) below the maximum that the economy is capable of producing. Thus, only N_3 workers are required to produce the commodities that will be purchased in the economy instead of either the N_5 who would be willing to work at the W^r_{20} level of real wages or the N_4 workers who would be employed at the maximum possible levels of production.

Similarly, unemployment levels of production due to an insufficient level of commodity purchasing are also possible when commodity prices are flexible and changes in the price level have a Pigou effect in the commodity market. Figure 13-4 represents such a situation. It depicts an example economy whose aggregate demand curve is based on the Pigou effect and whose aggregate supply curve is based on money wages that are inflexible downward. The economy is in equilibrium at unemployment levels of production.

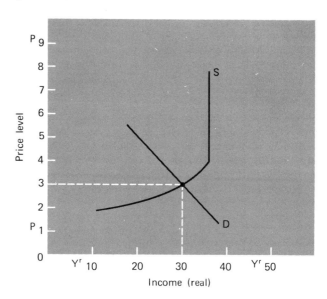

FIGURE 13-4
Unemployment equilibrium with the Pigou effect and money wages inflexible downward.

Flexible Prices and Wages: Keynes

Keynes rejected the idea that flexibility of both wages and prices would result in an economy automatically obtaining maximum levels of employment and commodity production. From his analysis of the influence of a wage and price deflation on the demand for commodities, discussed in Chapter 11, he inferred that it might even be fortunate that the wage levels of some economies were inflexible downward because this ensures that equilibrium will occur in these economies at some level of prices. It is fortunate because it averts the possibility of an infinite deflation with prices falling continuously as a result of the number of commodities supplied in these economies always exceeding the number of commodities demanded.

Figure 13-5 depicts the relationship of aggregate demand and supply which Keynes apparently thought could cause such a deflation when an economy has both flexible prices and flexible wages. Aggregate demand in the economy will not reach aggregate supply at any level of prices. Thus, with flexible wages and prices, the surplus of commodities caused by aggre-

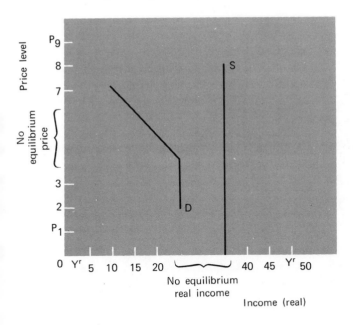

FIGURE 13-5
Infinite deflation with the Keynes effect and flexible money wages and prices.

gate supply's 'exceeding aggregate demand at every price level will result in a continual decline in wages and prices as producers and workers continually offer their commodities and labor at lower prices and wages in a futile attempt to find buyers and jobs.

Flexible Prices and Wages: Pigou

Pigou thought it conceptually possible that the levels of commodity production associated with the full employment of an economy's labor force and capital stock could be attained automatically if only prices and wages were flexible and would decline enough. His conclusion is based on his analysis of aggregate demand and the nature of aggregate supply when money wages and prices are flexible.

Figure 13-6 depicts such a situation with curves representing the nature of an economy's aggregate supply when money wages are flexible and aggregate demand when the level of prices affects the propensity to consume. It shows the economy in equilibrium at price level P_5 with the maximum

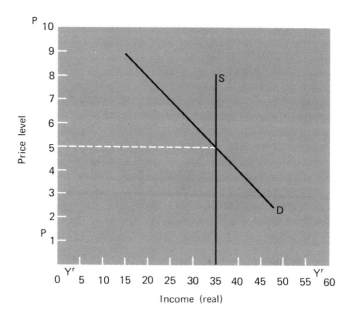

FIGURE 13-6
Full employment levels of production with the Pigou effect and flexible wages and prices.

possible amount of commodities being produced. Pigou did not advocate deflation as a cure for inadequate levels of production and employment. In fact, he thought that prices and wages were inflexible downward and that a general deflation was unlikely to occur. Thus, the importance of Pigou's analysis is theoretical; it refutes Keynes' conclusion that it is possible to have a less than full-employment level of income in a market economy where competitive forces brought into being by the existence of unsold commodities and unemployed labor cause wages and commodity prices to fall. In any event, as we earlier noted, the very process of wage and price deflation may itself lead to a reduction in the amount of commodities purchased in an economy. Specifically, if prices are falling and the reduction is expected to continue because full-employment levels of production have not yet been attained, purchasers may reduce the amount of commodities they purchase on the premise that they will be able to buy even more in the future when they expect prices to be even lower. On balance it appears that any production expanding real balance effects caused by deflation may well be swamped by the additional reduction in purchasing that will occur if prices are expected to be even lower in the future. Thus it is possible that even if deflation does occur, it might not eliminate unemployment caused by inadequate demand unless the deflation is expected to stop.

PRICES AND MONEY WAGES INFLEXIBLE DOWNWARD

The foregoing discussions have proceeded as if an economy cannot be in equilibrium until a level of prices is reached that will cause the amount of commodities demanded in the economy to be equal to the amount supplied. But will prices fall if business firms are willing to supply more commodities at some initial level of prices than are demanded? And will money wages fall if there is unemployment? They may not. Union pressure, long-term wage contracts, and minimum wage laws all tend to keep money wages from declining, while commodity prices may not fall due to lack of competition caused by government regulations and laws, private agreements between potential competitors, or the absence of competitors.

To appreciate the effect of inflexible prices, consider the situation depicted in Figure 13-7. Y^r_{18} is not the equilibrium level of real income in the economy if the price level is flexible upward and inflexible downward. For instance, if the price level is P_{15} and does not fall despite the fact that firms are willing to supply more commodities at that level than purchasers will buy, only Y^r_{12} commodities will be purchased. And if only Y^r_{12} com-

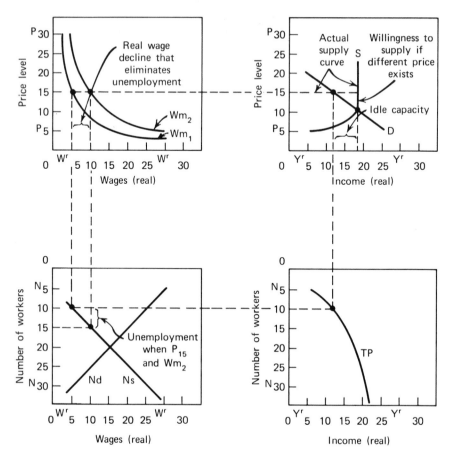

FIGURE 13-7
Inflexible prices.

modities are purchased, no more will be produced since firms will not produce commodities which they cannot sell. Furthermore, the production of Y^r_{12} commodities means that only N_{10} workers will be employed even though N_{15} workers are willing to work at the level of real wages that exists in the economy at money wage level Wm_2. Thus the economy is in equilibrium at price level P_{15}, income level Y^r_{12} and employment level N_{10}; there is no force to cause purchasers to buy more or fewer commodities and there is no reason why any other amount of production or employment should occur. For all practical purposes, then, the existence of downward price inflexibility means that the actual aggregate supply curve indicating the willingness of an economy's producers to supply goods and services should be perfectly horizontal at the existing level of prices until the maximum level of income that the economy's producers will provide is reached for that level of prices. In the Figure 13-7 example, the location of such an actual aggregate supply curve is initially identified with a heavy dotted line running from P_{15} to the initial aggregate supply curve. The relevant portion of the latter curve depicts how much the economy's producers would be willing to supply at different price levels above P_{15}.

Flexible Wages and Inflexible Prices

The effect of inflexible prices on the levels of production and employment in an economy remains basically unchanged by the existence of flexible money wages. All that would occur if there are unemployed workers at the real wages associated with the initial levels of money wages and commodity prices is that the level of money wages in the economy would decline until all the workers who are willing to work are able to find employment. Under the conditions reflected in Figure 13-7, the level of money wages in the economy will fall to Wm_1 as the unemployed workers compete for jobs. Then the economy's real wages will be so low that only N_{10} workers will be available to work; there will no longer be a surplus of labor to further bid down the level of wages. There are no other changes even though it is quite possible that there will be a reduction in the amount of commodities purchased by workers when their real wages are lower; the economy's aggregate demand curve already reflects the levels of purchasing that are associated with the levels of employment that occur at each level of real income. Thus, any tendency for less purchasing to occur in the Figure 13-7 economy when its level of real wages declines to W^r_5 is already depicted in the economy's aggregate demand curve.

Equilibrium at Maximum Levels of Production

Equilibrium at less than maximum levels of production is not the only possible fate of an economy which has some combination of inflexible prices and money wages. Indeed, the various possible situations of unemployment and less than maximum levels of production described in this chapter will not exist in an economy if its aggregate demand is sufficiently large. And aggregate demand can be large enough; conditions can exist in an economy's money and commodity markets which would result in total purchasing being high enough so that the economy's aggregate demand curve intersects the vertical axis of the aggregate supply curve.

For instance, consider an economy with the capacity to annually produce commodities that could be sold for $700 billion dollars; however, it is only producing $500 billion of them because that is all that can be sold at the existing level of prices. The attainment of maximum levels of production in the absence of a general deflation would require a $200 billion increase in the level of purchasing at the existing price level. But such an increase can occur and thus the economy can move from equilibrium at $500 billion to the equilibrium at $700 billion which will result in maximum levels of production. For instance, lower interest rates might encourage an increase in investment purchasing; lower personal income taxes might increase disposable income and result in more consumption; or the economy's governments might increase their purchasing. Furthermore, due to the multiplier effect, the initial change in purchasing may not have to be equal to the entire additional $200 billion.

The effect of an increase in demand is presented graphically in Figure 13-8. It represents an economy that initially is in equilibrium at an income level Y^r_{12}, employment level N_{10}, price level P_{15}, and money wage level Wm_1, with the nature of its aggregate demand represented by D_1 and its aggregate supply by S_1. But consider the effect of increasing aggregate demand in this economy to D_2: real income rises to the maximum level of Y^r_{18}, employment rises to N_{20} and unemployment disappears, money and real wages are bid up to Wm_2 and W^r_{15} respectively; but the economy's price level remains unchanged at P_{15}.

Demand increases and changes in aggregate supply. Figure 13-8 depicts an economy whose full employment level of production is restored by an increase in aggregate demand. The figure also indicates that the level of money wages in the economy will rise to Wm_2 as a result of the increase in the quantity of labor demanded caused by the increased ability of producers to sell goods and services. But the higher level of money wages means that there will be a change in the willingness of the economy's producers to supply commodities at the different possible price levels. Thus, a new aggregate supply curve (S_2) is needed to depict the producer's new willingness to supply. In the case of the Figure 13-8 economy, the increase in money wages to level Wm_2 means that the economy's producers will only be willing to supply full employment levels of production at price level P_{15} instead of at P_{10}. The reaction of the producers is predictable; they are still capable of the same physical levels of production but will now only

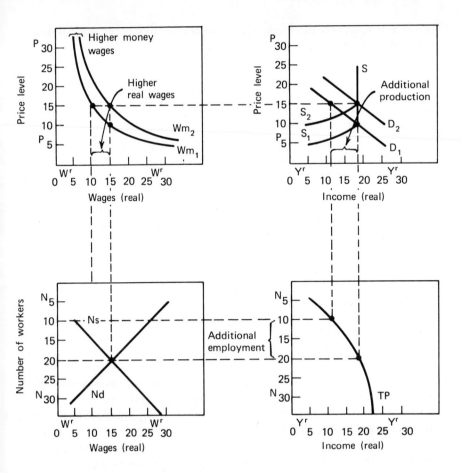

FIGURE 13-8
The effect of increases in demand.

be willing to provide it if they can get higher prices to cover their now higher costs of production.

WAGE AND PRICE FLEXIBILITY IN PERSPECTIVE

The conditions that were previously noted as sources of downward wage and price inflexibility were accepted by both Keynes and Pigou. Both Keynes and Pigou, despite their differences regarding the effect of lower prices and wages on the levels of an economy's production and unemployment, thought it unrealistic to expect wage and price deflation when total purchasing in an economy is not high enough to induce all the production of which the economy is capable. In other words, they thought it possible for an economy to be in equilibrium with less than maximum levels of production. Keynes was particularly pessimistic about the possibility that deflation would occur if an economy in such straits waited long enough. The pessimism fit the times in which he lived: England had for years been experiencing relatively substantial levels of unemployment and relatively little wage and price deflation. Furthermore, he noted that, since the only certain effect of deflation is an increase in an economy's real supply of money, deflation might not adequately increase the level of purchasing if the economy gets into the liquidity trap before it attains maximum levels of production. And in any event, said Keynes, the same effect of deflation can be had by increasing an economy's supply of money; therefore, there is no need to wait for deflation to occur.

Pigou's criticism of Keynes' reasoning was limited to whether it is conceptually possible for deflation to work if it ever did occur; he presented the real balance effect, which Keynes had omitted, in order to show that deflation could result in the purchase of the maximum amounts of commodities that an economy is capable of producing. But, owing to the lack of deflation that he observed during periods of unemployment, he neither advocated relying on deflation as a means of obtaining the purchase of all the commodities that the economy is capable of producing nor quarreled with the conclusion that an economy could be in equilibrium at less than maximum levels of production when prices or money wages are inflexible downward. Instead, he joined with Keynes and subsequent economists in accepting the tendency for downward rigidities in wages and prices and, thus, the need for greater amounts of money expenditures whenever an economy's production is below the level of which it is capable owing to insufficient amounts of commodities being purchased.

● REFERENCES

Davidson, Paul, "Income and Employment Multipliers and the Price Level," *American Economic Review*, **LII**, pp. 738–752 (1962).

Hansen, A., *A Guide to Keynes* (McGraw-Hill, 1953), Chapter 11.

Hahn, F. H., "Some Adjustment Problems," *Econometrica*, **XXXVIII**, pp. 1–17 (Jan. 1970).

Keynes, J., *The General Theory of Employment, Interest and Money* (Harcourt, Brace, 1936), pp. 303–304.

Kuh, E., "Unemployment, Production Functions, and Effective Demand," *Journal of Political Economy*, **LXXIV**, pp. 238–249 (1966).

Mundell, R., "A Fallacy in the Interpretation of Macroeconomic Equilibrium," *Journal of Political Economy*, **LXXIII**, pp. 61–66 (1965).

Patinkin, D., "Price Flexibility and Full Employment," *American Economic Review*, **XXXVIII**, pp. 543–564 (1948).

Economic Growth

14

A growing economy produces more commodities in each successive time period. One way growth occurs is when available but unused productive capacity in the form of unemployed labor and capital is restored to work by an increase in the amount of goods and services being purchased. In the long run, however, growth only occurs if an economy's productive capacity increases and the demand for its commodities is such that the additional capacity is used to produce more commodities.

Economists are concerned with an economy's growth and its growth rate for several reasons. First and foremost, growth means that more and more goods and services will be available to meet the needs of the economy. Furthermore, particularly in the United States, growth and the rate of growth are important because of the competition between different political and economic systems; many countries apparently are willing to emulate the system that is most successful in producing ever-increasing amounts of commodities.

THE GROWTH OF PRODUCTIVE CAPACITY

A host of factors influences the amount of commodities an economy is capable of producing when the maximum possible amount of labor is employed. Among them are such things as the quantity and quality of the capital stock with which the economy's labor force works, the level of education of the labor force, the cultural standards of the economy regarding the desirability of work, the degree to which competition exists to force producers to produce efficiently in order to keep their costs at competitive levels, and the level of technology with which the labor and other factors are combined in the productive process.

Over time it is possible that an economy's capacity to produce will be able to increase because of changes that might occur in either the size or the productivity of the economy's factors of production. For instance, so many newly produced capital assets might be purchased by an economy's investors that there is a net addition to the stock of capital in the economy. Alternately, growth may occur if an economy merely develops laws and patterns of behavior that are more conducive to high levels of commodity production. For example, judicial procedures might be strengthened to encourage more exact performance of contracts. Or the economy's labor force might become more accustomed to the punctuality required by such things as the need for periodic preventive maintenance.

Even if an economy's capacity to produce grows, there is still the possibility that production will not grow on a per person or per worker basis. For instance, there may be investment purchases that cause the capital stock of an economy to be expanded. But if the labor force grows at the same rate at which the stock of capital expands, each worker will tend to have the same amount of capital to use as before. Thus, although the economy will have the capacity to produce more commodities, there would be no reason for an increase to occur in the amount that could be produced by each worker. Increases in an economy's stock of capital which are accompanied by similar increases in the size of the labor force usually are referred to as "capital widening" additions to the economy's capital stocks. This is in contrast to the "capital deepening" which occurs when an economy's stock of capital grows faster than the size of the labor force so that, over time, the average worker in the economy has more and more capital assets with which to work.

HOW MUCH CAN AN ECONOMY GROW?

Economists have long attempted to determine how much an economy will grow, whether it will stop growing, and what it will be like when and if growth ceases. They are now generally optimistic about the possibility of continual growth. They concede, however, that there is an absolute limit to the amount of commodities which an economy's workers can produce at a given point in time. The limit is set by the existing quality of the economy's labor and its willingness to work, the quantity and quality of capital in the economy which is available for the workers to use, and the level of technology. On the other hand, these economists see no inherent reason to expect such an upper limit to remain unchanged over time. In the first place, forces exist in each economy which continually promote capacity-expanding increases in the quality of the economy's labor and the level of technology that the labor uses. Second, the wants of men for goods and services are thought to be so infinite in scope and quantity as to be insatiable. Consequently, there is no upper limit to the total amount of commodities desired by the residents of an economy and thus to the amount of purchasing that can occur.

The quality of labor rises as workers learn to use larger amounts of capital and higher levels of technology. Workers are under continuous pressure to develop their abilities to do this because of the larger incomes that increased productivity tends to bring. The basis for their continual efforts to improve their productive abilities is that the size of their incomes tends to determine both the amount of commodities which they will have available to meet their infinite needs and their social positions in the economy. Consequently, a man can satisfy more of his needs as well as tend to improve his position in society if he increases his ability to produce. Furthermore, other men who do not want him to move ahead of them socially must improve the quality of their own labor merely to keep their relative positions.

New and more productive technologies, on the other hand, tend to be sought by both the workers, who endeavor to enhance their value by increasing the amount of commodities they can produce, and employers, who expect to improve their profits and abilities to compete by increasing the amount of commodities that can be produced by the labor and capital they employ. An additional cause of the present optimism is the feeling that most economies can provide whatever amounts of additional capital that their labor forces may be able to use as a result of improvements in labor quality or technology. The stocks of capital can grow because not all incomes earned in producing commodities are completely spent for consumption purposes. Instead, some of the income is saved and thus, in essence, some commodities are not purchased by consumers but are available for economies' investors to purchase and use.

Needless to say, just because there is the possibility of growth it does not necessarily follow that it inevitably occurs. For many reasons, various economies, at different times, apparently have not grown. For example, the absence of an increase in demand prevents an increase in production and tends to retard the growth of an economy's productive capacity. No producer is going to produce additional commodities if he cannot sell them. And producers certainly will not be interested in expanding their plant and equipment if they expect it to stand idle due to a lack of purchasers.

Or economies may not grow because the quality of labor remains unchanged. For example, new technology and capital might be available but not used because individuals in the labor force are unmotivated due to such things as lack of education or the existence of a social structure requiring them to share any additional incomes which their production efforts might yield with entire families or villages. Still other economies may not grow because they cannot obtain the additional capital required to increase the productivity of their workers. This lack of capital is often observed in economies with low per-capita levels of commodity production and high rates of population increase. These economies' populations must consume just about all production in order to survive. Consequently, only a few commodities remain for use in replacing capital that is consumed during the production process and increasing the economy's capital stock. Then, as a result of the addition of only a small amount of capital to the economy's stock, total productive capacity increases little. Simultaneously, the populations of these economies also increase and the additional people consume the additional commodities that can be produced. Thus, such an economy is back where it started, having few commodities left that can be used as capital.

Economists have not always been so optimistic about the possibility of growth. The next sections of the chapter contain brief descriptions of a few of the more pessimistic views. Notice the diverse conclusions and how this diversity derives from the fundamentally different interpretations of the nature of market economies and their growth process.

The Stationary State

The English political economists of the nineteenth century basically adhered to the concept of the stationary state, as put forth by David Ricardo.[1] They thought that an economy's total production would tend to remain

---

[1] D. Ricardo, *The Principles of Political Economy and Taxation* (London, 1817). (Reissued by Everyman's Library, New York, 1955.)

stationary once it had grown to a certain size. Essentially, an economy's labor force receives wages for producing commodities with capital such as plant, equipment, and inventories that is owned and operated by the economy's capitalists. The level of wages is the key to growth because the more an economy's labor force is paid, the less profits are available for use by the economy's capitalists to obtain more capital assets. New capital assets, however, mean that more workers are needed and that wages will tend to rise and profits to fall. But any time workers' wages rise above the minimum subsistence level because of an increased demand for labor to operate new capital assets, these workers have more children who soon join the labor force. The new workers then compete for the available jobs and drive the level of wages in the economy back down toward the subsistence level.

But the additional children also mean that more food is needed in the economy and this causes food prices to rise to levels needed to cover the costs of bringing less productive land into cultivation. The higher food prices mean that the level of money wages in the economy will not drop as far before they reach the subsistence level as they had been previous to the initial wage increases that resulted in the larger population. Thus, each successive time period results in higher and higher money wage levels and smaller and smaller profits available for use to expand the amount of capital in the economy. Finally, labor costs will be so high owing to the high food prices that profits in the economy will only be high enough to replace used-up capital. No more capital will be accumulated and thus production will not rise. The economy's production will be in a stationary state.

The Marxian View

Marx saw economies where commodities are produced for purchasers by private producers as having two classes of people involved in the productive process—workers and capitalists.[1] The capitalists employ the workers and pay them wages. The difference between the wages which workers are paid and the value of the commodities which they produce Marx called "surplus value." It is the profit of the capitalists and, according to Marx, it exists because capitalists exploit their workers by paying them less in wages than the value of the commodities they produce. The capitalists will will use the surplus value to obtain even more commodities to use as capital in order to increase the productivity of their workers. Then, when the

[1]A detailed discussion of the Marxian view of capitalist development can be found in most histories of economic thought or economic development textbooks.

workers become more productive, fewer workers are needed to produce the commodities which the capitalists can sell.

According to Marx, the capitalists then will fire some workers in order to reduce wage costs. Furthermore, because idled workers are ready to take over the remaining jobs, the capitalists will be able to work the rest of the workers longer and harder for even lower wages. Each capitalist will take such actions because if he does not and the others do, they will have lower wage costs than he and he may no longer be able to sell his products at competitive prices and still remain in business. Needless to say, an economy's workers will be made more miserable by such activities.

Concomitant with the decline in wages there will tend to be a decline in the amount of commodities which the workers can purchase and thus a reduction in the number of commodities which the capitalists can sell. As a result of the reduced sales and lower prices caused by the competition to sell to the remaining buyers and their inability to wait until the situation improves, the smaller capitalists and those who do not reduce their workers' wages and work them harder will fail and join the unemployed workers in what Marx called the "Industrial Reserve Army."

Finally, as a result of more misery and fewer capitalists, those capitalists who are left again will tend to be making profits. But again this surplus value will be invested and again the workers will become more miserable and again some of the economy's capitalists will fail. In each time period this will occur until the whole system of production collapses and the ever more miserable workers finally assume control of the economy's production from the ever smaller number of capitalists.[1]

The Stagnationists

Keynes suggests in *The General Theory* that it is possible for an economy to become so fully stocked with capital assets relative to its technology and supply of labor that the MEC of any potential increment to the economy's stock would be equal to the economy's minimum rate of interest.[2] Then

---

[1] After the collapse, according to Marx, the production and distribution of commodities on the basis of purchasing will be eliminated. Instead, production and distribution will be based on communal cooperation and individual need after a temporary period of socialism during which all the institutions of capitalism are removed. Unfortunately for his followers, Marx wrote primarily about why market economies would fail. He left them with the dilemma of finding a way to organize an economy's production and distribution on the basis of cooperation and need.

[2] J. Keynes, *The General Theory of Employment, Interest and Money* (Harcourt, Brace, 1936), pp. 320–326.

---

there would be no investment purchasing except to replace the capital assets that are used up during the production process. Keynes, in essence, goes on to note that under these "full investment" circumstances there may not be enough nonconsumption purchasing to offset the savings that would occur in the economy at the full employment level of income that it had previously been obtaining as a result of investment purchasing to expand the stock of capital. As we have seen, the equilibrium level of income in such an economy would be below the full employment level. Figure 14-1

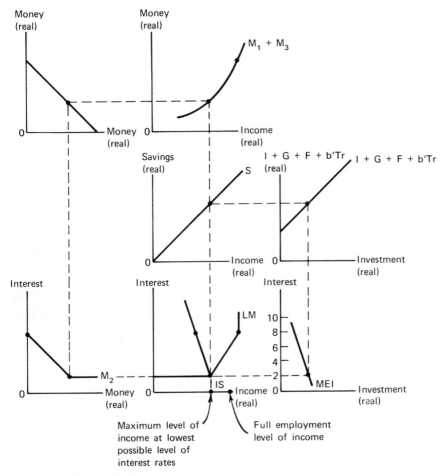

FIGURE 14-1
Full-investment levels of income.

depicts an economy under such circumstances. The economy's minimum rate of interest is 2 percent and the investment and other nonconsumption purchasing is insufficient to get the economy's equilibrium level of income to full employment.

Keynes, in fact, seems to attribute the depressions of the national incomes of Great Britain and the United States in the 1930's to the capital that previously was accumulated in such large amounts in these countries. The MEC's of the remaining potential additional capital assets tended to be below the existing low rates of interest and this, in turn, caused investment purchasing to be reduced to the replacement level and the economies to stagnate at income levels below those needed for full employment levels of production.

Alvin Hansen and others further expanded the "stagnation thesis" that there may not be enough investment and other nonconsumption opportunities to carry investment purchasing to the levels required to maintain full employment levels of total purchasing.[1] They emphasize several factors in their explanations of the absence of investment purchasing and, thus, the cause of the stagnation of the United States' economy in the 1930's. In the first place, they note that there was a reduction in the amount of capital required to support the technological advances occurring in the society. In the nineteenth and early twentieth centuries the new technology took the form of great new industries such as railroads, automobiles, and steel which required large amounts of capital. But by the 1930's, the technological advances primarily involved either new capital-saving methods of producing the products of the great industries or new and improved consumer durables, such as radios, whose production required relatively low amounts of capital per unit of output. Also contributing to the decline in the investment, according to these economists, was the decline in the rate of population growth and the end of the "frontier." These resulted in a reduction in the rate at which new houses, schools, and roads were purchased by individuals and governments.

THE RATE OF GROWTH

The rate at which the equilibrium levels of an economy's commodity production and purchasing can grow has been suggested by the work of various economists. In the following pages the analyses and reasoning of several of them will be examined. The analyses are based on oversimplified

[1] A. Hansen, *Fiscal Policy and Business Cycles* (Norton, 1941), particularly pp. 13–65.

assumptions concerning the nature of economies, but oversimplification is not bad in and of itself since reasoning and identification necessarily begin somewhere. Moreover, their analyses draw attention and understanding to various key aspects of the growth of modern, market-oriented economies.

Domar and the Dual Role of Investment

Evsey Domar's basic analysis[1] is an attempt to determine the rate at which investment purchasing must increase in an economy if full employment levels of production are to be maintained. The analysis relates to the dual nature of investment purchasing. Such purchasing has a dual nature because it not only influences the total amount of commodity purchasing in a given time period, but also it tends to increase the economy's stock of capital and thus to expand the economy's capacity to produce in subsequent periods.

To illustrate the implications of investment's dual role as seen by Domar, consider an economy having the following characteristics: every $4 of investment purchasing acquires enough capital to produce $1 of additional commodities in each subsequent time period; the average and marginal propensities to save are 40 percent of the level of income so that all investment purchasing has a multiplier effect of $2\frac{1}{2}$ on the level of total investment purchasing; wages and prices are inflexible downward; $36 billion of investment purchasing has just occurred; and the economy is in equilibrium at maximum levels of production with an income level of $90 billion. Following Domar, the $36 billion of capital commodities acquired with the investment purchasing will increase productive capacity by $9 billion to $99 billion in the subsequent time period because of the 4:1 capital to output ratio. Then, since the investment purchasing expands the capacity of the economy to produce, merely repeating the $36 billion of investment purchasing in the subsequent time period will not result in enough total purchasing to obtain full employment levels of production. Instead, a new and higher level of investment purchasing of $39.6 billion is needed. This higher amount of investment purchasing is required if the economy is to have the $99 billion of total purchasing it needs to attain the new full employment level of production.

Furthermore, the level of investment purchasing will have to be even larger in every subsequent period if full employment levels of production are to be maintained. For instance, in the next period the amount of investment purchasing will have to be $43.56 billion because the $39.6 billion

[1] E. Domar, "Expansion and Employment," *American Economic Review*, **XXXVII**, pp. 34–55 (1947). Reprinted in *Macroeconomic Readings* J. Lindauer, editor. (The Free Press, 1968).

that preceded it will increase the economy's productive capacity from $99 billion to $108.9 billion.

It is obvious from the previous example that, in the absence of other changes, in every time period the amount of investment purchasing in an economy must be larger than the amount that preceded it if full employment levels of production are to be maintained. But how much larger? Domar derives a formula that can be used to answer this question. But this formula has another use. Because he relates an economy's productive capacity to the capital that its investment purchasing obtains, Domar's rate at which an economy's investment purchasing must grow to provide full employment levels of production is also the rate at which the economy's productive capacity and income will grow when there is full employment. The following are the essences of the components with which Domar derives his formula.

The potential increase in capacity. The change in the amount of commodities which an economy can produce (ΔY_p) from one time period to the next depends on how much investment purchasing (I) occurs and on the relationship between the additional capital it provides and the economy's capacity to produce additional commodities. Domar depicts this relationship with the symbol σ. For example, an economy's σ or output to capital ratio is 1:4 if, on the average, it takes $4 of investment purchasing to give an economy the capacity to produce $1 more of commodities in each subsequent time period. The increase in capacity that will occur during any one time period can be depicted algebraically:

$$\Delta Y_p = \sigma I$$

The equation simply states that the increase in the amount of commodities which the economy can produce is equal to the amount of investment in the previous time period multiplied by the economy's ratio of output to capital. For example, if an economy's σ is 1:4 and investment purchasing of $100 billion occurs, the economy will be capable of producing $25 billion of additional commodities in each subsequent time period.

The necessary increase in demand. There must be an increase in the amount of commodities demanded in an economy if its additional capacity is to be utilized. In order to get such an increase in the absence of changes in the other factors, such as foreign purchasing, which affect the level of total purchasing, investment must be even higher than it was in the previous period of time. The amount by which investment purchasing must rise (ΔI) is determined by the multiplier and the increase in total purchasing that must occur if full employment levels of production are to continue (ΔY_d). Domar's multiplier is $1/\alpha$ where α represents the marginal propensity to save. Thus, algebraically, investment purchasing must rise, if full employment levels of production are to be maintained, so that:

$$\Delta Y_d = \Delta I \, \frac{1}{\alpha}$$

(The equation states that the increase in the amount of commodities demanded is equal to the increase in the level of investment purchasing times the multiplier. For example, if an economy's total purchasing must rise $25 billion and the multiplier is 5, the economy's investment purchasing must rise by $5 billion.)

The required proportion of new investment. The complete use of an economy's productive capacity requires that increases in the capacity to produce be exactly offset by increases in the demand for what it can produce. This identity can be depicted algebraically:

$$\Delta Y_p = \Delta Y_d$$

This requirement for full employment can be made somewhat more complex by substituting in the basic components of Y_p and Y_d. The result is Domar's "Fundamental Equation":

$$I\sigma = \Delta I \, \frac{1}{\alpha}$$

The equation can be solved for the proportion of an economy's total investment that must be additional investment (ΔI) in each time period by multiplying both sides by α, then dividing them by I. The result is simply:

$$\frac{\Delta I}{I} = \alpha\sigma$$

Thus, in an economy in which both the average and marginal propensities to save (α) are 40 percent and the ratio of output to capital (σ) is 1:4 or 25 percent, investment purchasing will have to increase from each time period to the next by 10 percent ($\Delta I/I$) if full employment and maximum levels of production are to be maintained. Then, since there is a constant relationship between additions to capacity and investment, each subsequent level of productive capacity will exceed the previous level by the same proportion.

That such increases must occur if full employment is to be maintained can be seen by examining the economy that was initially at full employment with an investment level of $36 billion and an income level of $90 billion. Then in the next time period, the economy went to $39.6 billion of investment and $99 billion of income. In other words, its investment purchasing rose by $3.6 billion or 10 percent of the previous level of investment and its total purchasing rose by $9 billion or to a level 10 percent above the previous level of income.

Full employment rates of growth are not inevitable. Investment purchasing in an economy does not automatically grow at the rate required to provide full employment levels of purchasing. And if it does not grow at that rate the result may be either excess productive capacity and unemployment, or inflation. For instance, if investment purchasing does not rise by the required rate, producers will not be able to sell all the commodities they are willing to produce. They then may tend to cut back on investment purchasing in subsequent periods since they do not need as much new capital. This will cause even lower levels of total purchasing and even further reductions in the amount of capital that will be acquired.

Consider what would happen if the example economy's investment purchasing and level of income are initially at $36 billion and $90 billion and then investment purchasing rises only to $38 billion instead of $39.6 billion. The capital acquired by the initial $36 billion of investment purchasing will increase the economy's capacity to produce to $99 billion, but total purchasing will rise only to $95 billion. Thus $4 billion of the economy's productive capacity will be idle. Then, if the economy's producers react to the excess capacity by cutting back their investment purchasing to $36 billion in the next period, the economy's purchasing will be reduced to $90 billion even though the previous $38 billion of investment purchasing increases the economy's productive capacity to $108.5 billion. Thus the proportion of idled productive capacity will be even greater in the subsequent time period.

On the other hand, if the economy's producers raise their level of investment purchasing faster than the required rate, they will find themselves short of capacity because of more commodities being demanded than are supplied. Their reaction to this probably will be to increase their investment purchasing at an even higher rate in order to take advantage of the existing sales opportunities. Should this occur, there will be a cumulative tendency toward inflation because the economy's prices will grow ever faster as the rate of increase in investment purchasing continually and futilely rises to provide all the commodities the purchasers desire.

Consider what would happen in the example economy if instead of investment purchasing being increased from $36 billion to $39.6 billion, it is increased to $44 billion. Productive capacity will have risen to $99 billion as a result of the $36 billion of investment purchasing in the previous time period, but total purchasing will rise to $110 billion. The resulting shortage of capacity might cause producers to increase investment at an even faster rate such as to $52 billion in the next period. But this would cause an even greater gap as the $44 billion of investment preceding it would increase productive capacity only by another $11 billion to $110 billion while the $52 billion would cause $130 billion in total purchasing.[1]

Domar and Harrod

Domar's work has such a strong similarity to that of Sir Roy Harrod that the two analyses often are lumped together and referred to as the "Harrod–Domar" analysis. Harrod's analysis[2] differs slightly in that it emphasizes the effect of expected changes in an economy's level of income on the amount of investment purchasing and thus on the actual level of income in the economy. It is based on the assumption that when producers expect an economy's level of income to rise, they will make investment purchases in order to be able to produce the additional amounts of commodities they think they will be able to sell. In essence, Harrod points out that if producers expect a certain increase in the future level of income, they will make investment purchases in the present time period which are just large enough to offset the savings at the present full employment level of income and so cause that level, in fact, to occur.

An example of Harrod's reasoning. Consider the economy in which $4 of capital is needed to produce $1 of commodities and the average and marginal propensities to save are 40 percent. Following Harrod, in each succeeding time period the level of income in the economy must be expected to be 10 percent higher than the level that existed in the previous period. Only if its producers expected income to rise by that rate will they make the investment purchasing needed to cause full employment levels of income.

For example, start with an economy in which full employment levels of production can be obtained in the present time period with $90 billion of

[1] The considerable problems of inflation, income fluctuations, and unemployment which might arise in an economy when such differences exist between the level of its purchasing and the size of its productive capacity will be discussed in detail in subsequent chapters.
[2] R. Harrod, "An Essay in Dynamic Theory," *The Economic Journal*, **XL**, pp. 14–33 (1939).

purchasing. If the producers expect the economy's income to reach $99 billion in the next period, they will desire to have $9 billion of additional productive capacity available by the beginning of that period. Harrod's point is that the $36 billion of investment purchasing which they will make in the present time period in order to expand capacity by $9 billion in subsequent periods is exactly the amount needed to offset the savings in the present time period and cause the economy's level of income to be $90 billion. Thus producers' expectations regarding the future level of income cause a full employment level of income to occur in the present period. Furthermore, if full employment levels of production are to be maintained in the next period, the producers will have to expect another 10 percent increase in the level of income to $108.9 billion. Only if the businessmen think that they will need $9.9 billion of additional capacity will they make the $39.6 billion of investment purchasing needed to cause the next full employment income level of $99 billion.

The warranted rate. The "warranted rate" is Harrod's term for the rate at which the level of income must be expected to increase in each time period if full employment levels of production are to be maintained. It is the only rate of increase in the level of income that actually warrants the expectation by causing the expected level of income to occur. And Harrod provides a basic formula for computing this proportion: $Gw = s/Cr$, where Gw represents the warranted rate, Cr represents the ratio of capital to output, and s is the average and marginal propensity to save. The value of the required proportion of the previous level of income that must be added if the economy continually is to grow fast enough to maintain full employment can be determined if the value of its Cr and s components are known; it is the only rate that results when s is divided by Cr. For example, if an economy's Cr is 4 to 1 because $4 of additional capital is required to produce $1 more of commodities and if its average and marginal propensities to save are 40 percent, its warranted rate or Gw is 10 percent since $.10 = .40/(4/1)$.

The Validity of the Harrod–Domar Type of Analysis

Both the Harrod and Domar analyses can be criticized on several counts. First, they make unrealistic assumptions to simplify their presentations. They use marginal and average propensities to save that are equal and do not change as the level of income changes. Harrod and Domar also over simplify as they define all nonconsumption purchasing as investment purchasing and assume that all such purchases have the same effects on the economy's productive capacity. In fact, it might be reasonable to expect that foreign and government purchasing would have a different effect on an economy's capacity to produce goods and services than would purchasing that acquires plant, equipment, and inventory. On the other hand, if a stable relationship exists between the level of income in an economy and the levels of government, foreign, and investment purchasing, then the Harrod–Domar use of a constant investment-output ratio would be reasonable. For example, if plant and equipment have a 2 to 1 output ratio and the economy's government and foreign purchasing provide the same proportion of the economy's level of income as does investment purchasing, then there would be $2 of government and foreign purchasing for every $2 of investment purchasing and a constant 4 to 1 ratio between nonconsumption purchasing and output.

A much more serious drawback, however, is the emphasis in the Harrod and Domar analyses on the importance of capital, however defined, to the productive capacity of an economy. Specifically, the analyses ignore the possibility of changes in an economy's productive capacity such as could be caused by technological improvements or changes in the size of its labor force. For instance, if an economy's labor force grows at the rate of 2 percent per year and its technology is such that there is a constant relationship in the economy between labor and capital, it means that the economy's stock of capital and thus its capacity for commodity production can grow a maximum of 2 percent per year.

Harrod labels as "the natural rate" the maximum rate at which an economy is capable of increasing its capacity to produce. Since the natural rate may be lower than the warranted rate, it is possible that the sales expectations of the producers may not be realized, and as a result, they will further reduce their investment purchasing to such an extent that the level of income in the economy actually will increase at a rate that is lower than the natural rate. This is possible, however, only if nothing else occurs in the economy to offset the tendency toward inadequate amounts of investment purchasing. But, as has been shown, total purchasing can be affected by various factors other than investment purchasing. And thus there is no inherent reason why an economy must stagnate with a low rate of investment and income growth just because there is an initial lack of investment purchasing.

Furthermore, even if investment purchasing is not large enough to prevent departure from the required rate of investment growth or the warranted rate of income growth, there will not necessarily be a cumulative move away from full employment. Instead, a host of automatic stabilizers might come into being to offset, at least partially, the effects of the inadequate amount of investment purchasing. For instance, as an economy's income falls due to a reduction in investment purchasing its taxes might fall and its transfers might rise, and the rate of interest in the economy might decline as less money is demanded for transaction purposes.

NEOCLASSICAL GROWTH THEORY

The classical Harrod–Domar analysis uses fixed capital-output ratios to suggest that the rate of growth of an economy's level of income will increase when there is an increase in the propensity to save and a corresponding increase in the level of investment purchasing. The neoclassical growth theorists agree that such an increase in an economy's stock of capital might tend to increase its productive capacity. But they do not think it is inevitable. They note, instead, that in the absence of technological changes, diminishing returns to increments of capital may occur as more capital is available for use by an economy's stock of labor. And if diminishing returns occur, the economy's productive capacity will not grow as fast as the rate at which capital is being accumulated. Thus to maintain a long run per person rate of income growth faster than that allowed by technological advances would require the impossible in the form of an ever increasing rate of capital accumulation. This is impossible in the long run for it means that at some point in time the required rate will have to be so high that all of the economy's income is devoted to capital. Furthermore, the neoclassical theorists note that at some point in time so much capital may be accumulated relative to the economy's stock of labor that a long-run productivity rate is reached wherein any additional savings that is devoted to investment will only increase the level of income an equal amount so that even in the long run no increase in consumption is possible. Then there would be no purpose served by accumulating additional capital until there is either an increase in the economy's labor supply or an increase in technology that raises the productivity of the economy's capital stock. One main point of the neoclassical economists is that an economy's growth rate cannot be permanently increased by increasing the percentage of income devoted to capital accumulation. Their second main point is that fewer goods and services will be available for noninvestment uses even if such investment efforts are made.

Figure 14-2 depicts the neoclassical analysis of capital accumulation. It depicts the effects of technological changes that increase the marginal productivity of capital per worker over time and specifically depicts an economy having technological changes sufficient to increase capital productivity per worker enough to have a 4 percent annual increase in the size of the stock of capital used by each worker without causing a reduction in the marginal productivity of capital. The economy opens in 1970 with an initial marginal productivity of capital based on a stock of capital per worker of 100. As a result of lower interest rates, the economy accumulates capital per worker at the rate of approximately 6 percent per year in 1972, 1973, and 1974 even though productivity only rises enough to allow for a 4 percent annual increase in the stock of capital per worker without causing a reduction in the marginal productivity of capital. After 1974 when the economy's capital stock per worker reaches 112.36, however, the capital stock per worker need only rise at the rate of 4 percent per year in order to obtain maximum levels of production, and still cover the long run rate of interest that is desired for the economy.

If the example economy's labor supply rises 2 percent per year and an additional 2 percent of each year's capital stock is consumed during the production process, then 8 percent is the optimum growth rate of investment purchasing to maximize production in the example economy as long as the

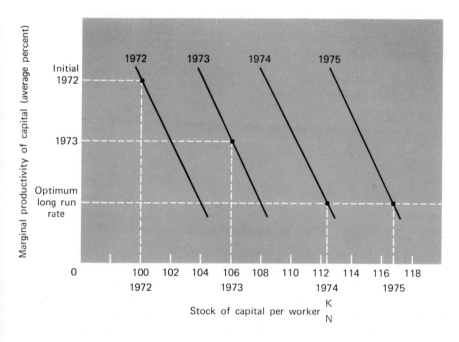

FIGURE 14-2
Neoclassical growth analysis.

technological advances require a 4 percent annual increase in the stock of capital per worker. The previous level of 10 percent is only maintainable until the economy reaches the optimum rate in 1974. Then the devotion of 92 percent of the economy's income to consumption and other noninvestment uses will provide the long run "Golden Path" of capital accumulation for the example economy so long as the nature and rates of growth of its labor force growth, technological change and capital consumption remain unchanged; a smaller propensity to consume means that more consumption will be lost than will be subsequently recaptured in the form of increased production and a higher propensity to consume means less consumption in the long run since it involves consuming commodities that could have been produced in the form of capital and used to subsequently produce an even greater amount of commodities.

The neoclassical growth theorists conclude that the primary concern of an economy over the long run is not to raise its propensity to save and encourage an expansion of the economy's stock of capital but to promote technological advances. But they note that there must be enough savings to allow the investment needed for modernization to occur. In the example economy, if less than an 8 percent growth in saving occurs, the economy will not have enough savings to allow its productive capacity to grow at the optimum rate associated with a 4 percent increase in the economy's per worker stock of capital. But even if its capital stock does not grow fast enough, an economy might still be able to obtain higher levels of production due to the arrival of new technology that allows it to more efficiently use its existing labor and capital. Whether an economy can continue to grow without investment depends upon whether the new technology arrives independently and allows vintage assets to be used more effectively or only arrives via new capital assets that both expand the economy's stock of capital and replace the less productive assets that have been consumed.

MEASURES OF GROWTH

The most commonly used measures of economic growth are related to an economy's GNP, or the total money value of the commodities actually produced and purchased during a given period of time. For instance, if an economy has moved from the purchasing and production of commodities worth $600 billion in one time period to those worth $660 billion in the next period, the money value of commodities produced in the economy has risen 10 percent. One major drawback to the use of such data to measure growth is that this approach excludes price changes from consideration. If both the GNP and the general level of commodity prices have risen 10 percent, no increase occurs in the amount of commodities produced in the economy from one time period to the next. The GNP data can be made more effective, however, by using them in conjunction with other data, such as the price level. For instance, if the money value of commodities purchased rises 10 percent and prices rise only 4 percent, it would indicate that the amount of commodities produced and purchased had grown about 6 percent.

On the other hand, several conceptual shortcomings are inherent in using the rate of increase in the real size of GNP as a measure of economic growth. One shortcoming is that changes in the size of an economy's real GNP make no allowance for population changes. For instance, if an economy's population has increased 6 percent and its real GNP has risen 6 percent, there has been no increase in the amount of commodities produced per person. In terms of measuring the growth of an economy's ability to meet the needs of its residents, a more appropriate measure of growth is the increase in real GNP per capita.

Another possible shortcoming of GNP estimates is that the value of certain newly produced goods and services may be arbitrarily omitted as part of GNP. This possibility was discussed in Chapter 2. To the extent that such exclusions occur in an economy, its GNP estimates not only understate the value of what is being produced in the economy, but also may not accurately reflect the rate at which the GNP is changing. For instance, government interest payments are not included as part of GNP by the United States. Yet they are payments to obtain the financing services of lenders, services which the government needs. Similarly, government subsidies are not included. Subsidies occur when a government makes payments to a producer in addition to those that he receives from the actual purchaser. A government is willing to do this because the commodity has a value to the entire economy which is over and above its value to the individual purchaser. For example, a commuter might value the services produced by a bus at only 15¢ per ride. But a government might reduce the bus line's tax liabilities by an additional 10¢ per ride because of the valuable services it provides by keeping down traffic jams and air pollution. Under the United States' system of estimating GNP, each ride would represent the existence of only 15¢ worth of commodities. But it is necessary to add the 10¢ subsidy to get a complete measure of the value of the services produced by the bus line.

As we have already seen, it is even conceptually necessary to include transfer payments as part of an economy's GNP. After all, rational men do not make money outlays unless they get something of value in return. In the case of transfers, those making them may get such valuable services as the feeling that they are good and moral or the security of knowing that the programs exist if they ever need them. These omissions have certain interesting implications for the United States' economy. Specifically, the sizes of some of these items have been growing much faster in the postwar period than has the economy's GNP as it is officially measured. Consequently, it is possible that the rate of growth in the value of the commodities actually produced in the United States has been understated by their exclusion.

The use of real GNP as a measure of growth also omits from consideration factors other than commodity production which are related to the well-being of the residents of the economy. First, it omits leisure. Thus it is possible that the ability of an economy to produce may grow from one time period to the next but that no additional commodity production will occur because the economy's residents prefer more leisure to additional commodities. Such an economy certainly is growing in terms of the well-being of its residents since it is providing additional leisure which the residents value more highly than the additional commodities made possible by their economy's increased ability to produce. Needless to say, a more appropriate rate of growth would be one that acknowledges additional leisure as well as additional commodities. One way this can be accomplished is by the use of real GNP on a worker-hour basis. Thus, if real GNP per worker remains the same in two successive time periods but the average work week declines from 40 to 36 hours, the rate of growth would be about 11.11 percent as $\frac{1}{9}$ more is produced per hour.

Furthermore, the use of GNP omits the effect of exported and imported commodities. Because the amount of commodities produced and exported can differ from the amount of commodities imported, the commodities actually available to an economy may differ from the amount it produces. This means that GNP-based measures of growth may not adequately reflect the changes occurring in an economy's ability to fill the needs of its residents. For instance, real GNP per person in an economy may rise 6 percent over a given period of time, but if all the additional purchasing is from abroad, foreigners are obtaining the additional commodities produced and there is no increase in the amount of commodities available to satisfy the needs of the producing economy.

It is possible, however, to modify growth estimates to take into account the difference between the amount of commodities which the economy actually has available for use and the amount it produces. For example, using one type of measure, an economy whose real GNP per person rises from $2,000 to $2,100 per year has a growth rate of 5 percent. But if that initial real GNP of $2,000 per person includes $400 of exports and $200 of imports per person, the total real value of commodities actually available for use is $1,800 (the $1,600 produced as part of GNP which is not sent abroad to foreign purchasers plus the $200 in commodities received from abroad). Then, if the subsequent $2,100 again includes $400 in exports but $300 in imports, the amount of commodities actually available per person in the example economy will have risen from $1,800 to $2,000 for a growth rate of more than 10 percent.

There are various implications to this approach. For instance, it has been suggested that the prices of commodities exported by underdeveloped countries have been falling relative to the prices of goods and services exported by the modern industrial countries. This means that, over time, there is a tendency for an industrial economy to be able to buy more commodities abroad and at the same time to have to give up fewer of its own to foreign economies. Under these conditions it is possible that the rate of growth in the amount of commodities actually acquired by a relatively modern industrial nation (such as Great Britain) which engages extensively in international trade may be substantially understated.

Another drawback of using changes in some GNP-related measure of the rate of growth is that the GNP estimates include commodities that are merely replacing those used up in the production process. A better measure of the growth of an economy's ability to meet the needs of its residents would include only the commodities acquired by the economy which it can consume without tending to reduce production in the future. This would be accomplished by subtracting an estimate of the real value of commodities exhausted in the production process from the GNP or whatever other base is used to compute the economy's rate of growth.

GOVERNMENT POLICIES TO PROMOTE GROWTH

Government policies regarding the growth of an economy's production and productive capacity can be either permissive or positive. The decision to expand production under a permissive government is left entirely to the individual producer, and the government makes no special effort to encourage him other than to keep the level of purchasing in the economy high enough so that producers in general do not lack customers. The private sector of the economy thus is left free to decide whether to introduce new techniques of production and whether to use the available factors of production to produce consumer goods or to expand the economy's productive capacity so that even more commodities can be produced in the future.

Once there is an adequate level of aggregate demand, as a permissive government ensures, the only way in which more commodities can be devoted to the expansion of an economy's productive capacity is that fewer are used for consumption purposes. Thus each income recipient in such an economy affects the rate at which the economy's capacity and production will grow as he decides whether to consume or to temporarily surrender his purchasing power control over commodity production to a producer so that he might be able to have a higher level of income in the future.

A positive government program for the growth of per capita incomes can take numerous interrelated forms: birth control programs so that there will not be as many people to share the economy's production; tax and subsidy incentives to promote more investment than otherwise would occur; government-supported research to develop new technologies; lower interest rates for investors; and rewards such as patents to encourage the private development of new products and production techniques.

A major problem is associated with such a positive program; it may be necessary to reduce the amount of commodities purchased by an economy's consumers so that more will be available for investment and other uses related to growth. Such a reduction can be accomplished in several ways: higher rewards for savings such as higher interest rates; and tax inducements such as deferred tax payments on income saved; higher taxes so that the income recipients have less disposable income; rationing or permitting inflation so that money incomes of a given size will not buy as many commodities. The drawback to such positive programs is that they may cause less present and more future consumption than its residents would voluntarily choose in the absence of such policies.

● REFERENCES

Akerloff, G. and W. Nordhaus, "Balanced Growth—A Razor's Edge?" *International Economic Review*, **VIII**, (Oct. 1967).

Atkinson, A. and J. Stiglitz, "A New View of Technological Change," *Economic Journal*, **LXXIX**, pp. 573–578 (Sept. 1969).

Conley, R., "Some Remarks on Methods of Measuring the Importance of Sources of Economic Growth," *Southern Economic Journal*, (Jan. 1969).

Conlisk, J., "A Neoclassical Growth Model with Endogenously Positioned Technical Change Frontier," *Economic Journal*, **LXXIX**, pp. 348–362 (June 1969).

Cornwall, J., "Three Paths to Full Employment Growth," *Quarterly Journal of Economics*, **LXXVII**, pp. 1–25 (1963).

Denison, E., "How to Raise the High Employment Growth Rate by One Percentage Point," *American Economic Review*: Papers and Proceedings, **LII**, pp. 67–75 (1962).

Domar, E., "Expansion and Employment," *American Economic Review*, **XXXVII**, pp. 34–35 (1947).

Fellner, W., "Measures of Technological Progress in the Light of Recent Growth Theories," *American Economic Review*, **LVII**, pp. 1073–1097 (Dec. 1967).

Green, H., "Embodied Progress, Investment, and Growth," *American Economic Review*, **LVI**, pp. 138–151 (March 1966).

Griliches, Z., and Dale Jorgenson, "Source of Measured Productivity Change: Capital Input," *American Economic Review*: Papers and Proceedings, **LVI**, pp. 50–61 (1966).

Hahn, F., "On Money and Growth," *Journal of Money, Banking and Credit*, **I**, pp. 172–187 (May 1969).

———, "On Warranted Growth Paths," *Review of Economic Studies*, **XXXV**, pp. 175–184 (April 1968).

Hamberg, D., "Full Capacity vs. Full Employment Growth," *Quarterly Journal of Economics*, **LXVI**, pp. 444–449 (1952).

Hansen, A., "Economic Progress and Declining Population Growth," *American Economic Review*, **XXIX**, pp. 1–15 (1939).

Harrod, R., "An Essay in Dynamic Theory," *Economic Journal*, **XLIX**, pp. 14–33 (1939).

———, "Domar and Dynamic Economics," *Economic Journal*, **LXIX**, pp. 451–464, (1959).

Kaldor, N., and J. A. Mirrlees, "A New Model of Economic Growth," *Review of Economic Studies*, **XXIX**, pp. 174–192 (1962).

Keiser, N., *Macroeconomics, Fiscal Policy, and Economic Growth* (John Wiley, 1964).

Komiya, R., "Economic Growth and the Balance of Payments: A Monetary Approach," *Journal of Political Economy*, **LXXVII**, pp. 35–48 (Jan.–Feb. 1969).

Koopmans, T. C. "Objectives, Constraints, and Outcomes in Optimal Growth Models," *Econometrica*, **LXXVII**, pp. 1–15 (Jan. 1967).

Levhari, D. and D. Patinkin, "The Role of Money in a Simple Growth Model," *American Economic Review*, **LVIII**, pp. 713–753 (Sept. 1968).

_____ and E. Sheshinski, "The Relation Between the Rate of Interest and the Rate of Technical Progress," *Review of Economic Studies*, **XXXVI**, pp. 363–379 (July 1969).

Lorentzen, R., "On Efficient Consumption Paths in a Class of Simple Growth Models," *Journal of Economic Theory*, **I**, pp. 92–98 (June 1969).

Marty, A. L., "Some Notes on Money and Economic Growth," *Journal of Money, Credit, and Banking*, **I**, pp. 252–265 (May 1969).

Meltzer, A., "Money, Intermediation, and Growth," *Journal of Economic Literature*, **VII**, pp. 27–56 (March 1969).

Nagatani, K., "A Monetary Growth Model with Variable Employment," *Journal of Money, Credit, and Banking*, **I**, pp. 188–206 (May 1969).

Neher, P., "Natural Rates of Economic Growth and International Interest Rates," *Kyklos*, **XXI**, pp. 326–497 (1968).

Nelson, R. and E. Phelps, "Investment in Humans, Technological Diffusion, and Economic Growth," *American Economic Review*: Papers and Proceedings, **LVI**, pp. 69–75 (1966).

Oshima, H. T., "Income Originating in the Models of Harrod and Domar," *Economic Journal*, **LXIX**, pp. 443–450 (1959).

Phelps, E., "The Golden Rule of Accumulation: A Fable for Growthmen," *American Economic Review*, pp. 638–643 (Sept. 1961).

_____, "The New View of Investment: A Neoclassical Analysis," *Quarterly Journal of Economics*, **LXXVI**, pp. 548–567 (Nov. 1962).

Pilvin, H., "Full Capacity vs. Full Employment Growth," *Quarterly Journal of Economics*, **LXVII**, pp. 545–552 (1953).

_____, "A Geometric Analysis of Recent Growth Models," *American Economic Review*, **XLII**, pp. 594–599 (1952).

Robinson, J. and K. Naqui, "The Badly Behaved Production Function," *Quarterly Journal of Economics*, **LXXXI**, pp. 579–591 (Nov. 1967).

Sato, R., "Stability Conditions in Two-Sector Models of Economic Growth Theory," *Journal of Economic Theory*, **I**, pp. 107–117 (June 1969).

Selowsky, M., "On the Measurement of Education's Contribution to Growth," *Quarterly Journal of Economics*, **LXXXIII**, pp. 449–463 (Aug. 1969).

Sidravskie, M., "Inflation and Economic Growth," *Journal of Political Economy*, **LXXV**, pp. 796–810 (Dec. 1967).

Wassom, J. C., "Inflation as a Tool for Promoting Growth," *Nebraska Journal of Economics and Business*, **VIII**, pp. 34–43 (Winter 1968–69).

Income Fluctuations

15

Economies such as that of the United States may be able to have ever-increasing levels of aggregate demand and aggregate supply. But, with the possible exception of instantaneous price adjustments, there are no forces that ensure the level of purchasing in such an economy will always change in concert with the economy's capacity to supply so that the economy will always be in equilibrium with full-employment levels of production. Instead, conditions may arise that cause fluctuations in the economy's level of income. The resulting divergences that such fluctuations cause between the level of aggregate demand in the economy and the economy's aggregate capacity to supply goods and services may periodically or permanently result in price-level changes and unemployment levels of production.

How experiences and changes in expectations may cause an economy's investment and income levels to fluctuate so that they differ from the requirements of full employment and result in either inflation or unemployment levels of production have already been covered in the discussion of the Harrod–Domar analysis. Other causes of income fluctuations are described

313

below along with the types of changes that might be experienced by economies that are affected by them. Subsequent chapters examine the effects of such income changes on prices and production, analyze the possibility of stabilizing an economy's prices and incomes at desired levels, and consider policies that might be implemented for stabilization purposes.

MONETARY THEORIES OF INCOME FLUCTUATIONS

Central banks, financial intermediaries, and the holders and users of money and credit can all modify their behavior and cause changes in an economy's level of income. For example, new credit arrangements could change the demand for an economy's money and credit, or the economy's central bank could change the supply. Alternately, the participants in an economy may modify their activities in response to the economy's monetary characteristics.

Such monetary influences and changes in responses to monetary conditions have been used to explain the fluctuations observed in certain economies' levels of income. One of the earliest explanations of the monetary origins of income fluctuations is provided by R. G. Hawtrey who emphasizes the effect of inventory changes in response to changes in the level of interest rates that might occur in an economy.[1] The main villain in his analysis and most others that explain income fluctuations in terms of changes in an economy's interest rates is the economy's central bank. It causes the level of income to expand as it lets the economy's commercial banks have additional excess reserves. Then it stops creating additional excess reserves and the level of income in the economy contracts.

Hawtrey theorized that lower interest rates encourage retailers and wholesalers to engage in additional purchasing in order to build up inventories since interest is the major expense of acquiring and holding them. In turn, the increased inventory purchasing means higher incomes for the producers of the inventoried goods and thus further increases in the purchasing of both the producers and the owners of the factors that are employed in the production process. Furthermore, the additional inventory and other purchasing also raises the level of sales out of inventories and leads to even more purchasing as even larger inventories are desired so that their holders will be able to handle the new and now higher levels of business that they are experiencing. The upturn in the economy's level of income is further fueled

---

[1]Hawtrey presented his ideas in various publications. See, for example, *The Art of Central Banking* (Longmans, Green and Co., Inc.), 1936.

by the price increases that occur as a result of the increased purchasing. The higher prices result in higher profits for both the producers when increases in their wages and other costs lag behind their price increases and the retailers and wholesalers who are able to sell goods out of their inventories that were purchased earlier before prices began to rise. The entire business community is, therefore, encouraged to make an effort to purchase even more goods in order to further build up their inventories before prices rise even higher.

The upturn comes to an end when the commercial banks start to run out of excess reserves and begin to increase their interest rates. How soon the banks run out of excess reserves depends on the economy's central bank and its willingness and ability to supply excess reserves to the banks. The higher interest rates reduce the stock of inventory that is desired, and as a result, the sales of the wholesalers and producers begin to decline so that they desire even lower levels of inventories. Since less inventory is desired, goods sold out of inventories are not replaced and there is a decline in both purchasing from manufacturers and the desire to borrow money from banks. Finally, enough loans will be repaid and the amount of money needed for transactions purposes in the economy will be sufficiently reduced to that the banks have such excess reserves that they begin to lower their interest rates in order to compete for loan customers. Inventory buildups are then encouraged and the income fluctuating cycle begins anew.

UNDERINVESTMENT AND OVERINVESTMENT THEORIES

Fluctuations in an economy's level of income can also occur as a result of investment purchasing either rising above or falling below and the amount required to offset the savings generated by the economy's initial level of income. Investment may tend to fall below the required level of savings when saved monies flow into the possession of commercial banks and other financial intermediaries and are prevented from being completely loaned out by the regulatory activities of the economy's central bank. On the other hand, investment in excess of the required level of savings tends to occur when investment purchasing is financed by the creation of loanable funds in addition to the funds provided by savings out of income. The creation of additional funds tends to occur, for example, when a central bank makes open market purchases or reduces reserve requirements in order to increase the excess reserves of commercial banks and thus their abilities to make loans. A central bank may be encouraged to engage in these procedures by the commercial banks which inevitably desire higher earnings and need to make additional loans in order to get them.

Some theorists emphasize the possibility that excess investment caused by monetary changes is the source of income fluctuations and the cycle from prosperity to inflation to recession that most economies seem to periodically experience. These "monetary overinvestment theorists" feel that the lower interest rates that will tend to result from an expansion of money and credit will encourage an economy to adopt more capital-intensive methods of production and that the resulting increases in autonomous investment will launch the economy into a cycle of inflation and recession.

When investment increases in an economy, the level of monetary income is driven higher and higher until it generates enough savings to offset the new and higher level of investment. But only so much production can occur in an economy at any point in time. Thus, if the economy is already at full employment as the early monetary overinvestment theorists assumed, only prices in the economy will be increased as a result of the additional investment purchasing. The higher prices mean that fewer noncapital goods and services can be purchased by factor owners and other purchasers in the economy whose money incomes lag behind the increases in the levels of income and prices in the economy. Such a lag is assumed to occur, and it is the forced savings caused by the higher prices that reduces the amount of commodities purchased for noncapital purposes and allows more labor and capital to be devoted to the production of plant and equipment.

But the lagging factor incomes do eventually rise and, as they do, there is more and more demand for noncapital goods so that prices and profits rise in these industries. Simultaneously, the rising factor incomes mean higher costs of production in the capital goods industry so that its profits tend to be reduced. With their rising profit margins the noncapital industries are then able to bid factors back away from the capital-goods industry. Furthermore, as the level of income rises and the additional excess reserves are loaned out, interest rates in the economy may begin to rise so that the level of investment purchasing is further contracted. The higher interest rates and lower profit margins discourage further borrowing, and investment begins to decline below the level needed to maintain the new and higher level of money income. The economy is now in a condition of underinvestment and its level of income declines until the reduced demand for loans causes interest rates to fall; simultaneously, profits on the production of capital goods rise as a result of the reduced demand for consumer and other noncapital goods that leads their producers to be less competitive for the available factors of production. Then investment begins to rise, and the cycle begins again.

Changes in investment purchasing can obviously occur in an economy as a result of central bank activities that affect the economy's supply of money and credit. But the cyclical return of the level of income may not occur as the monetary overinvestment theorists described because costs and interest rates may not change. After all, it is possible both that production costs per unit may not change as a result of changes in the economy's stock of capital and that the economy's monetary authorities can continue to change the supply of money and credit so that interest rates in the economy will not change as the economy's level of income changes.

SCHUMPETER AND THE ENTREPRENEURS

Innovative changes in the structure of an economy are the source of income fluctuations, according to Joseph Schumpeter.[1] He begins with an economy in equilibrium with every factor fully employed and every firm producing efficiently with product prices equal to average and marginal costs. Then, in an effort to obtain profits, an entrepreneur disturbs the equilibrium by introducing an innovative modification such as a new technique of production or a new product. The innovation is an effort to commercially apply an invention or idea that others may have developed but that is not yet used by the economy's producers because they are fearful of unprofitable results.

If the entrepreneur is successful, he makes profits. And the profits attract imitators who seek to share them by duplicating the original innovation. It is the alteration of an economy's structure as the result of an innovation that is the essence of economic development, according to Schumpeter. But innovation has cyclical effects as well. The initial purchasing by the entrepreneur who must bid factors away from other uses and the subsequent increases in investment spending by the imitators drive the economy's levels of income and prices higher. Finally, the increase in prices and incomes is reversed by both the tendency for the imitators to complete their wave of additional investment purchasing and the increase in production that may begin to flow from the new facilities and processes. The economy then turns back toward an equilibrium with a new and more productive structure.

Further influencing the economy's price and income movements is the possibility that the optimism generated during the period of expansion may lead both to the innovation of other modifications and to an expansion of production in the unmodified sectors as a result of the general increases in purchasing. However, once the upswing of income stops and the decline

[1] Schumpeter presented his theory in several publications. See, for example, his *The Theory of Economic Development* (Harvard University Press, 1934).

sets in, certain producers whose success and existence are based on producing goods and services for the expansion become overextended and fail. Lenders become pessimistic in view of the declining income levels and business failures and loans to entrepreneurs are held in abeyance so that the downturn is a period of net lender repayments. But while the repayments are causing loanable funds to pile up in the hands of the lenders, more and more inventions are occurring to open up additional innovative possibilities for entrepreneurs. Finally, the economy's entrepreneurs begin to be able to get the funds that they need to introduce new innovations, and another upturn occurs in the economy's income cycle.

THE PRINCIPLE OF ACCELERATION

The accelerator principle is a theory of fluctuating income and investment that relates investment purchasing to the changes in an economy's level of income that affect its optimum stock of capital. Specifically, if an economy has already obtained its optimum capital stock for its existing level of income, then investment purchasing in excess of replacement needs will only occur if the level of income in the economy is increased so that more capital is needed to efficiently produce the additional goods and services that can be sold at the higher level of income. Such additional investment purchasing then affects the level of income and may cause it to further increase. But the increased level of income is difficult to maintain because it is based on investment purchasing in excess of replacement needs. If there are no forces to keep the level of income expanding fast enough, investment purchasing will begin to decline and the level of income in the economy will tend to fall. Then, since a smaller stock of capital is needed to produce the goods and services that can be sold at the lower levels of income, capital assets that wear out may not be replaced so that investment purchasing and thus the level of income will decline further. Finally, enough capital will wear out and investment purchasing will begin again for replacement purposes. Then, even more investment purchasing will have to occur in order to provide the capital stock needed to produce the now higher level of production that can be sold.

The acceleration effect on investment and income under such conditions is depicted in Table 15-1 for an economy with a $2:1$ capital-output ratio whose level of income permanently rises \$10 billion in time period T_3 due to some extraneous change such as an increase in foreign purchasing. Investment in each time period is based on the capital consumption and changes in the optimum stock of capital that occurred in the previous time period. It is also assumed that $1 of capital will have to be replaced for every $5 of production and that, except for the initial $10 billion income increase, all changes in the economy's level of income are caused by changes in the level of investment purchasing. The latter restriction will be removed in the next section which adds the multiplier effects of responding to the accelerator changes in investment purchasing.

The initial $10 billion increase in purchasing results in a 2 percent increase in the level of income of the Table 15-1 economy in time period T_3 and a 22 percent increase in the economy's investment purchasing in time period T_4. The economy's level of income in time period T_4 thus rises by the amount of the additional investment purchasing and, as a result, even more investment purchasing occurs in subsequent time periods. The economy reaches an income peak in time period 6 and then begins to decline as the

TABLE 15-1
The Acceleration Effect (Billions of Dollars)

TIME PERIOD	GNP	OPTIMUM CAPITAL STOCK	DESIRED NET CAPITAL ADDITION	REPLACEMENT INVESTMENT	TOTAL INV.
1	500	1000	0	100	100
2	500	1000	0	100	100
3	510	1020	0	100	100
4	532	1064	20	102	122
5	560.4	1120.8	44	106.4	150.4
6	578.9	1157.8	56.8	112.1	168.9
7	562.8	1125.6	37	115.8	152.8
8	490.4	980.8	−32.2	112.6	80.4
9	410	820	−144.8	98.1	0*
10	410	820	−160.8	82.0	0*
11	410	820	0	82.0	0*
12	448.5	897	0	82.0	38.5*
13	576.7	1193.4	77	89.7	166.7
14	825.7	1651.4	296.4	119.3	415.7
15	1033.1	2066.2	458.0	165.1	623.1
16	1031.4	2062.8	414.8	206.6	621.4
17	612.9	1225.8	3.4	206.3	202.9
18	410	820	−837.0	122.6	0
19	410	820	−405.8	82.0	0

*Total investment is less than the economy's replacement requirements because capital consumed need not be replaced since the economy's actual stock exceeds its optimum stock.

growth in the economy's level of income is insufficient to encourage enough additional investment purchasing. The level of income bottoms out in time period 9 and begins to rise again in period 12 when the economy has finished consuming the capital stock that is not required at the low levels of income and begins to experience investment for replacement purposes. The resulting increase in the level of income accelerates investment purchasing and the cycle begins anew.

THE ACCELERATOR–MULTIPLIER INTERACTION

An economy's level of investment purchasing may be both affected by changes in the level of income and have a multiplier effect on the level of income. Thus what happens to an economy when something causes an initial change in purchasing depends upon the resulting interaction between

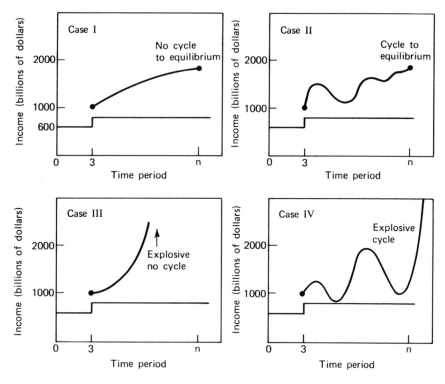

FIGURE 15-1
Accelerator–multiplier cases and the level of income.

the economy's multiplier and accelerator effects. The general nature of the income effects associated with the four major types of multiplier–accelerator interactions are depicted graphically in Figure 15-1. Each curve represents the multiplier–accelerator effects that would result from an initial increase in the level of income that begins in time period 3 when the economy is initially at an equilibrium of $1,000 billion level of income. The floor under each curve represents the level of income that will occur in the economy if there is no investment purchasing.

Notice that the economy only moves to a new and higher equilibrium level of income in cases I and II and that it explodes to infinitely high levels of income in cases III and IV. The various combinations of multiplier and accelerator values associated with each case are identified in Figure 15-2. The "k" on the horizontal axis of Figure 15-2 is the accelerator value relating induced investment in the economy being considered to changes in the economy's level of income. It is the economy's marginal capital/output ratio. For example, k = 1.5 if it takes $30 billion of additional investment purchasing to provide the additional capital stock required to produce the additional goods and services that can be sold in each subsequent time period if the economy's level of income rises $20 billion. The value of the economy's income multiplier is measured on the vertical axis of Figure 15-2. Thus if the economy's marginal propensity to consume is 0.5Y, 0.2Y of replacement investment is required to maintain the economy's stock of capital, and if there are no other components related to the economy's level

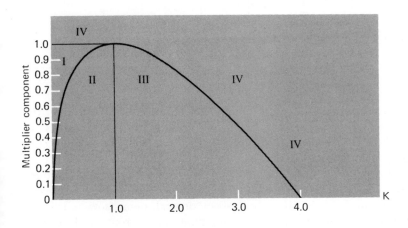

FIGURE 15-2
The accelerator–multiplier case values.

of income, the vertical axis would measure .7 and the economy's income multiplier would be $1.0/1.0 - 0.7 = 3.33$.

Tables 15-2 through 15-5 present the time-period-by-time-period changes in an example economy's levels of investment and income that will occur

TABLE 15-2
Case I Multiplier–Accelerator Interaction k = 0.1

PERIOD	Y	C	I	G	F	I_r	I_i
1	1,000	500	200	200	100	200	0
2	1,000	500	200	200	100	200	0
3	1,100	500	200	300	100	200	0
4	1,180	550	230	300	100	220	10
5	1,234.0	590	244	300	100	236	8.0
6	1,269.2	617	252.2	300	100	246.8	5.4
7	1,292.0	634.6	257.4	300	100	253.8	3.5
8	1,306.6	646.0	260.7	300	100	258.4	2.3
9	1,316.1	653.3	262.8	300	100	261.3	1.5
10	1,322.2	658.1	264.2	300	100	263.2	.9
11	1,326.2	661.1	265.1	300	100	264.4	.6
12	1,328.7	663.1	265.6	300	100	265.2	.4
13	1,330.4	664.4	266.0	300	100	265.7	.3
14	↓	↓	↓	↓	↓	↓	↓
15							
n	1,333.3	666.67	266.66	300	100	266.66	0
(equilibrium reached)							

with different combinations of multiplier and accelerator values when the example economy experiences a $100 billion initial change in its level of income. The example economy is described below. It is assumed that consumption purchasing and replacement investment purchasing in each time period will depend upon the income level of the preceding period. Furthermore, following our discussion of the accelerator concept, induced investment purchasing (I_i) is also assumed to depend upon how much the level of income changed in the previous time period from the level that

existed in the prior period. Algebraically, if we separate accelerator investment purchasing from autonomous investment:

$$Y = C + I_a + I_i + I_r + G + F$$
$$C = c(Y_{t-1})$$
$$I_r = r(Y_{t-1})$$
$$I_i = k(Y_{t-1} - Y_{t-2})$$
$$I_a = I_o$$
$$G = G_o$$
$$F = F_o$$

The example economy is initially in equilibrium with a $1000 billion GNP
with:

$$C = \$500 \text{ billion}$$
$$I_r = \$200 \text{ billion}$$
$$I_i = \$0$$
$$I_a = 0$$
$$G = \$200 \text{ billion}$$
$$F = \$100 \text{ billion}$$
$$c = .5$$
$$r = .2$$

Then the level of government purchasing rises to $300 billion in time
period 3. Notice that the subsequent income levels associated with the
different k values correspond to the different multiplier–accelerator cases
depicted in Figures 15-1 and 15-2.

TABLE 15-3

Case II Multiplier–Accelerator Interaction k = .9

PERIOD	Y	C	I	G	F	I_r	I_i
1	1,000	500	200	200	100	200	0
2	1,000	500	200	200	100	200	0
3	1,100	500	200	300	100	200	0
4	1,260	550	310.0	300	100	220	90.0
5	1,426	630.0	396.0	300	100	252.0	144.0
6	1,547.6	713.5	434.6	300	100	285.2	149.4
7	1,592.8	773.8	418.9	300	100	309.5	109.4
8	1,555.6	796.4	359.2	300	100	318.6	40.6
9	1,455.4	777.8	277.6	300	100	311.1	−33.5
10	1,328.7	727.7	201.0	300	100	291.1	−90.1
11	1,216.0	664.3	151.6	300	100	265.7	−114.1
12	1,149.8	608.0	141.8	300	100	243.2	−101.4
13	1,145.3	574.9	170.4	300	100	230.0	−59.6
14	1,197.6	572.6	226.0	300	100	230.1	−4.1
15	1,285.4	598.8	286.6	300	100	239.5	47.1
16	1,378.9	642.7	336.1	300	100	257.1	79.0
17	1,449.3	689.4	359.9	300	100	275.8	84.1
18	1477.9	724.6	353.3	300	100	289.9	63.4
19	1,460.2	738.9	321.3	300	100	295.6	25.7
20	1,406.3	730.1	276.1	300	100	292.0	−15.9
21	↓	↓	↓	300	100	↓	↓
22				300	100		
23				300	100		
n (equilibrium reached)	1,333.3	666.66	266.66			266.66	0

TABLE 15-4

Case III Multiplier–Accelerator Interaction k = 2.0

PERIOD	Y	C	I	G	F	I_r	I_i
1	1,000	500	200	200	100	200	0
2	1,000	500	200	200	100	200	0
3	1,100	500	200	300	100	200	0
4	1,370	550	420	300	100	220	200
5	1,899	685	814	300	100	274	540
6	2,787.3	949.5	1,437.8	300	100	379.8	1,058
7	4,127.7	1,393.7	2,334.1	300	100	557.5	1,776.6
8	5,970.2	2,063.9	3,506.4	300	100	825.5	2,680.8
9	8,264.2	2,985.1	4,879.1	300	100	1,194.0	3,685.0
10	10,772.8	4,132.1	6,240.7	300	100	1,652.8	4,587.9
11	12,958.3	5,386.4	7,171.9	300	100	2,154.6	5,017.3
12	13,841.7	6,479.1	6,962.6	300	100	2,591.7	4,370.9
13	11,856.0	6,920.8	4,535.2	300	100	2,768.3	1,766.8
14	6,328.0	5,928.0	0*	300	100	2,371.2	−3,971.3
15	3,564.0	3,164.0	0*	300	100	1,265.6	−11,056.0
16	2,181.0	1,782.0	0*	300	100	712.8	−5,528.0
17	1,491.9	1,091.0	0*	300	100	436.4	−2,764.0
18	1,145.5	745.5	0*	300	100	298.2	−1,382.0
19	972.8	572.8	0*	300	100	229.1	−691.0
20	886.4	486.4	0*	300	100	194.5	−345.5
21	↓	↓	↓	300	100	↓	↓
22				300	100		
23				300	100		
n	∞	∞	∞	300	100	∞	∞

(No equilibrium reached. Oscillates to ever higher levels.)

*Total investment is zero because the capital assets used up in the production process can be replaced from that portion of the existing stock that is no longer needed.

TABLE 15-5

Case IV Multiplier–Accelerator Interaction k = 6.0

PERIOD	Y	= C	+ I	+ G	+ F	I_r	I_i
1	1,000	500	200	200	100	200	0
2	1,000	500	200	200	100	200	0
3	1,100	500	200	300	100	200	0
4	1,770	550	820	300	100	220	600
5	5,659	885	4,374	300	100	354	4,020
6	27,695.3	2,829.5	24,465.8	300	100	1,131.8	23,334
7	↓	↓	↓	↓	↓	↓	↓
8	↓	↓	↓	↓	↓	↓	↓
n	∞	∞	∞	300	100	∞	∞

(No equili-
brium reached)

● REFERENCES

Chow, G., "The Acceleration Principle and the Nature of Business Cycles," *Quarterly Journal of Economics*, **LXXXII** (Aug. 1968).

————, "Multiplier, Accelerator, and Liquidity Preference in the Determination of National Income in the United States," *Review of Economics and Statistics*, **XLIX**, pp. 1–15 (Feb. 1967).

Ferguson, C., "On Theories of Acceleration and Growth," *Quarterly Journal of Economics*, **LXXIV**, pp. 79–99 (Feb. 1960).

Hahn, F. and R. Matthews, "The Theory of Economic Growth: A Survey," *Economic Journal*, **LXXIV**, pp. 779–902 (Dec. 1964).

Hamberg, D. and C. L. Schultze, "Autonomous vs. Induced Investment: The Inter-Relatedness of Parameters in Growth Models," *The Economic Journal*, **LXXI**, pp. 53–65 (March 1961).

Hawtrey, R., *The Art of Central Banking* (Longmans, Green & Co., Inc., 1933).

Hicks, J. R., *A Contribution to The Theory of The Trade Cycle* (Clarendon Press, 1950).

Kaldor, N., "A Model of the Trade Cycle," *Economic Journal*, **L**, pp. 78–92 (March 1940).

Lovell, M. and E. Prescott, "Money, Multiplier Accelerator Interaction, and the Business Cycle," *Southern Economic Journal*, **XXXV** (July 1968).

Matthews, R. C. O., "Duesenberry on Growth and Fluctuations," *The Economic Journal*, **LXIX**, pp. 749–765 (Dec. 1959).

Rose, H., "Real and Monetary Factors in the Business Cycle," *Journal of Money, Credit and Banking*, **I**, pp. 138–152 (May 1969).

————, "Expectations and Stability in Neo-Keynesian Growth Theory," *Quarterly Journal of Economics*, **LXXVII**, pp. 71–94 (1963).

Samuelson, P., "Interactions Between the Multiplier Analysis and the Principle of Acceleration," *Review of Economics and Statistics*, **XXI**, pp. 71–94 (1939).

Sato, R., "Stability Conditions in Two-Sector Models of Economic Growth Theory," *Journal of Economic Theory*, **I**, pp. 107–117 (June 1969).

Schumpeter, J., *The Theory of Economic Development* (Harvard University Press, 1934).

Smithies, A., "Economic Fluctuations and Growth," *Econometrica*, **XXV**, pp. 1–52 (Jan. 1957).

Stein, J., " 'Neoclassical' and 'Keynes-Wicksell' Monetary Growth Models," *Journal of Money, Credit and Banking*, **I**, pp. 153–171 (May 1969).

Weintraub, R., "The Stock of Money, Interest Rates, and the Business Cycle, 1952–1964," *Western Economic Journal*, **V**, pp. 257–270 (June 1967).

Inflation and Unemployment

16

Various conditions may arise to cause an economy to experience rising prices—*inflation*—or less than maximum levels of production and employment. These are more than just conditions of academic interest. They are cornerstones of concern in terms of whether the economy will provide the commodities needed to satisfy the needs of its residents. They determine, for example, whether or not men will be roaming the streets looking for employment to earn the wages needed to provide food and shelter for their families or whether the slim pension of an aged couple will be adequate to provide the necessities of life.

The way in which changes in certain conditions affect an economy's prices, production, and employment can be discussed using the graphic model developed in the previous chapters. How and why these conditions affect an economy are examined in this chapter. In subsequent chapters we shall discuss the possibility of implementing policies that might prevent or reduce inflation and unemployment.

CHANGES IN DEMAND

One economic condition that may cause an economy to experience inflation is an increase in the amount of commodities that buyers are willing to purchase at the level of prices existing in the economy. Such an increase could be caused by a multitude of factors. For instance, taxes may be reduced so that individuals in an economy have larger disposable incomes to spend for consumer goods; or the transactions demand for money might be reduced by an increase in the use of credit cards and thus result in an increase in the levels of investment and other purchasing as an economy's interest rates decline. Furthermore, as we have already discussed, any such initial change in spending may well have a subsequent multiplier effect on the level of total purchasing. For example, increased auto purchases tend to mean higher incomes for auto workers who, in turn, may buy more houses.

The effect of increased purchasing on an economy's production, employment, prices, and wages depends on the initial state of the economy. Consider the economy depicted in Figure 16-1. It is initially in equilibrium at price level P_{10} and money wage level Wm_1 with the maximum possible levels of production $(Y^r{}_{18})$ and employment (N_{20}). An increase in purchasing in this economy, since its full employment level of real income is already occurring, will only result in the prices of those goods and services being bid up to higher levels. This will occur as those desiring to purchase additional commodities find none available since the economy's producers are already selling all the commodities which they are willing to produce at the existing level of prices. Thus these purchasers will have to offer to pay higher prices to obtain the commodities they desire. The economy's prices will continue to rise so long as more commodities are demanded than are supplied. For example, if demand rises from D_1 to D_2 in the Figure 16-1 economy, the result will be inflation as the increased purchasing bids up the level of commodity prices in the economy: specifically, the price level will rise from P_{10} to P_{20}. At the same time, the level of money wages in the economy will be bid up since the higher price level and the initial level of money wages (Wm_1) would otherwise result in a lower level of real wages so that more workers are demanded than are supplied. Only when the level of money wages is bid up to Wm_2 as a result of the tendency toward a shortage of workers will the level of real wages be restored to $W^r{}_{15}$. Then the economy's producers will no longer desire to employ more workers than are willing to work.

Because an increase in demand pulls an economy's price level upward as

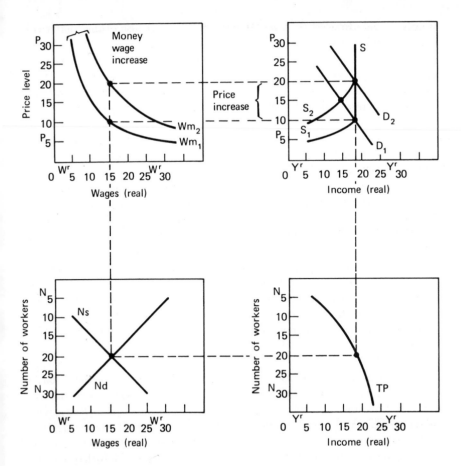

FIGURE 16-1
Demand-pull inflation.

the increased purchasing bids up the prices of the limited amount of available commodities, such inflation typically is referred to as "demand-pull" in nature. It is important to note that, even though an economy's levels of money wages and prices rise when its purchasing increases under such demand-pull conditions, there is no effect on either the number of commodities purchased and produced in the economy or the number of workers employed and the level of real wages that they receive. The only certain change that occurs in the structure of an economy as a result of demand-pull inflation is the decreasing willingness of the economy's producers to supply commodities at each lower level of prices because of the higher costs of production caused by the resulting increase in money wages. Such a change is depicted in the Figure 16-1 economy by a shift in the economy's aggregate supply curve from S_1 to S_2; it shifts upward to the extent that higher prices are needed at each level of production to cover the now higher production costs caused by the increase in the level of money wages. After all, once an economy's money wages increase the economy's producers will only be willing to produce the various possible levels of production at the higher prices needed to cover the higher production costs that will now occur at each production level.

Inflation may also have other kinds of effects on the behavior of an economy's participants. First, it may change the participants' propensities to save if the inflation is expected to continue. After all, why should an individual save if he expects to get less in the future with his savings than he can get now? Second, higher prices may encourage savings because they reduce the real amount of savings that individuals have accumulated. Third, higher prices tend to cause a redistribution of purchasing power away from individuals such as pensioners who are living on fixed incomes; they cannot obtain as many commodities with the disposable income they receive, and thus more commodities are available for individuals whose disposable incomes rise as the price level rises.

Demand-pull inflation is not the inevitable result of an increase in the level of commodity purchases. As was shown in Figure 13-8, there may be no effect on an economy's level of prices if increased purchasing occurs when less than maximum levels of output and employment have been existing due to a previously inadequate amount of purchasing. Instead, production and employment will rise as the economy's business firms use their previously idle capacity to produce the additional commodities which they can now sell.

Decreases in Demand

Reductions in the level of output that will be purchased in an economy at every level of prices may result from a variety of causes. For instance, the level of interest rates might rise and less investment purchasing occur as a result of a reduction in the supply of money or an increase in the amount of money demanded. Or the level of taxes in an economy might be increased so that the level of its disposable income is reduced and the level of its consumption purchasing declines.

Whatever the cause, the effect of a decline in the level of real income in an economy at a given level of prices depends on the flexibility of the economy's wages and prices. Consider the effect of reducing demand in an economy in which prices are inflexible downward such as the one reflected in Figure 16-2. Initially this economy is in equilibrium at a full employment level of production Y^r_{18} with price level P_{15}, money wage level Wm_1, and the employment of N_{20} workers. But if demand declines from D_1 to D_2, only Y^r_{11} commodities will be purchased in the economy at price level P_{15}. Thus, if the economy's commodity prices are not bid down, the econ-

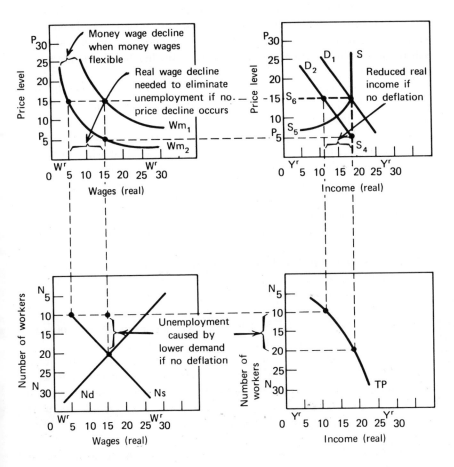

FIGURE 16-2
Decreases in demand.

omy's producers will only be willing to produce a Y^r_{11} level of output and, as a result, only N_{10} workers will be employed. When prices are inflexible downward, whether unemployment occurs along with the less than maximum level of commodity production depends on the flexibility of money wages. If they remain at Wm_1 despite the decline in production, more workers will be willing to work at the existing level of real wages than will be employed. On the other hand, if money wages are flexible and do decline as the unemployed compete for the available jobs, the level of money wages in the economy will be reduced (to Wm_2) until the level of real wages is low enough (W^r_5) so that only the N_{10} workers for whom employment is available will be willing to supply their labor. Then all the workers who are willing to work will be able to find employment, and there will be no surplus of unemployed workers to further bid down the level of money wages.

There is every reason to expect that a reduction of aggregate demand in an economy will indeed lead to unemployment and less than maximum levels of production. Prices tend to be inflexible downward as a result of long-term price agreements, noncompetitive producers, government-determined prices, and production costs such as wages that do not decline when there is a reduction in the level of production. Wages may be inflexible downward due to minimum wage laws and long-term labor contracts such as are traditionally negotiated by unions and professors.

When aggregate demand declines in an economy and the economy's wages and prices do not fall, no commodities will be supplied at price levels below the existing level. Such an economy's aggregate supply curve thus has the form of S_6 in Figure 16–2. It indicates that increases in output can occur in the example economy at the existing price level of P_{15} until the Y^r_{18} full employment level of real income is reached.

Wage and price flexibility. Reductions in the level of output demanded at each price level will not cause less than maximum levels of production if commodity prices and money wages are sufficiently flexible downward. For example, if aggregate demand declines from D_1 to D_2 in the economy depicted in Figure 16-2, all that will occur is a general wage and price deflation which restores the economy to full employment and maximum levels of production at a lower level of money wages (Wm_2) and prices (P_5).

Nevertheless, even though the levels of production, employment, and real wages remain the same, a general deflation does affect an economy; it means an increase in the real incomes of those individuals with fixed money incomes and an increase in the real value of savings which have been accumulated in the form of assets with fixed money values. This means that individuals receiving the fixed money incomes will be able to obtain a larger proportion of the commodities produced in the future and that individuals with their savings in the form of such assets will be closer to filling their savings goals and thus under less pressure to save. On the other hand, if price deflation is expected to continue, savings may increase as purchasers wait to buy later when prices are even lower.

Wages inflexible and prices flexible downward. If the level of money wages in an economy is inflexible downward, an even different effect will occur when a reduction in demand causes the economy's price level to decline. Consider the economy depicted in Figure 16-3. This economy is initially in equilibrium at price level P_{15} with a full employment level of real income Y^r_{18}. A decline in demand from D_1 to D_2, when prices are flexible downward and money wages are not, will result in a new level of prices slightly above P_{11}, the production of Y^r_{15} commodities, and the employment of only N_{15} workers since that is the number needed to produce the commodities that can be sold at the wage level and income distribution associated with Y^r_{15}. Furthermore, a reduction in the level of an economy's prices in conjunction with the retention of the economy's initial level of money wages means that an even higher level of real wages will occur and, perhaps, more workers will be willing to work even though fewer will be able to find employment. For example, the decline of prices to approximately P_{11} in the Figure 16-3 economy and the retention of money wage level Wm_1 mean that the level of real wages in the economy will rise from W^r_{15} to W^r_{20}. As a result, the number of workers willing to work will increase from N_{20} to N_{25} even though employment drops from N_{20} to N_{15} as a result of the reduction in aggregate demand. In this case, a reduction in demand means lower prices, a reduction in the level of real income as fewer commodities are purchased and produced, and a higher level of real wages. It also means the existence of involuntary unemployment as workers are willing to work but cannot find positions because of the higher real wages and because not all of the commodities which the producers in the economy are willing to supply can be sold.

PRODUCTIVITY INCREASES

An economy's productive capacity tends to rise in response to improvements in such things as the skill and quality of its labor, the quantity and quality of

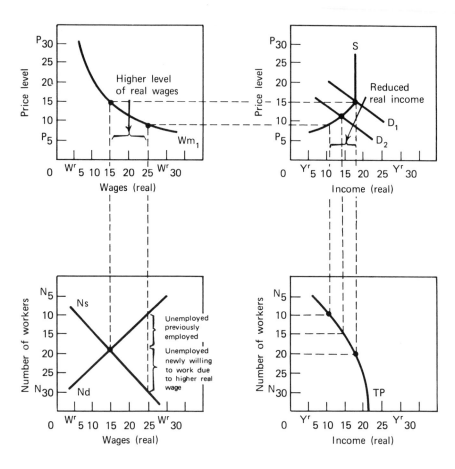

FIGURE 16-3
Decline in demand with flexible prices and inflexible wages.

the capital and other materials used by the labor, and the technology or way in which the labor uses the economy's stock of capital and other materials in the production processes. Productivity increases may be depicted in the basic model by changes in both the production function and the labor demand curve. Specifically, the curve representing the production function rises to represent the new and higher level of commodities that can be produced with the employment of each amount of labor, whereas the labor demand curve rises to the extent that each subsequent worker will contribute more commodities in excess of the other costs of production associated with his employment.

An example of the changes in the nature of an economy's aggregate supply which would result from productivity increases is depicted in Figure 16-4. The curves representing conditions in the economy prior to the productivity increases are identified with the subscript 1, and those for the conditions in the economy after the increase with the subscript 2. The aggregate supply curve that results from the productivity increases lies to the right of the economy's original aggregate supply curve since the increased productivity

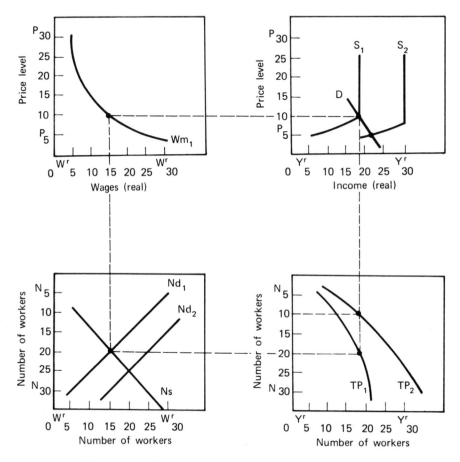

FIGURE 16-4
Increased productivity.

means that larger amounts of goods and services can be produced in the economy at every level of prices. The increase in the maximum level of commodity output that can be supplied is caused by the increase in labor productivity and by more workers' supplying their labor at the new and higher level of real wages associated with full employment.

The Effects of Productivity Increases

Increases in the productivity of an economy's labor force, however, are not enough to ensure a higher level of commodity production in the economy. Instead, such increases can and will cause unemployment if aggregate demand in the economy is not sufficiently increased. After all, businessmen only produce goods and services that they can sell. Therefore, the additional commodities that can be produced actually will be produced only if there also is a sufficient increase in the amount of newly produced goods and services that is purchased. And if demand does not increase, fewer of the now more productive workers will be needed to produce the level of output that can be sold.

Consider the economy depicted by Figure 16-5. Initially this economy is in equilibrium at price level P_{10}, and its full employment level of real income is Y^r_{18}. Then labor productivity in the economy increases in the manner depicted by production function TP_2 and other labor demand curve Nd_2. The result is a new and greater willingness on the part of the economy's producers to supply commodities at each level of prices. This is depicted by aggregate supply curve S_2. If aggregate demand in the economy does not change and its commodity prices are flexible while its money wages are not, the level of prices in the economy will fall to a new equilibrium level of P_5 while the level of output purchased and produced at the resulting wage level and income distribution will rise to Y^r_{21}.

Even though the new equilibrium level of real income is larger than the level that existed before the productivity increase, it still falls short of the economy's new maximum potential level of output of Y^r_{30}. Notice also that fewer workers, N_{15}, are needed to produce the larger amounts of commodities than the N_{20} required to produce Y^r_{18} before the productivity increase. Furthermore, despite the decline in the number of workers employed, additional workers will be attracted into the economy's labor market because of the higher real wages resulting from the decline in prices and the continued payment of the initial level of money wages to those individuals fortunate enough to find employment.

On the other hand, should the economy's commodity prices be inflexible

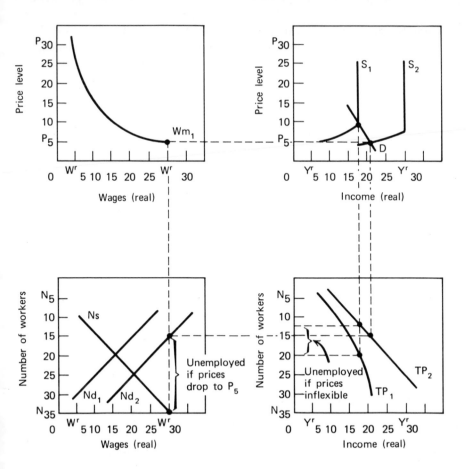

FIGURE 16-5
Some possible effects of productivity increases.

downward and such an increase in labor productivity occur, the amount of commodities that will be purchased and thus produced in the economy will remain unchanged at Y^r_{18}. Under these conditions, even fewer workers, about N_{12}, are needed to produce the amount of commodities that can be sold; all the rest who are willing to work at the existing level of real wages will remain unemployed because the additional output that they could provide cannot be sold.

Unemployment and less than maximum levels of production are not the inevitable fate of an economy that experiences productivity increases. Instead, the level of commodity purchasing may rise so that the economy's producers are willing to raise their output of commodities to the new and higher levels that they are capable of producing. Consider for instance, the economy depicted in Figure 16-6. Initially the level of money wages is Wm_1, and the economy is in equilibrium at P_{10} and Y^r_{18}; then the productivity of the economy's labor force rises so that the curve representing the willingness of its producers to supply commodities shifts from S_1 to S_2. No unemployment or less than maximum levels of production will result if the demand for the economy's commodities also increases from D_1 to D_2.

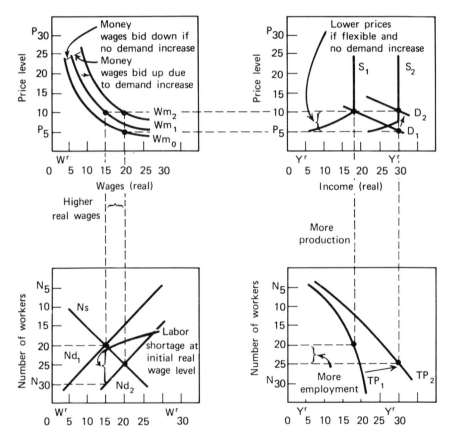

FIGURE 16-6
Productivity increases offset by demand increases.

Indeed, prices will remain stable at P_{10} and the economy's output will rise to the new maximum possible level of Y^r_{30}. Nevertheless, other changes will occur because the increased demand for labor means a shortage of labor at the original real wage level of W^r_{15}. Thus producers will bid up money wages as they compete for the available labor. The level of money wages will rise to Wm_2 before the surplus is eliminated at the resulting higher real wage level of W^r_{20}. Furthermore, more labor, N_{25} instead of N_{20}, will be employed than before the productivity and demand increases. In other words, it is possible for wages and employment to rise in an economy without causing inflation. Thus increases in expenditures to purchase commodities are not the only way by which maximum levels of commodity production can be obtained in economies that experience productivity increases. For instance, the same production and employment results will occur in the economy initially depicted in Figure 16-6 if there is a sufficient deflation of money wages and prices. Specifically, if wages and prices are flexible downward in the example economy, its level of prices will fall to P_5 when productivity increases to TP_2. The level of prices in the economy falls as the economy's producers bid down prices as they compete to sell the additional commodities they are now willing to produce at each price level. The economy's money wages will similarly fall. They will decline to a level of Wm_0 as workers in the economy bid down money wages as they compete for the available jobs. Maximum levels of production and employment will occur when the wage and price deflation is completed: N_{25} workers will be employed, and the employed workers will receive the higher level of real wages W^r_{20}.

Policy alternatives. Two basic policy alternatives exist when increased productivity causes unemployment. The first alternative is to increase the amount of commodities purchased in the economy. This is typically accepted as desirable since it results in a larger amount of commodities being available to satisfy the needs of the economy and eliminates any problems that might be associated with unemployment. How such an increase might be accomplished without a general wage and price deflation will be discussed in detail in Chapter 19.

The other alternative is to eliminate or offset the increase in the productivity of labor. This can be accomplished by such techniques as cutting the length of the work week, forcing early retirements of men and machines, and insisting upon the retention of traditional methods of production. It is interesting to note that a substantial portion of the American labor union movement has continually advocated such policies. Apparently they believe that only so many commodities can or will be produced in an economy during a given period of time, and thus that any improvements in worker productivity mean a reduction in employment and consequently labor unemployment. The advocates of such policies, in essence, ignore the first alternative and, more surprisingly, the higher wages that might accompany it.

HIGHER COSTS OF PRODUCTION

Still another economic condition that may arise to cause both inflation and unemployment in an economy is an increase in the costs of producing commodities. Such higher costs can be caused by increases in wages, taxes, interest rates, and other cost factors. For example, an economy's labor unions may bargain for and receive higher money wages, or its governments may raise interest rates and property taxes or engage in price support programs that increase the prices of materials used in production. The initial effect of cost increases that are not offset by lower costs in other areas is that while the economy's producers may still physically be able to produce as many commodities as before the increase, they will be willing to produce them only if they can get higher prices to cover their now higher costs. The willingness of producers to supply the same amount of commodities but only at higher prices is depicted by a new and higher aggregate supply curve; it will shift upward to higher prices by the amount of the additional costs that must be covered if production is to occur.

Figure 16-7 presents the effect of higher money wages. It depicts an economy that is initially in equilibrium at price level P_{10}, money wage level Wm_1, and full employment level of real income Y^r_{18}. Aggregate supply curve S_1 represents the amounts of commodities that the economy's producers initially are willing to supply at each level of prices. On the other hand, aggregate supply curve S_2 represents the amounts of commodities that will be supplied in the economy at each price level if the level of money wages is Wm_2. The figure indicates that an increase in the level of money wages from Wm_1 to Wm_2, and thus a change of the economy's willingness to supply commodities from S_1 to S_2, will cause the level of prices in the economy to rise from P_{10} to P_{15}, the equilibrium level of real income to decline from Y^r_{18} to Y^r_{15}, and unemployment to occur as the amount of labor employed is reduced from N_{20} to N_{15}. Additionally, even though the level of employment will decline to N_{15} from N_{20} since less will be purchased at P_{15} and the resulting wage level and income distribution, the number of workers willing to supply their labor rises to N_{25} owing to the increase in the level of real wages from W^r_{15} to W^r_{20}.

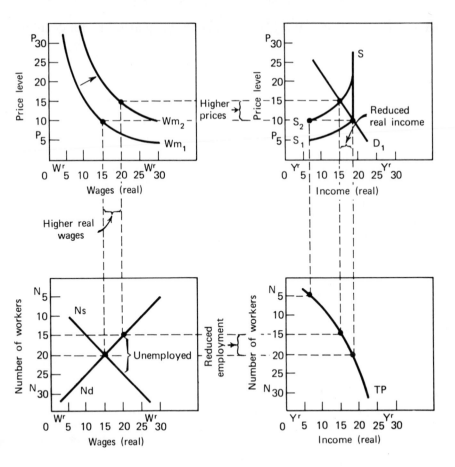

FIGURE 16-7
Cost-push inflation and unemployment caused by higher money wages.

These changes traditionally are referred to as "cost-push inflation and unemployment" since both prices and unemployment, in a sense, are "pushed up" as a result of the higher costs. Technically, however, the price level in an economy tends to rise when costs increase because the economy's producers are not willing to supply as many commodities at the initial price level as purchasers are willing to buy; thus the purchasers bid up the price level as they compete for the fewer goods and services the producers are willing to supply. In the Figure 16-7 economy, for instance, prices will tend to be bid up beyond the initial level of P_{10} because at that price level the producers will only be willing to supply Y^r_6 commodities when they have to pay the higher Wm_2 level of wages while purchasers still desire to purchase Y^r_{18}.

Cost Increases Other Than Wages

Cost increases that are not directly related to the level of wages in an economy may mean that a worker will produce fewer commodities in excess of those needed to cover the other costs that accompany his employment. For instance, consider the worker whose employment will result in the production of ten additional commodities as well as costs in addition to his wages which are equivalent to four commodities. Since he would make a net contribution of six commodities, this worker will be hired if he will work for a real wage equivalent to six or fewer commodities. But what if the other costs associated with his employment rise to the equivalent of six commodities owing to increased taxes or material costs? Then the worker will be employed only if he will work for a real wage equivalent to four commodities or less. In other words, such cost increases result in a decline in the demand for labor by the amount of additional costs associated with each subsequent worker's employment.

The effect of such cost increases on an economy's prices, production, and employment is depicted in Figure 16-8 for an example economy in which aggregate supply surve S_1 represents the commodities that will be supplied in the economy at each price level before a cost increase. The economy is initially in equilibrium at price level P_{10}, money wage level Wm_1, and full employment level of income Y^r_{18}. Aggregate supply curve S_2 represents the commodities that will be supplied in the economy if the additional costs associated with the employment of each subsequent worker rise in the manner depicted by the decline in the labor demand curve from Nd_1 to Nd_2. Examination of the latter aggregate supply curve indicates that if costs rise in the manner depicted, the level of prices in the economy will rise from P_{10} to P_{12}. They will be "pushed up" by the higher costs because the economy's producers will no longer hire workers and produce all the commodities that purchasers desire to buy at price level P_{10}. They will not produce as much because fewer workers will be able to make net contributions equal to or larger than the real wages that will exist at price level P_{10}. Furthermore, the equilibrium level of income will decline from Y^r_{18} to Y^r_{13} and unemployment will occur as the level of employment is reduced from N_{20} to approximately N_{12}. Notice also that fewer workers are willing to work in the economy at the lower level of real wages which are caused by the higher price level, and that, as a result, the new aggregate supply curve lies to the

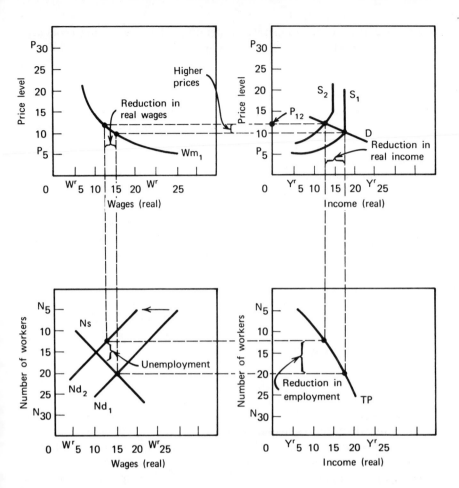

FIGURE 16-8
Cost-push inflation and unemployment caused by cost increases other than wages.

left of the initial curve to indicate that less production will occur at the new full employment level of real wages.

Changes in Costs and Changes in Demand

Increases occur in the proportion of an economy's output that can be purchased by workers or the owners of other factors of production when money payments to them increase faster than the level of the economy's prices. For example, the level of money wages in an economy could double while other costs remain unchanged in money terms so that the economy's price level is only pushed up 50 percent. Under such circumstances there would be a redistribution of purchasing power at every level of real income. The redistribution is away from individuals, businesses, and governments whose money incomes either increase less than the increases in prices or decrease as a result of unemployment caused by the increased costs. It is toward the individuals, businesses, and governments whose money incomes increase more than prices increase. Then, if the marginal propensities to spend of those receiving increases in purchasing power are higher than those experiencing reductions, there would be an increase in the economy's aggregate demand associated with every level of real income.

In terms of the Figure 16-7 economy, for example, an increase in money wages to Wm_2 could result in a new willingness to purchase commodities at every level of price if it changes the distribution of income at the different possible levels of production. Such a change would be depicted by a new aggregate demand curve that would lie above or below the existing curve D_1 depending on propensities to spend of the income recipients and the degree of redistribution that occurs at each level of output if money wages rise from Wm_1 to Wm_2.

The Cost-Push Dilemma

The dilemma arising when a cost-push situation occurs is presented in Figure 16-9 which represents an economy that has experienced a cost-push situation. Specifically, as a result of higher money wages, the level of prices has risen from P_{10} to P_{15} and the equilibrium level of real income has fallen from the maximum possible level of Y^r_{18} to a lower level of Y^r_{15}. Under these circumstances, the maximum level of real income of Y^r_{18} can be regained only by increasing the economy's aggregate demand from its original level of D_1 to the new and higher level of D_2. But this causes the even higher price level of P_{20}. On the other hand, restoration of the initial level of prices in order to avoid any of the drawbacks of inflation requires a reduction in aggregate demand to D_3. But this causes the even lower level of real income of Y^r_6. Thus a choice must be made among fighting inflation at the expense of maximum levels of production, eliminating the less than maximum levels of production at the expense of inflation, or doing nothing and accepting some of each.

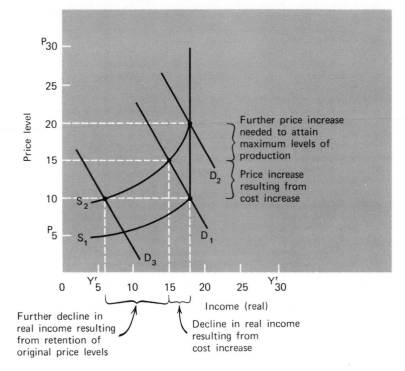

FIGURE 16-9
The cost-push dilemma.

On the premise that production, not prices, is more important in meeting the wants of men, some economists hold that if a cost-push situation does occur, demand should be raised so that the economy can avoid unemployment and less than maximum levels of production. Other economists, however, are not so sure that the best interests of an economy are served when demand is increased in a cost-push situation. They note, first, that acceptance of the need to increase aggregate demand also may mean accepting changes in the distribution of the economy's commodities. That is, a larger share of the economy's total production may go to individuals who have been able to raise their money wages and other incomes while, correspondingly, a smaller share goes to those such as the retired who cannot raise their money incomes to offset the higher commodity prices. Second, they foresee almost immediate new cost increases if prices are allowed to increase since money wages often are tied to the price level by cost-of-living indexes; they fear a continual "wage-price inflationary spiral" with the government continually ratifying the efforts of those groups who are able to increase their money wages to gain control of more of the economy's commodities. Furthermore, they see a possible adverse effect on the nature of the commodities being purchased for investment purposes as, in addition to the profit expected from its operations, a criterion of a good investment commodity becomes its ability to increase in price as fast or faster than the spiraling commodity prices.

Some of the economists who oppose government actions to restore maximum levels of production in a cost-push situation advocate the immediate reduction of demand so that a wage-price spiral does not begin. They feel that such policies are necessary to discourage behavior that could cause a cost-push situation; they advocate demonstrating to those who are causing the cost-push problem by trying to gain a larger share of production that they will not be able to accomplish their goal in that manner. Despite the hopes of these economists, however, a general decrease in demand will not discourage efforts to increase incomes faster than productivity. After all, the individuals who remain employed still will be able to gain by obtaining higher wages for themselves and so there is no reason to expect that they will stop trying.

Avoiding Cost-Push Inflation and Unemployment

Higher money wages, as Figure 16-6 indicates, do not necessarily cause cost-push inflation in an economy if they are accompanied by a sufficient increase in the productivity of the economy's labor force. The reason that the prices do not rise when both wages and productivity increase is that, even though the workers are paid more, they also are producing more so that the cost of each commodity they produce tends to remain the same. These conclusions also hold for increases in other costs of production. For instance, assume that the price of a major metal such as steel rises 3 percent but that technological advances occur so that 3 percent less steel is used in the production of each commodity. Under these conditions, the cost of the steel used to produce each commodity does not increase and there is no tendency toward cost-push inflation and unemployment.

It is interesting to note that the United States' government, in an attempt to avoid cost-push inflation and unemployment, at times has estimated the average annual increase in labor productivity and then persuaded both workers and employers to agree to wage increases that do not exceed this productivity estimate. Supposedly, if labor receives wage increases that do not exceed the government's productivity estimates, there is no reason for commodity producers to raise their prices because per unit costs will not be higher. The use of productivity estimates as guidelines for noninflationary wage increases, however, may be an exercise in futility which merely causes any inflation and unemployment occurring in the United States' economy to be attributed to factors unrelated to higher costs. In fact, cost-push inflation might well occur even if the government's wages guidelines are computed accurately and followed assiduously.

The cost-push inflation and unemployment pressures continue to exist because the productivity of labor in each circumstance may differ from the average for the economy as a whole. For example, the productivity of an economy's barbers might not go up at all during a given year, whereas the productivity of its auto workers might rise 10 percent. Then, if the economy's government estimates that the average productivity gain in the economy has been 3.8 percent, both barbers and auto workers as well as their employers will be urged, following the guidelines, to accept wage increases that do not exceed 3.8 percent. But a 3.8 percent increase in barbers' wages without an increase in their productivity means an increase in the cost of producing a haircut. Then the economy's barbershops will tend to provide such services only if they can get prices high enough to cover the increased costs. On the other hand, a 3.8 percent increase for auto workers means a reduction in the labor cost of each automobile produced in the economy and the absence of wage-induced cost-push pressures in the economy's automobile industry. But there does not have to be a price increase in the auto industry for inflation to occur. After all, if one price such as that of haircuts rises and the others stay the same, the general level of prices in the economy rises.

Inflation can be avoided under these conditions only if increases in the prices of the commodities experiencing higher unit costs are offset by reductions in the prices of commodities whose costs decline. In other words, only if the higher prices of items such as haircuts are offset by the lower prices of items such as automobiles will inflation tend not to occur. In many industries, however, there apparently is not enough competition among producers to cause price reductions when costs decline. Furthermore, the government pressure typically has been concentrated on holding wage increases within the guidelines, not on encouraging price reduction where productivity has increased faster than the guidelines. Thus any price increase that occurs because productivity has increased slower than the government guideline rate may not be offset by price reductions where productivity has increased faster. In other words, the general level of prices in the United States may be pushed up by higher wages even if none of the wage increases exceeds the government guideline.

CHANGES IN THE SIZE OF THE SUPPLY OF LABOR

An increase in the size of an economy's supply of labor has somewhat the same effect on unemployment as an increase in productivity. Such an increase can result from such things as population increases, the removal of leisure-time incentives not to work, and increases in the number of years of employment allowed by employers and the government. For instance, 65 years of age is the conventional retirement age in the United States. But would the labor force not increase if that upper limit were extended to 70? It probably would if workers previously had been retired involuntarily at age 65. Whatever the cause of the expansion, an increase in either the number of workers willing to produce commodities at each level of real wages or the amount of labor supplied by each worker may cause unemployment. On the other hand, such increases also may cause increased production and and even lower commodity prices. What actually happens in a particular economy when its supply of labor increases, as will be demonstrated presently, depends on the flexibility of its wages and prices and whether the demand for its commodities also increases.

Figure 16-10 represents an economy in which money wages are inflexible downward before and after it obtains a larger labor force for some reason. The initial levels of aggregate demand and aggregate supply are represented by D_1 and S_1, and the economy is initially in equilibrium with a price level slightly above P_7, the employment of N_{15} workers, and the purchasing and production of Y^r_{21} commodities. The subsequent increase in the number of people who are willing to work at every level of real wages is represented by the shift of the labor supply from its original position of Ns_1 to a new position of Ns_2. One result of such a shift is that the full employment level of real wages is reduced from W^r_{20} to W^r_{10}. The new aggregate supply curve resulting from such an increase in the size of the economy's labor supply is S_2. It indicates that the effect of an increase in the economy's supply of labor is to increase the maximum amounts of commodities which can be produced in the economy but that when money wages are inflexible downward, the new and higher levels of production will occur only at a price level that is higher than the initial price level; higher prices are needed to lower the level of real wages received by the labor force to the new and lower full employment level of W^r_{10}.

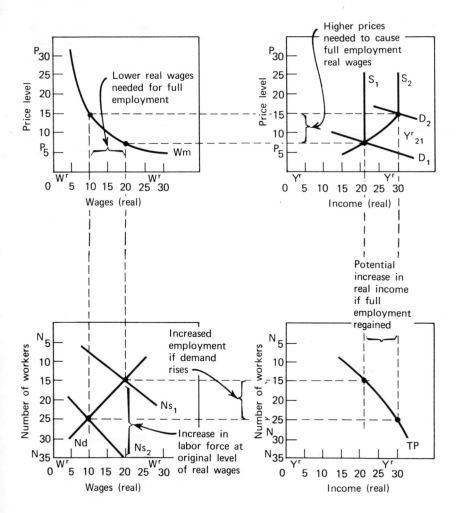

FIGURE 16-10
An increase in the labor force.

The Effects of an Increase in the Supply of Labor

Increases in the size of an economy's labor supply do not necessarily affect the equilibrium levels of the economy's employment, prices, and production. Instead, in the absence of any other changes, the economy will remain in equilibrium at the original levels of prices and real income. No changes will occur in the amount of commodities produced and the number of workers employed because no changes occur in the amount of commodities purchased. Thus the additional workers will remain unemployed, and the additional commodities which they could provide for the economy will go unproduced. The additional labor remains unemployed because the economy's employers are already hiring all the labor they desire to employ at the level of real wages associated with the initial levels of money wages and commodity prices.

Unemployment and less than maximum levels of production need not occur in an economy if its supply of labor increases when its money wages are inflexible downward. They can be avoided if the economy's aggregate demand is increased so that its commodity prices rise enough to cause the real wages of its workers to fall to the level at which all the workers in the economy will be hired. For the Figure 16-10 economy, this requires increasing aggregate demand to the level represented by D_2. The result will be an increase in production to Y^r_{30} as the production of the additional workers is added to the previous totals, an increase in the level of employment to N_{25}, and a decline in the full employment level of real wages to W^r_{10}. Notice that the increase in employment from N_{15} to N_{25} is less than the additional amount of workers who have joined the labor force. The smaller increase occurs because the lower level of real wages leads some previously employed workers to drop out of the labor force; the new level of real wages is too low to induce them to give up their leisure.

Flexible wages and prices. An increase in demand is not the only way in which an economy can obtain the requisite reductions in real wages and increases in employment and production. The same results can be obtained if its money wages will decline as additional workers compete for the available jobs and if the possibility of producing additional commodities causes the economy's producers to compete for sales by bidding down prices. Figure 16-11 depicts the effects of lower wages and prices in an economy with flexible wages and prices which has experienced an increase in the size of its labor force. The increased labor force expands the maximum amount of commodities which the economy's producers are willing to supply at each price level from S_1 to S_2. As a result, the economy's price level falls from slightly above P_7 to P_5 before all the additional commodities are purchased; and its level of money wages declines from Wm_2 to Wm_1 before the level of real wages in the economy is low enough for all workers who are willing to work to actually find employment.

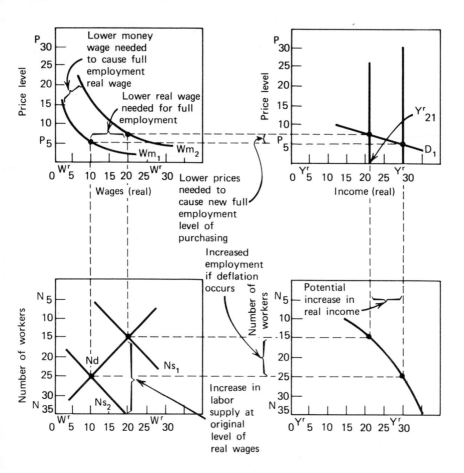

FIGURE 16-11
An increased labor supply with flexible wages and prices.

Productivity increases. It is possible that productivity increases can cause the demand for labor in an economy to rise even faster than the economy's labor supply. Should this occur, the full employment level of real wages will tend to rise, and it becomes conceptually possible for an economy to obtain its maximum possible levels of production without experiencing inflation.

For example, consider the economy represented by Figure 16-12. The curves and values depicting the initial conditions in the economy are denoted by the subscript 1. The conditions after an increase in the size of the labor force, an increase in the productivity of labor, and an increase in aggregate demand are identified by the subscript 2. Notice that no inflation has occurred, but real wages have risen, money wages have risen, more commodities are being produced, and yet there is no unemployment. As long as purchasing increases adequately an expanding labor force does not necessarily mean either unemployment or inflation when an economy's wages and prices are inflexible downward.

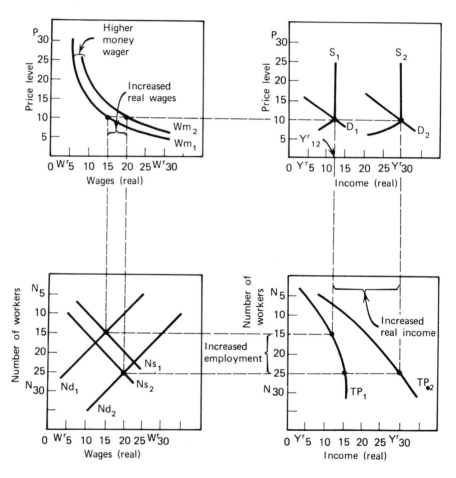

FIGURE 16-12
Labor increases, productivity increases, and demand increases.

ADMINISTERED PRICES

The prices of some commodities may be set as the result of arbitrary administrative decisions rather than determined in competitive markets by the forces of supply and demand. Inflation tends to result when such "administered prices" are increased. It occurs because an increase in one or more administratively determined prices while other prices remain unchanged means an increase in the general level of commodity prices. And unemployment also will tend to occur if the higher individual prices result in a decline in the amount of commodities that their producers can sell and thus in the number of commodities they are willing to produce.

"Administered prices" cannot occur when price competition exists among the producers of each type of commodity. They cannot occur because any arbitrary increase in prices will result in a surplus of unsold commodities that will cause prices to be bid back down to the equilibrium level. But competition does not exist in the production and sale of every commodity. If it does not exist, the economy's noncompetitive producers might be expected to arbitrarily raise their prices whenever the decline in their revenues from not selling as many commodities is more than made up by the higher prices they received from those commodities they do sell and the lower costs associated with the production of fewer commodities. Prices also may be raised if commodity producers agree among themselves to set prices higher and then not compete to drive them down, or if the economy's governments, perhaps associating high prices with prosperity or at the behest of the producers, arbitrarily raise the prices of certain commodities by law or decree and do not permit the economy's producers to bid them down. Higher administered prices in the United States' economy, for instance, would occur if General Motors arbitrarily raised all its car prices $100 or if a government passed a law or engaged in activities that effectively raised the price of haircuts from $2 to $3.

Figure 16-13 reflects the effects of administered prices. It portrays an economy that is initially in equilibrium at price level P_{10} with N_{20} workers producing Y^r_{18} commodities. Then certain prices are increased by administrative activities so that the general level of commodity prices in the economy rises to P_{15}. The amount of commodities that will be purchased and thus produced declines to Y^r_{11} which requires the employment of N_{10} workers, and the level of real wages declines from W^r_{15} to W^r_{10}. Furthermore, unemployment occurs in the Figure 16-13 economy because its money wages are inflexible downward. (If money wages were flexible downward, they would eliminate the unemployment by declining until only N_{10}

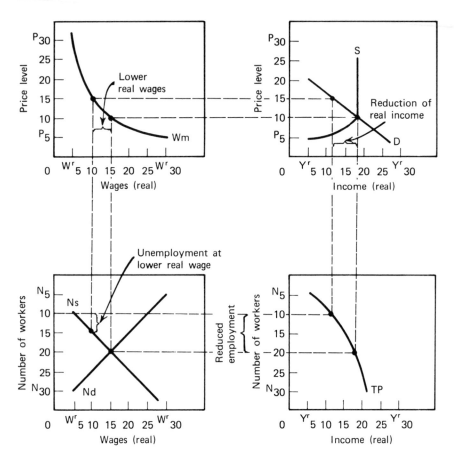

FIGURE 16-13
Administered prices.

workers were willing to work.) In any event, no change occurs in the nature of either the economy's aggregate demand or its aggregate supply curves when price levels are increased arbitrarily. This is true because nothing has occurred to change the amount of commodities that would be purchased in the economy at each price level or the maximum amounts of commodities that the economy's producers would be willing to produce at each price level if the price level should ever be, in fact, in existence.

The inflation and unemployment levels of production caused by increases in administered prices can be ended by eliminating the method by which administered prices are installed. This can be accomplished by promoting competition among noncompeting producers, by withdrawing government price regulations, and by regulating producers without possible competitors so that they price and behave as if they were operating under competitive conditions. Obviously, in the absence of policies to eliminate the causes of the administered prices, an economy confronted with inflation due to administered prices is faced with a dilemma similar to that which exists in a cost-push situation; it must choose among doing nothing, raising demand to eliminate unemployment by having more commodities purchased and thus produced, or lowering demand in an effort to fight the rising prices. And if purchasing is raised or lowered, a problem still remains in deciding whether to change it just for the affected commodities or have general changes that will affect all commodities.

For instance, a general reduction in taxes for the purpose of restoring demand to the full employment level tends to increase the purchases of all commodities rather than just those whose production was reduced because their prices were increased arbitrarily. But if maximum amounts of the other commodities whose prices were not raised are already being produced, attempts to increase the purchases of these items will only cause their prices to rise. Then as the prices rise, their producers may be willing to hire more labor and capital and produce more commodities. Under such circumstances the effect of administered prices not only is inflationary but also, when the unemployment they cause is eliminated, may change the composition of the goods and services produced in the economy.

FRICTIONAL UNEMPLOYMENT

The vertical portion of the aggregate supply curve used in this and other chapters represents the maximum amount of commodities that can be produced in an economy at a specific point in time. It is the amount of production that will occur when the economy is fully employing its factors of production. But is it actually possible for a full employment level of commodity production to occur? Probably not, even though it is conceptually possible. Instead, it is reasonable to believe that there always will be some labor and capital which is unemployed because they have not yet reached an available position which their owners are willing for them to hold. Unemployment for this reason typically is referred to as "frictional unemployment" because it is caused by various interferences or frictions that prevent job seekers from instantaneously reaching available jobs.

Among the possible frictions that cause temporary delays in reaching available employments are such things as the need to move to another geographic location or an inadequate dissemination of information about available jobs. Obviously, such unemployment will not be eliminated by changes in aggregate demand or worker productivity. But it can be minimized by anything that causes the rapid communication of job information and the rapid transportation of workers and capital to the site of new jobs.

STRUCTURAL UNEMPLOYMENT AND INFLATION

Various changes may occur in the structure of an economy which affect the levels of certain prices and types of employment even though the economy generally remains unchanged. Such changes may involve a shift in consumer preferences and purchasing from one type of commodity to another, or a change in the optimum location of producing a commodity, or a technological development that changes the type of labor and capital required by its producers. In the United States, for instance, there has been an increase in the demand for services and a decline in the demand for rail transportation; many coal deposits have been exhausted in certain areas of Appalachia where coal mining once flourished; and mechanical pickers have substantially replaced migrant farm laborers.

Such changes have various possible effects. First, there may be "structural unemployment" as the labor and capital associated with certain types of commodities or areas become unemployed due to structural changes. For instance, the decline in purchasing of commodities such as coal and railroad passenger service may mean that less labor and capital will be needed to produce them. Furthermore, the labor and capital that are no longer needed may remain unemployed because they are not adaptable to other locations or production techniques. What this means, in essence, is that illiterate farm migrants may lose their jobs due to the development of crop-picking machinery and not be able to find other employment; similarly, unemployed miners in West Virginia's coal fields, though they may be willing and able to work, may never be able to find comparable positions in the area.

A second possible effect of structural changes is inflation. A general rise in the level of an economy's commodity prices will occur if increases in demand for relatively favored commodities causes an increase in their prices at the same time that business practices, unchanged demand, or the need to cover unchanging costs of production prevent a drop in the prices of the now relatively unfavored products. After all, a continual increase in the prices of some of an economy's commodities due to structural changes without offsetting decreases in the prices of other commodities means a continual increase in the general level of prices in the economy.

An economy faced with such structural changes has several choices. It can attempt to solve the problem by resisting the development of new products or methods of production since a static society is not as likely to experience such changes. For instance, it can pass laws or tolerate pressures that ensure that a railroad fireman is used on each train even though there are no more fires for him to tend. Or it can encourage competition so that the prices of commodities that become relatively undesired will fall to offset any increases in those that become favored. Or it can encourage structurally unemployed labor and capital to move into new positions by providing subsidies for retraining, so the workers can take new jobs, and for moving, so they can go to new locations. Finally, in the absence of such programs, an economy can attempt to deal with the resulting inflation by lowering aggregate demand or with the resulting unemployment by raising demand. Of course, efforts to eliminate either of these effects may tend to aggravate the other. For instance, an increase in total purchasing sufficient to substantially reduce unemployment among an economy's former railroad firemen and coal miners might be enough to cause inflation as prices and wages are bid up in areas where maximum levels of production are already occurring. Some of the considerations related to choosing among these and other alternatives will be considered in subsequent chapters which deal with the level of government activity.

● REFERENCES

Ackley, G., "Administered Prices and the Inflationary Process," *American Economic Review:* Papers and Proceedings, **XLIX**, pp. 419–450 (1959).

Adekunle, J., "Rates of Inflation in Industrial, Other Developed, and Less Developed Countries 1949–65," *International Monetary Fund Staff Papers*, **XV**, pp. 531–559 (Nov. 1968).

Adelman, M. A., "Steel, Administered Prices, and Inflation," *Quarterly Journal of Economics*, **LXXV**, pp. 16–40 (Feb. 1961).

Akerloff, G., "Relative Wages and the Rate of Inflation," *Quarterly Journal of Economics*, **LXXXIII**, pp. 353–374 (Aug. 1969).

————, "Structural Unemployment in a Neoclassical Framework," *Journal of Political Economy*, **LXXVII**, pp. 399–407 (May–June 1969).

————— and J. Stiglitz, "Capital, Wages, and Structural Unemployment," *Economic Journal*, **LXXIX**, pp. 269–281 (June 1969).

Barth, P., "Unemployment and Labor Force Participation." *Southern Economic Journal*, **XXXIV**, pp. 375–382 (Oct. 1967).

Bowen, W. G., and S. H. Masters, "Shifts in the Composition of Demand and the Inflation Problem," *American Economic Review*, **LIV**, pp. 975–984 (Dec. 1964).

Bronfenbrenner, M., and F. Holzman, "Survey of Inflation Theory," *American Economic Review*, **LIII**, pp. 593–654 (Sept. 1963).

Council of Economic Advisers, "The Gap between Actual and Potential GNP," in *The Annual Report of the Council of Economic Advisers*, 1965 (Washington, D.C.: U.S. Government Printing Office, 1965), pp. 81–84.

Depodwin, H. J., and R. Selden, "Business Pricing Policies and Inflation," *Journal of Political Economy*, **LXXI**, pp. 116–127 (Feb. 1963).

Duesenberry, J., "The Mechanics of Inflation," *Review of Economics and Statistics*, **XXXII**, pp. 144–149 (May 1950).

Gallaway, L., "Labor Mobility, Resource Allocation, and Structural Unemployment," *American Economic Review*, **LIII**, pp. 694–716 (Sept. 1963).

—————, "The Wage-Push Inflation Thesis, 1950–1957," *American Economic Review*, **XLVIII**, pp. 967–972 (Dec. 1958).

Hansen, W., "The Cyclical Sensitivity of The Labor Supply," *American Economic Review*, **LI**, pp. 299–309 (June 1961).

Holzman, F., "Inflation: Cost-Push and Demand-Pull," *American Economic Review*, **L**, pp. 20–42, 723 (March 1960).

Kessel, R. A., and A. A. Alchian, "The Meaning and Validity of the Inflation Induced Lag of Wages behind Prices," *American Economic Review*, **L**, pp. 43–66 (March 1960).

Lewis, J. P., "The Lull That Came to Stay," *Journal of Political Economy*, **LXIII**, pp. 1–19 (Feb. 1955).

Machlup, F., "Another View of Demand-Pull and Cost-Push Inflation," *Review of Economics and Statistics*, **XLII**, pp. 125–139 (May 1960).

Perlman, R. (Ed.), *Inflation, Demand-Pull or Cost-Push* (Heath, 1965).

Phelps, E., "Wage-Price Dynamics, Inflation, and Unemployment. The New Microeconomics in Inflation and Employment Theory," *American Economic Review*, **LIX**, pp. 124–134 (May 1969).

Reder, M., "The Theory of Frictional Unemployment," *Economica*, N.S. **XXXVI**, pp. 1–28 (Feb. 1969).

Schultze, C. L., "Recent Inflation in the United States," Study Paper No. 1, in *Study of Employment, Growth, and Price Levels*, Joint Economic Committee, 86th Congress, 1st Session (Washington, D.C.: U.S. Government Printing Office, 1959), pp. 4–16.

Selden, R., "Cost-Push vs. Demand-Pull Inflation, 1955–1957," *Journal of Political Economy*, **LXVII**, pp. 1–20 (Feb. 1959).

Simler, N. J., "Long-Term Unemployment, the Structural Hypothesis and Public Policy," *American Economic Review*, **LIV**, pp. 985–1001 (1964).

Weiss, L., "Business Pricing Policies and Inflation Reconsidered," *Journal of Political Economy*, **LXXIV**, pp. 177–187 (April 1966).

Yordon, W. J., "Industrial Concentration and Price Flexibility in Inflation: Price Response Rates in Fourteen Industries, 1947–1958," *Review of Economics and Statistics*, **XLIII**, pp. 287–294 (Aug. 1961).

Stabilization
Analysis

17

Economic analysis suggests that inadequate levels of employment and production can be caused by inappropriate levels of wages, prices, and total purchasing. Thus it is in the best interest of an economy to stabilize its prices, wages, and purchasing at whatever levels and rates of growth will most enhance the economy's attainment and retention of the most desirable levels of employment and production. But each economy has unique structures and institutions. Thus, in order to make rational stabilization decisions, it is necessary to identify both the ways in which each economy's employment and production are related to its prices, wages, and purchasing and the most desirable levels of production and employment in the economy. Only when these relationships are known can reasonable policies be selected to provide the appropriate levels of prices, wages, and purchasing.

THE PHILLIPS ANALYSIS

In 1958 Professor A. W. Phillips presented his now famous examination of the relationship between unemployment and the rate of change of money-wage rates in the United Kingdom during the preceding century.[1] His analysis indicated that the rate of change in the economy's money-wage rates depended primarily on the level of unemployment. He also found that the rate of change in the economy's money-wage rates was influenced by changes in the cost of living as indicated by changes in the level of the economy's retail prices and the state of the economy's business cycle as indicated by the direction and rate of change of the economy's rate of unemployment.

Phillips explained his findings as being caused by competition among the employers of labor that resulted in wages being bid up faster and faster as the supply of unemployed labor dwindled while, on the other hand, the economy's workers were reluctant or unable to offer their services for less even when unemployment existed and was growing. He also reasoned that as prosperity was arriving and unemployment declining the employers bid more vigorously for labor and the workers pressed more vigorously for wage increases than they would at the same rate of unemployment if prosperity was receding and the economy was experiencing or expecting employment reductions.

The Basic Procedure

A Phillips' analysis begins by plotting points representing each year's combination of the rate of change in the economy's level of money-wage rates and the annual labor unemployment rate onto a scatter diagram. Then the basic relationship between unemployment and wage increases during the time period under consideration is obtained by fitting a curve to the observed combinations. Examples of the type of relationships found by Phillips and the economists who subsequently developed and extended his analysis are presented in Figures 17-1a and 17-1b. The dotted loops around the fitted curves trace out the move from one year's observed combinations to the next. The loops indicate the degree to which the actual combinations deviate from the fitted curves at any particular time during the time periods under consideration.

[1]A. W. Phillips, "The Relation between Unemployment and the Rate of Change of Money Wage Rates in the United Kingdom, 1861–1957," *Economica*, **XXV**, pp. 283–300 (1958); reprinted in *Macroeconomic Readings* (The Free Press, 1968), John Lindauer, editor. Also see R. G. Lipsey, "The Relation between Unemployment and the Rate of Change of Money Wage Rates in the United Kingdom, 1862–1957: A Further Analysis," *Economica*, **XXVII**, pp. 1–31 (1960).

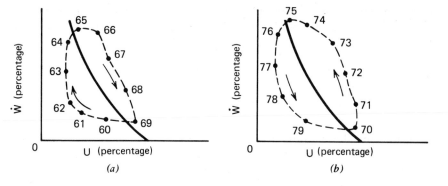

FIGURE 17-1
Example Phillips curves (*a*) 1960–1969, (*b*) 1970–1979.

The Nature of Phillips Curves

Most curves fitted to actual wage and labor unemployment data for the U.S., U.K., and Canada have the basic shape depicted in the Figure 17-1 examples. Their positions to the right of the vertical axis is explained by the frictional and structural unemployment whose existence ensures that some labor unemployment will exist no matter how anxious employers are to hire workers and how fast wages rise. The curve for countries such as the U.K. lies closer to the vertical axis than do those of the U.S. and Canada because it has less frictional and structural unemployment. There are several possible explanations for the observed differences in the curves for the different economies during the same time period. First, the geographic size of the U.K. is smaller so that it takes less time and effort to move from one position to the next. Second, it may be that tradition is more binding in terms of long term occupation and employer relationships. And, third, perhaps the U.K. economy is less dynamic and the labor force better prepared to handle alternative opportunities so that fewer are left behind as unemployable when the structure of the economy changes.

Shape of the Curves. Rapidly rising wage rates have been found in all three economies at relatively low rates of unemployment. This can be explained, in the best market tradition, as occurring because wages tend to be bid higher when the supply of available labor is relatively low. Except for the war years and special efforts by the U.K. in response to its balance of payments problems, all three economies have generally been free from government restrictions on raising wages, and their employers have generally been unable to sufficiently organize themselves to stop competing for the economies' stocks of labor. On the other hand, however, wages have risen in all three economies at times when unemployment apparently existed in excess of the structurally and frictionally unemployed.

Wages would be bid down in a competitive labor market whenever unemployed workers compete for the available jobs and only bid up whenever there is no additional surplus labor and employers still desire to hire more workers. Thus the Phillips curve for a perfectly competitive economy should be a vertical line positioned to the right of the vertical axis by the amount of the frictional and structural unemployment. Curve ABCD in Figure 17-2 is an example of such a curve.

If workers tend to resist wage competition for the available jobs when there is general unemployment in excess of the example economy's frictional and structural unemployment, then the Phillips curve for the economy would have the ABCE form presented in Figure 17-2. This would be the case where union and minimum wage laws allow money wages to increase if employers bid them up but are partially successful in keeping wages from falling where there is general unemployment. If an economy's money wages absolutely could not fall, the economy's Phillips curve would have the form ABCF.

Portions of the actual Phillips curves for the U.S., U.K., and Canada lie above the horizontal axis even though there was general unemployment in the economies during the time period considered. The curves take the form ABG. The fact that an economy's Phillips curve lies above the horizontal axis when general unemployment exists in the economy could be caused by pressures such as those caused by various union activities or government activities that force wages up even in the face of a labor surplus, or if the economy's labor submarkets have temporarily different levels of labor unemployment so that an increase in the demand for labor puts workers back to work in some markets where there is unemployment. In others, where labor is already fully employed, the increased demand merely bids up wages.

Shifts in the Curves. The differential unemployment explanation of Phillips curves that lie above the horizontal axis, however, rests on the existence of imperfectly adjusted markets. Thus there will be no more unemployment once wages have risen enough to sufficiently reallocate labor into the areas and occupations where wages are being bid up. When an economy's wages have once risen enough to induce labor from everyone who wants to work except the frictionally unemployed and the residual of

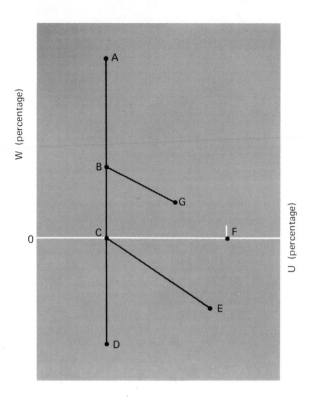

FIGURE 17-2
Alternative shapes of Phillips curves.

the structurally unemployed who will not or can not take other jobs at any wage, the economy's labor force will be properly allocated and, in the absence of nonmarket forces, its wages will not tend to be bid up in subsequent periods until all of the general unemployment in the economy is eliminated. In other words, the economy's Phillips curve will be shifted down until its vertical portion intersects the horizontal axis at the level of frictional and structural unemployment. But such a proper allocation of labor may never be attained. The more dynamic an economy is in terms of creating structural changes and the less the economy has been operated at capacity to insure the continual reallocation of labor appropriate to its new structures, the more the economy's wages will rise in each time period at a given rate of unemployment.

Shifts in an economy's Phillips curve also occur when additional nonmarket pressures are added to its wage-determination processes. For example, several studies have indicated that the existence of unions have added approximately one percent to the rate of wage increases that could otherwise have been expected in the United States at each level of unemployment.

Wage Increases and the Business Cycle

Employers in market economies are apparently more willing to agree to pay higher wages if they expect to have to hire more workers than if they expect sales to decline in the future so that they will have to decide which workers will be terminated. Thus the degree of wage increases and decreases in an economy at a particular point in time not only depends on the level of unemployment in the economy but is also influenced by the direction and speed of changes in the level of economic activity in the economy. Various studies have been made relating the rates at which unemployment levels have changed to the state of an economy's business cycle. The studies generally suggest that their cyclical position was a major factor influencing the rate at which money wage levels changed in the U.S., U.K., and Canada prior to World War I and that the importance of cyclical fluctuations of income and employment in explaining wage rate changes dwindled substantially after the war.

The basic analysis relating Phillips curves to the effects of the cycle is in terms of the loops joining the actual combinations of unemployment and rates of change in money wages. The speed and direction of the cycle and other factors such as changes in the cost of living explain why different rates of wage changes might occur in an economy at the same level of unemployment. Notice the change in the levels of unemployment and rates of wage increases occurring from one year to the next in the Figure 17-1 example economies. Both economies move through an entire cycle starting and returning to a high rate of unemployment. These changes and the position of the specific combinations of wage increases and unemployment suggest the nature of the cycles that confronted the economies. In the Figure 17-1*b* economy, for example, the wage increase and unemployment combination for the earlier years lie above the economy's Phillips curve during the upswing of the cycle toward prosperity and then in the later years lie below it during the downswing toward extensive labor unemployment and the lower levels of production that unemployment implies. Such a move suggests that the cycle initially begins with the economy either possessing differential levels of unemployment in its submarkets or experiencing increases in the activities that affect specific submarkets of labor. The level of money wages in the economy rises relatively rapidly as wages are bid up in the submarkets that are initially short of labor while employment lags behind the expanding demand and output as unemployment continues to exist in other locations and occupations. The decline in the rate of increase in the level of money wages during the second half of the decade occurs after labor has been reallocated in response to the higher wages in certain submarkets.

The Figure 17-1a economy depicts just the opposite situation. Its wage rates initially rose relatively little as its unemployment declined. Either its unemployment was initially spread more uniformly over the economy or the initial increases in activity occurred in those sectors with the greatest unemployment. Once the Figure 17-1b economy reached the prosperity peak of its cycle and turned down, however, the decline in activity was concentrated in relatively few sectors so that the number of unemployed in the economy rose even though employment pressures and sales opportunities in the other sectors kept their wages, and thus the general level of wages in the economy, rising relatively rapidly.

Wage Increases and Changes in the Price Level

Phillips did not attribute most of the wage increases he observed to increases in the level of prices that would cause increases in the wage-earners' costs of living. He felt instead that an economy's wages can rise as fast as its productivity increases and that higher prices will have no effect as long as they do not rise faster than wages. In essence, he assumed that labor will remain content as long as it is not asked to accept a reduction in real wages. The only exception to the neutrality of inflation occurred when prices rose faster than productivity alone would allow wages to increase. This happened on only a few occasions and then, he thought, due to extraneous forces such as a change in import prices. Subsequent economists have disagreed with his conclusions. They find that price changes became an important cause of wage behavior after the 1900's and that by the post-World War II era were a major determinant of the rate at which money wages rose in the U.S., U.K., and Canada.

Prices and Unemployment

Paul Samuelson and Robert Solow extended the Phillips approach to relate the level of an economy's unemployment to the rate of changes in the economy's level of prices.[1] An example of their modified Phillips curve is presented in Figure 17-3. The curve in the figure indicates that the economy

[1] Paul A. Samuelson and Robert M. Solow, "Analytical Aspects of Anti-Inflation Policy," *American Economic Review: Papers and Readings*, **L**, pp. 177–194 (1960). Reprinted in *Macroeconomic Readings* (The Free Press, 1968), John Lindauer, editor.

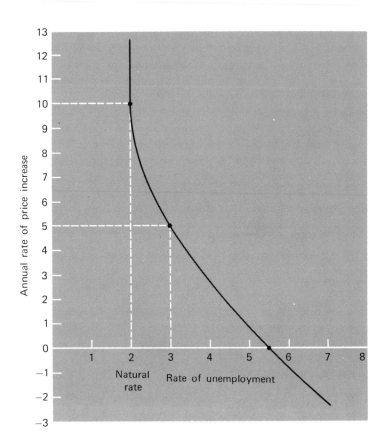

FIGURE 17-3
A modified Phillips curve.

depicted would have to accept a 5 percent annual increase in prices if it desires to maintain a 3 percent level of unemployment. Based on their findings of the United States' past expenses, Samuelson and Solow initially estimated that the American economy would have to have a 4–5 percent increase in prices if it were to have a 3 percent rate of unemployment and that the economy's price level would remain stable if its unemployment rate were approximately $5\frac{1}{2}$ percent. Subsequent analysts suggest that their estimate of the unemployment rate required for price stability is overly optimistic in view of the dynamic nature of the economy's structure and the apparent downward inflexibility of commodity prices. Others, however, suggest that such past experiences during periods of unstable growth are not applicable to economies enjoying periods of sustained full employment. They feel that certain "natural rates" of wage and price changes with magnitudes lower than those of the past can occur in the long run in economies that move from income fluctuations to sustained income growth.

THE NATURAL RATES

The Phillips curves for an economy are based on the alternative combinations of unemployment, inflation, and wage increases that occurred in the economy in the past. But such combinations are averages based on incomes and unemployment rates that have fluctuated in a cyclical manner. Thus they may not adequately reflect the conditions that will exist when monetary, fiscal, and other policies are implemented in order to prevent such fluctuations. After all, the past may not have been one of sustained stability with wage- and price-induced reallocations smoothly occurring. Instead, the reallocations inherent in a dynamic market economy and the wage and price increases associated with them may only have occurred sporadically whenever the economy got close enough to prosperity to exhaust the available supply of labor and commodities in certain submarkets.

Natural rates of unemployment and wage changes. The goal of maximum production requires that an economy be able to employ its willing and able productive factors in the production process. Higher wages tend to assist in accomplishing this employment to the extent that they are able to induce the structurally unemployed to leave their traditional homes and occupations and engage in productive activities in other areas or of other types. But full employment is impossible due to both frictional unemployment and the unemployable portion of the structurally unemployed.

A Phillips curve for an economy could be based on stable unemployment rates and the wages and price changes associated with them. It would then depict the trade-offs between unemployment and wage or price increases when there is sustained employment stability so that the periodic one-time effects of price and wage changes accumulated from previous changes in the structure of the economy are eliminated in favor of continual smooth adjustments. The derivation of such a curve requires that only wage-increase data be used for unemployment rates that were stable for a relatively long period of time. Such a "stable Phillips curve" would indicate the economy's alternatives between wage increases and unemployment rates if the economy were able to permanently stabilize its rate of unemployment, and it would tend to lie below the economy's historical Phillips curve if the economy had previously experienced periodic wage and price increases to reallocate factors when unemployment fell toward the lowest possible rates.

The natural rate of unemployment for an economy is the proportion that the economy's frictionally unemployed and structurally unemployable is of its total labor force. The natural rate of unemployment is 3 percent in the Figure 17-4 example economy. And if that economy's natural rate of unemployment is 3 percent, its natural rate of wage increase is 9 percent. Nine percent is the lowest rate of wage increase that can be obtained if unemployment is stabilized with the existence of only frictional unemployment and the unemployable portion of structural unemployment.

The natural rate of inflation. Stable Phillips types of curves can also be developed that relate the rate of price increase experiences of an economy to various rates of unemployment that have remained stable for a

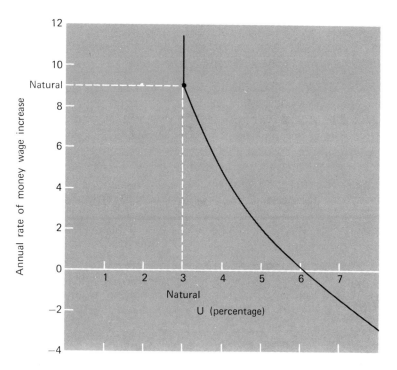

FIGURE 17-4
Stable and historical Phillips curves.

period of time. Such stable curves would retain the basic shape as Samuelson and Solow's modified version of the Phillips curve. First, if individual prices tend to be inflexible downward, generally higher and higher price levels would be required if particular prices were to rise enough to change relative prices and cause the economy's producers to dynamically adjust to new products, techniques, and preferences. Second, it would retain the basic Phillips shape because the higher rates of wage increases associated with lower rates of unemployment would produce greater and greater cost-push effects at lower unemployment rates.

Figure 17-5 presents a stable Phillips type curve for the economy initially depicted in Figure 17-4. Notice that the stable curve becomes perfectly inelastic at a 3 percent rate of unemployment: no matter how much the economy's relative prices adjust or its absolute prices rise, the frictional and residual structural unemployment cannot be elininated.

An economy can choose to operate at its natural rate of unemployment

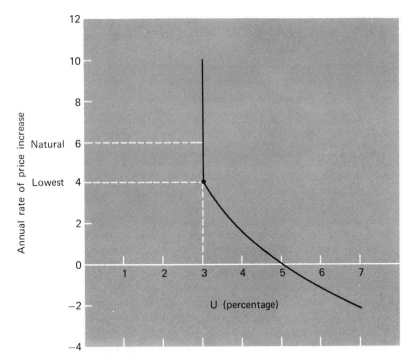

FIGURE 17-5
Modified Phillips curve.

and maximize its production. But consider the price level dilemma that this causes in the economy depicted in Figures 17-4 and 17-5. The natural rate of wage increases in this economy is 9 percent while the lowest possible rate of price increase that can be associated with its natural rate of unemployment is 4 percent. Thus, if the economy's annual increase in productivity is 2 percent and if the economy chooses to operate at its 3 percent minimum rate of unemployment and to keep its rate of price increase minimized at 4 percent and its rate of wage increase minimized at 9 percent, there will be a steady redistribution of income to the labor sector at the rate of 2 percent of the labor sector income. This economy must then choose between redistribution or letting the economy's prices rise at the rate of 6 percent in order to prevent redistribution. Six percent is the economy's natural rate of inflation. It is the lowest rate that allows both maximum production without redistribution and the wage and price increases needed to obtain structural change and factor reallocation.

INTERNAL AND EXTERNAL STABILITY

Both monetary and fiscal policies may be used in an effort to stabilize an economy with fixed exchange rates, such as that of the United States, at full employment levels of income and balance of payments equilibrium. And either type of policy could conceivably be used in an effort to obtain either goal. For example, lower interest rates and lower taxes could be used during a period of unemployment to restore an economy's performance internally by increasing its income to the full-employment level. On the other hand, higher interest rates and higher taxes may reduce purchasing and could be used both internally to avoid levels of income so high that they would result in demand-pull inflation and externally to restore equilibrium by eliminating a balance-of-payments deficit.

The Policy Combination

The problem of simultaneously stabilizing an economy both internally and externally is that policies that improve an economy's balance of payments position also tend to reduce its level of income and, conversely, policies that expand the level of income may lead to balance-of-payments deficits. Furthermore, there are various combinations of interest rate levels and fiscal restraints that would yield full-employment levels of income and other combinations that would yield equilibrium in the economy's balance of payments. Analysis of the various combinations suggests that there is one combination of monetary and fiscal policies that simultaneously yields both internal equilibrium at full employment without inflation and external equilibrium without a balance-of-payments deficit or surplus.[1]

Internal stability. Full employment levels of income can be attained with various combinations of interest-rate levels and fiscal restraints on the level of income. The more that an economy's fiscal activities such as higher taxes tend to reduce total purchasing, the lower that the economy's level of interest rates can be without causing demand-pull inflation. The internal equilibrium curve in Figure 17-6 represents the various combinations of monetary ease and fiscal restraint that will lead to full employment levels of income without inflation. Points to the right of the curve represent combinations of interest rates levels and fiscal restraint that are so great that they will yield unemployment levels of income. Points to the left of the curve represent combinations of interest rate levels and fiscal restraint that are so low that they will yield inflation. The curve slopes down and to the right since lower and lower levels of fiscal restraint are offset by the monetary conditions associated with higher and higher interest rates.

External stability. The lower levels of income that tend to be associated with greater degrees of fiscal restraint in an economy mean that fewer products will be purchased abroad and that the economy will tend to run a balance-of-payments surplus. On the other hand, lower levels of interest rates tend to mean that a balance-of-payments deficit will occur. Since various combinations of fiscal restraint and interest rate levels can lead to balance-of-payments equilibrium, the greater the fiscal restraint, the lower the level of interest rates can be without causing a balance-of-payments deficit. The external equilibrium curve in the Figure 17-6 example economy depicts the various combinations of interest rate levels and fiscal restraint that will lead to balance-of-payments equilibrium.

The external equilibrium curve slopes down and to the right to indicate that a balance-of-payments equilibrium can occur with higher levels of interest rates when there are lower levels of fiscal restraint to curb purchasing abroad and other expenditures. Furthermore, the external equilibrium curve tends to be more inelastic than the internal equilibrium curve. Specifically, if both purchasing abroad and domestic purchasing depends on the level

[1] This analysis is derived from Robert Mundell's "The Appropriate Use of Monetary and Fiscal Policy for Internal and External Stability." It originally appeared in the *International Monetary Fund Staff Papers* (1962) and is reprinted in *Macroeconomic Readings* (The Free Press, 1968), John Lindauer, editor.

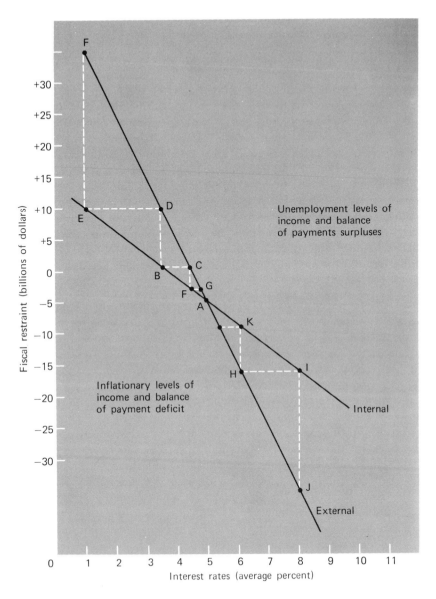

FIGURE 17-6
Internal and external stability.

of income in an economy and changes in proportion to changes in the economy's income, then both the internal and external curves would have the same slope. But the external curve will be more inelastic to the extent that the movement of monetary assets from abroad affects the economy's balance-of-payments position more than its level of income so that it takes a smaller interest rate increase to restore equilibrium in the economy's balance of payments with a given reduction in fiscal restraint than would be required to internally restore full employment with such ·a reduction in fiscal restraint.

The Policy Requirements

There is only one combination of interest rate levels and fiscal restraint that will simultaneously result in both internal and external equilibrium. In the Figure 17-6 example economy, for example, the combination that will simultaneously result in both internal and external equilibrium is identified as point "A." All other combinations would, at best, result in the attainment of only one type of equilibrium.

The equilibrium requirements for the Figure 17-6 economy also suggest that fiscal policies should be used to internally stabilize such an economy with fixed exchange rates while monetary policies should be reserved for use in stabilizing the economy externally. Consider the combination represented by point "B" so that the economy would be internally in equilibrium at a full-employment level of income without inflation even though the degree of fiscal restraint and the level of interest rates are inadequate to prevent a balance-of-payments deficit. The balance-of-payments deficit could only be eliminated with an increase of BC in the level of interest rates or an increase of BD in the degree of fiscal restraint. But while the additional fiscal restraint would solve the balance-of-payments problem as it takes the economy to the combination represented by point D, it would also provide an equilibrium level of income that would result in unemployment. Then an even greater reduction in the level of interest rates of DE would be required to restore full employment. But then the economy's balance of payments would again have a deficit, and its elimination would require an increase in fiscal restraint of EF that is even greater than the initial increase of BD. And the stabilization requirements would continue to grow without simultaneously yielding external and internal equilibrium as long as monetary policy is used in an effort to get internal equilibrium and fiscal policy is used to get external equilibrium.

Consider, on the other hand, the effect of reserving monetary policies for the attainment of external balance. Initially, the interest-rate levels in the Figure 17-6 economy would have to be increased from B to C in order to eliminate the balance-of-payments deficit. Then the degree of fiscal restraint would have to be reduced by CF to restore full employment. But the reduction in fiscal restraint to the level depicted by "F" means another tendency for a balance-of-payments deficit that would require a FG reduction in the level of interest rates and thus a further reduction in the degree of fiscal restraint. The important aspect of this analysis is that the degree of monetary and fiscal changes required to restore equilibrium is getting smaller and smaller and the economy is approaching the point "A" combination that will simultaneously put it into internal and external equilibrium.

STABILIZATION EFFORTS

One of the least considered aspects of monetary, fiscal, and other governmental activities is that they may affect the level of prices in an economy such as that of the United States by directly changing the prices or costs of production of certain commodities. For example, certain taxes such as sales, excises, and property taxes directly affect the level of expenditures needed to acquire taxed items and are reflected in the consumer price index that is often used as a measure of the degree of price stability in the United States. Furthermore, increases in these and other taxes may raise the cost of production either directly as they increase the cost that suppliers must bear if they are to produce goods and services or indirectly to the extent that they reduce the incomes of the producers below the level of normal profits that the producers require in order to be willing to produce. Interest rate changes have the same effect. Higher interest rates, for example, tend to increase the consumer price index to the extent that they cause greater levels of expenditures to be needed to obtain housing and the ownership of automobiles. Finally, in response to the conditions and policies that exist and are expected to occur, governments may raise the prices of items such as water and sewage that they sell in order to finance their outlays without raising taxes, or they may raise the regulated prices of their constituents so that the regulated constituents will be able to participate in an existing or anticipated inflation.

The possibility that government stabilization and pricing activities may directly cause inflation and the level of unemployment associated with the higher prices means that each potential degree of stabilization activity must be evaluated both in terms of its ability to counter the conventional causes of inflation and unemployment and the degree to which it directly causes inflation and unemployment. Obviously care must be taken that the degree of stabilization effort that could offset the forces that would otherwise cause one level of inflation and unemployment do not directly cause even greater levels.

Figure 17-7 depicts the trade-off between the direct and indirect effects of different degrees of stabilization effort. D_5 represents the economy's initial level of aggregate demand and so represents the willingness of its producers to supply goods and services. The economy is initially in equilibrium at price level P_{100} with the economy's factors of production fully employed producing a real income of Y^r_{500}. Now assume that increases in investment caused by changes in expectations will increase demands to D_0 so that the economy's price level will rise to $P_{112.5}$ unless some degree of additional monetary and fiscal restraints are implemented. Aggregate demand curves D_2 and D_3 represent the effects of two of the various degrees of monetary and fiscal restraint that might be implemented in response to those demand-pull influences. Increases in the degree of restraint to degree 5 would tend to stabilize the economy's price level at P_{100} in the absence of any cost or direct effects. But such cost or direct effect may exist. And, if they do, the efforts to stabilize prices may not be successful.

The various aggregate supply curves such as S_2 and S_3 depict the cost effects of the various degrees of stabilization efforts that might be implemented in an effort to prevent the demand-pull inflation. The extent to which costs change with different degrees of stabilization efforts depends on the composition of whatever monetary and fiscal activities are undertaken which, in turn, depend upon the preferences and abilities of the policy decision-makers. In the Figure 17-7 economy, for example, stabilization to degree 5 is associated with cost increases that would tend to push up the example economy's price level to P_{105} and reduce the level of its income to Y^r_{450}.

The direct price effects associated with the various possible degrees of stabilization effort to the other determinants of prices and employment are depicted by the A and B points in Figure 17-7. The A points represent the higher levels of prices that will result from the addition of the direct effects of the various degrees of stabilization efforts and governmental pricing responses; they indicated that the greater the degree of stabilization effort and governmental pricing responses, the more the level of prices in the economy will be above the level that would otherwise exist in their absence. The B points indicate the levels of income for which there will be sufficient aggregate demand at the levels of prices associated with each degree of stabilization effort. Thus a curve joining them would represent the trade off

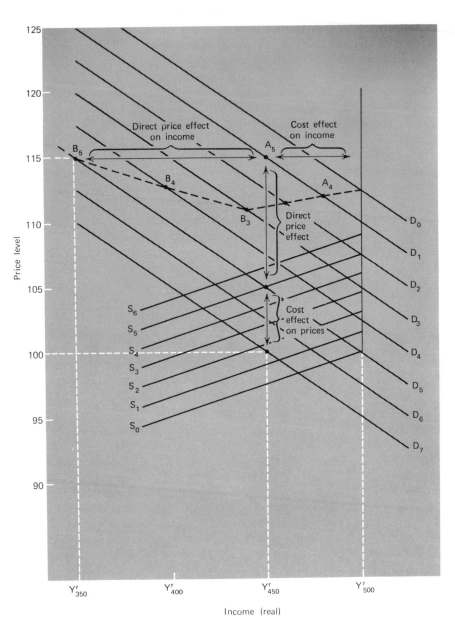

FIGURE 17-7
The effect of stabilization efforts.

between prices and unemployment under the new conditions assumed to exist in the economy. Notice, for example, that the cost changes and direct effects of the policies to degree 5 that would be implemented in an effort to restrict aggregate demand to the original level and prevent prices from rising to $P_{112.5}$ will result in both an even higher P_{115} level of prices and a reduction in the level of real income to Y^r_{350}. In this case, the most acceptable stabilization mix to reduce aggregate demand in order to fight demand-pull inflation directly increases prices to such an extent that the government, if it cannot adopt another set of policies that would have substantially less of a direct effect on prices, would provide a greater degree of price stability if it would not try to prevent the economy's aggregate demand from increasing. Obviously, the more that an economy's stabilization policies take forms that do not directly increase prices and costs, the more likely it is that the policies will be successful in stabilizing an economy's prices at full employment levels of production without inflation.

The United States' Experience

The United States' price level experiences during the late 1960's and early 1970's may be an example of the inflationary aspects of governmental stabilization policies and other governmental activities in response to inflation or inflation anticipation. First, publicity was given to the possibility of a demand-pull inflation as a result of budgetary deficits and increased expenditures for the war in Viet Nam. Then, as a result, interest-rate levels were continually increased, certain excise tax reductions were restored, the 7 percent investment credit was eliminated, and a surcharge was added to income taxes. Unfortunately the higher excise taxes and interest rates implemented to fight inflation were responsible for a substantial portion of the increase in the consumer price index; they directly increased the amounts of money that consumers had to pay to acquire housing, automobiles, and various taxes items such as cigarettes and transportation. Additionally, the increased taxes and interest rates caused production costs to rise, and the higher interest rates and the elimination of the investment credit tended to cause labor to be substituted for capital in the productive process and thus extraordinary cost-push pressures to develop in labor-intensive industries such as services. Furthermore, throughout the time period the various governmental regulatory agencies responded to the publicity and campaign rhetoric about inflation; they increased the prices of the producers they regulated so that the producers would be able to keep their relative income positions when the inflation arrived. Thus, the higher taxes, higher interest rates, higher government-regulated prices, and the changes that occurred in wages due to the tendency for labor to be substituted for capital, may have been responsible for a substantial portion of the increases in the consumer price index and caused the prices of newly produced goods and services to exceed the increases that would have occurred in the absence of these efforts. In other words, it is possible that the main cause of this particular inflation was the governmental efforts to fight it and the governmental price-fixing that occurred because governments thought that the efforts to prevent it would not be completely successful.

Ironically, there may not have been any demand-pull pressures in the economy that would have required either the implementation of such monetary and fiscal policies or increases in government-determined prices in order that relative income positions would be maintained. Instead, the productive capacity of the economy may have been growing as fast as demand increased. Thus, unfortunately, the main stabilization effect of the monetary and fiscal policies that were implemented may have been to cause inflation and to provide the economy with inadequate levels of aggregate demand that tended to stabilize the economy in a recession with high rates of unemployment, low rates of growth, and unexpectedly large budgetary deficits caused by the resulting lower levels of tax collections and the higher levels of transfer payments to the unemployed and unprofitable. Furthermore, the resulting recession tended to aggravate the inflation as state and local governments responded to their unexpected deficits by increasing their sales, excise, and property tax rates.

Prices did rise in the United States prior to the implementation of the stabilization efforts. But the increases were moderate and may well have resulted from the normal increases associated with the changes in relative prices inherent in a dynamic economy and, beginning in 1966 and 1967, an additional one-time burst of structural change that resulted from the preceding, relatively long period of prosperity without recession convincing many of the economy's participants of the permanency of prosperity and causing them to further readjust the structure of their purchasing and production.

• REFERENCES

Adams, J., "The Phillips Curve, A 'Concensual Trap,' and National Income," *Western Economic Journal*, **VI**, pp. 145–149 (March 1968).

Archibald, G. C., "The Phillips Curve and the Distribution of Unemployment," *American Economic Review*, **LXIX**, pp. 124–134 (May 1969).

Cargill, T. F., "An Empirical Investigation of the Wage-Lag Hypothesis," *American Economic Review*, **LIX**, pp. 806–816 (Dec. 1969).

Corry, B., and D. Laidler, "The Phillips Relation: A Theoretical Explanation," *Economica*, N.S., **XXXIV**, pp. 189–197 (May 1967).

Hansen, B., "Excess Demand; Unemployment, Vacancies, and Wages," *Quarterly Journal of Economics*, **LXXXIV**, pp. 1–23 (Feb. 1970).

Hines, A. G., "Unemployment and the Rate of Change of Money Wage Rates in the United Kingdom—1862–1963: A Reappraisal," *Review of Economics and Statistics*, **L**, pp. 60–67 (Feb. 1968).

Holt, C. C., "Improving Labor Market Trade-Off Between Labor and Unemployment," *American Economic Review*, **LIX**, pp. 135–146 (May 1969).

Liebling, H. S., and A. T. Cluff, "U.S. Postwar Inflation and Phillips Curves," *Kyklos*, **XXIV**, pp. 232–250 (1969).

Lipsey, R. G., "The Relation between Unemployment and the Rate of Change of Money Wage Rates in the United Kingdom, 1862–1957: A Further Analysis," *Economica*, **XXVII**, pp. 1–31 (Feb. 1960).

Lucas, R. E., Jr., and L. A. Rapping, "Price Expectations and the Phillips Curve," *American Economic Review*, **LIX**, pp. 342–350 (June 1969).

Phelps, E. S., "Phillips Curves, Expectation of Inflation and Optimal Unemployment Over Time," *Economica*, N.S., **XXXIV**, pp. 254–281 (Aug. 1967).

Phillips, A. W., "The Relation between Unemployment and the Rate of Change of Money Wage Rates in the United Kingdom, 1861–1957," *Economica*, **XXV**, pp. 283–299 (Nov. 1958).

Pierson, G., "The Effect of Union Strength and the U.S. 'Phillips Curve,' " *American Economic Review*, **LVIII**, pp. 456–467 (June 1968).

Samuelson, P., and R. M. Solow, "Analytical Aspects of Anti-Inflation Policy," *American Economic Review: Papers and Proceedings*, **L**, pp. 177–194 (May 1960).

Simler, N. J., and A. Tella, "Labor Reserves and the Phillips Curve," *Review of Economics and Statistics*, **L**, pp. 32–49 (Feb. 1968).

Vanderkamp, J., "The Phillips Relation: A Theoretical Explanation— A Comment," *Economica*, N.S., **XXXV**, pp. 179–183 (May 1968).

Income Distribution

18

Income received from the sale of goods and services produced in an economy tends to be initially distributed to the owners of the economy's factors of production on the basis of the contribution made by their factors to the production process. The essence of the relationship between an economy's production and purchasing and its income distribution is that the receipts from the sale of goods and services tend to go as incomes to the owners of the factors that produce them. The owners then voluntarily or involuntarily redistribute a portion of such purchasing power with their transfers, voluntary savings, and tax payments.

The nature of the initial distribution and subsequent redistribution of the income received from the sale of goods and services produced in an economy is important in a macroeconomic sense for several reasons. First, the desire to obtain purchasing power that can be used to acquire commodities that satisfy their own needs and those of their heirs and beneficiaries may encourage an economy's participants to develop and acquire factors of production. Second, the level of aggregate demand in an economy is affected by the degree to which the incomes received in the economy are taxed, transferred, or saved. Such receipts, for example, could end up in the hands of individuals with low propensities to consume or in financial institutions with high reserve requirements or be held by corporations in the form of retained earnings.

The effects of the taxes, transfers, and financial intermediaries in terms of how they might influence the manner in which initial income receipts are redistributed through an economy have already been discussed. Thus the discussion in this chapter emphasizes the principles underlying the initial distribution of an economy's income.

THE INITIAL DISTRIBUTION

Figure 18-1 and Table 18-1 depict example distributions of the income received as a result of expenditures to purchase an economy's production.[1] Initially (column 1) the example economy is in equilibrium at full employment with a real GNP of $600 billion and the employment of 60 million workers who are paid an average real wage of $5,000 for their production efforts. Notice that the owners of the economy's labor initially earn incomes totaling $300 billion, and that this is sufficient purchasing power to obtain 50 percent of the value of the economy's production.

The distributional effects of a reduction in the level of income in such an economy depends upon the downward flexibility of the economy's wages and prices. The data in columns 2, 3 and 4 of Table 18-1 depict several possible distributional alternatives that might occur if the example economy's gross national product recedes from $600 billion to $450 billion so that the economy's production is depressed below the full employment level and the number of workers required to produce the saleable goods and services falls to 40 million.

---

[1] The receipts of the capital owners, profit makers, and governments are each divided into two parts in order to better depict the existence of the diverse services that result in such receipts. The inclusion of indirect business taxes and capital consumption allowances as part of the receipts of governments and capital owners preserves the identity between the economy's levels of purchasing and income and allows the distribution of all purchasing expenditures to their initial recipients to be considered. Government payments made to obtain the services of productive factors used in the production of government products are added to the receipts of the owners of these factors. Thus the government net-income component contains only the balance of the income received from the sale of goods and services produced by governments and only measures the level of purchasing power that governments end up with as a result of their productive activities.

Distribution with Factor Price Inflexibility

Column 2 in the table depicts an example distribution of the $450 billion when the economy's factor prices are inflexible downward so that the 40 million workers who remain employed receive $200 billion. The other factor owners are similarly affected, and the data in the column indicate

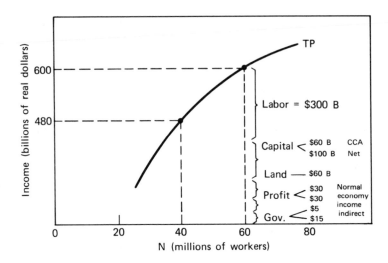

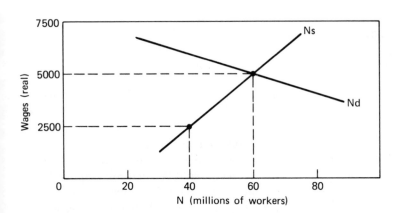

FIGURE 18-1
The initial distribution of receipts from the sales of goods and services.

TABLE 18-1

The Initial Distribution of Receipts from the Sale of Goods and Services
(Billions of Dollars)

NATURE OF THE ECONOMY	(1) FULL EMPLOY-MENT	(2) UNEM-PLOYMENT INFLEXIBLE FACTOR PRICES	(3) UNEM-PLOYMENT FLEXIBLE FACTOR PRICES	(4) UNEM-PLOYMENT WAGES INFLEXIBLE FIXED FACTOR PAYMENTS
Gross National Product (billion $)	600	450	450	450
Employment (millions)	60	40	40	40
Wage Level	5000	5000	2500	5000
Labor Force	300	200	100	200
Capital				
Consumption	60	50	50	50
Net Income	100	85	65	110
Land	60	50	40	60
Profit				
Economic	30	25	155	−30
Normal	30	25	25	25
Government				
Income	5	5	5	5
Indirect Tax	15	10	10	10
Total Receipts	600	450	450	450

that the initial incomes of all the distributive sectors will be reduced. For instance, the receipts of the owners of the economy's land and capital decline as a result of the reduction in the number that are employed even though the prices paid for the land and capital that remain on the job do not fall. On the other hand, a more uneven distribution of the economy's lower level of income would occur if legal or contractual rigidities cause some of the economy's participants to receive the same level of receipts even though there is a decline in the level of production. Column 4 depicts such an effect with the owners of the economy's land and capital continuing to receive their initial levels of income even though the economy's GNP substantially declines. Under these circumstances the position of the economy's capital owners is enhanced by the depressed level of income in the economy since less capital is consumed as a result of the reduction in the economy's level of production. The major burden of the income and employment recession, in this case, falls on the profits of the producers who bring together the economy's land, labor, and capital to produce commodities; although the producers have laid off workers and sales prices have not fallen, their profits are being squeezed by the rigidity of their payment obligations to the economy's land and capital. If such rigidities can be maintained by law or contracts that provide such things as guaranteed annual wages, land payments, or capital payments, factor owners may have a vested interest in a recession while the employers of the factors do not.

Distribution with Factor Price Flexibility

The possible effects of flexible factor prices and employment are depicted in Column 3. In this example, the incomes of the various factor owners decline substantially, but the economy's producers benefit as their profits rise far above the level that would exist at full employment. The profits rise because the cost of acquiring the factors needed for the production of the goods and services that can be sold decline further than do the economy's sales revenues. How far costs decline depends, of course, upon the amount of each type of factor that is needed for production purposes and the price elasticity of the supply of these factors. The distributions depicted in columns 3 and 4 are significant because they represent situations where an economic group would benefit from macroeconomic policies that depress an economy's level of income below the requirements of full employment.

Commodity Price Flexibility

Changes in the levels of an economy's commodity prices would have no effect on the initial distribution of the purchasing power received from the sale of the economy's goods and services if all sectors of the economy participate equally in the change. But such equal participation may not occur. Instead, the initial income distribution that results from a change in the level of an economy's commodity prices depends upon the state of the economy and the flexibility of the economy's factor prices. For example, an economy's commodity prices might rise when its factors such as labor and land are already under long-term contracts for specific monetary amounts.

An inflation under such circumstances would tend to reduce the real income of the factor owners and increase the purchasing power of their employers whose profits would rise since their sales prices are higher while their production costs are not. In terms of the example economy with money wages such that its level of real wages is initially at the $5,000 level, a doubling of the price level would be the same as reducing the level of real wages to $2,500. Thus inflation can be an alternative to downward factor-price flexibility. Whether such a reduction and the income distribution associated with it actually occur as a result of an inflation depends upon the state of the economy. If the level of real income associated with the higher prices in the example economy is $450 billion, for instance, the distribution depicted in column 3 will tend to occur. But if the level of income is $600 billion, the lower level of real wages will cause a shortage of labor and, if competition exists among the buyers, they will bid the level of money wages higher in an effort to obtain workers until the $5000 full employment level of real wages is restored.

A reduction in commodity prices would have the opposite effect. If factor prices are inflexible downward, the initial income shares of the factor owners would rise while those of their employers would fall. On the other hand, if commodity prices decline and the resulting tendency for unemployment to occur due to the higher real levels of factor prices leads to competition among the factor owners for the available jobs, factor prices would tend to be bid down in proportion to the change in commodity prices, and there would be no change in the initial distribution of income.

STABILIZATION AND DISTRIBUTION

An economy's aggregate demand for newly produced goods and services at each level of prices is based on the initial distribution of the sales revenues that will occur at each price level and the extent and manner in which the initial recipients redistribute their receipts through transfers, savings, and taxes. Thus a change in an economy's income distribution could cause a change in aggregate demand.[1] As a result, changes in an economy's income distribution could be used as an alternative to the monetary and fiscal policies that might be implemented to affect aggregate demand. Furthermore, since changes in income distribution may occur when there are

---

[1] In the Table 18-1 example economy it was assumed that the different initial distribution did not change the example economy's aggregate demand. In other words, it was assumed that any reduction in purchasing that tended to occur due to a decline in the initial income receipts of one sector was offset by the increase caused by the higher levels of income in other sectors.

changes in the flexibility of commodity and factor prices, policies that add or remove such flexibilities could be implemented for the purposes of affecting aggregate demand. Distributional changes as an alternative to monetary and fiscal policies, however, are of questionable value since ideally an economy's income is already being distributed in the most desirable manner. Thus, there may be a conflict between the goals of adequate income distribution and adequate aggregate demand. And, since there are other means of affecting the level of demand in an economy, the optimum distribution of income should occur and then other policies be implemented as required to obtain adequate levels of aggregate demand.

● REFERENCES

Davidson, P., *Theories of Aggregate Income Distribution* (Rutgers University Press, 1960).

Hotson, J., "Neo-Orthodox Keynesianism and the 45° Heresy," *Nebraska Journal of Economics and Business*, pp. 34–39 (Autumn 1967).

North, D., *Growth and Welfare in the American Past* (Prentice-Hall, 1966).

Weintraub, S., "A Macroeconomic Approach to the Theory of Wages," *American Economic Review*, **XLVI**, pp. 835–856 (Dec. 1956).

————, *An Approach to the Theory of Income Distribution* (Chilton, 1958).

————, *Employment, Growth, and Income Distribution* (Chilton, 1958).

Macroeconomic Policies

19

Most participants in an economy probably would consider the ideal level of total purchasing to be the one that results in full-employment levels of production without causing inflation. But that alternative is not realistically open to them since, for frictional, structural, and institutional reasons, there may well be no level of purchasing that can result in both full employment and stable prices. Instead, different levels of total purchasing may result in different combinations of price changes and unemployment. This situation exists, for example, when levels of total purchasing that are high enough to reduce unemployment among an economy's factors of production are also so high that they cause prices and wages to be bid up in sectors of the economy where high levels of production have already been attained. Furthermore, if an economy's wages and prices tend to be inflexible downward, the changes in relative prices inherent in a dynamic market economy will constantly move the economy's prices to higher levels. In any event, the optimum level of total purchasing for an economy at any one point in time is whatever level yields the combination of inflation and unemployment that is most acceptable to the economy's participants.

The basic goal of macroeconomic policies is the efficient use of the economy's labor and capital. In the past, the macroeconomic performances of many economies have been sadly lacking. In the United States, for example, hundreds of billions of dollars of goods and services were not produced in the post World War II period due to inadequate levels of aggregate demand that periodically occurred and resulted in unemployment. This performance resulted despite the 1946 act of Congress directing that full employment was to be the major economic goal of the economy.

There was no reason for United States' purchasing to periodically be at levels below those needed to cover full-employment levels of production. But the various macroeconomic policies implemented by the congresses and administrations that governed the economy made them inevitable. However, there is no need for such unemployment to occur in the future; monetary, fiscal, and other policies can be implemented to ensure that adequate levels of purchasing will occur.

FISCAL POLICIES

In addition to the decisions by the people of an economy concerning what government purchases they wish to be made and what government transfers granted, there also must be decisions as to how the governments are to acquire the money they need to pay for these purchases and transfers. When governments collect the same amounts of money from taxes as they disburse for transfers and purchases, their budgets are balanced. But even if optimum amounts of government transfers and purchases occur, such balanced budgets do not necessarily solve all the problems of the economy. In particular, it is still possible for the various types of purchasing in an economy to add up to a level of total purchasing that differs from the amount that will yield the results desired by the residents of the economy. After all, there is no reason to believe that the rates of taxation that will balance the budgets of an economy's governments will also provide the levels of disposable income and purchasing incentives that will result in the most desirable level of total purchasing.

The Fiscal Choices

An economy's governments have three basic choices when confronted with a situation in which their budgets are balanced with optimum amounts of purchases and transfers but do not result in the most desirable level of total purchasing. First, they can accept the situation. This means that optimum amounts of government purchases and transfers occur and that they are financed completely by the collection of an equal amount of taxes. It also means that an undesirable level of total purchasing will exist unless the performance of the economy is influenced in some other manner. Second, one or more of the governments can change the amounts of their purchases or transfers in order to generate the desired level of total purchasing. This may or may not be accompanied by a similar change in taxes so that budget balancing is maintained, but it certainly results in a level of government purchasing or transfers that differs from the levels that would exist in the absence of total purchasing considerations. Third, one or more of the governments can maintain their purchasing and transfers at the optimum levels and adjust the level of tax collections until the desired level of total purchasing occurs. This, of course, means that these governments' tax revenues will differ from the amount of their outlays; they will have to either cope with budget surpluses or run deficits and thus be forced to use other sources of financing.

Since an optimum level of total purchasing must occur if high employment levels of production are to exist without intolerable levels of inflation, and since sources other than taxes exist to finance government outlays, "Functional Finance" is the basic governmental fiscal approach favored by most economists. It involves the maintenance of the optimum level of government purchasing and transfers along with adjustments in the amount of taxes so that the optimum level of total purchasing is attained. The advocates of functional finance consider the drawbacks of financing deficits or coping with surpluses to be relatively minor compared with those associated with undesirable levels of total purchasing or other than optimum amounts of government purchases and transfers. In other words, they prefer the existence of deficits or surpluses to the existence of unemployment and inflation. And instead of preferring that the governments buy either unneeded missiles and roads when total purchasing is too low or too few missiles and roads when it otherwise would be too high, they prefer the deficits or surpluses that result from adjusting the amount of taxes without changing the level of government outlays. Stated yet another way, they consider the optimum level of taxes to be that which results in the optimum level of total purchasing rather than the level needed to finance government outlays; they prefer not to have labor and capital wasted by standing idle or producing less desirable commodities merely to "make work" for otherwise unemployed labor and capital.

Determining the Optimum Level of Taxation

It is possible to use the equilibrium income formula to determine the optimum level of taxes when tax adjustments are to be used to obtain a desired level of total purchasing. The appropriate amount of taxes is determined by putting the various components into the income-estimating equation equal to the desired level of total purchasing and then solving for the rate of taxation that will yield that total. The resulting rate of taxation then can be used to determine the amount of tax revenues that will yield the desired level of total purchasing.

For example, consider an economy whose equilibrium level of income is initially $600 billion and whose tax revenues and total government expenditures for purchases and transfers are equal because $a = \$10$ billion, $I_a = \$30$ billion, $I_r = .20Y$, $BS = .10Y$, $F_a = \$20$ billion, $F_i = .10Y$, $G_a = \$80$ billion, $G_i = \$12$ billion $- .03Y$, $Tr_a = \$20$ billion, $Tr_i = \$25$ billion $- .05Y$, $Tx_a = \$30$ billion, $Tx_i = .11667Y$ so that $70 billion of induced taxes are collected, $b' = .80$, and the MPC out of the remaining disposable income is .60. Then, if a $700-billion level of total purchasing is necessary for this economy to attain full-employment levels of production and is to be obtained through a reduction in induced taxes, the tax rate will have to be reduced from an average of 11.667 percent of the level of total purchasing to an average of 6.105 percent since:

1. $Y = a + b(Y - BS - Tx_a - Tx_i) + b'Tr_a + I_a + I_r + G_a + F_a + F_i + b'Tr_i + G_i.$
2. $Y = \$10 + .60(Y - .10Y - \$30 - tY) + .80(\$20) + \$30 + .20Y + \$80 + \$20 + .10Y +$ potentially excluded $.80(\$25 - .05Y) + (\$12 - .03Y).$

Substituting in the desired level of Y:

3. $\$700 = \$726 - .60(t \cdot \$700)$ if G_i and Tr_i are excluded.
4. $.60(t \cdot \$700) = \$26.$
5. $t = 6.105$ percent.

And the amount of taxes that will be collected when $Y = \$700$ billion:

6. $\$30 + .06105 (\$700) = \$72.735$

Thus the reduction in the rate of taxation to 6.105 percent will cause the level of total purchasing in the economy to rise to $700 billion. It also will move the economy's governments from a situation involving $100 billion

---

each of government outlays and taxes to an unbalanced budget situation involving a net deficit of $27.265 billion. In a sense, then, acceptance of the deficit and the need to finance part of the government outlays in some manner other than taxes is the price that must be paid by the example economy if it is to obtain the production of $100 billion of additional goods and services while retaining the optimum levels of government purchasing and transfers.

Fiscal Drag and the Full Employment Surplus

The example economy described above would have a "full employment surplus" of $11.667 billion if its original tax rates are applied to the $700 billion level of income required for full employment. The potential $11.667 billion surplus is a measure of the degree of "fiscal drag" placed on the economy by its efforts to balance its budget. But removal of the drag of the full employment surplus is not sufficient to ensure that an economy will attain full employment levels of purchasing. For example, if the full employment surplus in the example economy is removed by a tax reduction of $11.667 billion, the level of income in the economy will only rise to $630.4 billion. Furthermore, the elimination of the drag of a full employment surplus may still result in a deficit since the increment of additional taxes caused by applying the economy's tax rates to the higher level of income that results from the tax cut only recaptures a portion of the tax reduction. For instance, if the entire tax cut in the example economy was in the autonomous taxes, additional revenues from induced taxes of only $3.550 billion would occur to offset the $11.667 billion reduction in revenues from autonomous taxes. Thus there would be a net deficit of approximately $8.117 billion. Of course, if the initial reduction was attained by reducing the induced tax rates, the deficit would be greater since there would be even less of a tax recapture. Yet, deficits are not inevitable at full employment. For example, the new and low tax rates that caused the example economy to reach the full employment level of income at $700 billion will yield a balanced budget when the level of income in the example economy grows to $1146.6 billion and a surplus at income levels higher than that.

The Maximum Size of Government Indebtedness

Continued government borrowing caused by repeated deficits means that the total amount of government debt and interest payments will rise to higher and higher levels. But is there an upper limit to the size of government debt and interest? The question is important because, if answered affirmatively, it means that there is a limit to how long an economy can engage in such practices.

The answer depends on the type of government. There is no debt or interest limit for governments that can create money; lenders are always willing to lend money to such governments because they know that these governments will always be able to repay their debts with interest since, if necessary, they can create the requisite sums of money. And in any event, such governments do not need to borrow in order to finance their deficits because they or their agents literally can create all the money they need. For instance, in the United States the Federal Reserve System at times has deliberately financed the federal government's deficits or created bank reserves for the purpose of financing them. On the other hand, governments that cannot create money may have an upper limit to their indebtedness; they are like individuals in that, at some total amount of debt, they may be unable to borrow any additional money if lenders feel that they will no longer be able to acquire the money necessary to pay off their debts.

Government Surplus Accumulation

A growing public debt and the capacity of an economy to finance it may not be a long-run problem in economies such as the United States. Instead, functional finance may require that the taxes collected in such economies exceed the governmental expenditures for transfers and purchasing. If such a condition develops on a permanent basis as might well be the case if there is sustained prosperity and a desire in the economy for relatively low interest rates in order to encourage capital intensive modes of production, the economies experiencing it will be forced either to engage in nontax policies to restrict purchasing or to tax and accumulate a growing budget surplus. If a surplus is accumulated, the economy will be vulnerable to calls for the reduction of taxes in order to balance the governmental budgets and for the expenditure of any accumulated balances.

The source of the spending pressures that would tend to require budgetary surpluses may already exist in the United States. First, there may be an income-elastic demand for government purchasing that could result in a growing proportion of income being devoted to government. Second, the economy's propensities to consume and invest may increase as economic sophistication grows to the point that rational macroeconomic policies are continually implemented so that the economy's participants have reason to expect that sustained full employment will occur on a permanent basis.

With such expectations, for example, there might be an increase in the propensity to consume caused by a reduction in saving for precautionary purposes.

A Less Desirable Fiscal Alternative

When for some reason tax adjustments are not possible in an economy and the situation is basically one of optimum government outlays, balanced budgets, but less than optimum levels of total purchasing, many economists favor the implementation of fiscal policies involving the expansion of government transfers and purchasing past the levels that would exist if total purchasing were not a consideration. Such an expansion is thought to be appropriate because, even though the additional commodities purchased by the governments are relatively less desirable than others that could be produced with the labor and capital used in their production, there is a positive effect on the production of other, more desirable commodities.

For instance, an increase in government purchasing in order to obtain unneeded missiles and roads simply to make work for the economy's unemployed because total purchasing is inadequate may, indeed, be wasteful. But the producers of these goods and services will earn incomes. And their purchases with their incomes can cause the production of additional commodities that are desired. Thus a government purchase of an absolutely useless forest trail means that the labor and capital employed in its construction are wasted. But the owners of that wasted labor and capital earn incomes by building the trail and they can use these incomes to buy the commodities they prefer. If they desire automobiles, their purchasing will tend to result in more autos being produced. Furthermore, the resulting increase in the incomes of auto workers may lead them, in turn, to buy such things as houses. In other words, the economy gains not only a useless forest trail but cars that are desired by some individuals and houses that are desired by others. Thus, although the trail is wasted in the sense that it is relatively useless, the additional government outlays that cause its production tend to expand the production of other, relatively desired commodities.

MONETARY POLICIES

Monetary policies are generally implemented to change an economy's supply of money and credit in order to affect either the level of purchasing in the economy or the economy's balance of payments position. Primarily, the implementation of monetary policies takes the form of open market operations or changes in reserve requirements. There are, of course, other forms of activity that monetary authorities may use to affect economic behavior in an economy. For example, consumption purchasing in an economy may be affected by changes in margin requirements that influence the level of stock prices and, thus, change both the degree to which existing and new issues of stock attract savings and the money value of these financial assets in the hands of the economy's consumers.

Monetary policies usually transmit their effects through interest-rate changes and changes in the sizes and amounts of the money balances and other financial assets that are held by the economy's participants. If an increase in purchasing is needed, for example, the monetary authorities may increase the supply of money and credit in order to drive down interest rates and encourage the forms of purchasing that are influenced by the resulting changes in interest rates and the size of the supply of money and credit.

Monetary Policies and the Optimum Levels of Fiscal Activity

The concept of an optimum level of taxation is based on the desirability of an economy's obtaining an optimum level of total purchasing. It is possible, however, that the policies of an economy's monetary authorities will result in a situation in which the optimum level of taxation to get the desired level of total purchasing is also the level needed to balance the budgets of the economy's governments. After all, if the governments' budgets are balanced and total purchasing is too high or too low, an economy's monetary authorities can encourage changes in the level of total purchasing by effecting changes in the supply of money. For example, if total purchasing is too low so that unemployment and less than maximum levels of production are occurring, the authorities could implement monetary policies designed to increase the supply of money. This would tend to cause reductions in the level of interest rates in the economy and thereby encourage investment and other forms of purchasing. Furthermore, even if there is a minimum level of interest rates and it is reached by expanding an economy's money supply, subsequent additions to the money supply may still tend to have an expansionary effect on the level of purchasing since they would increase the real value of money balances in the economy and consequently tend to increase the amounts of commodities that consumers are willing to purchase. Needless to say, the optimum amount of money is the amount that results in the optimum level of total purchasing. Furthermore, if an economy's monetary authorities provide that optimum amount, its governments will not need to pursue fiscal policies resulting in either unbalanced budgets or government outlays that differ from the most desirable levels. It should be noted, however, that an economy's governments may voluntarily engage in such activities in order to change the size of the economy's optimum supply of money and thus change the conditions that will exist in the economy's money market.

The Use of Monetary Policies

The role of monetary policies, according to some economists, is to provide a stable background for the operation of an economy. Based on the past monetary experiences of the United States, for example, they do not favor reliance on the use of discretionary activities on the part of the economy's monetary authorities in order to offset fluctuations in total purchasing. Furthermore, so long as an economy has fixed exchange rates, there is a potential conflict between domestic and foreign considerations. For example, it might be necessary to expand the stock of money and credit in an economy in order to drive down interest rates and cause an increase in the level of purchasing in the economy while at the same time the economy has a deficit in its balance of payments and needs an even higher level of interest rates in order to attract additional foreign deposits and eliminate the deficit.

In the past, the monetary authority of the United States, the Federal Reserve, has always proclaimed that domestic prosperity was its major goal. But often, whenever the Federal Reserve has been confronted with even the possibility of a conflict between balance of payments considerations and domestic employment and production considerations, it has acted to alleviate the balance of payments problems and left the domestic problems to fiscal policies. Such a reaction is rational according to our examination of the stability requirements for internal and external equilibrium in the previous chapter. But it does assume that fiscal policy will act to assure full employment levels of income and such an assumption may be unwarranted since the deliberate implementation of fiscal activities in order to achieve full employment levels of purchasing has rarely occurred in the United States.

Monetary Policies May Conflict with Fiscal Policies

The government of an economy may cause inflationary pressure to develop if it sufficiently increases its spending or reduces its taxes. The appropriate monetary policy under such circumstances is to tighten up on the supply of money and credit in order to offset the expansionary effects of the fiscal activities. But such fiscal activities also tend to mean the occurrence of budgetary deficits that the government must finance by issuing debt instruments. The government may then desire that the economy's monetary authorities assist in the financing of the deficits by either creating money and exchanging it for the resulting government debt or expanding the excess reserves of the economy's financial institutions so that these institutions will be able to buy the debt and finance the government. If the economy's monetary authorities do not cooperate, the government debt will compete for the available funds in the economy's money market and tend to drive down bond and asset prices and increase interest rates. The higher interest rates and lack of money and credit will tend to discourage investment and consumption purchasing as well as increase the interest expenses of the government. On the other hand, if the economy's monetary authorities do cooperate in the financing of deficits, the additional money and credit that is created will add to the inflationary pressures that already exist in the economy unless the deficits are directly financed by the monetary authorities who simultaneously engage in open-market operations and reserve-requirement changes in order to prevent the total stocks of money and credit in the economy from increasing the supply.

The Critical Rate Concept

Monetary policies may have a gap in their effectiveness at some critically high level of interest rates. An economy's monetary authorities cause the economy's interest rates to rise as they tighten up on the economy's supply of money and credit relative to the economy's demand for money and credit. Normally, such "tight money" policies are used to restore balance-of-payments equilibrium or to offset domestic pressures for an excessive amount of purchasing that would otherwise cause demand-pull inflation. But if some of the economy's financial intermediaries have statutory interest rate maximums that set an upper limit on the interest rates that they can pay to obtain deposits, while other intermediaries do not, the level of interest rates in the economy may rise to a critically high level. Such a level, as we discussed in chapter eight, is so far above the maximum rates that can be paid by the regulated intermediaries that the nonregulated intermediaries and those with higher maximums will be willing to pay more for the available savings than the regulated intermediaries can pay. If this occurs, savers and wealth holders responding to the higher interest-rate payments may shift their wealth from the assets of the regulated intermediaries to those of the nonregulated intermediaries.

Typically it is the commercial banks that have the highest reserve requirements and the lowest interest rate maximums in terms of what they are allowed to pay for deposits. Thus, at some level of interest rates, funds may begin flowing out of the banks and into the intermediaries with lower reserve requirements so that a substantial expansion of an economy's supply of money and credit can occur in response to any further increase in the demand for money and credit. Furthermore, the regulatory activities of an economy's monetary authorities tend to be concentrated on the economy's commercial banks so that the efforts of the economy's monetary authorities to offset the expansion of money and credit that might occur at the critical level of interest rates may result in a further deterioration of the role of the banks as financial intermediaries. For example, instead of an initial $100 deposit going into a commercial bank and $80 being loaned out because the bank has a 20 percent reserve requirement, the $100 may be led by higher interest rates into another intermediary which loans out $95 and holds $5 in reserve by depositing it in a bank which, in turn, loans out $4 and holds (20 percent) one dollar in reserve. The maximum expansion of money and credit with the initial $100 deposit is $10,000 if it goes through our example process as compared to $500 if it goes only through the banking system. Furthermore, the ability of the economy's monetary authorities to control the economy's supply of money and credit becomes severely limited when interest rates cause a change from banks to other intermediaries. For example, the monetary authorities would only reduce the expansion of money and credit to a ten times greater increase of $5000 if the bank reserve requirements are doubled in order to halve the supply of monetary assets available to be held as reserves.

THE IMPLEMENTATION OF MONETARY AND FISCAL POLICIES

The residents of every economy have a vested interest in seeing that inflation does not develop, that potential production actually occurs, and that growth is not thwarted. This self-interest tends to lead to the implementation of government monetary and fiscal policies whenever the absence of such activities would result in the existence of undesirable circumstances. Certain problems and considerations must be resolved, however, before it is possible to determine the appropriate monetary and fiscal policies for an economy under a given set of economic circumstances. Some of these problems and considerations have been alluded to in the preceding chapters and sections.

The Choice of Goals

There are areas of conflict regarding the goals which the governments of an economy should try to attain with their monetary and fiscal policies. Needless to say, these conflicts necessitate the economy's choosing goals that it considers to be the most desirable before it can select the monetary and fiscal policies appropriate to attain them. For instance:

1. Is it more desirable that purchasing rise or fall when there is inflation and unemployment due to higher costs or administered prices? More purchasing may be desirable because it means more production, but undesirable if it means more inflation. On the other hand, less purchasing may be desirable because it counters inflation but undesirable because it means fewer commodities will be purchased and thus fewer produced.
2. Should balance-of-payments deficits be eliminated by monetary policies that cause interest rates to rise so that foreign funds are attracted? Such policies not only tend to eliminate the payments deficits and so solve certain international financial problems, but also tend to reduce the purchasing of investment and other commodities; thus they cause a decline both in the number of commodities presently purchased and produced in the domestic economy as well as in its future productive capacity.
3. Should the existence of unemployment caused by structural changes or frictional conditions lead to policies that expand total purchasing until all or part of those unemployed locate jobs? Or should more selective means such as the "War on Poverty" be used to counter such unemployment?
4. Should there be a redistribution of income and wealth? Transfers, taxes, inflation, and unemployment all may cause such a redistribution to occur. Redistribution from potential purchasers with a particular marginal propensity to consume to other potential purchasers with another marginal propensity to consume may change an economy's consumption purchasing in a manner that tends to keep the economy closer to its full-employment level of income. But, on the other hand, such a redistribution might also change consumers' incentives to produce in order to earn incomes and, thus, change the economy's productive capacity and rate of growth.
5. Should an economy produce for the present or for the future? Lower interest rates may encourage investment purchasing and thus the adoption of new techniques of production that will allow more goods and services to be produced in the future. But more investment purchasing

in an economy already operating at maximum levels of production means that fewer commodities will be left over to satisfy the present needs of the economy's residents.

Workable Policies

There may be difficulties in choosing policies that will attain a goal even if the goal is identified; neither monetary nor fiscal policies may work at all times. This can be seen by examining the equilibrium conditions in the economy depicted by Figure 19-1. If the IS and LM curves representing the possible equilibrium conditions in the economy's commodity and money markets intersect along section "a" of the LM curve, fiscal policies such as tax cuts, whose effect is reflected by shifting the IS curve to the right, can indeed result in higher equilibrium levels of income. But policies of monetary expansion cannot have such an effect on the level of income if the only influence of money on the level of total purchasing is an indirect one through changes in the level of interest rates. Graphically, their effect is represented

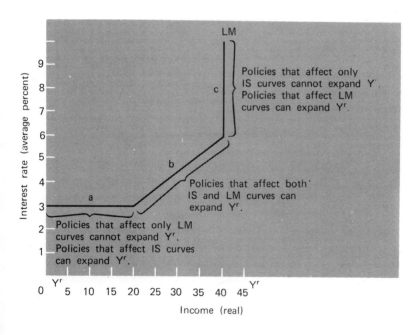

FIGURE 19-1
Workable policies.

by a shift of the LM curve farther to the right without changing the point at which the LM and IS curves intersect. There is no change in the equilibrium level of total purchasing because the minimum level of interest rates already has been reached; the economy is in the liquidity trap, and any additional money that might be placed in it will not be used to bid up the price of assets, causing interest rates to fall and investment and other purchasing to increase. Thus expanding the money supply under these conditions will not increase the equilibrium level of income via lower rates of interest.

It is also possible, of course, that an increase in an economy's money supply will have an effect that would be depicted by a shift in the IS curve since there is no need for deflation to have a real-balance effect. Instead, the same increase in the real value of money assets that might increase total purchasing can be obtained with the existing price level by increasing the supply of money in the economy.

Both monetary policies whose effects are represented by shifts in the LM curve and fiscal and monetary policies that shift the IS curve can increase an economy's total purchasing if the initial equilibrium conditions in the economy are similar to those represented graphically by section "b" of the LM curve. Any move in one market of an economy under these conditions, however, will generate offsetting "secondary" effects in the other market. Thus lower taxes or more government purchasing tends to increase the equilibrium level of income in an economy at every level of interest rates and thus shift the economy's IS curve to the right. But the increased demand for transactions money at the higher levels of purchasing may partially offset the expansionary effect of the initial change by causing higher interest rates and thus a tendency toward less purchasing.

Finally, only monetary policies can expand the level of income if the economy is initially in equilibrium under the conditions represented by the inelastic "c" portion of the LM curve. Owing to the lack of money available to handle additional transactions, fiscal policies that have the effect of shifting the IS curve to the right will only cause changes in the level of interest rates. This occurs because implementation of the expansionary fiscal policies when all the money in the economy is already being used for transactions purposes merely causes the economy's interest rates to be bid up as additional money is demanded at each rate of interest. The level of interest rates will rise until the amounts of investment and other types of expenditures desired by purchasers are cut back to the level at which all available money in the economy is used for transaction purposes.

Offsetting developments. Even if a monetary or fiscal policy is implemented which is basically workable in terms of accomplishing some goal, it still may be offset and thus not achieve the desired results. For instance, the implementation of a monetary policy designed to expand the excess reserves of commercial banks is no guarantee that the commercial banks whose excess reserves are expanded actually will lend out their additional excess reserves or, for that matter, that there will be any customers to borrow them. Conversely, a decline in the availability of money may be offset by the introduction of new credit arrangements between producers and purchasers so that less money is needed. Similarly, changes in taxes or transfers are no guarantee that purchasing will change; purchasers are free to do as they please, and they may decide to save less and not cut their purchases, or to save more and not raise them. Similarly, a workable policy being implemented to attain one goal might be offset by the implementation of other workable policies designed to attain other goals. For instance, the United States Congress might cut taxes to increase purchasing in order to eliminate unemployment and raise production while the Federal Reserve is decreasing the supply of excess reserves to force up interest rates and reduce purchasing in order to combat inflation.

Time lags. There is no guarantee that otherwise workable policies can even be put into effect in time to have any positive influence: there may be a tremendous time lag between the need for action and its arrival. First, the problem has to be seen; then analyzed and a policy formulated; then the policy put into effect; and finally be in effect long enough to achieve the desired results. And circumstances may be different by the time the policy has any influence. For instance, the economy may have moved into an inflationary period caused by too much purchasing by the time activities designed to eliminate a previously perceived shortage of purchasing begin to have their impact.

Temporary changes. It should be obvious from the example of the unneeded forest trail that temporary changes in government fiscal activities, such as the increases in purchasing historically employed in the United States to "prime the pump and get the economy going again," may not cause a lasting change in the level of purchasing and production. Once the temporary purchasing of forest trails ceases, their construction will stop and the incomes earned in this production will be eliminated. Then the producers will not be able to buy cars and the auto workers will not be able to buy houses. In other words, in the absence of other changes, the economy will return to its original position of inadequate levels of total purchasing once the temporary "pump priming" ends.

Appropriate Policies

Even though macroeconomic goals have been selected and there are workable policies that can lead to their attainment, the use of some policies proves more appropriate than the use of others. As suggested earlier, it is inappropriate to change government purchasing or transfers merely to influence the level of purchasing unless changes in the level of taxation are impossible. The basis for this suggestion is the lack of relationship between the need for government transfers and purchasing activity to alleviate distress or provide enough commodities for public use and the need for activity to affect total purchasing.

Even if the policies generally are appropriate and can achieve the economy's goals, they may be undesirable if they discriminate in their effects on the different sectors of the economy. For instance, monetary policies may be implemented which keep interest rates up and curb purchasing in order to hold back inflation or prevent the loss of gold. Such policies, however, may hardly affect either established businesses that internally generate the funds required for their expansion or public utilities whose higher interest costs can be passed on to their customers. On the other hand, such policies fall heavily on those sectors of an economy that depend on outside sources for financing: new and expanding business firms that do not yet generate enough funds from depreciation and operations, state and local governments, and housing.

Politically Feasible Policies

The whole area of macroeconomic policies is complicated further because the application of fiscal and monetary policies cannot be considered or advocated solely on the basis of technical economic considerations. Various politically oriented forces within an economy such as that of the United States shape the size and nature of the fiscal and monetary policies that are politically feasible for solving macroeconomic problems. These forces, often based on irrational fears arising from lack of knowledge and understanding, are nonetheless potent; failure to consider them can result in the advocacy of policies that cannot and will not be adopted. Primary among these forces in the United States is the desire for balanced government budgets. A large proportion of the electorate seems unaware of the nature of debt creation and the effect of its existence; neither does it understand that the problem of financing government budget deficits and the interest expenses associated with their existence are the prices that may have to be paid at times by an economy if it is to obtain optimum levels of total purchasing without having undesirable levels of government transfers or purchases. The fact that national debt may be deliberately brought into existence as a by-product of fiscal policies has already been discussed in some detail as has the fact that there is no upper limit to the size of national debt or the interest that can be paid by governments that can create money. The latter aspect means that the concept of "bankruptcy" due to an inability to pay debts as they come due does not apply to a national economy; it can always use fiscal policies to attain the optimum level of purchasing even though such policies constantly result in deficits and thus an ever-growing national debt.

If there are adverse effects of national debt they must come into being when the debt arrives, exists, or is paid off. But debt is brought into existence to get "enough" purchasing, not too much; thus it is not associated with policies that lead to inflation and unemployment. When debt exists, however, it is used in open market operations and, in the absence of offsetting forces, may tend to change the distribution of income and wealth in an economy as it transfers purchasing power in the form of interest to the holders of the debt. Finally, neither the interest payment nor any debt payoffs need to be a burden since they can be financed with additional indebtedness rather than with taxes.

As well as the fears already mentioned, many people seem to credit unbalanced budgets, and particularly those of the federal government, with causing inflation, unneeded government transfers and purchases, and the end of free enterprise. For the latter to happen, of course, one or both of the following conditions would have to result from an unbalanced budget. First, unbalanced budgets somehow would have to discourage or prevent individual business firms from competing for sales by efficiently producing the types and amounts of commodities that individuals in the economy are willing to purchase. Second, such activities would have to prevent or discourage individuals from being led by their own self-interest to work where they get the largest incomes and then to use their incomes in such a manner as to get the greatest satisfaction. Needless to say, the monetary and fiscal activities described earlier as possible means of attaining optimum levels of total purchasing have no such effects. A general reduction in personal income taxes, for instance, merely leaves more disposable income in the hands of potential purchasers. These individuals are then free to attempt to buy more of whatever commodities they prefer. And producers remain free to attempt to produce and sell such commodities.

Even though unbalanced budgets do not adversely affect the existence of free enterprise in an economy, fiscal policies involving balanced budgets might be quite desirable if such budgets somehow were to encourage that form of economic organization. But this is not inevitably the case. After all, the total amount of purchasing in a free enterprise economy when governmental budgets are balanced may be so high as to cause inflation or so low that there is unemployment and low levels of production. And these conditions certainly would not cause the residents of such an economy to marvel how well the economy was doing and thus be determined to maintain that form of economic organization. Quite the contrary, they would probably, and with justification, become dissatisfied with their economy's performance and thus willing to consider other forms of economic organization. Indeed, it is the individuals who support the monetary and fiscal policies that result in optimum levels of purchasing who are advocating policies that tend to conserve a free enterprise form of economic organization; the policies they advocate would maintain high levels of employment without intolerable price increases while not interfering with the basic decision-making power of individual producers and purchasers. But whatever the reason for the public's preferring no debt, the political need of democratic governments to be responsive to the desires of their electorates makes it difficult to use changes in the amount of taxes to obtain the optimum level of total purchasing while simultaneously maintaining the most appropriate levels of government purchasing and transfers.

Similar to the desire for no deficits or national debt, a substantial portion of the American public seems to urge that the nation's supply of gold not be reduced. These individuals seem to have mystically accepted gold as determining the value of the nation's money. We know that the size of the United States' money supply is absolutely unrelated to the size of its stock of gold and that the value of the money depends on what it will buy. But if a substantial portion of a democratic economy's citizenry insists that the economy's gold stock be maintained, policies such as lower interest rates that result in balance of payments deficits and a loss of gold are not politically feasible solutions for the economic problems that might confront governments who periodically must answer to their electorates.

Even if a government could disregard such views of debt and gold, it would have to weigh the advantages of fiscal policies that cause an increase in national debt or a loss of gold against the disadvantage of possible changes in behavior that may arise from individual fears and uncertainties about the results of a debt increase or gold loss. For instance, a move to a higher national debt might cause public uncertainty and panic which could result in even lower levels of total purchasing than those existing before taxes were cut in the attempt to raise total purchasing. Or a loss of gold might cause an inflationary increase in purchasing as the holders of money rushed to spend it because of their fear that it would lose its value.

ALTERNATIVES TO MONETARY AND FISCAL POLICIES

It may not be necessary for an economy's government to implement monetary and fiscal policies whenever inflation or unemployment exists or is threatening. Instead, governments may be able to use other means to maintain high levels of production without inflation or to head off the need for changing the level of purchasing. Aspects of some of the alternatives that are discussed in this section have already been examined in earlier chapters as have the alternatives of deflation, redistribution, and wage-price guidelines.

International Trade

If the level of total purchasing in an economy is too low, the government controlling the rate at which the economy's money exchanges with the money of other economies might change the exchange rate in order to reduce the amount of foreign money needed to obtain the money of the economy that needs additional purchasing. Alternately, the government could do such things as raise the economy's tariff barriers in order to discourage the economy's residents from buying abroad or give additional credit to foreign purchasers.

Then, as discussed in Chapter 5, both local residents and foreigners would tend to buy more of the economy's commodities. Great Britain, for instance, followed this policy in the 1930's when her production and employment were depressed owing to a lack of purchasing. Unfortunately, her exchange rate efforts to export her depression, by having foreigners buy in her economy instead of their own, met with failure as other countries retaliated with their own exchange rate and tariff changes in order to offset the British efforts.

Controls and Intervention

The United States has used various techniques other than fiscal and monetary policies to deal with nonoptimum levels of prices and employment. In the middle of the 1960's, for instance, when the amount of commodities demanded at the existing level of prices apparently exceeded the capacity of the economy's producers to supply commodities, the Johnson administration used direct personal appeals and threats to unions, businesses, and industries in an effort to keep prices stable and wages from increasing faster than productivity. The appeals were in the name of the national interest and the threats took the form of promises to investigate firms and industries for anti-trust violations and to sell commodities from government stockpiles and make purchases from domestic and foreign producers with lower prices.

The indirect intervention of the 1960's contrasts to the United States economy's Second World War experience when rigid price and wage controls and rationing were used in an attempt to prevent inflation when the amount of commodities demanded in the economy substantially exceeded the amount supplied. One problem associated with such price and wage controls is that purchasing power may be accumulated due to a lack of spending opportunities until a later time period. Then, when the controls are relaxed, excessive purchasing occurs as the economy's participants rush to purchase the goods and services that they have previously been unable to obtain. A more significant drawback to the use of controls, however, is that they eliminate the changes in relative prices and wages needed to efficiently allocate labor and capital into the production of the goods and services most desired by purchasers. The efficient allocation of scarce factors is the genius of the market economies; its elimination through controls thus eliminates the very essence of free enterprise.

Direct Aid Programs

Despite their sporadic implementation of monetary, fiscal, and other policies, economies such as that of the United States have periodically experienced inflation and unemployment because of nonoptimum levels of total purchasing. Quite often, the governmental response was to succor those who had been adversely affected rather than to implement monetary and fiscal policies to eliminate the conditions that led to their difficulties. Thus, for example, a complex unemployment insurance program has evolved to provide relief to unemployed individuals such as those who lose their jobs because of inadequate total purchasing. Of course, an insurance payment does partially alleviate the individual's distress when he is no longer earning an income. But it typically does not provide as much as the individuals were earning, and reliance on such programs in lieu of policies to raise total purchasing results in fewer commodities being produced to meet the needs of the economy's residents.

MONETARY AND FISCAL REFORMS

At the beginning of both the 1960's and 1970's, purchasing in the United States economy was so low that unemployment and less than maximum levels of production not only existed but apparently were getting worse as the economy's capacity to produce grew faster than its commodity purchases. Furthermore, because purchasing was growing slowly, total production was growing slowly and other economies seemed well on their way to overtaking the United States in terms of per capita output. Despite this situation, expansionary monetary policies were not pursued aggressively because the monetary authorities feared that demand-pull inflation would result from an expansion of the economy's money supply and that the resulting lower interest rates would tend to keep foreigners from sending their money to the United States and thus lead to even larger balance of payment deficits and an accelerated loss of gold. On the other hand, Congress hesitated on fiscal changes such as tax cuts because of public and political fears regarding unbalanced budgets. In the 1960's, in a series of moves extending over several years, Congress reduced the general rate of taxation. Personal and business income tax rates were reduced, certain excise taxes were removed or reduced, and businessmen were allowed to avoid up to 25 percent of their federal tax liabilities through a procedure wherein they received tax credits equal to 7 percent of certain types of new investment. Needless to say, the latter program was designed to encourage investment purchasing by offering tax reductions to those who invested. The various tax reductions were effective despite the threat at one time by the monetary authorities that they would implement offsetting monetary activities in order to fight the inflation which they thought would result.

Subsequently, in the middle of the 1960's after a period of relatively rapid growth and prosperity, total purchasing became so high as a result of the additional spending on the war in Asia and the changes in behavior that resulted from the existence of sustained growth that inflation was thought to threaten. Now, however, tax rates were not increased because of political considerations; the government did not want to alienate voters by increasing taxes. Instead, the economy depended on restrictive monetary policies to keep total purchasing from being so high as to cause inflation. Unfortunately, the monetary efforts were not completely adequate and some inflation did occur for reasons other than the existence of excessive amounts of aggregate demand. But there were other effects. The resulting high interest rates substantially depressed purchasing and productive activity in many sectors of the economy, particularly housing. Furthermore, the higher interest rates directly caused inflation as it is measured by the consumer price index because they increased the sizes of the payments needed to acquire such things as housing, automobiles, and consumer durables. Finally, because they attracted so much money from foreigners, the high interest rates also tended to reduce the outflows of gold and international reserves which the economy had been experiencing.

Because of the difficulties experienced in implementing policies and because of the significance of noneconomic considerations, various reforms in tools and techniques have been suggested to improve the effectiveness and acceptability of the United States' monetary and fiscal policies. These proposed changes are important because economies that basically are free enterprise in nature may be lost by default to other forms of economic organization if inadequate policies result in unemployment that alienates workers, or a lack of sales that discourages producers, or inflation that wipes out individual and business savings. Brief discussions follow for a few of the reforms relating to the general level of monetary and fiscal activity in the United States' economy. Most of them apply to the federal government since it is the only government responsible for the economic state of the entire economy. Other potential reforms are not examined here because they have in effect, been previously considered in this and other chapters. They include the elimination of interest rate maximums in order to prevent a rapid expansion of money and credit at some critical level of interest rates and the adoption of freely fluctuating exchange rates in order to eliminate balance of payments' constraints on the use of monetary policies.

Standby Fiscal Activities

Changes in the fiscal activities of the United States government require congressional approval. And Congress traditionally is slow in approving them. This means that economic problems may remain unresolved for an extended period of time. As a means of reducing the time required for a fiscal response to a problem, it has been suggested that Congress determine standby changes in the sizes and composition of federal taxes, transfers, and purchasing which could be put into effect by the President if appropriate circumstances arise. Alternatively, Congress could pass such legislation in advance and then tie its implementation to some index of need such as a rate of unemployment or level of prices. For instance, Congress could allow the President to put into effect a 10 percent reduction in personal income tax rates if the rate of labor unemployment exceeds 6 percent.

Monetary Rules

Another possible reform involves the supply of money. Changes in the size of the United States' money supply currently are effected by the Federal Reserve System. Supposedly the Federal Reserve acts to ensure a supply of money that will cause high levels of employment, stable prices, and growth. Historically, however, the Federal Reserve often has managed to do just the opposite. During the United States' depression it managed on at least one occasion to constrict the money supply in order to fight inflation. Then, in the immediate postwar era when demand-pull inflation existed as money was spent which had been saved during the war years, the Federal Reserve contributed to the inflation by allowing the money supply to expand rapidly.

Some economists fear the continuation of such policies. Thus, to prevent more of such experiences, they have for some time proposed governing the size of the United States' money supply by some simple and easily understood "rule" rather than leaving it to the discretion of the Federal Reserve. In other words, they propose that the nation's money supply no longer be altered by the whims of those who govern the activities of the Federal Reserve or by the decisions of bankers to lend or not to lend their excess reserves.

Various rules have been suggested for governing the supply of money, among them that it be kept constant or that it be changed only as needed to stabilize some index of prices. The most seriously discussed rule, however, has been that the money supply be increased at some constant rate. Typically, this rate is described as being the rate at which the demand for money would grow if there were full employment without inflation. Obviously, if the money supply is to increase at some constant rate or, for that matter, to be governed by any rule, not only would the discretionary activities of the monetary authorities have to be ended, but also the money-creating and money-destroying capabilities of the banking system would have to be eliminated.

Proponents of the "rules" approach to the supply of money feel that such changes can, indeed, be made. For instance, the banks' ability to affect the money supply can be reduced substantially by removing the present fractional reserve requirements and, instead, requiring them to hold 100 percent of their deposits in reserve. The deposit of a given amount of cash then will merely change the composition of the economy's money supply but it will not expand it; instead of some proportion of the deposit becoming excess reserves that can be lent out to expand the money supply, the bank would be required to hold all of the deposit in reserve. The proponents of rules also suggest as a means of further eliminating money creation on the part of banks that the Federal Reserve cease all forms of rediscounting and asset purchasing. Then the banks will be unable to sell assets to the monetary authority for money which the authority might create for that purpose.

The advocates of basing monetary activity on rules seem to feel that neither temporary changes in the supply of money nor changes in fiscal activities will be needed to stabilize total purchasing once the rules are in use. They argue that the security of knowing that neither the monetary authorities nor the banks will be able to interfere adversely with the money supply will tend to eliminate cyclical fluctuations in total purchasing. The fluctuations will be eliminated, supposedly, because they occur primarily in response to either changes in the policies of the banks and monetary authorities or because of changes in the public's expectations about future policies. The big drawback to accepting such rules is that fluctuations may occur despite their existence. And while it is true that at least the fluctuations would not be intensified by poor monetary policies such as occurred in the past, they also could not be countered by appropriate policies.

Capital Budgets

Still another reform lies in the area of the budget. Currently the annual administrative budget of the United States government lumps together all the expenditures that are funded by congressional appropriations. It has been suggested that this budget might better be separated into an operating budget and a capital budget. For example, the capital budget could contain expenditures on real capital assets whose useful life extends for more than one year and the operating budget could provide the funds for operations whose benefits are not spread over more than one year.

The advantages of such a division are that it would more clearly identify the uses to which expenditures are put as well as make it politically easier to have a deficit whenever one is necessary to attain a level of total purchasing that ensures high levels of production. It would be easier to have a deficit because it could be assigned to the capital budget so that any increase in debt liabilities would be directly associated in the public's and politicians' minds with a simultaneous increase in the value of publicly owned capital assets. Furthermore, the value of a debt-financed asset could be depreciated over its life; each subsequent operating budget could include an amount needed to pay off the portion of the debt that represents the value of the acquired capital that is used during the time period covered by the budget.

Thus there would never be a government debt that was not backed by a government-owned asset of equal or greater value. Finally, the payment of the debt over the life of the asset would enable any particular deficit to be defended on the basis that, in the long run, the government's budget would be balanced as the debt was paid.

Expanding the Scope of Federal Reserve Operations

Also possible are reforms involving additional responsibilities for the Federal Reserve System. For one, the Federal Reserve might be allowed to make "voluntary tax payments" to the federal government in any amounts it deemed appropriate. It then could choose to allow the federal government to balance its budget in periods of declining total purchasing even though the government's tax revenues from other sources had fallen or its outlays had increased to offset a decline in total purchasing. Public fears of an unbalanced budget thus could be allayed and the government could fully utilize its fiscal tools without the panic or uncertainty that might accompany a deficit.

Such voluntary "taxes" also could add an additional element of stability in that the Federal Reserve could be allowed to file an "amended return" at some subsequent, appropriate time and receive all or part of the funds back. The repayment would amount to forcing the government to increase its expenditures at a time when the Federal Reserve felt it appropriate for the government to do so. The element of the "amended return" would make assets of the tax receipts the Federal Reserve would receive when making payment; thus any liabilities that the Federal Reserve would create in association with making tax payments would simultaneously be offset by the presence of an additional asset.

Public Developing Banking. Another possible reform could involve empowering the Federal Reserve and its agents to make direct loans to governments in order to help them finance the purchase of capital assets or, in order to circumvent the legal or political debt restrictions of some government units, to enter into rental contracts wherein it would purchase the assets and "rent" them to the governmental units for a fee sufficient to cover all charges. It has been suggested that only capital projects proposed to it by political units with taxing and contractual powers should be accepted by the Federal Reserve and that no funds should be provided for administration, maintenance, or operations. This would ensure that assets would be in existence to offset every liability that the Federal Reserve might create to finance such operations.

Not only would such a reform provide the basis for encouraging and discouraging government purchasing when it was appropriate to do so, but also the Federal Reserve's power to solve macroeconomic problems would be enhanced by its ability to release funds for governmental capital formation on a flexible basis. For instance, projects could be encouraged in those areas in which factor utilization had fallen and discouraged where demand would tend to be of an inflationary nature. Or the Federal Reserve could require selective increases or decreases in the rate of repayment. Furthermore, the reform might have a positive psychological influence in that there would be a tendency toward governmental budget surpluses as the Federal Reserve's operations replaced governmental capital expenditures financed by taxes. This last aspect is additionally important because increased Federal Reserve activity when total purchasing is low might make it politically feasible for the affected governments also to change the level of their taxation without moving away from optimum levels of government purchasing.

● REFERENCES

Ablin, R., "Fiscal-Monetary Mix: A Haven for The Fixed Exchange Rate," *National Banking Review*, **IV** (Sept. 1966).

Alhadeff, D., "Credit Controls and Financial Intermediaries," *American Economic Review*, **L**, pp. 655–671 (Sept. 1960).

Anderson, L., "The Influences of Economic Activity On The Money Stock. Additional Empirical Evidence on the Reverse Causation Argument," *Federal Reserve Bank of St. Louis Review*, **LI**, pp. 19–24 (Aug. 1969).

————, and J. Jordan, "Monetary and Fiscal Actions: A List Of Their Relative Importance in Economic Stabilization," *Federal Reserve Bank of St. Louis Review*, **L**, pp. 11–23 (Nov. 1968).

Bach, G. L., and C. J. Huizenga, "The Differential Effects of Tight Money," *American Economic Review*, **LI**, pp. 52–80 (1961).

Bator, F., "Budgetary Reform: Notes on Principles and Strategy," *Review of Economics and Statistics*, **XLV**, pp. 115–120 (May 1963).

Beard, T. R., "Debt Management: Its Relationship to Monetary Policy, 1951–1962," *National Banking Review*, **II**, pp. 61–76 (1964).

Boughton, J., E. Braw, T. Naylor, and W. Yohe, "A Policy Model of the United States Monetary Sector," *Southern Economic Journal*, **XXXV**, pp. 333–346 (April 1969).

Break, G., "Fiscal Policy in a Fully Employed Economy," *Journal of Finance*, **XXII**, pp. 247–260 (May 1967).

Bristow, J., "Taxation and Income Stabilization," *Economic Journal*, **LXXVIII**, pp. 299–311 (June 1968).

Brunner, K., "The Role of Money and Monetary Policy," *Reserve Bank of St. Louis Review*, pp. 9–24 (July 1968).

———, and A. H. Meltzer, "What Did We Learn From U.S. Monetary Experience in the Great Depression?" *Canadian Journal of Economics*, **I**, pp. 334–348 (May 1968).

Cagan, P. and A. Gandolfi, "Monetary Theory. The Lag in Monetary Policy As Implied by the Time Pattern of Monetary Effects on Interest Rates," *American Economic Review*, **LIX**, pp. 277–284 (May 1969).

Committee for Economic Development, *Fiscal and Monetary Policy for High Employment*, pp. 7–37 (1962).

DeLeeuw, F., and E. M. Gramlich, "The Channels of Monetary Policy," *Federal Reserve Bulletin*, **LV**, pp. 472–491 (June 1969).

Dobell, A., and Y. C. Ho, "An Optimal Unemployment Rate," *Quarterly Journal of Economics*, **LXXXI**, pp. 675–683 (Nov. 1967).

Francis, D. R., "An Approach to Monetary and Fiscal Management," *Federal Reserve Bank of St. Louis Review*, **L**, pp. 6–10 (Nov. 1968).

———, "Monetary Policy and Inflation," *Federal Reserve Bank of St. Louis Review*, **LI**, pp. 8–11 (June 1969).

Friedman, M., "A Monetary and Fiscal Framework for Economic Stability," *American Economic Review*, **XXXVIII**, pp. 245–264 (June 1948).

———, "Post War Trends in Monetary Theory and Policy," *National Banking Review*, **II**, pp. 1–9 (Sept. 1964).

———, "The Role of Monetary Policy," *American Economic Review*, **LVIII**, pp. 1–17 (March 1968).

Gurley, J. G., "Federal Tax Policy (A Review Article)," *National Tax Journal*, **XX**, pp. 319–327 (Sept. 1967).

Guttentag, J., "The Strategy of Open Market Operations," *Quarterly Journal of Economics*, **LXXX**, pp. 1–30 (1966).

Hageman, H. A., "Reserve Policies of Central Banks and Their Implications for U.S. Balance of Payments Policy," *American Economic Review*, **LIX**, pp. 62–77 (March 1969).

Holt, C., "Linear Decision Rules for Economic Stabilization and Growth," *Quarterly Journal of Economics*, **LXXVI**, pp. 20–45 (1962).

Johnson, H. G., "The Case for Flexible Exchange Rates 1969," *Federal Reserve Bank of St. Louis Review*, **LI**, pp. 12–24 (June 1969).

Kareken, J., "The Mix of Monetary and Fiscal Policies," *Journal of Finance*, **XX**, pp. 241–246 (May 1967).

Kawaja, M., "The Economics On Statutory Ceilings on Consumer Credit Charges," *Western Economic Journal*, **V**, pp. 157–167 (March 1967).

Keran, M. W., and C. T. Babb, "An Explanation of Federal Reserve Actions (1933–68)," *Federal Reserve Bank of St. Louis Review*, **LI**, pp. 7–20 (July 1969).

Laird, W., "The Changing Views on Debt Management," *Quarterly Review of Economics and Business*, **III**, pp. 1–17 (1963).

Leijonhufvud, A., "Keynes and the Effectiveness of Monetary Policy," *Western Economic Journal*, **VI**, pp. 97–111 (March 1968).

Leveson, S. M., "The Potential vs. Performance Gap in Monetary and Fiscal Policy," *Nebraska Journal of Economics and Business*, **VII**, pp. 18–30 (Autumn 1968).

Mundell, Robt. A., "Should the United States Devalue the Dollar," *Western Economic Journal*, **IV**, pp. 247–259 (Sept. 1968).

Niehans, J., "Efficient Monetary and Fiscal Policies in Balances Growth," *Journal of Money, Credit, Banking*, **I**, pp. 228–251 (May 1969).

Palomba, N., "Unemployment Compensation Program: Stabilizing or Destabilizing," *Journal of Political Economy*, **LXXVI**, pp. 91–100 (Jan.–Feb. 1968).

Perry, G. L., "Wages and the Guidposts," *American Economic Review*, **LVII**, pp. 897–904 (Sept. 1967).

Read, L. M., "The Measure of Total Factor Productivity Appropriate to Wage Price Guidelines," *Canadian Journal of Economics*, **I,** pp. 349–358 (May 1968).

Ross, M. H., and R. E. Zelder, "The Discount Rate. A Phantom Policy Tool," *Western Economic Journal*, **VII**, pp. 341–348 (Dec. 1967).

Schlesinger, J., "Monetary Policy and Its Critics," *Journal of Political Economy*, **LXVIII**, pp. 601–616 (1960).

Shaw, G., "Monetary-Fiscal Policy for Growth and The Balance-Of-Payments Constraint," *Economics N.S.*, **XXXIV**, pp. 198–202 (May 1967).

Smith, P. E., "Taxes, Transfers, and Economic Stability," *Southern Economic Journal*, **XXXV**, pp. 157–166 (Oct. 1968).

Starleaf, D. R., and J. A. Stephenson, "A Suggested Solution To The

Monetary-Policy Indicator Problem: The Monetary Full Employment Interest Rate," *Journal of Finance*, **XXIV**, pp. 623–641 (Sept. 1969).

Steindl, F., "Fiscal Policy Over the Postwar Business Cycles," *National Tax Journal*, **XX**, pp. 258–269 (Sept. 1967).

Takayama, A., "The Effects of Fiscal and Monetary Policies Under Flexible and Fixed Exchange Rates," *Canadian Journal of Economics*, **II**, pp. 190–209 (May 1969).

Tanner, J. E., "Lags in The Effect of Monetary Policy: A Statistical Investigation," *American Economic Review*, **LIX**, pp. 794–805 (Dec. 1969).

Thurlow, L. C., "A Fiscal Policy Model for the United States," *Survey of Current Business*, **XLIX**, pp. 45–64 (June 1969).

Tsiang, S. C., "A Critical Note On The Optimun Supply of Money," *Journal of Money, Credit and Banking*, **I**, pp. 266–280 (May 1969).

Tucker, D., "Credit Rationing, Interest Rate Lags, and Monetary Policy Speed," *Quarterly Journal of Economics*, **LXXXII**, pp. 54–84 (Feb. 1968).

Willes, M., "The Inside Lags of Monetary Policy: 1952–1960," *Journal of Finance*, **XXII**, pp. 591–593 (Dec. 1967).

Classical
Macroeconomics

20

The general form of macroeconomics described in this book was initially presented in 1936 by Lord Keynes. Preceding him as macroeconomists were the "classical economists" who identified various forces which they thought would automatically ensure an economy's operation at full employment and maximum levels of commodity production. Unlike Keynes and most subsequent economists, the classicists generally accepted any move from this optimum as a temporary phenomenon occurring only while the economy was in the process of adjusting to some new situation. As a result, they could see no need for the implementation of monetary and fiscal policies whenever there were departures from the optimum.

Classical macroeconomics is characterized by three entirely separate and self-contained parts: purchasing; wages, employment, and production; and prices. In discussing each, we shall present a consensus of the fragmented ideas of these earlier economists rather than the complete statement of any one of them.

PURCHASING

The classical economists believed that there could be no lack of purchasing to cause production of less than the maximum amounts of commodities. Three major lines of reasoning led to this conclusion: "Say's Law"; the classical theories of interest and savings; and the flexibility of commodity prices.

Say's Law

Jean Baptiste Say, a French nineteenth-century economist, asserted, in essence, the impossibility of unemployment due to inadequate aggregate demand. He noted that an individual's production is either for his own use or for bartering for commodities produced by others. Since men do not work merely for the sake of working, it is the possibility of making such an exchange that leads an individual to produce more of certain commodities than he himself can consume. Thus the supply of goods each individual puts on the market is equal to his demand for the surplus production of others. When the activities of all individuals are summed, the total demand for commodities produced in an economy must be equal to the aggregate amount supplied. A simple summary of this line of reasoning has been designated as "Say's Law of Markets." In its simplified form, the law states that an economy's "supply creates its own demand."

Say's Law was accepted by the classical economists as also being appropriate in a money economy in which each individual sells his surplus production for money and then uses the money to buy the surplus production of others. Individuals will still produce more of a commodity than they themselves can consume only for the purpose of selling the surplus production to get money with which to buy other commodities. According to the classical economists, if an individual does not want any other commodities, he will not produce any surplus for sale because all he will get for his efforts will be money that has no value to him since he does not want any other commodities.

Interest and Savings

Savings occurs when individuals supply their own surplus commodities but wait to claim the surplus commodities of others. Such delays in obtaining the surplus commodities of others basically occur, according to the classical economists, when individuals are offered an interest payment for waiting. The payment is paid by those who want to use the saved commodities even

---

though they have no surplus commodities of their own to exchange for them. Saved commodities are desired for several reasons. First, they can be used in the form of capital such as plant and machinery to produce even more commodities. As a result, their users can repay the savers an amount of commodities equivalent to the ones they initially did not claim and also pay the interest reward needed to get them to wait. Second, they are desired by people who want at present to consume more commodities than they could obtain with their own surplus production. These people may desire to consume commodities because they optimistically feel that their surpluses in the future will be sufficient to repay the additional commodities and the required amount of interest, and still leave enough so that they will be able to consume as they wish.

The classical economists held, furthermore, that the fundamental conclusion of Say's Law remained unaltered if savings occurred in an economy. They thought that the economy's interest rates would act to equate the amounts of saved commodities supplied and demanded; the existence of an imbalance between the amounts supplied and demanded at a given level of interest rates would result in the rates being bid up or down until an equilibrium level of rates was reached at which they were equal. For example, consider a situation in which an economy's general level of interest rates is so high that large amounts of savings occur though few saved commodities are desired. The level of interest rates in the economy will decline because there will be an excess of savings; the savers who cannot earn any interest at all at those rates because of the lack of investment and other demand will begin to offer their savings for lower rates of interest. The economy's interest rates will continue to fall until they reach a level at which there is no longer a surplus to continue to drive them down.

Figure 20-1 depicts the classical theory of how the level of an economy's interest rates is determined by the supply and demand for savings. Notice that the curve representing the economy's savings slopes upward to indicate that higher rates of interest induce greater amounts of savings; conversely, the curve representing the demand in the economy for such savings slopes down to the right to show that more and more savings are desired at lower levels of interest rates. More savings are desired at lower rates of interest because, first, some potential investments yield only enough additional commodities to pay low rates of interest. These investments take place only if the rates of interest in an economy are low enough. Second, because of the lower rates of interest, more people will expect their future surpluses to be high enough to enable them to repay the saved commodities they consume and pay the smaller amount of interest. Notice further that the curves

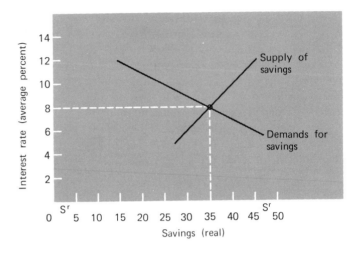

FIGURE 20-1
The classical rate of interest.

representing the demand for savings and the supply of savings intersect at a positive level of interest rates. It never occurred to the classical economists that the nature of an economy's savings supply and demand could be such that the curves would not intersect at some positive level of interest rates. Instead, they assumed that there would always be an amount of savings demanded equal to the amount supplied since any decline in the amount demanded because of savings would be offset by the additional demand of those who wanted to use the savings. Then, since all commodities that could be supplied in an economy would be demanded, there would never be involuntary unemployment resulting from a general lack of demand for commodities.

Savings and investment. An alternative classical approach to the rate of interest and the amount of savings emphasized only the investment use of saved commodities and defined saved commodities as those not used for consumption purposes. This approach results in exactly the same level of interest rates as the foregoing method. For example, in the first approach, at some equilibrium level of interest rates, 20 commodities might be saved by those entitled to them, of which 5 are used by consumers who expect to be able to repay the commodities plus interest out of their future incomes and 15 are desired for investment uses because they are productive.

With the alternative approach, 15 commodities are not used for consumption purchases but are all desired for investment purposes. Thus, whichever definition of savings is used, the same level of interest rates is the equilibrium level with the same amount of savings supplied and demanded.

Loanable funds. The foregoing description of interest and savings was in terms of commodities. But the results remain fundamentally unchanged in a money economy. Basically, in a money economy, an individual supplies his excess commodities, receives money in payment for them, and then uses the money to obtain the surplus commodities of others. The money represents the individual's right to the surplus commodities of others. He can use it to obtain the commodities or he can wait to obtain them and instead temporarily lend his money to someone else so that the borrower can use it to obtain the commodities accessible to the lender. The monies made available by such waiting are the "loanable funds" of the economy. They are supplied in return for interest by individuals who save rather than use them to purchase the surplus commodities of others. And they are demanded by those consumers and investors who are willing to pay interest in order that they may get the funds they need to buy the commodities they desire. Since the loanable funds represent the value of the saved commodities and the means to purchase them, the same equilibrium level of interest rates obviously exists whether the loanable funds representing the saved commodities or the commodities themselves are directly considered.

The natural rate at Interest. Certain classical economists, however, accepted the possibility that other levels of interest rates might temporarily exist in an economy which differ from the "natural" level of rates that would equate the amount of saved commodities supplied and demanded. One cause of these other levels of interest rates is the ability of the economy's financial institutions to cause the total supply of loanable funds to differ from the amount of funds saved. Rather than remain at the natural rate when such differences occur, the level of the economy's money rates of interest will adjust to equate the total supply of loanable funds from all sources with the amount demanded. The financial institutions can cause such differences—and thus levels of interest rates that differ from the natural level of rates—either by accepting deposits from savers and then not lending them, or by creating new money and lending it in addition to the loanable funds available as a result of saving. Differences between the amount of funds made available by savings and the total amount of loanable funds also occur if individuals "hoard" the money they receive from selling their surplus commodities instead of either using it to purchase the surplus commodities of others or making it available as loanable funds so that someone can buy the surplus commodities of others. In other words, in an economy in which the total supply of loanable funds differs from the amount of funds saved, the money rates of interest will adjust to equate the total supply of loanable funds from all sources (savings, dis-hoarding of previously hoarded money, newly created money) with the amount of loanable funds demanded rather than remain at the natural rate.

The importance of the activities that cause the level of an economy's money rates of interest to differ from the natural level of interest rates is that more or less money is lent to those who wish to buy the saved commodities than actually is needed to buy all of them. For example, if the supply of loanable funds from not buying the surplus commodities is $100 billion but $20 billion of this is hoarded so that only $80 billion is available for investors and others to use in buying these surplus commodities, not all the surplus commodities will be purchased. Instead, the amount of commodities actually saved (which has a money value of $100 billion) will exceed the amount of commodities purchased by the borrowers (which has a money value of only $80 billion). Since these surplus commodities cannot be sold, they will not be produced; thus there is a tendency for "gluts" of unsold commodities and unemployment to result. Of course, the same effect will occur if financial institutions set the interest rate they will pay to savers at a level that causes $100 billion in savings and then, through ignorance or design, lend only $80 billion to investors and other consumers.

Loanable funds and the bond market. Bonds are the promises of repayment that a borrower gives when he borrows funds. An alternative classical approach to the loanable funds description of an economy's rates of interest involves the use of bonds. It simply looks on the demand for loanable funds as the willingness to supply bonds and the supply of loanable funds as the demand for such bonds. Thus the demand for bonds in an economy (the economy's supply of loanable funds) is high when the bonds yield high interest rates and low when the interest rates are low. Figure 20-2 reflects this relationship.

Flexible Prices

The classical economists thought that flexible commodity prices would ensure the purchase of an economy's entire full employment level of commodity output even if the economy's rate of interest did not equate savings and investment. They believed that in the event of a level of interest rates so high that savings exceeded investment and resulted in an unpurchased

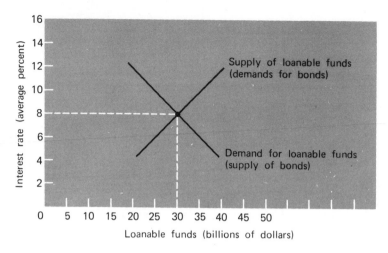

FIGURE 20-2
Loanable funds and bonds.

surplus of commodities, commodity prices would be bid down by competition from the unsuccessful sellers until total spending at the high rates of interest was enough to purchase all the commodities being produced.

Automatically attaining full employment levels of purchasing through such a decline in commodity prices requires that money wages also fall so that the full employment level of real wages is maintained. If money wages do not fall, commodity prices will not fall because producers will not have the lower costs that enable them to produce the same number of commodities and sell them at lower prices. Second, since such a decline in money wages may cause a further decline in commodity prices owing to the lower levels of purchasing that lower money wages may cause, money wages must fall faster than any subsequent decline in the level of commodity prices caused by the initial wage reduction. The most sophisticated classical economists, particularly those, such as Pigou, who followed Keynes, pointed to the real balance effect as ensuring that the subsequent decline in commodity prices would be less than any decline in the level of money wages.

WAGES, EMPLOYMENT, AND PRODUCTION

The classical economists' views on wages, employment, and production are similar to those presented in the chapter on aggregate supply. Basically, they held that the number of workers employed in an economy and the level of real wages they receive will be determined in the economy's labor market by the supply of and demand for labor. The supply of labor depends on the level of real wages; more people will be willing to sacrifice leisure for work if real wages are higher. Furthermore, they believed that the number of workers demanded depends on the productivity of the workers and the level of real wages that they receive since employers will hire employees only so long as the amount of additional commodities each worker adds in excess of the additional costs caused by his employment are larger than the real wages it takes to obtain his services. The productivity of labor is determined by its skills, the quantity and quality of capital, and the level of technology.

Unlike Keynes and his followers, the classical economists assumed that there could be neither a shortage nor a surplus (involuntary unemployment) of labor. They based this assumption on their belief that money wages were flexible upward and downward and would automatically adjust to a given level of commodity prices in order to yield a full employment real wage. Thus, if the level of prices in an economy changes and yields a level of real wages so high that there is involuntary unemployment, the economy's unemployed will bid down money wages as they compete for the available jobs until real wages are reduced to the point where all workers who want to work at that level of real wages can find work. And if real wages are too low and there is a shortage of labor, employers attempting to maximize profits will offer higher and higher money wages until the full employment real wage is reached.

Once the level of money wages yields a full employment level of real wages, the number of workers employed at those real wages and their productivity will determine the total amount of commodities that will be produced in the economy. Prices have no effect on the level of physical production since any change in the prices of commodities will result only in whatever changes in money wages are needed to regain the full-employment level of real wages.

PRICES: THE QUANTITY THEORIES OF MONEY

The classical economists related the level of an economy's commodity prices to the quantity of money in the economy and the level of its commodity production. Two very similar "quantity theory" formulations usually were used to explain the level of prices.

The Transactions Formulation

The transactions formulation of the quantity theory of money begins on the premise that the total amount of money that will be spent in transactions involving the purchase of newly produced commodities in an economy is determined by the quantity of money in the economy (M) and by its "velocity" (V). The classical economists usually defined the quantity of money to include coins, currency, and demand deposits. The velocity of money is the number of times the average unit of money in the money supply is respent over and over again in a time period as it is used in one transaction to purchase a newly produced commodity and then respent by its recipients or others to purchase additional such commodities. The total volume of money expenditures to purchase newly produced commodities during a given period of time thus is the quantity of money (M) multiplied by the number of times it is spent for such purposes (V). Total purchasing thus equals MV.

On the other hand, the total amount of money received from the sale of the purchased commodities in an economy is PY^r since the amount of receipts equals the number of commodities produced (Y^r) multiplied by the average price at which the commodities are sold (P). Since the amount of money expenditures to purchase commodities is the same as is received from selling them, MV must be equal to PY^r. Furthermore, the values of M, V, and Y^r were thought to be relatively stable and independent of the levels of purchasing and income: the supply of money because it is determined by the monetary authorities and institutions; the velocity of money because it is determined by how fast transactions are completed and how many intermediate transactions occur before the money gets into someone's hands who will spend it on new commodities; and the level of commodity production because the only amount that will be produced is that which occurs in an economy at full employment. Because M, V, and Y^r are stable and unaffected by the level of expenditures or income, it is an economy's level of commodity prices that must adjust so that $MV = PY^r$.

Consider an economy during a given period of time in which 5 billion commodities are produced, there is a money supply of $20 billion, and the average dollar is spent to obtain newly produced commodities and then respent so that the velocity of money in the economy is 2. Total money outlays to purchase the 5 billion commodities thus will be $40 billion. The average level of commodity prices in this economy cannot be $10 because only 4 billion commodities would be purchased at that price with an outlay of $40 billion; one billion commodities would remain unsold, and competition to sell them would cause their prices to fall. Only when the average price level reaches $8 will all the commodities be purchased. Nor can commodity prices fall below an average of $8. For example, they cannot be $4 because at that average price, money outlays of $40 billion would buy 10 billion commodities, and less than that are available. The competition at that price level to buy the available commodities would cause their prices to rise. Only when the average price rises to $8 will purchasers stop bidding up prices in an effort to obtain the commodities they are willing to buy.

The Cash-Balances Formulation

The cash-balances formulation of the quantity theory is based on the observation that the cash or money income of consumers and firms arrives periodically such as on paydays, whereas they must pay out cash continually as their debts come due and commodities are needed. This means that cash balances equal to some portion of the total money expenditures (PY^r) are always being held to bridge the gaps between the periodic arrivals of cash. The percentage of total money expenditures that is held in the form of cash balances is usually designated by "k." Thus cash balances are equal to k percent of PY^r, and the total amount of money that will be held in an economy is kPY^r.

The "cash-balances economists" thought that forces existed to change prices until levels of prices and total money expenditures were reached that required the entire supply of money in an economy to be held in cash balances to fill the gaps in time. They noted that commodity prices would be bid up any time the quantity of cash in an economy exceeded the amount of cash needed to fill the gaps, since the individuals who held cash in excess of their needs would use it in an attempt to obtain more commodities. This process would continue until the quantity of money actually available in the economy equalled the amount the economy needed to fill the gaps in time. Algebraically, they thought that prices would change until they reached the level at which $M = kPY^r$. For instance, consider the economy in which 5 billion commodities are produced and the money supply is $20 billion. Also assume that the economy desires to hold one-half of its total money outlays in cash balances to bridge the gap in time so that k = .50. Only if the average price is $8, so that money outlays are $40 billion, will all $20 billion be held in cash balances. Prices cannot be any lower or higher with that quantity of money. For example, if the average price is $5 so that the total money expenditures needed to purchase the 5 billion commodities are $25 billion, the economy will desire to hold only $12.5 billion in cash balances; the other $7.5 billion will be used then in an attempt to buy more commodities. But the additional purchasing only drives up the price level. And it will rise until the average price reaches $8 so that the economy's money outlays are $40 billion, and all of the economy's money supply is desired for cash balances, leaving none for use in the further bidding up of prices.

Changes in the Level of Prices

According to the classicists' explanation of the level of commodity prices, changes in prices can be caused by changes in any of the four components $(M, Y^r, V, \text{ or } k)$ that determine the level of prices. Inflation thus can be caused by increases in the quantity of money, decreases in the amount of commodities available to be purchased, or decreases in the proportion of money expenditures that are held to bridge the gap in time (or increases in the velocity of money if the transactions approach is used instead of the cash-balances approach). For example, in the economy described in which the average price is $8, a tripling of the money supply to $60 billion with velocity remaining at 2 would mean total money outlays of $120 billion to purchase 5 billion commodities. Prices would thus be bid up to an average of $24 since that is the only price at which exactly 5 billion commodities can be purchased for $120 billion. Notice that the price level has changed proportionally to the change in the quantity of money. Exactly the same results occur when the cash-balances approach is used; prices rise initially as more money is available than is desired in order to bridge the gaps in time. The extra money is spent and prices are bid up until they reach an average of $24 so that total money expenditures are high enough for all $60 billion to be desired for cash balances.

The same price increase will occur if either the velocity increases to 6 while the initial quantities of money and commodities remain unchanged or if the quantity of money and the velocity remain unchanged but the number of commodities that the resulting expenditures could buy is reduced by two-thirds. The classical economists, however, generally did not attribute price changes to changes in these latter items. They noted that these items tended to remain stable in value because they were rooted in the economy's institutions and productive capacity. Thus they generally attributed price changes to proportional changes in the quantity of money (whose size could be changed since it is affected by the actions of the governments and banks) and advocated the maintenance of a stable money supply in order to avoid inflation or deflation.

Figure 20-3 presents a graphical representation of the various levels of total money expenditures which the existence of different quantities of money will cause. Money is measured on the horizontal axis and money expenditures on the vertical axis. A line (kPY^r) depicts the amount of cash balances that the economy desires to hold for each level of money expenditures. Because the line relates cash balances to money expenditures, it can be used to depict the level of money expenditures that each amount of money to be held in cash balances will cause. For example, $40 billion of money available to be held in cash balances will support and cause $120 billion of money outlays.

The level of prices associated with each quantity of money can be found by dividing the level of total money expenditures that each quantity of money supports, such as the $120 billion in Figure 20-3 by the number of commodities sold in the economy. For instance, if the quantity of money is such that money outlays of $120 billion will occur during a given period of time, the average price will be $6 if the economy produces and sells 20 billion commodities in that time; $34 if it produces and sells 5 billion; and $1 if it produces and sells 120 billion.

Figure 20-4 presents a "price-possibility" curve (PP) representing the level of money outlays ($80 billion) that an economy's money supply can support. The PP curve depicts the various combinations of prices and commodities the economy can have with that particular level of money outlays; it has the

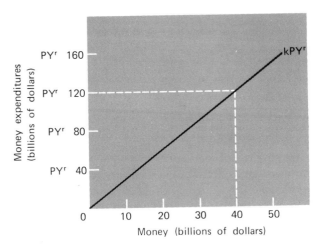

FIGURE 20-3
The quantity of money and the size of money expenditures.

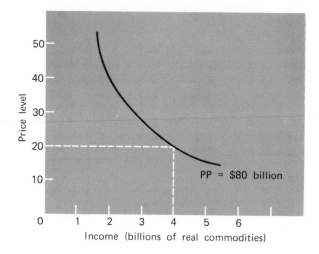

FIGURE 20-4
A price-possibility curve.

shape of a rectangular hyperbola since a change in the amount of commodities being purchased results in a proportional change in the level of prices. Other amounts of money outlays would be represented by other curves. Such curves are valuable because they can be used to identify the level of prices for a given amount of money outlays and a given amount of commodities. This identification is accomplished by moving to the curve representing the level of money outlays from the number of commodities on the horizontal axis and then moving to the vertical axis where price is measured. For instance, Figure 20-4 indicates that with money outlays of $80 billion, the average commodity price will be $20 if the level of real income in the economy is 4 billion commodities.

A CLASSICAL MACROECONOMIC SYSTEM

A complete classical macroeconomic system having the characteristics just described is presented graphically in Figure 20-5. The various components of the system depicted by each graph as well as their behavior according to the classical economists have already been explained in the text. Basically, the system operates in the following fashion:

1. The level of real wages and the amount of labor that will be employed in

an economy are determined in the economy's labor market by the forces of labor demand and labor supply. Only one level of real wages can exist. Higher levels of real wages are not possible because the resulting surplus of labor would compete for the available jobs by working for lower real

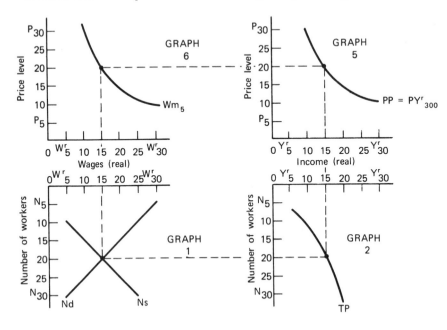

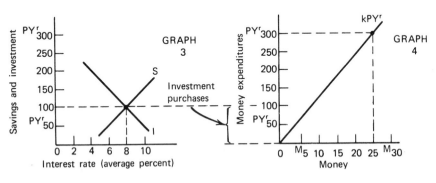

FIGURE 20-5
A classical macroeconomic system.

wages (by accepting lower money wages). Lower levels of real wages are not possible because the resulting shortage of labor would cause employers to offer higher real wages (by raising money wages) in order to get the acquiescence of workers they desire to employ. In the economy depicted in this figure the level of real wages is W^r_{15} and the amount of labor is N_{20}.

2. The amount of labor employed and its productivity determine the total level of commodity production. Y^r_{15} commodities will be produced in the the Figure 20-5 economy with N_{20} workers employed.

3. The quantity of money in the economy and the proportion of total money expenditures that must be held to fill gaps in time determine the total level of money expenditures for the commodities produced. In this economy, the quantity of money M_{25} results in PY^r_{300} of money expenditures.

4. The desires to save and invest determine the level of interest rates and the amount of total money outlays to be diverted from the purchase of commodities for consumption purposes and instead used to obtain commodities for investment purposes. In the Figure 20-5 economy, the general level of interest rates will be 8 percent, and PY^r_{100} of investment purchasing will occur.

5. The level of money expenditures divided by the number of commodities produced and purchased determines the level of commodity prices. It has already been shown that PY^r_{300} of money expenditures will occur in this economy (of which PY^r_{100} will be for the purchase of investment commodities) for the purpose of purchasing Y^r_{15} commodities. Thus the price level will be P_{20}.

6. The level of commodity prices and the level of real wages determine the level of money wages that producers will pay and workers will receive when full employment occurs. The level of commodity prices in the Figure 20-5 economy is P_{20}; thus the economy's money wages will adjust to the level Wm_5 which is required if the W^r_{15} level of real wages is to occur in the economy.

Cases in the Use of the Classical Model

Case 1. The money supply of an economy is increased: more money is now available than people want to hold, so money expenditures in the economy rise to purchase the goods produced in the economy. The only effect is that the economy's prices are continually bid up until people want to hold all the additional money to fill gaps in time. The higher prices mean that the level of real wages in the economy will fall, leading to a shortage of workers. The shortage of workers means that the economy's producers will bid up the level of money wages in the economy as they compete for the services of workers, money wages will increase until they yield the original full employment real wage. The level of interest rates and the number of commodities saved and devoted to investment uses will remain unchanged even though the higher level of prices means a proportional increase in the amount of money desired for investment purposes since more investment expenditures are needed to get the same amount of commodities for investment use. They do not change because the increased prices also mean a proportional increase in money received from the sale of commodities, and thus a proportional increase in the amount of money that savers are willing to provide at every rate of interest.

The initial effect of a larger quantity of money in an economy is a proportional change in the level of the economy's money expenditures. Subsequent effects include an upward shift in the price-possibilities curve proportional to the change in the quantity of money to show that proportionally higher prices will exist at every level of commodity production. They also include a similar proportional, upward shift in the level of money wages to offset the increase in commodity prices so that the full employment level of real wages is restored, and a similar proportional shift in the supply of loanable funds and the investment demand for loanable funds so that the same interest rate is maintained and the same amount of consumption and investment commodities are purchased at the higher price levels.

Case 2. The desire to invest increases: there is now a shortage of savings at the original level of interest rates. The result is that the economy's investors bid up the economy's interest rates until a level is reached that induces enough savings to offset the investment desired at that level. No other changes occur except that a larger proportion of total money expenditures is for the purpose of purchasing investment commodities; thus a larger proportion of total production is diverted into investment goods.

The initial change and its effects are depicted by a shift of the investment demand curve and the establishment of a new equilibrium level of interest rates and quantity of money savings and investment.

KEYNES' CRITICISM OF CLASSICAL MACROECONOMICS

The classical economists thought that the various forces just described ensured that an economy could be in equilibrium only at full employment levels of production. Thus they held that any situation of unemployment and less than maximum levels of production could exist only temporarily while the economy was in the process of readjusting to full employment. Keynes rejected this conclusion. Instead, he provided an alternative analysis, the essence of which was contained in the previous chapters, leading to the conclusion that it is indeed possible for an economy to be in equilibrium at less than full-employment levels of production. The basis for Keynes' rejection of the classical economists' conclusions was his rejection of the classical reasoning regarding Say's Law and the role of interest in maintaining it when savings occurred, and the classical reasoning regarding flexible money wages and prices.

Say's Law and the Rate of Interest

Keynes rejected Say's Law that it is impossible for producers to supply more commodities than will be demanded. First, he noted that various psychological reasons, discussed in the chapter on consumption, lead individuals to save a portion of the income they earn from the sale of their surplus production; thus some amount of production tends to go unpurchased unless other purchasers appear who will buy that amount of commodities. Second, he emphatically disagreed with the classical economists' belief that the rates of interest in an economy would adjust to equate the amounts of savings and investment so that the amount of commodities demanded remained equal to the amount supplied. In essence, he noted first that the level of interest rates in an economy is set in its money market by the supply and demand for money rather than by the supply of savings and demand for savings. Second, he held that the amount of savings occurring in an economy did not depend on the interest rates as the classical economists thought, but primarily on the level of income in the economy. Third, he pointed out that money was demanded as an asset for speculative and precautionary purposes as well as for transactions purposes to bridge the gaps in time. He then emphasized that the speculative demand for money balances in an economy would become infinitely large at some low level of interest rates and that this would keep the economy's interest rates from falling below some minimum level, a minimum level below which the classical system might require it to fall in order to equate savings and investment. Finally, he thought it was not the rates of interest but the level of income that adjusts until a level of savings occurs that exactly equals the total amount of investment purchasing. (Recall that the total investment determinant of an economy's equilibrium level of income also includes G, F, and b'Tr.)

Flexible Money Wages and Commodity Prices

Keynes, in a discussion emphasizing money wages, also rejected the classical belief that unemployment due to inadequate demand would automatically be eliminated by a decline in money wages and commodity prices even if an economy's interest rates did not adjust to equate the supply of savings and the demand for savings. First, in essence, money wages will not fall if there is unemployment; they are inflexible downward because of institutional barriers such as minimum-wage laws and long-term wage contracts. Second, even if there were a decline in money wages, Keynes held that it would not inevitably guarantee an increase in the number of commodities purchased and the amount of labor needed to produce them. Keynes reached the second conclusion by examining the effect of a decline in money wages on the determinants of the amount of commodities purchased for consumption and investment purposes: the consumption function, the MEI, and the rate of interest. He found no inherent reason why the consumption function or the MEI[1] would inevitably change in such a manner as to ensure the sale of the additional goods and services that the unemployed could produce. He did find some tendency for this to be attained through changes in the level of interest rates, noting that lower wages (and the lower commodity prices that might occur with lower wage costs) reduced the amount of money needed for transactions purposes so that if there were a fixed amount of money in an economy, its level of interest rates would tend to fall and its purchasing would rise. He went on to note, however, that purchasing would rise only so long as the interest rates were falling and that the level of interest rates in an economy would fall only until some minimum level was reached; then all additional money freed by falling wages and prices would be held without a further decline in the level of interest rates.

Thus flexible wages and prices may work to ensure full employment levels of commodity purchasing so long as the economy is not in the liquidity trap. But once in the liquidity trap, deflation will not work. Furthermore, if the liquidity trap is reached without an economy's attaining full employment, infinite deflation will occur as wages and prices continually fall because of the futile search for jobs and sales. Keynes, however, overlooked the possibility brought out by Pigou that the declining commodity prices that possibly accompany declining money wages would increase the amount of commodities purchased for consumption purposes because they increased the

---

[1]Keynes discussed the MEI and MEC as one concept titled "The MEC." Subsequent economists established the difference between stocks of capital and flows of investment.

real value of money assets in the economy and thus reduced the amount of additional savings needed to meet savings goals.

THE KEYNES-CLASSICAL DIFFERENCES

Basically, the Keynesian macroeconomic system that allows for the possibility of involuntary unemployment due to inadequate demand departs from the general consensus of the classical system in the following four areas:

1. It adds the speculative and precautionary demands for money.
2. It has the level of interest rates determined by money supply and money demand rather than by savings and investment. Furthermore, some minimum level of interest rates exists, at least in the short run.
3. It adds the consumption function: the level of savings depends on the level of income rather than the rates of interest. And it is the level of income that adjusts to equate savings with I, G, F, and b'Tr rather than the rates of interest.
4. It assumes that the general levels of an economy's money wages and commodity prices are inflexible downward.

The Most Important Difference

Keynes apparently felt that the speculative demand for money together with the resulting liquidity trap and minimum level of interest rates was the most significant change he made in macroeconomic theory; it explains why an economy's interest rates cannot fall low enough to equate savings and investment, why wage and price flexibility is no guarantee that all the commodities that can be produced in an economy can be sold, and why monetary policies might not be effective in attaining the purchasing required for full-employment levels of production. The Pigou or real balances effect, however, makes this difference of less importance since it makes it conceptually possible for full-employment levels of commodity purchasing to be reached with wage and price flexibility or with the implementation of policies that expand the supply of money.

Many of today's economists disagree, however, with Keynes' opinion of what was his most significant contribution. Some point to the realism of Keynes' assumptions regarding inflexible money wages and prices which make it possible for an economy to be in equilibrium with unemployment and less than maximum levels of production. Other economists feel that latter contribution was not so important. They note that classical macroeconomics would yield the same results with these assumptions. For instance, unemployment would occur in the classical system if the level of interest rates became so high that money expenditures declined but prices did not; fewer commodities then would be purchased and fewer workers would be employed. Furthermore, these economists note that the classical description of flexible wages and prices was a reasonable description of the conditions that existed when the classical economists were writing. They note that there were then fewer interferences with wage flexibility, such as labor unions and minimum wages laws, and that the markets were more competitive so that prices could not be prevented from rising or falling by the administrative actions of a few producers. Nevertheless, Keynes went into great detail to deny that rigid wages and prices were required before there could be unemployment. He pointed out that a decline in money wages and prices, if it occurred, only had the effect of creating more money that might just be caught in the liquidity trap. Keynes did overlook the Pigou effect, however, and if it exists, the classical economists were correct in saying that flexible wages and prices could lead to full employment.

Most economists, however, consider the consumption function to be Keynes' most important contribution, and thus the most important difference between his system and that of the earlier classical economists. They emphasize that it is an economy's consumption function that determines the equilibrium level of income, and thus the levels of production and employment that will occur when there are specific levels of I, G, F, and b'Tr. Further, it destroys Say's Law by showing that savings might occur so that supply does not necessarily create its own demand. And finally, it eliminates the possibility of the rate of interest equating savings and investment since the level of savings in an economy is a function of the level of income.

● REFERENCES

Belassa, B., "Mill and the Law of Markets," *Quarterly Journal of Economics*, **LXXIII**, pp. 263–274 (1959).

Clower, R., "Keynes and the Classics: A Dynamical Perspective," *Quarterly Journal of Economics*, **LXXIV**, pp. 318–323 (1960).

Hansen, A., *A Guide to Keynes* (New York: McGraw-Hill, 1953), pp. 3–25, 140–153, 173–182.

Hawtrey, R. G., "Public Expenditure and the Demand for Labour," *Economica*, **V**, pp. 38–48 (1925).

Hicks, J. R., "Mr Keynes and the Classics: A Suggested Interpretation," *Econometrica*, **V**, pp. 147–159 (1937).

Johnson, H. G., "The General Theory after Twenty-Five Years," *American Economic Review*, **LI**, pp. 1–17 (1961).

Keynes, J., *The General Theory of Employment, Interest and Money* (New York: Harcourt, Brace, 1936), Chapters 2, 14, 19.

Klein, L. R., *The Keynesian Revolution* (New York: Macmillan, 1947), Chapters 3–5.

Knight, F., "Capital, Time and the Interest Rate," *Economica*, **I**, pp. 257–286 (1932).

Marshall, A., *Principles of Economics*, 8th ed. (New York: Macmillan, 1948).

Mill, J. S., *Principles of Political Economy*, II (London: Longmans, Green, 1929), Book III, Chapter 14.

Neisser, H., "General Overproduction: A Study of Say's Law of Markets," *Journal of Political Economy*, **XLII**, pp. 433–465 (1934).

Pigou, A., "The Classical Stationary State," *Economic Journal*, **LIII**, pp. 343–351 (1943).

————, *Employment and Equilibrium* (London: Macmillan, 1941).

Schlesinger, J. R., "After Twenty Years: The General Theory," *Quarterly Journal of Economics*, **LXX**, pp. 581–602 (1956).

Index

445

Money (*continued*)
  total demand, 211–213
  transactions demand, 201–204
Money market, 223–231
Money wages, 258–269
Morgan, J. M., 74
Multiplier, and accelerator, 320–326
  balanced budget, 171–173
  complete, 179–180
  formula, 133–136
  nature, 132–133
  tax, 164–165
  time period, 136–137
  transfer, 158–161
Mundell, R., 15, 120, 285, 374–378, 420
Musgrave, R., 181

Nagatani, K., 310
Naqui, K., 310
National Bureau of Economic Research, 39
National Debt, 408–411
National Income, accounts, 17–39
  components, 30–31
  defined, 29
  and GNP, 31–34
Natural rate of growth, 301
Natural rates, 371–374
Naylor, T., 418
Neher, P., 310
Neisser, H., 443
Nelson, R., 310
Neoclassical growth theory, 302–304
Niehans, J., 420
Net business savings, defined, 71–72
  and government borrowing, 170
Net exports, 22–23, 114–115
Net taxes, 167
New Deal, 8
New Economics, defined, 13
  See also Keynes and Macroeconomics
Nonconsumption purchasing, and the level
  of income, 138–149
Nordhaus, W., 308
Normal income, 69–70

Ohlsson, I., 39
Open market operations, 190–191
Ophir, T., 120

Optimum stock of capital, 97–105
Oshima, H., 310
Output potential, 255–269
Overinvestment and income fluctuations,
  315–317

Patinkin, D., 197, 285, 309
Peltzman, S., 253
Perlman, R., 360
Permanent income, 69–70
Perry, G. L., 74
Personal savings, 37–38
Peston, M., 181
Phelps, E., 109, 253, 310, 360, 383
Phillips, A., 363–371, 383
Pierson, G., 383
Pigou, A., 250–251, 253, 273, 276, 278–279,
  440–441, 443
Pilvin, H., 310
Planned economies, as alternative to market
  economies, 12–13
Policies, alternatives, 374–378, 411–412
  conservative, 8
  fiscal, 394–399, 403–411
  monetary, 399–411
  reforms, 413–418
Politically feasible policies, 408–411
Population, and growth, 305
Power, J., 253
Prescott, E., 326
Precautionary demand for money, 210–211
Present value, 81–83
Price possibility curve, 434–435
Prices, flexibility and equilibrium, 279–284
  flexibility and income distribution,
    389–390
  quantity theory, 430–435
  relative and absolute, 95–97
  and wage increases, 363–371
Problems of market economies, 11–12
Production, classical view, 429–430
  function, 257–258
  stock of capital, 97–101
  See also Aggregate supply and
    Productivity
Productivity, effects of increases, 335–342,
  353–354
  of labor, 257–258